LAW AND THE PRECARIOUS HOME

This book explores the emergent and internationally widespread phenomenon of precariousness, specifically in relation to the home. It maps the complex reality of the insecure home by examining the many ways in which precariousness is manifested in legal and social change across a number of otherwise very different jurisdictions. By applying innovative work done by socio-legal scholars in other fields such as labour law and welfare law to the home, *Law and the Precarious Home* offers a broader theoretical understanding of contemporary 'precarisation' of law and society. It will enable reflections upon differential experience of home dependent upon class, race and gender from a range of local, national and crossnational perspectives. Finally it will explore the pluralisation of ideas of home in subjective experience, social reality and legal form. The answers offered in this book reflect the expertise and standing of the assembled authors who are international leaders in their field, with decades of first-hand practical and intellectual engagement with the area.

Oñati International Series in Law and Society

A SERIES PUBLISHED FOR THE OÑATI INSTITUTE FOR THE SOCIOLOGY OF LAW

Recent titles in this series

Delivering Family Justice in the 21st Century
Edited by Mavis Maclean, John Eekelaar and Benoit Bastard

Regulatory Transformations
Rethinking Economy-Society Interactions
Edited by Bettina Lange, Fiona Haines and Dania Thomas

Life Imprisonment and Human Rights
Edited by Dirk van Zyl Smit and Catherine Appleton

Trust in International Police and Justice Cooperation
Edited by Saskia Hufnagel and Carole McCartney

Human Rights Encounter Legal Pluralism
Edited by Eva Brems, Giselle Corradi and Mark Goodale

Transitional Justice and the Public Sphere: Engagement, Legitimacy and Contestation
Edited by Chrisje Brants and Susanne Karstedt

Criminologies of the Military: Militarism, National Security and Justice
Edited by Andrew Goldsmith and Ben Wadham

For the complete list of titles in this series, see 'Oñati International Series in Law and Society' link at www.bloomsburyprofessional.com/uk/series/onati-international-series-in-law-and-society

Law and the Precarious Home

Socio Legal Perspectives on the Home in Insecure Times

Edited by
Helen Carr, Brendan Edgeworth
and Caroline Hunter

Oñati International Series in Law and Society

A SERIES PUBLISHED FOR THE OÑATI INSTITUTE
FOR THE SOCIOLOGY OF LAW

•HART•
OXFORD • LONDON • NEW YORK • NEW DELHI • SYDNEY

HART PUBLISHING

Bloomsbury Publishing Plc

Kemp House, Chawley Park, Cumnor Hill, Oxford, OX2 9PH, UK

HART PUBLISHING, the Hart/Stag logo, BLOOMSBURY and the Diana logo are trademarks of Bloomsbury Publishing Plc

First published in Great Britain 2018

A catalogue record for this book is available from the British Library.

Library of Congress Cataloging-in-Publication Data

Names: Law and the Precarious Home (Conference) (2015 : Oñati International Institute for the Sociology of Law) | Carr, Helen (Law teacher), editor. | Edgeworth, Brendan, editor. | Hunter, Caroline (Barrister), editor. | Oñati International Institute for the Sociology of Law, sponsoring body.

Title: Law and the precarious home : socio legal perspectives on the home in insecure times / edited by Helen Carr, Brendan Edgeworth and Caroline Hunter.

Description: Oxford : Portland, Oregon : Hart Publishing, 2018. | Series: Oñati international series in law and society | Based on a workshop "Law and the Precarious Home" hosted by Oñati International Institute for the Sociology of Law, July 2015.—ECIP acknowledgments. | Includes bibliographical references and index.

Identifiers: LCCN 2017056848 (print) | LCCN 2017057314 (ebook) | ISBN 9781509914586 (Epub) | ISBN 9781509914609 (hardback : alk. paper)

Subjects: LCSH: Housing—Law and legislation—Social aspects—Congresses.

Classification: LCC K3550.A6 (ebook) | LCC K3550.A6 L39 2015 (print) | DDC 344/.063635—dc23

LC record available at https://lccn.loc.gov/2017056848

ISBN: HB: 978-1-50991-460-9
ePDF: 978-1-50991-457-9
ePub: 978-1-50991-458-6

Typeset by Compuscript Ltd, Shannon

Acknowledgements

This book would not have been possible but for the support of the Onati International Institute for the Sociology of Law, who hosted a workshop entitled 'Law and the Precarious Home' in July 2015. We thank the Institute, and its then Director, Professor Adam Czarnota, for all they did to support the staging of the workshop, but also for their more general assistance with accommodation and transport for the participants. We are particularly grateful for the administrative support and guidance of Malen Gordoa Mendizabal, ably supported by Cristina Ruiz. Special thanks also to Emily Braggins and her team from Hart Publishing/Bloomsbury who have been a pleasure to work with and the two post-graduate students from the Universities of York and Kent, Cameron Giles and Joanne Pearman, who helped with editing.

Contents

List of Contributors

Laura Binger is a doctoral candidate at Kent Law School, University of Kent. Her research focuses on housing activism, and she holds a JD from Harvard Law School.

Sarah Blandy is a solicitor and Professor of Law at the University of Sheffield.

Danie Brand (BLC LLB, LLM, LLD), is Professor of Law, University of Pretoria.

Helen Carr is a Professor at Kent Law School. Her interests lie in the regulation of housing and homelessness and she has a broader concern with social welfare law. She has recently completed a research project on shared ownership (with Professor David Cowan from Bristol University and Alison Wallace, York University).

Grabriele D'Adda is a doctoral student at Kent Law School, where he works on the relationship between social movements, legal framework and right to housing in Spain. He has a Master in Social Development from Université Paul-Valéri of Montpellier and he graduated in Political Science at Università degli Studi di Milano.

Nestor M Davidson, a graduate of Harvard College and Columbia Law School, holds the Albert A Walsh Chair in Real Estate, Land Use and Property Law at the Fordham University School of Law, where he is also the Faculty Director of the Urban Law Center.

Lucia Delgado is an independent researcher, social activist for the right to housing, is one of the founders of PAH—*Plataforma Afectados por la Hipoteca*.

Ann Dupuis (MA (Hons), PhD), is an Honorary Research Fellow, School of People, Environment and Planning, College of Humanities and Social Sciences, Massey University, New Zealand.

Brendan Edgeworth is a Professor in the Faculty of Law, University of New South Wales, Sydney, Australia.

Wei Gong is a visiting fellow at the School of Law, University of Sheffield. He holds a PhD in Law from Renmin University, China. He had practised law for more than 12 years in China before coming to the UK.

Richard Goulding is a PhD candidate and early careers researcher at the School of Law, the University of Sheffield. Focusing on how finance acts to reshape cities, his research interests include neoliberal urbanism, legal geography and critical political economy.

Magdalena Habdas (Dr Hab. MSc, MA) is an Associate Professor at the University of Silesia in Katowice, Poland in the Faculty of Law and Administration, Department of Civil and Private International Law. A licensed Polish property valuer, attorney-at-law, and active participant in the Common Core of European Private Law project, she was also director of the Polish-Czech-Slovak team for the TENLAW project (EU Framework 7) and the Social Rental Agencies in Poland project (The National Center for Research and Development).

Caroline Hunter is a Professor at York Law School, University of York, UK. Her research interests lie at the intersection of housing law, policy and practice. She has conducted a number of empirical studies on evictions, regulation of antisocial behaviour and homelessness. She has published extensively on these subjects and is a co-author of *Arden and Partington's Housing Law* (Sweet & Maxwell).

Dr Edward Kirton-Darling is a Lecturer in Law and Solicitor (non-practising) at Kent Law School, University of Kent.

Jed Meers is a Lecturer at York Law School, University of York.

Eduard Sala is a doctoral student at the Universitat Autònoma de Barcelona, where he researches the mortgage crisis in Spain and the empowerment of the social movements. He has a Masters in Spatial Planning from the same university and graduated in geography from the Universitat de les Illes Balears.

David C Thorns (BA (Econ) MA DLitt) FRSNZ ONZM, is Emeritus Professor of Sociology, University of Canterbury, New Zealand.

Suzanne Vallance (PhD) is Lecturer in Urban Studies, Faculty of Environment, Society and Design, Department of Environmental Management, Lincoln University, New Zealand.

Richard Warren is a doctoral student at the University of Kent, where he is also an Assistant Lecturer, Research Assistant and Immigration and Asylum Caseworker. He has a BA in Social Anthropology and an MSc in Cross-Cultural Research Methods and is accredited by the Law Society as a Senior Caseworker in Immigration and Asylum Law.

Ting Xu is a Senior Lecturer at the School of Law, University of Sheffield and 'Changbaishan Scholar' Visiting Professor at the School of Law, Jilin University. She holds LLM and PhD degrees from the London School of Economics and Political Science.

1

Introducing Precarisation: Contemporary Understandings of Law and the Insecure Home

HELEN CARR, BRENDAN EDGEWORTH
AND CAROLINE HUNTER

I. INTRODUCTION

PRECARIOUSNESS AND INSECURITY are provocative ideas and for many are key signifiers of our times. When juxtaposed with the security that is implicit in common understandings of 'home' they become particularly unsettling. The chapters in this collection explore aspects of that dissonance and the work that law does in ameliorating or intensifying it.

This introductory chapter has two purposes. First, it sets out the rationale for the book and explains our approach to the term 'precarious home' (sections II to IV). It outlines changes in the broader social, economic and political landscape that provide extensive evidence of contemporary 'insecure times'. It will consider the various ways in which the home, and the legal framework by means of which it is defined and regulated, nationally and locally, formally and informally, have been affected by these changes, that we characterise as a growing 'precarisation'. The chapter will situate the current position by reference to a constellation of recent changes across advanced industrialised societies that arguably render the home precarious, and to various socio-legal responses to the problem.

The sections V to IX of the chapter explores different dimensions of precarisation as analysed in the various chapters of the book. These dimensions are manifold. They include, first, a jurisdictional dimension, as different state regulatory regimes engage with insecurity of and in the home in different ways. Secondly, there is a political dimension, as groups across society experience highly divergent levels of precariousness of home. The role of government will be examined, for example, by reference to the conditions under which housing is provided by the state to the disadvantaged, and the ways in which the state seeks to balance the rights of private owners and tenants, as well as the state's role in forcing populations to leave traditional homelands or deciding if and when claims to home are recognised. Thirdly, a wide range of unpredictable events can operate to undermine the security that might otherwise characterise the home. Natural disasters, homelessness and death all contribute to the precariousness of home, highlighting the contingency of any security the home may be presupposed to offer. Law, in its broadest sense, may or may not help in mitigating this 'precarity', and—as our book shows—can contribute to it. Fourthly, there is a temporal dimension to the precarious home. Not only is a sense of enduring relationships arguably implicit in the meaning of home, for some home is replete with nostalgia, located somewhere in the past, while for others it is an aspiration and a future location. Fifthly, there is a spatial dimension, as Ferreri et al suggest: 'Precarisation … needs to be understood as a spatial process that generates and sustains a varied geography of insecurity, flexibility and temporariness, at once intensifying and normalising precarity.'[1]

The potential of precarity as a focus for understanding the times in which we find ourselves notwithstanding, the contributions to this collection also acknowledge its limits. So, for instance it is clear that for many people, in many parts of the world, experiences of home have always been characterised by insecurity. The illustrations of this point in the chapters on South Africa, China and Poland in this collection are particularly important. Moreover, even within the arguably exceptional security offered by liberal welfare states there has been considerable variation both in the protections offered, and the people who are deemed worthy of protection. The rationale of the book then is not to offer without critique a contrast between a secure past and a precarious present, but to suggest that precarity might offer a useful starting point for socio-legal scholars questioning contemporary modes of governing. One further caveat: in identifying a new precariat, or new precarious ways of living, we wish to avoid equating the precarious with victimhood. Several contributors specifically focus on strategic responses to precarious homes, and the political potential of precarity.

II. THE HOME

This book focuses on 'home', an idea that is apparently universally understood. However, theorists have demonstrated that 'home' is a disputed and controversial notion. For some, the idea of home beyond its physical form is 'purely phantasmal', a 'chimera'.[2] For others it is more complex. Mallett noted in 2004 that 'research on the meaning and experience of home

[1] M Ferreri, G Dawson and A Vasudevan, 'Living precariously: property guardianship and the flexible city' (2016) 41 *Transactions of the Institute of British Geographers* 246.

[2] Stephen Merrett and Fred Gray, *Owner-occupation in Britain* (Routledge & Kegan Paul, 1982) 65.

has proliferated over the past two decades, particularly within the disciplines of sociology, anthropology, psychology, human geography, history, architecture and philosophy.'[3]

These researchers approach the home in a 'multitude of ways.'[4] For Easthope what is common to many is that home is something other than the physical structure of the dwelling or the surrounding built environment. 'While homes may be located, it is not the location that is "home". Instead, homes can be understood as "places" that hold considerable social, psychological and emotive meaning for individuals and for groups.'[5] This perspective on home suggests it provides security and a place from which to flourish.

Fox's influential formulation of the 'home = house + *X*',[6] with the conceptual challenge to 'unravel [this] enigmatic "*X* factor"' illustrates a socio-legal response to the concept of home. For her, law should give a specific value to 'X'. However, the literature points consistently to the difficulty of defining or knowing what it is about the home that provides security, due to its complex, subjective construction.[7] Is there a minimum that is globally pertinent, if home is dependent on the perceptions of both the individual and the society?

A different approach, which moves away from these problems, is to acknowledge the essentially contested[8] nature of the concept. The focus moves to the question of how law and policy often require low-level administrative workers, legal actors, or even home occupiers themselves to 'know'—and in some cases articulate—aspects of the meaning of home.[9] This can allow subjective, 'common sense' understandings to be acknowledged.

It can also mean that the negative experience of the home can rest beside the often positive portrait of home in much of the literature. Feminist thinkers have long pointed to the home as a place of violence and abuse and they have had to be continually vigilant in efforts to persuade the state to acknowledge its role in protecting vulnerable people within the home.[10]

[3] Shelley Mallett, 'Understanding Home: A Critical Review of the Literature' (2004) *Sociological Review* 62.

[4] Hazel Easthope, 'A place called home' (2004) 21 *Housing, Theory and Society* 128, 135.

[5] Ibid.

[6] Lorna Fox, 'The Meaning of Home: A Chimerical Concept or a Legal Challenge?' (2002) 29 *Journal of Law and Society* 580, 590.

[7] Lewin Fereshteh, 'Elderly Migrants and the Concept of Home: A Swedish Perspective' in GD Rowles and H Chaudhury (eds), *Home and Identity in Late Life: International Perspectives* (Springer Publishing Company, 2005) 135.

[8] Walter Gallie, 'Essentially Contested Concepts' (1955) 56 *Proceedings of the Aristotelian Society* 167; John S Dryzek, 'Can There Be a Human Right to an Essentially Contested Concept? The Case of Democracy' (2016) 78 *The Journal of Politics* 357.

[9] Jed Meers, *Reconceptualising Home: A study on the UK Bedroom Tax* (Unpublished PLO., University of York, 2018).

[10] Molly Warrington, '"I Must Get out": The Geographies of Domestic Violence' (2001) 26 *Transactions of the Institute of British Geographers* 365.

For others, even without the reluctantly acknowledged violence of the home, home is a site of repression. Take for instance Rushdie's essay 'Out of Kansas'[11] where Rushdie berates the 'conservative homily' at the end of the *Wizard of Oz*, that there is no place like home:

> Are we to believe that Dorothy has learned no more on her journey than that she didn't need to make such a journey in the first place? Must we accept that she now accepts the limitations of her home life, and agree that the things she doesn't have there are not loss to her? *Is that right*? Well excuse me, Glenda, but it isn't ...

Home can also be an exclusionary notion, particularly at a time of global movement. Telling migrants to go home or denying legal rights on the basis that the claimant's home is not here but somewhere else are useful examples. For Banky this points to a precarity of place, which relates to the possibility or impossibility of remaining in a specific place. For Banky,

> the permission to remain in one's physical place is perhaps paradoxically at the core of a concept of national assignment of privileges and benefits. 'Precarity of place' describes the absence of such permission and can be defined as vulnerability to removal or deportation from one's physical location.[12]

In order to avoid the discriminatory consequences of a static notion of home, some scholars have written of home as a process, something that emerges over time, through practices, rituals and stories, independently of a fixed location.[13] Migrants and others in transition can experience the opposite process, home *unmaking*, the '*precarious process* by which material and/or imaginary components of home are unintentionally or deliberately, temporarily or permanently, divested, damaged or even destroyed.' (emphasis added)[14]

In this collection we have not sought to limit the understanding of home, but we note that whatever approach to the meaning home is taken, the home can be—and is perhaps simultaneously—a place of security and insecurity, of fulfilment and repression, of inclusion and exclusion, of mobility and immobility. Law, once more broadly understood, is deeply implicated in these multiple experiences of home. What is interesting in our collection is how, for some of our contributors, the notion of the precarious home

[11] Salman Rushdie, 'Out of Kansas' in Rushdie, *Step Across This Line: Collected non-fiction 1992–2002* (Jonathan Cape, 2002) p 1.

[12] Susan Banky, 'Precarity of place: a complement to the growing precariat literature' in Matthew Johnson (ed), *Precariat: labour, works and politics* (Routledge, 2015).

[13] Nigel Rapport and Andrew Dawson, 'Home and Movement: a polemic' in NJ Rapport and A Dawson (eds), *Migrants of Identity: Perceptions of Home in a World of Movement* (Berg, 1998) 3–38.

[14] Richard Baxter and Katherine Brickell, 'For Home *Un*making' (2014) 11 *Home Cultures* 133–44, 134.

ceased to be productive. Instead inspired by Butler, they see 'precarity' as an ontological condition. As Butler notes,

> [p]recariousness implies living socially, that is, the fact that one's life is always in some sense in the hands of the other. It implies exposure both to those we know and to those we do not know; a dependency on people we know, or barely know, or know not at all.[15]

This framing raises difficult questions about the links between life and home—is home a construct to resist the precariousness of life? Is security therefore inevitably illusory? Can, in such cases, the home ever be seen as precarious itself, separated from life? How might an acceptance of precariousness as a condition of existence reshape or reconfigure accounts of home?—and these are themes which are explored throughout the collection.

III. INSECURE TIMES

One starting point for this book is an examination of what we mean by 'insecure times'. What is it that makes current social arrangements and institutions apparently more marked by 'insecurity' today than at any other time? The question might seem to be particularly relevant to the legal sphere, characterised as it is by its aspirations for fixed and stable institutions, practices and norms, where security would appear to be among its inherent features. This notion of security is acutely pertinent to rights to the home, as these rights have traditionally been presumed to be the most secure of all rights. From William Blackstone's characterisation of property as being a right of 'sole and despotic dominion' over things, and Bentham's 'property is security' to Charles Reich's formulation of property as providing a secure 'zone of privacy' for the individual,[16] the home has been conventionally seen by legal theorists as the paradigm case of the individual property right.

Yet, a closer examination of legal history as well as the socio-legal reality of property rights, particularly in relation to the 'home', reveals pervasive insecurity and precariousness.[17] Moreover, this insecurity is arguably increasingly evident. A burgeoning academic literature has begun to focus on the contemporary sociological phenomenon of 'precarisation' or 'precarity'. This concept first emerged a decade or so ago in the sphere of

[15] Judith Butler, *Frames of War: When is Life Grievable?* (Verso, 2009).

[16] W Blackstone, *Commentaries on the Law of England*, Bk 2, Ch 1; Jeremy Bentham, *The Theory of Legislation* (Kegan Paul, 1931) ch 2: C Reich, 'The New Property' (1964) 73 *Yale Law Journal* 733.

[17] See N Piska, *The Precarization of Real Property Law: an Essay on the Evisceration of Equity and Financial Capitalism* (unpublished, 2017) paper with author.

industrial relations to describe the effects of the broad changes consequent on the 'deregulation' of the economies of advanced industrialised societies from the 1980s onwards, and corresponding transformations of the post-war welfare state. More specifically, the deregulation of labour markets was central to the legal transformation of the post-war welfare state. As late modern economies shifted from Fordist to post-Fordist patterns of production, that is to say, where plant size is reduced, and mass production is less pronounced, union membership decreased and workforces became, or were forced to become, more 'flexible'.

Further, the widespread political rejection by governments over the last three decades of collectivist solutions to social problems in favour of more individualist policies has progressively undermined the legal entitlements of employees in the workplace.[18] Despite large differences across different states, the new model is manifested by principles that give greater primacy to *individual* rights in the workplace, and 'the rediscovery of the individual in labour law'.[19] These rights include the right of individual employees not to be members of unions, and the right to negotiate directly with an employer as to rates of pay and conditions of work without union collective bargaining over rights and obligations in the workplace; the labour contract takes on more of the characteristics of the traditional individual contract. The 'freer', contractual rights reflect the parties' respective strengths, so tend to be accompanied by a reduced package of statutory rights in relation to such matters as redundancy payments, minimum wage requirements, rights to security of employment and protections against unfair dismissal. The general process that some writers referred to as 'the death of contract' that accompanied the rise of the regulatory and welfare state[20] has started to give way to 'the rise' of freedom of contract, as contract assumes an increasingly dominant place in the landscape of employment relations.[21]

In this changed landscape, the post-war process that Glendon referred to as the 'occupational bonding' reflecting the enhanced legal security given to many (but not all) employees in welfare-regulatory states started to wane. The growing bundle of rights of employees, which assumed the form of 'new property',[22] has come to be progressively eroded with the incorporation of individualist market-oriented principles into labour law. Where once

[18] Lord Wedderburn, M Rood, G Lyon-Caen, W Daubler and P Van der Heyden, *Labour Law in the Post-Industrial Era: Essays in Honour of Hugo Sinzheimer* (Dartmouth, 1994).

[19] S Simitis, 'The Rediscovery of the Individual in Employment Law' in R Ragowski and G Teubner (eds), *Reflexive Labour Law: Studies in Industrial Relations and Employment Regulation* (Kluwer, 1994) 183.

[20] P Atiyah, *The Rise and Fall of Freedom of Contract* (Oxford University Press, 1979); G Gilmore, *The Death of Contract* (Ohio State University Press, 1974).

[21] FH Buckley (ed), *The Fall and Rise of Freedom of Contract* (Duke University Press, 1999).

[22] MA Glendon, *The New Family and the New Property* (Butterworths, 1981) 143–70.

labour unions, usually within a corporatist political framework, would offer nationwide representation to workers, in the newly disorganised environment, employment contracts, and therefore wages and conditions, reflect local, individual and increasingly insecure, conditions.[23] Similarly, the heavily due-process-driven 'industrial justice', widely institutionalised at the height of the regulatory welfare state,[24] has been progressively dismantled. The result is an increasingly precarious existence for workers. As Leah Vosko puts it: 'In the early 21st century, precarious employment encompasses forms of work characterised by limited social benefits and statutory entitlements, job insecurity, low wages, and high risks of ill-health.'[25]

Importantly, Vosko insists on examining the legal dimensions of this development in order to understand fully the way in which it operates:

> Legal definitions are central to any conception of precarious employment. They relate to whether workers confront insecurity because of whom a given law or policy is designed to cover, the parameters around which it is framed, and how it is applied. They are critical to revealing how and in what ways law and policy on the books shape, mirror, or contrast law and policy in practice.[26]

Although Vosko's analysis is confined to the labour market, the phenomenon of ever more fragile workers' rights in employment has come to be paralleled across society as a whole over the last four decades or so, as the central elements of post-war regulatory welfare states have been subjected to radical transformation. One manifestation of the change, closely inter-related to the changes in employment, is the transformation of welfare. Universal entitlements to social welfare, being the 'cradle to grave' rights characteristic of the fully-fledged social citizenship of post-war Keynesian welfare states, have been progressively pared back. Welfare rights have become increasingly curtailed, or made conditional, as social welfare safety nets have become less a policy priority for governments in recent decades, leading to lower levels of legal security.[27] While different jurisdictions experience these processes in widely divergent ways, some shared factors link them. For example, rights to many benefits are now harder to obtain, and harder to retain. Moreover, the administration of welfare increasingly places

[23] S Lash and J Urry, *The End of Organised Capitalism* (Polity, 1987); Ben-Israel, 'From Collective to Individual Justice' in J Beellace and M Rood (eds), *Labour Law at the Crossroads* (Kluwer, 1997) 27–34; Leah F Vosko, *Precarious Employment: Understanding Labour Market Insecurity in Canada* (McGill-Queen's Press, 2006).

[24] P Selznick, *Law, Society and Industrial Justice* (Transaction Books, 1969).

[25] LF Vosko, *Precarious Employment: Understanding Labour Market Insecurity in Canada* (McGill-Queen's Press, 2006) 11.

[26] Ibid, 12. See also N Kountouris, 'Legal Determinants of Precariousness in Personal Work Relations: A European Perspective' (2013) 34 *Comparative Labor Law & Policy Journal* 21.

[27] C Pierson, *Beyond the Welfare State* (Polity Press, 1991).

in jeopardy the rights of recipients, as states seek to rein in welfare expenditure, a process that fuels greater insecurity of income.[28]

These reforms have not only entailed the retraction of many welfare programmes, they are accompanied by the imposition of more restrictions and obligations on the receipt of social security, particularly unemployment benefits, and the establishment of ever harsher and more punitive compliance regimes.[29] These reforms reflect an accelerating global trend of withdrawal of support for the Keynesian welfare state, and the forms of economic and financial security that went with it, as a newly-configured 'workfare' state comes into being.[30] But this novel state form begins to insinuate itself into increasing domains of social life. The overall result, according to Isabell Lorey, is that

> precarization is not a marginal phenomenon, even in the rich regions of Europe … Precarization means more than insecure jobs, more than the lack of security given by waged labour. By way of insecurity and danger, it embraces the whole of existence, the body, whole modes of subjectivation. It is threat and coercion, even as it opens up new possibilities of living and working. Precarization means living with the unforeseeable, with contingency.[31]

The welfare-regulatory state's universalised social rights effected a significant reversal of class inequality.[32] By contrast, as Kosonen concludes, in summarising trends in Europe, the former capacities of welfare states to ameliorate class disadvantage have faded where 'unemployment rates and poverty rates have increased, public social security has weakened, and a shift toward private arrangements has occurred'.[33] This point was made over two decades ago; more recent studies reveal even more acute levels of inequality and poverty.[34] It may be that in some cases the new regimes reverse a debilitating dependency by encouraging a more active citizenry

[28] P Henman and M Fenger, 'Introduction' in Paul Henman and Menno Fenger (eds), *Administering Welfare Reform: International Transformations in Welfare Governance* (Policy Press, 2006) 1.

[29] Ibid. See also, L Wacquant, *Punishing the Poor: The Neoliberal Government of Social Insecurity* (Duke University Press, 2009); KS Gustafson, *Cheating Welfare: Public Assistance and the Criminalization of Poverty* (New York University Press, 2011).

[30] *Social Citizenship and Workfare in the United States and Western Europe: The Paradox of Inclusion*, JF Handler (Cambridge University Press, 2004); G Esping-Andersen, 'After the Golden Age? Welfare State Dilemmas in a Global Economy' in G Esping-Andersen (ed), *Welfare States in Transition: National Adaptations in Global Economies* (Sage, 1996) 1; B Kus, 'Neoliberalism, Institutional Change and the Welfare State: The Case of Britain and France' (2008) 47 *International Journal of Comparative Sociology* 488.

[31] I Lorey, *State of Insecurity: Government of the Precarious* (Verso, 2015) 1.

[32] T Marshall, *Sociology at the Crossroads* (Heinemann, 1963).

[33] P Kosonen, 'European Welfare State Models: Converging Trends' (1995) 25 *International Journal of Sociology* 81, 99.

[34] See generally, J Stiglitz, *The Price of Inequality* (Penguin, 2010), Thomas Piketty, *Capital in the Twenty First Century* (Harvard University Press, Arthur Goldhammer (trans), 2014).

to participate productively in labour markets; but much of the empirical evidence suggests that the primary consequence of getting claimants off the register leads to a substantial growth in the number of the working poor.[35] Overall, the combination of privatisation, deregulation and diminishing welfare rights lead to a growing insecurity of the more vulnerable citizens in the emergent contracting state. For the political philosopher Nancy Fraser these recent changes, in combination, have the effect of, to some extent, displacing the notion of the 'poor' as a social category, insofar as the latter term tends to obscure the factors that cause poverty. A far better term, she suggests, 'is the "precariat". This expression suggests multiple degrees and forms of inclusion/exclusion … it stresses their shared vulnerability and the ease with which those in the relatively favoured categories can slip back into the disfavoured ones.'[36]

At this moment it might be useful to consider the relationship between vulnerability[37] and precariousness. Berg, in her study of global labour migration, places the precariousness engendered by immigration law in the closely connected frames of 'precariousness', 'vulnerability' and 'dependency' developed in feminist legal and political theories. These take a more holistic approach to precariousness, recognising that insecurity in inherent in human life.[38]

Similarly, the chapters in this volume use this 'wider lens of precariousness' to consider the current position of particular housing situations in a range of advanced industrialised societies.

IV. THE HOME AND INSECURE TIMES

This creeping, society-wide precarisation can be argued to be evident not only in the context of workers' rights, but also in the context of housing provision. Many western liberal democracies following the Second World War attempted to advance general security by increasing housing security across each of the various forms of tenure, by increasing levels of traditional home ownership, increasing protection for tenants in private residential

[35] M Matsuda, 'Were You There? Witnessing Welfare Retreat' (1997) 31 *University of San Francisco Law Review* 779.

[36] N Fraser, 'Social Exclusion, Global Poverty, and Scales of (In)Justice: Rethinking Law and Poverty in a Globalising World' in S Liebenberg and G Quintot (eds), *Law and Poverty: Perspectives from South Africa and Beyond* (Juta, 2012) 19. See also, and generally, G Standing, *The Precariat: the New Dangerous Class* (Bloomsbury, 2011).

[37] See, for example, MA Fineman, 'The Vulnerable Subject and the Responsive State' (2010) 60 *Emory Law Journal* 251–75; Emory Public Law Research Paper No. 10–130. Available at SSRN: https://ssrn.com/abstract=1694740.

[38] L Berg, *Migrant Rights at Work: Law's Precariousness at the Intersection of Immigration and Labour* (Routledge, 2015) 9.

markets, and providing much greater levels of social housing. There were always those who were excluded or at best conditionally included: women, the disreputable working class, the vagrant and the migrant. Nonetheless these efforts were important in democratising the legal security of the home, although housing has been characterised as the 'wobbly pillar' of the welfare state.[39] Just as labour rights have been eroded, these attempts to provide housing security have been measurably weakened in recent years.[40]

For example, the rights of tenants have been widely reduced in a manner generally consistent with the precarisation of employment and welfare provision, as market principles have increasingly intruded. First, state provision of public housing has been significantly curtailed. In contrast to the post-war boom in public housing provision for the poor at heavily state-subsidised rents, states now have reduced or even reversed these policies. The most dramatic example is the United Kingdom where a comparatively large public housing stock has been sold off in recent years so that tenants' rights in the nature of public rights against the state, based on need, have become private rights of ownership in the property market.[41] At the same time, this shift in the direction of the market has been complemented by greater reliance on market rents by public housing authorities in many countries.[42] Furthermore, in the private sector, the former redistributive features of laws that gave tenants security of tenure and rights to affordable rents have been diluted. Increasingly, security of tenure is measured not by legal rules limiting landlord's rights to terminate, based on a tenant's long-term need, but simply by contractual agreement between landlord and tenant.[43] Equally, rents increasingly are determined by market pressures, as mechanisms for rent control are gradually dismantled.[44]

The growing resort to market-based solutions—to what some have referred to as a 'neoliberal' approach to economic and social problems that originated in the 1970s—has been further accentuated by the onset of the

[39] Ulf Torgersen, 'Housing: The Wobbly Pillar under the Welfare State' (1987) 4 *Scandinavian Housing and Planning Research* 116; Peter Malpass, 'Housing and the New Welfare State: Wobbly Pillar or Cornerstone?' (2008) 23 *Housing Studies* 604. However, see Binger's contribution (Chapter fourteen below) for an argument that the wobbly pillar may be more positively understood.

[40] See, for example, in England: Suzanne Fizpatrick and Beth Watts, 'Competing visions: security of tenure and the welfarisation of English social housing' *Housing Studies* On-line: http://dx.doi.org/10.1080/02673037.2017.1291916 (2017).

[41] R Forrest and A Murie, *Selling the Welfare State: The Privatisation of Housing* (Routledge, 1988).

[42] J Kemeny, *From Public Housing to the Social Market: Rental Policy Strategies in Comparative Perspective* (Routledge, 1995) 114–25.

[43] R Cranston, *Legal Foundations of the Welfare State* (Weidenfeld and Nicolson, 1985) 116; A Bradbrook, 'Residential Tenancies: The Second Stage of Reforms' (1998) 20 *Sydney Law Review* 402–34.

[44] R Cranston, *Legal Foundations of the Welfare State* (Weidenfeld and Nicolson, 1985) 116–17.

global financial crisis in 2008. The responses of governments across the world has largely been to adopt 'austerity' packages, which have had the effect of shifting bulk of the burden of restoring state finances, and paying off corporate debt, onto the most disadvantaged members of the community. The result has generally been to reduce further levels of social security and social housing provision, while leaving the incomes and property rights of the most advantaged largely intact, with enormous subsidies or tax breaks now available for middle-income home-owners or real estate investors. Yet, pro-poor housing assistance policies struggle on meagre budgets, and concern with evictions in the public and private sector has lessened. The overall result of these legal reforms is that housing has become the especially 'wobbly pillar' under the welfare state.[45]

For Marcuse and Madden[46] something else, closely connected, has happened, that is global in extent. Their starting point is that housing is a precondition both for work and leisure. But because the home has become commodified there is a 'conflict between housing as lived, social space and housing and housing as instrument for profitmaking—a conflict between housing as *home* and as *real estate*.'[47] This commodification exacerbates precarity.

In these respects, the growing 'precarity' reflects broader tendencies of contemporary societies to exhibit greater extremes of poverty and inequality, actively supported or at least tolerated by their governments and legal systems.[48] Precarisation, both in general, and specifically in relation to the home, is an agent of inequality, a phenomenon that affects only certain groups in society. The increasing insecurity of the home impacts differentially: women, migrants, the poor, ethnic minorities and others who are socially excluded suffer disproportionately from increasing domestic insecurity.

While the more recent forms of legal insecurity represent a novel historical phenomenon, or perhaps the reappearance in novel forms, of older patterns of employment insecurity, there are aspects of insecurity that have always beset what might otherwise be the security offered by the home. In particular, various social, economic and environmental factors produce different types of insecurity for home-dwellers. The various chapters in the book below examine the many aspects of this broad, if uneven, trend of historical, sociological and legal change. They measure the extent of precariousness of the contemporary home, but they also consider the theoretical

[45] Torgersen, n 39 and Malpass, n 39 above.
[46] D Madden and P Marcuse, *In Defence of Housing* (Verso, 2016).
[47] Ibid, 4.
[48] See generally, Joseph Stiglitz, *The Price of Inequality* (Penguin, 2010), Thomas Piketty, *Capital in the Twenty First Century* (Harvard University Press, Arthur Goldhammer (trans), 2014).

potential of re-imagining the home in precarious times. The authors suggest that an understanding that the home is precarious could lead to much more imaginative engagements with the notion of home. In doing so, different strategies might be considered to deal with this emerging condition.

We now turn to provide an overview of how the chapters in the book address these issues.

V. UNDERSTANDING PRECARISATION

Responding to the theme of the 'precarious home', the collection starts with Sarah Blandy's focus on home 'sharing'. Her chapter uses sharing as a lens for interrogating the idea of the precarious home. She explores a range of risk factors associated with sharing the home, starting with a consideration of how 'home' is conceptualised in contemporary Western culture and specifically in the United Kingdom. First, the chapter explores three distinct meanings of the concept of sharing. At its simplest, it means a 'one-off allocation' as when there is a grant of property rights in a building used as a home. It may also mean 'to possess or use a resource in common with others'. Finally, it may mean 'to participate or contribute to', which suggests a more active and wider meaning that can be applied to housing issues more generally. The chapter then moves on to examine different tenure types, from owner-occupation to squatting, which determine the extent of the property rights a resident enjoys in their home and therefore their degree of security. In the final section of the chapter, the specific meaning of to 'share' that expresses the idea of collaboration and participation and collaboration will come to the fore in an exploration of political and protest alliances around housing issues. The continuum of sharing identified sheds light on the home's precariousness, and the precarity of different groups in relation to the home.

This chapter is followed by Nestsor Davidson's exploration of psychological aspects of property in general, and how these might bear on a sense of insecurity. Like all legal institutions, property requires justification. One dominant set of normative justifications emphasises the relationship between property and the self. Another related approach invokes Aristotelian virtue ethics[49] to emphasise the role played by property in human flourishing. Both approaches appear to have psychological elements to them. But what if those psychological underpinnings were empirically suspect? Might a more grounded, empirically validated set of findings about human nature yield a different type of property law? To rely on psychological realism can open

[49] See generally, Gregory S Alexander and Eduardo Penalver, *An Introduction to Property Theory* (Cambridge University Press, 2012).

new possibilities for understanding the normative underpinnings of property. In the case of home, the insights of positive psychology would highlight the nature of home, less as a source of individual attachment, and more as a locus for positive experiences and a forum for the development of human relationships. Home in this view is a means to an end, and less a question of individual identity than a resource for what might connect and add meaning to people's lives. Accordingly, when the home becomes insecure, it generates very specific forms of psychological harm. The chapter argues that we can add to our existing normative understandings of property law's foundations a grounding generally in empirical psychology and more specifically in what has been shown in the research to support flourishing. This more realistic approach adds important nuance to prescriptions for the structures of property law in general, and for secure rights to the home in particular.

VI. RENTAL SECURITY

The next Part focuses on the rented home. Continuing the theme of 'insecure times', Caroline Hunter and Jed Meers examine an emergent form of particularly precarious housing in Western Europe; namely property guardianship. The growth in property guardians may be seen as 'a form of unregulated, semi-formal housing in the context of the growing shift of many housing practices from marginal to mainstream.'[50] They use the example of property guardians to examine the legal determinants of housing precarity for non-owners (tenants and those with less security), mirroring the work of Nicola Kountouris[51] on the legal determinants of precariousness in work relations. Using a framework of immigration status, tenure/time, control, cost, and conditions, they illuminate the elements that can exacerbate precarity. They highlight how two intersecting dimensions of precariousness—'organisational precariousness' and 'legal uncertainty'—can be useful in highlighting how the legal dimensions can compound precariousness. The third section of their chapter focuses of the role of local authorities as a particular organ of the state, using some empirical data. They conclude that it is clear that the state is less concerned in the tenure/time dimension, whether by local authorities using property guardian firms for their own empty properties or at a national level stripping way that dimension for tenants. The position in terms of conditions is more ambivalent.

In the second chapter of this Part Brendan Edgeworth, using the State of New South Wales in Australia as a case study, points to a decisive shift in

[50] Mara Ferreri et al, n 1 above.

[51] Nicola Kountouris, 'Legal Determinants of Precariousness in Personal Work Relations: A European Perspective' (2013) 34 *Comparative Labor Law & Policy Journal* 21.

legal regimes which have unfolded, from the 1970s onwards, in the sphere of social housing. He shows how the formerly secure legal framework of tenancy law in favour of tenants, reflecting the 'politics of redistribution' characteristic of welfare states,[52] has been progressively stripped away. As a result, tenants face increasing insecurity as the state more vigorously polices tenant behaviour, rendering tenants more vulnerable than ever. A core change in the legal framework has been the move from decision-making in the courts to a residential tenancies tribunal. The tribunal's more informal mechanisms for dispute resolution, far from reducing the impact of law on the resolution of conflict, actually increase it, and in ways that render public housing tenancies more, rather than less, insecure.

The final chapter in this Part is a provocation. It suggests that not only may the relentless pursuit of owner-occupation be counterproductive, but also the legislative insistence on security for tenants. By taking the Polish residential market as a case study, Magdalena Habdas argues that the lack of long-term housing policies, promoting only owner-occupation, and disregarding the need to strike a balance between the general and the individual interest of landlords, have hampered the development of the residential tenancy market and have left many housing issues, specifically issues of supply and quality, unresolved. The courts both nationally and particularly internationally (in the guise of the European Court of Human Rights) have ensured a different balance.

VII. THE HOME AND GOVERNMENTAL PRECARISATION

In this Part of the collection the contributors examine the contemporary socio-legal landscape of the home by focusing more carefully on governmental precarisation in the context of the home. By 'governmental precarisation' we mean laws and policies specifically enacted and implemented by states that bear directly on the capacities of citizens to remain secure in their homes.[53]

In the first chapter of this Part Helen Carr suggests a long and complex history to the precarious home and expands the notion of security beyond the right not to be evicted. Her examination of the interrelationship between the precarious home and 'thermal comfort' notes how the English home appears to be peculiarly vulnerable to the characteristic cold and damp of the local climate and that this porousness to the weather impacts particularly on the poor and the vulnerable. 'Excess winter deaths' because of governmental failure do not appear to have been given priority by governments,

[52] Nancy Fraser, 'From Redistribution to Recognition: Dilemmas of Justice in a "Postsocialist" Age' (1995) 212 *New Left Review* 68–93.

[53] Lorey, n 31 above, 13.

which have either sought to solve other housing problems such as limited supply or chosen to prioritise the privatisation and affordability of domestic energy supplies. The chapter uses the thermally precarious home as a lens through which to challenge accounts of the emergence of social problems which fail to interrogate the role of power and ideology.

In the next chapter in this Part, Richard Goulding examines another recent phase of UK social housing policy, at odds with the organising presumptions of earlier decades. Specifically, he looks at the reshaping of social housing providers as an example of financialisation through the imposition of housing insecurity, drawing on contemporary debates in critical urbanism. Financialisation of housing is an inherently spatial and temporal process, and recent years have seen growing calls for research into the specific connections between states, real estate actors and financial markets in structuring patterns of accumulation.[54] This has been facilitated by neoliberal reforms through which the state actively restructures both itself and other arenas of social life along market and quasi-market lines.

De-municipalisation of public housing and reforms to social housing development finance from the 1980s onward facilitated the spread of new commercial models and the use of derivatives for larger, predominantly London-centred housing associations—non-government organisations registered with the state's housing regulator and able to provide social housing. The adaptability of financialisation following the 2008 crisis can be seen in how a renewed housing bubble, centred on London, has allowed capital markets to become a new source of finance, while state-implemented urban austerity policies have restricted non-commercial provision through weakened tenant protections and slashed welfare incomes. This has entailed uneven development, exposed the sector to new sources of risk as it becomes dependent on real estate markets tied into global capital flows, and increased the precariousness of everyday life as growing numbers of people are excluded from accessing social housing.

Written in the immediate aftermath of the fire at Grenfell Tower in West London, Edward Kirton-Darling's chapter examines the accounts of precarity and precarisation in the work of Lorey[55] and Butler[56] through an in-depth analysis of the deaths of three women and three children in a fire at Lakanal House, South London, in 2009. The analysis unpicks the responses of government to concerns set out by the Coroner in letters following the conclusion of the inquests into those deaths, and focuses on the way in which these deaths at home and the role of law and ownership

[54] Manuel B Aalbers (ed), *Subprime Cities: The Political Economy of Mortgage Markets* (Wiley-Blackwell, 2012).

[55] Lorey, n 31 above.

[56] Butler, n 15 above and Judith Butler, *Precarious Life: the Powers of Mourning and Violence* (Verso, 2004).

in those deaths reveal aspects of the governance of contemporary life. The discussion highlights that a general account of precariousness risks glossing over important nuances, including the importance of distinguishing different approaches by 'the state'. In addition, the case study demonstrates the importance of examining the relationship of space and law in efforts to compartmentalise life and property, and argues that Lorey's emphasis on the hegemony of governmental precarisation misses the ways in which liberal protection continues to exist as a strategy of governance.

VIII. GLOBAL/LOCAL PRECARIOUSNESS

This Part of the collection contains chapters that reflect on the precariousness which is the consequence of global events or conditions which are, or appear to be, outside of local control.

So, Richard Warren examines the United Kingdom's increasingly restrictive approaches to resettlement of migrants. The chapter considers, through a legal lens, what home might mean in contemporary times for the migrant to the UK. The argument is that there has been a shift from an understanding that the UK seeks to integrate migrants and provide them with a secure and permanent home, to a position where migrants enjoy, at best, institutionalised insecurity and a highly conditional 'home'. This shift is not productive, but contradictory and destabilising and with serious consequences for the indigenous, as well as the migrant population.

The chapter reflects on the etymology of precariousness, suggesting that its original meaning reveals a connection with the exercise of arbitrary power, which usefully illuminates the migrant's encounters with the law. It then provides some examples of how the law works to create the new migrant precariat, and how, contrary to the argument by Habdas, legal counter-narratives, such as those deriving from Article 8 of the European Convention on Human Rights, have failed to protect migrants. The author then considers recent policy shifts from social integration to conditionality, before focusing on the prevailing neoliberal rationalities which underpin these shifts. In the final section of the chapter Warren argues not only that we should resist the creation of a migrant precariat but points to the contradictions and broader consequences.

Another instance of precariousness of home arises where migration is not from one country to another, but from one part of one country to another. So, in contemporary China, mass migration from the country to the city has been occurring for many decades. To address the problem of housing the rural migrants, in many areas in China a de facto property market is emerging that consists of affordable properties called 'minor rights properties'. This does not constitute a formal legal concept. These sorts of properties are built by farmers on collectively owned land that is reserved for agricultural purposes or farmers' residential use, and which cannot be commodified in the sense of being transferred on the formal property market according to relevant provisions of the Land Administration Law (2004) and the Property Law (2007). Buyers of such properties can obtain an ownership certificate issued by the township government. However, the legality of such ownership certificates is highly questionable, as according to the law, only governments at the county level or above have the authority to issue these ownership certificates and register these properties. Ting Xu and Wei Gong's chapter explores the nature of the minor rights properties and the ways in which it is linked to the inequality embedded in the urban–rural divide, the government and property developers' pursuit of profits, and the manner in which central and local government wrestle for power. Specifically, it adopts a legal pluralist analysis, examining the interplay of legal and extra-legal property rights, and of state law and informal norms, and their implications for the understanding of informality and extra-legality in perceiving the idea of property. It argues that we should recognise extra-legal property as legitimate, drawing upon the continuum of land rights approach adopted there.

In the final chapter of this Part, Ann Dupuis, Suzanne Vallance and David Thorns consider how trust and certainty in social institutions can be rebuilt after a natural disaster such as New Zealand's Canterbury earthquakes in order that people can recreate and maintain their sense of ontological security. The chapter raises further challenges to the notion of ontological security in circumstances of a 'natural', rather than a 'human-made' disaster. Their suggestion is that the home is better understood, not as a haven, but rather as a socio-legal space and they argue that the earthquakes have exposed new vulnerabilities that were previously almost unimaginable. As a consequence the notion of the home takes on new meanings. Because of the many complex insurance issues to do with damage and remediation, this chapter presents a new framing of 'the home' as a site co-constituted in and through socio-legal processes. This view has implications for the way the home is secured and serviced and raises major questions of where responsibility lies in these processes.

IX. RESISTANCE AND STRATEGIES

This final Part of the collection concentrates on strategies that the precarious use in order to manage or reduce their precarious status.

In the first chapter, Laura Binger takes us back to a period which may be seen as the 'golden age' of the welfare state, where nonetheless a group of homeless families were housed in an isolated and bleak hostel (King Hill) in the south of England in the 1960s. The residents started a campaign, and negotiated with local government for a charter of rights. Using Lorey's[57] framework for thinking about precariousness, Binger analyses the King Hill Hostel Campaign in raising questions about the conditions of life at the hostel and the relationships in which that precariousness existed. She argues for a shift away from assuming that a precarious welfare state only leads to its erosion; rather it allows for an analysis of the power relationship between the institutions of the welfare state and the people who encounter it in their everyday lives, and that shift is important to understanding struggles like the Campaign and more generally to allowing us to see the agency of the residents of the hostel.

Gabriele D'Adda, Lucia Delgardo and Eduard Sala take us to the mortgage crisis in Spain and the work of PAH (*Plataforma Afectados por la Hipoteca*) to help owner-owners to avoid evictions and to negotiate directly with banks to obtain a resolution of their cases through different strategies. Using empirical evidence from the Barcelona PAH, they argue that PAH challenges the system by rejecting the public blame of people affected and instead involving them in a process of awareness and empowerment. By-passing Spanish mortgage law, which exclusively protects the creditors, PAH has successfully promoted thousands of individual and direct negotiations between owners and creditor banks. These negotiations are preceded and accompanied by a collective awareness and empowerment process developed through the weekly welcome assembly but also during the actions, the interventions to block evictions and the mobilisations promoted by PAH. The affected people gradually lose their sense of guilt and the fear of losing their home that often accompanies them when they first arrive at PAH. At the same time, they realise that they are not alone and, listening to other people's situations, they learn strategies that they can use in their own negotiation. Furthermore, by taking part in actions and mobilisation, affected people feel a sense of community and they become aware that, being part of the PAH, they can count on other people and on the forces of the movement. It is a tale of resistance outside of the law.

The collection finishes with Danie Brand's chapter. He uses a South Africa Supreme Court of Appeal case—*The Baphiring Community v Tswaranani Projects CC*[58]—to focus on the contentious issue of restitution of land rights in post-Apartheid South Africa. This process is intended to rebalance the scales of justice. Successful restitution claimants may be awarded either the rights to the actual land that they lost, rights to alternative land, or monetary compensation. In a growing number of cases before South African courts, claimants who were seeking returned access to the actual land they had lost—their erstwhile homes—have been awarded alternative land, as

[57] Lorey, n 31 above.
[58] *The Baphiring Community v Tswaranani Projects* CC [2013] ZASCA 99.

return to the original land was held not to be 'feasible'. On offer was a different tract of land roughly of the same size and productive capacity.

Against their claim, arguments were raised that their return to the land would not be economically feasible or desirable—not in the sense that it would be too expensive to acquire the land, but that it would in a more macro-economic sense be detrimental to national food and general agricultural production. The chapter argues that the notion of restoration of home and of the spiritual, historical, communal and emotional links to a certain physical place has been progressively elided by the courts in favour of supposedly ideologically empty notions of efficiency and 'feasibility'. This development can be seen as part of a broader development in the local jurisprudence dealing with access to basic resources, of regarding rights as that which is possible rather than as ideals, and regarding justice as efficiency. The chapter concludes with a critique of the notions of efficiency, feasibility and the possible, and problematises the idealistic notions of home, community and history.

X. CONCLUSION

This collection does not aim to provide a definitive analysis of precarity and the home. Indeed, when the editors are all too conscious of gaps and limitations in the approaches taken to precarity, particularly the insufficiency of attention paid to feminist analysis of the home, and to the relationship between race, home and precarity, it would be foolish to make any such claim. Instead, the collection has a much more limited aim: it seeks to suggest that the notion of the precarious home offers socio-legal scholars a particular perspective that is worth interrogating, and that the theoretical insights developed in the context of labour relations may be worth applying to the home, whether understood as a space or a form of entitlement. Moreover, at a time when those of us who are United Kingdom-based are in shock about the tragic loss of life at Grenfell Tower, in the Royal Borough of Kensington and Chelsea, one of the wealthiest boroughs in the world, we would also suggest that socio-legal scholarship has an important role in revealing that the security inherent in the concept of home may be illusory. The anger and sense of betrayal resulting from the failure of the state to provide secure homes for some of its most vulnerable citizens are significant. But so too are suggestions that there may be progressive possibilities within the concept of precarity. If the collection stimulates thoughtful responses to the interface of home, precarity and law we will consider that it has succeeded.

Part I

Understanding Precarisation

2

Precarious Homes: The Sharing Continuum

SARAH BLANDY*

I. INTRODUCTION

THIS CHAPTER EXAMINES sharing as a strategy for managing insecurities of the home, and the consequences of this response to the age of austerity. The role of law and government in enabling, regulating and managing how people share in relation to the home is analysed, bringing out the differential experiences of particular groups. A theoretical framework for understanding sharing as a continuum is applied to the lived realities of precarious homes. The chapter examines different forms of sharing in relation to the home, including sharing as a form of collective resistance to precariousness resulting from particular features of the contemporary economic, social and legal landscape.

Approaching precariousness from its opposite is a useful starting point: what would constitute a completely secure home? I hypothesise a home belonging to the outright owner of an island, living alone and financially unencumbered. There are no other island residents to deal with; nor are there any other potentially complicating property rights in the island, such as easements or leasehold interests; and no risk of losing the island to a lender, as the owner has no financial indebtedness secured against the home. The sea provides natural boundaries which eliminate the risk of disputes over or across boundaries with adjoining properties. This imagined completely secure home thus avoids the more common risks and causes of precariousness. Strikingly, these all arise from sharing property or property rights with other people or institutions. Sharing and precariousness of the home are evidently closely entwined.

In this chapter I have adopted Judith Butler's distinction between precariousness (meaning uncertainty) and the concept of 'precarity', which she uses to mean 'that politically induced condition in which certain populations

* Professor of Law, School of Law, University of Sheffield.

suffer from failing social and economic networks of support more than others … precarity is thus the differential distribution of precariousness'.[1] In relation to the home, some policies and practices discussed in this chapter have increased the precarity experienced by certain groups. Further, while precariousness is experienced individually, resistance to precarity is collective, as it involves intentional sharing in the sense of participation in a demonstration or social movement. This chapter is also informed by the way in which Butler uses the concept of performativity—when 'an utterance brings what it states into being',[2] and its relevance to understanding the effect of words and actions in accessing, occupying and sharing residential space.[3]

Although the focus of the chapter is on the UK, there are many similarities across Europe and other developed countries where the welfare safety net has been, to a greater or lesser extent, withdrawn. An increasing number of people are experiencing their homes as precarious, following the 2008 financial crash.[4] One-third of working families in England would not be able to pay more than one more month's rent or mortgage if the main earner lost their job.[5] After housing costs, typical real incomes among low- to middle-income households and those aged 24–35 are no higher in 2016–17 than they were 15 years earlier.[6] Other key factors contributing to the precariousness of home include a more general move towards urban living with consequent higher density[7] and scarcer availability of housing. Increased property values now affect many areas in the UK, rather than being concentrated in London.[8]

Sharing residential accommodation may seem an ostensibly rational response to these larger forces. However, it is shown that such arrangements may actually increase precariousness of the home and occupiers. A wide range of sources are used to illustrate the arguments in this chapter, which is structured as follows. First, I look at the idea of 'sharing', then

[1] Judith Butler, *Notes Toward a Performative Theory of Assembly* (Cambridge MA, Harvard University Press, 2015) 33.

[2] Ibid, 28.

[3] Ibid, 218.

[4] Except for the top one per cent of the UK population, whose fast-rising incomes mean they have now recovered from the crash: Resolution Foundation, 'The Living Standards Audit 2017' (London, Resolution Foundation, 2017): www.resolutionfoundation.org/publications/the-living-standards-audit-2017.

[5] BBC, 'Many families could not afford a month's rent if they lost job—Shelter', *BBC News* (9 August 2016): www.bbc.co.uk/news/uk-england-37017254.

[6] Resolution Foundation (n 4 above).

[7] Office for National Statistics, '2011 Census: Population and Household Estimates for England and Wales, March 2011' (ONS, 16 July 2012): www.ons.gov.uk/peoplepopulationandcommunity/populationandmigration/populationestimates/bulletins/2011censuspopulationandhouseholdestimatesforenglandandwales/2012-07-16#how-densely-england-and-wales-were-populated.

[8] Stephen Clarke, 'Home ownership struggle reaches Coronation Street' (*Resolution Foundation*, 2 August 2016): www.resolutionfoundation.org/media/blog/home-ownership-struggle-reaches-coronation-street/.

I consider how 'home' is shaped by different tenures. The chapter then analyses a range of sharing property relationships within and around the home, and the different models and meanings of sharing with which these may be associated. The subsequent section addresses political and protest alliances around housing issues, before conclusions are reached on sharing, precariousness and precarity in the context of the home.

II. SHARING

The concept of the 'sharing economy'[9] has been recently popularised, and accompanying legal expertise has been developed,[10] so this section begins by considering its relevance to the issues discussed here. The term refers to digital platforms which enable 'access-based consumption transactions … in which no transfer of ownership takes place'.[11] For example, Airbnb, one of the most successful of these online enterprises, profits from both property owners and their guests, describing both as 'members of our global community'.[12] However, those sites which operate on the basis of economic exchange (such as Airbnb) have been described by Belk as 'a business relationship masquerading as communal sharing'.[13] Two kinds of digital platform are considered here in relation to sharing and the home: those which operate on the basis of trust; and those run by profit-seeking entrepreneurs. The tendency of the latter to spot the commercial potential of the former and then adopt their ideas to establish 'pseudo-sharing' enterprises[14] is a contemporary phenomenon of which examples are identified in this chapter.

The nuanced, alternative meanings of 'sharing' shape my broader discussion and analysis of sharing and its consequences for precariousness of the home. The verb to share can mean 'a one-off allocation', such as the grant of property rights in the home; or it can refer to 'possession or use of a resource in common with others', such as when there is a continuing relationship between co-residents of a home or between people holding rights in the same property; and it can have the wider, more active meaning of 'to participate in or contribute to'. The chapter refers to and illustrates each of these meanings.

[9] Arun Sundararajan, *The Sharing Economy: the End of Employment and the Rise of Crowd-based Capitalism* (Cambridge MA, MIT Press, 2016).

[10] Janelle Orsi, *Practicing Law in the Sharing Economy: Helping People Build Cooperatives, Social Enterprise, and Local Sustainable Economies* (Chicago, American Bar Association Books, 2012).

[11] Fleura Bardhi and Giana M Eckhardt, 'Access-based Consumption: The Case of Car Sharing' (2012) 39 *Journal of Consumer Research* 881, 881.

[12] Sign-off in email received from Airbnb by the author, an occasional user of the site.

[13] Russell Belk, 'Sharing Versus Pseudo-Sharing in Web 2.0' (2014) 18 *Anthropologist* 7, 11.

[14] Ibid.

More generally, the idea of sharing usually conveys warmth, co-operation, and other similar positive values such as 'mutuality, trust and openness'.[15] Yet sharing may also imply discomfort, lack of privacy, and a lack of control over your home and possessions. The island home example has already highlighted the risks implicit in a range of sharing relationships with other people, whether a family arrangement or a more formal legal relationship with those holding simultaneous or subsequent rights in the same property, such as a landlord or mortgagee. These will be discussed in more detail in the following section.

The theoretical framework for understanding sharing in relation to the home which is put forward in this chapter, explains sharing as a continuum. At different points along this continuum three different modes of sharing can be distinguished: *involuntary* (being forced into sharing by external circumstances); *uninformed* (sharing by choice, but without being aware of the implications); and *intentional* (a deliberate and positive choice to share, on the basis of full information). These are ideal types, with many possible variations and combinations along the continuum. Drawing on empirical research data from my study of shared residential space[16] and on a wide range of sources from scholarly literature to social media, these models and meanings of sharing are applied here to everyday instances of sharing: homes, property rights and protests about housing insecurities.

III. TENURE AND THE HOME

To a lawyer, the most obvious cause of precariousness in the home is any tenure less than full ownership. Although the tenure of a home can undoubtedly make it more secure or alternatively more precarious, this chapter points to the additional effects of legislation, regulation, financialisation and governance, which are layered over tenure.[17] The UK government's policies include the performative encouragement of home ownership by successive governments, to the extent that there is now a sense of shame involved in not being an owner-occupier.[18] The effect has been to push up rates of

[15] Nicholas A John, 'The Social Logics of Sharing' (2013) 16 *The Communication Review* 113, 128.

[16] British Academy SG-45089, 'The role of legality in multi-occupied residential settings'. All interview respondents quoted in this chapter are derived from this research project, unless otherwise stated.

[17] See Sarah Blandy, Susan Bright and Sarah Nield, 'The Dynamics of Enduring Property Relationships in Land' (forthcoming) *Modern Law Review*.

[18] David Cowan and Morag McDermont, 2006, *Regulating Social Housing: Governing Decline* (Abingdon, Routledge-Cavendish, 2006) 163.

owner-occupation to over 70 per cent in the early 2000s.[19] The ideals of control, autonomy and exclusion have become associated with the tenure of home ownership. The privately owned home is now equated with 'sovereign control over territorial space' on a domestic, personal scale.[20]

However, an owner-occupied home may also prove precarious. Firstly, property rights are always 'shared' with the state, which may decide to exercise its rights such as compulsory purchase. In an unusual example from Guernsey, Mr and Mrs Gillow were refused a licence to occupy the home they owned. The language used by the European Court of Human Rights is telling. The state's action was described as transforming the home from a resource which should provide 'personal security and well-being' into its opposite, something 'precarious'.[21] Secondly, and far more commonly, the owner-occupied home risks becoming precarious because of money borrowed by way of mortgage. A 'one-off allocation' of property rights means that the mortgagor and mortgagee in effect share the same property. Their different but simultaneous 'rights of property are ... a bundle of powers, capable of being separately enjoyed'.[22] Thirdly, the owner's home can become precarious because of unpredicted life-changing events such as illness, divorce or redundancy. Fourthly, uncontrollable external events, for example changes in interest rates, may affect the owner-occupied home, whether freehold or leasehold tenure. A time-limited leasehold estate is by definition more precarious than freehold ownership. Even where the owner has a 999 year lease of their home, a greater 'estate' or bundle of rights in the property is held by someone else, usually the freeholder but possibly by an intermediate superior leaseholder.

Shorter term tenancies are also a leasehold interest, in property law terms. Housing legislation has introduced many variants of this tenure. The social rented sector encompasses two types of landlord: local authorities and housing associations (now officially known as Private Registered Providers) which both once let properties on lifetime 'secure tenancies',[23] making this the least precarious tenure in the UK. However, precarity has subsequently been introduced into this sector through sequential legislation establishing a range of increasingly insecure tenancy types. First, the Housing Act 1998

[19] Stephen Clarke, Adam Corlett and Lindsey Judge, 'The Housing Headwind: The Impact of Rising Housing Costs on UK Living Standards' (London, The Resolution Foundation, 2016) www.resolutionfoundation.org/publications/the-housing-headwind-the-impact-of-rising-housing-costs-on-uk-living-standards/.

[20] Kevin Gray and Susan F Gray, *Elements of Land Law* (5th edn, London, Butterworths, 2009) 105.

[21] *Gillow v UK* [1986] 11 EHRR 335, [55], [57].

[22] Sir Henry Summer Maine, *Village-communities in the East and West: six lectures delivered at Oxford* (London, John Murray, 1881) 133–34.

[23] Housing Act 1980.

introduced 'assured tenancies', with less security, for new housing association tenants. Then, with the Housing Act 1996, came 'introductory tenancies' for local authorities (the equivalent for housing association tenancies were 'starter tenancies') with no security for the first year of occupation. The possibility of insecure 'demoted tenancies' was established by the Anti-Social Behaviour Act 2003; Article 8 of the European Convention on Human Rights can only be used to challenge a decision to demote a tenancy in 'very highly exceptional cases'.[24]

'Flexible tenancies' of a maximum of five years were introduced by the Localism Act 2011, ending the concept of the lifetime tenancy in the social rented sector. The much-contested Housing and Planning Act 2016 has brought in mandatory five-year fixed-term tenancies. At the same time, financialisation of the housing association sector (discussed by Goulding, Chapter eight of this volume) has seen many instances of displacement of existing tenants under the banner of regeneration.[25] Despite these legislative changes and increasing precarity in terms of security of tenure, there were 1.18 million households on the waiting list for social rented sector homes in England.[26] There are now fewer such homes, as the social rented sector has shrunk considerably over the past few decades, from 31 per cent of all households in 1980 to 17 per cent in 2015–16.[27] This decrease is 'due to Right to Buy sales and the large-scale voluntary transfers of local authority stock to Private Registered Providers'.[28]

In contrast to the social rented sector, the private rented sector has dramatically increased its share of the residential market, from 10 per cent in 2002 to 20 per cent in 2015–16.[29] Ironically, nearly 40 per cent of former council properties bought under the Right to Buy[30] are now rented out by private landlords, at much higher rents.[31] Much media and popular attention is paid to 'Generation Rent', young people under 40 who share rented housing in non-related groups of a similar age. In fact, the largest demographic group living in the private rented sector is single people under the age of 65; 'it is not possible to identify whether [their choice to do so] is elective or forced'.[32] However, one factor is likely to be due to fewer

[24] *Manchester City Council v Pinnock* [2010] UKSC 4, Neuberger LJ at [53].

[25] See for example, Stuart Hodkinson and Chris Essen, 'Grounding accumulation by dispossession in everyday life: The unjust geographies of urban regeneration under the private finance initiative' (2015) 7 *International Journal of Law in the Built Environment* 72.

[26] Department of Communities and Local Government, 'Local authority housing statistics: year ending March 2016' (London, DCLG, 2016).

[27] Department of Communities and Local Government, 'English Housing Survey Headline Report 2015–16' (London, DCLG, 2017).

[28] DCLG (n 25 above) 1.

[29] DCLG (n 26 above) 2.

[30] Introduced by the Housing Act 1980.

[31] Pete Apps, 'Revealed: 40% of ex-council flats now rented privately', *Inside Housing* (14 August 2015).

[32] Nigel de Noronha, 'Living in the private rented sector: changing patterns of solo living?' (2014) 111 *Radical Statistics* 21, 33.

houses being available for purchase, and at higher prices. The proportion of owner-occupying households has fallen off markedly from its 2003 peak of 71 per cent, to 63 per cent in 2015–16,[33] the same rate as in 1986. This decrease affects not only London, where most would-be buyers are priced out of the market, but unexpectedly, also the traditionally cheaper areas of the North and the West Midlands.[34]

The private rented sector provides the most precarious homes in terms of security, and is known for its poor conditions and high rents. The standard form of private tenancy is a six-month 'assured shorthold' which the landlord can terminate on two months' notice, without any need to prove fault such as rent arrears; and there is little or no rent control.[35] A particular sector of private tenants, migrants to the UK, suffer an extra layer of precarity under the Immigration Acts 2014 and 2016: landlords are now required to check immigration documents, and can evict on a month's notice anyone without the 'right to rent' due to their immigration status.[36] The unpopularity of the private rented sector is remarkable. When asked to explain why they felt it was unlikely they would buy a home in the future, two-thirds of renters said they wanted to but were unable to afford it; only one per cent preferred the flexibility of renting, and only nine per cent liked their current rented home too much to move.[37]

The UK government policy on the de-regulation of short-term rented accommodation in London[38] has embraced the possibilities that the sharing economy may bring. A report commissioned by the Department for Business, Innovation and Skills suggested that the development of digital platforms can unlock under-used assets, for example empty spare rooms.[39] Occupiers of such accommodation will be licensees, rather than tenants. Licensees have no property rights, just a personal right to occupy the property without any security of tenure at all. In the UK, the most common type of licence arrangement is where a lodger lives in the home of their landlord or landlady; they can be asked to leave immediately if there has been a serious breakdown of the relationship of trust. This makes their position precarious, irrespective of other risk factors associated with sharing.

[33] DCLG (n 27 above) 5.

[34] Clarke et al (n 19 above).

[35] Housing Act 1988, as amended.

[36] Carlos Vargas-Silva, 'Briefing: Migrants and Housing in the UK: Experiences and Impacts' (Oxford, Migration Observatory Briefing, COMPAS, 2015).

[37] Department of Communities and Local Government, *English Housing Survey: First Time Buyers and Potential Home Owners Report, 2014–15* (London, DCLG, 2016).

[38] Department of Communities and Local Government, *Promoting the sharing economy in London: Policy on short-term use of residential property in London* (London, DCLG, 2015).

[39] Debbie Wosskow, 'Unlocking the sharing economy: An independent review' (London, Department for Business, Innovation and Skills, 2014): www.gov.uk/government/publications/unlocking-the-sharing-economy-independent-review.

It is difficult to categorise trespassing, more commonly known as squatting, as a type of tenure. It is now a criminal offence[40] and an extremely precarious way to occupy a home. Apart from the constant threat of eviction, nearly 600 homeless people were arrested by the police and at least 200 prosecuted, with 51 convicted, between 2013 and 2015.[41] However, given the cost and scarcity of housing, it is understandable why some people turn to squatting in empty accommodation. In the final section of the chapter, squatting is considered again, as a collective political protest and response to precarity.

This section has summarised the various tenure sectors which may provide homes, and different degrees of security. If one building is shared by occupiers with such different property rights, it becomes almost impossible to manage effectively. At the time of writing, the terrible tragedy at Grenfell Tower in Kensington and Chelsea had recently revealed how fatally precarious for all residents such circumstances could be. The mix of residents there included 'social tenants, long leaseholders, private tenants, lodgers and many other, less formal arrangements'[42] such as illegal subletting or sofa surfing, all sharing the same tower block as home.

IV. SHARING RELATIONSHIPS AND THE HOME

The chapter now looks at different scenarios of sharing, moving spatially outwards from intimate relationships, through households, to sharing space and facilities within and around the home, and finally to shared boundaries between the home and other properties.

A. Sharing a Bedroom and the Home

Sharing the home with an intimate partner should represent an ideal form of intentional sharing, in the sense of possessing and using resources in common. But a high degree of risk is involved: what happens if the relationship breaks down, particularly if the home is owned in one person's sole name, and particularly if the couple are not married? The emotional difficulties of relationship breakdown and practical difficulties of finding alternative accommodation are exacerbated by the inadequacies of the law

[40] Legal Aid, Sentencing and Punishment of Offenders Act 2012.

[41] SQUASH (Squatters' Action for Secure Homes), 'Homes, Not Jails' (SQUASH, 2015): www.squashcampaign.org/docs/Homes%20Not%20Jails_SQUASH%20April%202015.pdf.

[42] Helen Carr, 'Grenfell Tower and the unravelling of forty years of housing ideology' *Countercurrents: Critical Law at Kent* (Kent University, 21 June 2017) blogs.kent.ac.uk/countercurrents/2017/06/21/grenfell-tower-and-the-unravelling-of-forty-years-of-housing-ideology.

to deal effectively with the property rights of cohabitees.[43] Court decisions are gender-biased against women, whose economic position is still weaker than men's.[44] Women also suffer disproportionately from domestic violence, which is a significant cause of homelessness.[45] The risks associated with intimate relationships in the home are differentially distributed between the genders in a clear instance of precarity.

Financial considerations can lead to continued, enforced, sharing of a home in which there is no individual private space, with a partner from whom you would rather separate:

> [O]ften what keeps people together is money. Living in London, in particular, is so gallingly expensive, I can see why if you lived with the monetary cushion of a partner, the leap to solo occupancy could seem incomprehensible. Impossible even?[46]

Enforced sharing of a different kind is revealed by analysis of the traffic on digital platforms set up to facilitate finding accommodation. This shows that rented accommodation in London has become so scarce and expensive that some tenants are sharing their bedroom with strangers, restricting personal space to a bunk bed. On the SpareRoom site[47] searches of this kind increased by 71 per cent in the two years to 2015, while over 93,505 adverts were placed on Kangaroom[48] by people looking to share twin or even triple bedrooms in 2014, an increase of 48 per cent over the previous year.[49] The degree of precariousness is inevitably much greater when the tenant shares a bedroom in a rented house with a person or people previously unknown to them.

B. Living as a Household

Sharing an owner-occupied home as a family, or a rented home with one or more friends sounds like a successful form of intentional sharing. However, these scenarios may disguise some very precarious homes, which challenge the third meaning of sharing as participation and contribution.

[43] House of Commons Library, '"Common Law Marriage" and Cohabitation' (Briefing Paper 03372, House of Commons, 9 March 2016).

[44] Simone Wong, 'Would You "Care" to Share Your Home?' (2007) 58 *Northern Ireland Law Quarterly* 268.

[45] Department of Communities and Local Government, *Statutory homelessness and homelessness prevention and relief, England: January to March 2017* (London, DCLG, 2015) 6.

[46] Alison Taylor, 'I'll take single over suffering any day', *The Independent Magazine* (London, 1 November 2014).

[47] www.spareroom.com.

[48] www.kangaroom.com.

[49] Nicola Slawson, 'Tenants in London forced to share rooms by sky-high rents', *The Guardian* (London, 25 January 2015).

The 'full-nest' household of different generations sharing a privately owned home is by no means a new phenomenon, but due to the economic recession and high property values for scarce accommodation, the number of 20 to 34 year olds living with their parents has increased by 20 per cent since 1997.[50] Half a million people, more than a quarter of that age range, have either never left the parental home or have returned there. Research found that 62 per cent of these adults are providing financial support for their adult children living at home, and half have cut back financially in order to manage the higher living costs.[51] The more positive side of this sharing phenomenon is that most 'boomerang kids' express gratitude, and more than half expect to provide their parents with support later in life as a way to repay the help they are currently receiving. One in five even expects their parents to move in with them later in life. The report concludes that:

> many people in our focus groups also speak warmly about how they enjoy living with their grown-up kids. On the other hand, a small but significant number of full nesters do feel unhappy about how much support they must offer their children.[52]

There is clearly a range between intentional and enforced sharing of the home by full-nest households.

In the private rented sector, SpareRoom and Kangaroom (already referred to), are just two of many digital platforms ostensibly devoted to making the process of finding shared rented homes easier, but whose real aim is profit. These sites offer flat-shares to 'young professionals', who are internet-savvy and not dependent on Housing Benefit, looking for an enjoyable home-sharing experience akin to the iconic TV series *Friends*. Room-seekers upload details of their requirements, personality and lifestyle, and can search the online profiles of those offering a spare room for shared interests or even friends in common. This performativity is designed to mitigate the risk inherent in sharing a kitchen and bathroom with people who were previously strangers, even if you can withdraw into your own bedroom.

SpareRoom, 'the #1 Flatshare site in the UK', warns that:

> If there are any issues that cause problems, try to avoid leaving notes around the house. This is unlikely to resolve anything as, even with the best of intentions, your tone can be misinterpreted. Best to sit down over coffee and talk it through.[53]

[50] Office for National Statistics, *2011 Census: Population and Household Estimates for England and Wales, March 2011* (ONS, 16 July 2012): www.ons.gov.uk/peoplepopulationandcommunity/populationandmigration/populationestimates/bulletins/2011censuspopulationandhouseholdestimatesforenglandandwales/2012-07-16#how-densely-england-and-wales-were-populated.

[51] Centre for the Modern Family, 'Meet the Full Nesters' (2014): reference.scottishwidows.co.uk/docs/cmf_report_oct_2014.pdf, 17.

[52] Ibid, 21.

[53] www.spareroom.co.uk.

Successful flat-sharing, it seems, depends on the residents being rational, articulate and communicative with each other, willing to share their expectations and irritations as well as their home. And it is not just the tenants who are sharing; Weroom, for example, describes itself as 'a friendly community of share-seekers, room-renters, landlords and letting agencies gathered around a simple, intuitive and homely platform sharing a common vision'.[54] These varied interests are not usually aligned, but the language of this pseudo-sharing digital platform defines 'community' broadly, using the warm and friendly connotations of sharing for commercial profit.

In a different part of the private rented sector, single rooms in a building with shared facilities are offered to less affluent, perhaps unemployed, tenants. An interview carried out with a young man living in this type of accommodation produced some interesting reflections on the meaning of home when you share the kitchen and bathroom with strangers:

> Everyone's bedroom is theirs and then the rest is all shared. Obviously as time goes on you become more accustomed to sharing … I don't feel it's 'mine' but I feel comfortable in the bathroom or the kitchen.
>
> [*Q: Does it feel like home?*]
>
> No but … it'll never feel like you've got full responsibility and full control over things … you're aware that it's not yours and it's someone else's and anyone could come in (to the kitchen) at any time.

This respondent had a short tenancy agreement, at his own request. He was prepared to put up with sharing, which could be described in his case as intentional but temporary. A more enforced form of sharing, due to financial necessity, was experienced by families with young children who also occupied one room in the same building, sharing other essential living rooms with strangers.

The relationship between lodger and landlord or landlady is more precarious, because one is living in the other's home and as a licensee has fewer rights than a tenant. A lodger described in interview how she carefully negotiated her use of the shared kitchen, bathroom and living room around the needs of the owner: she said the key to a successful lodging relationship is 'finding out what matters to people'. In her case the arrangement was very informal: 'nobody's signed anything, I just pay a standing order each month', and while she was very conscious of the inequality of power in this sharing arrangement, she concluded that this meant 'I don't feel responsible and that's a real plus, actually'.

[54] www.weroom.com.

The landlady of a different house explained how she vetted and chose her lodgers:

> I show them round and explain how I use the space and explain what sort of resources they'll have and then we both sit down with a cup of tea and ask each other any questions that might crop up, but meanwhile we're obviously sizing each other up a little bit as people as well.

This process is the embodied version of examining and matching the online profiles offered by the flat-sharing websites. A more formal process, administered by a third party, operates in the Homeshare scheme[55] to match a younger person looking for accommodation with an elderly person living alone. The licensee occupies a spare room in exchange for companionship and some domestic help, plus a contribution to household bills. Whether this is intentional or enforced sharing, for either or both parties, is dependent on their individual circumstances. A sordid and precarious version of home-sharing is offered by some advertisers of accommodation on the Craigslist website: for example, 'rent free accommodation for a girl … I would expect a relationship in lieu of rent'.[56] Only desperation would lead to acceptance of this form of enforced sharing.

Couch, or sofa surfing is a form of temporary licence, insecure because it is intended to be extremely transient. Three distinct forms are identified here, which have very different implications. First is international couchsurfing, through which travellers wanting free lodgings in a foreign country, maybe for only one night, are connected online with local people offering to share their home on a very temporary basis. The Couchsurfing organisation[57] has nine million members globally, aged 28 on average, and provides 'a remarkably safe, legit form of alternative accommodation'.[58] Its digital platform was created as a non-profit organisation promoting the art of sharing but in 2010 it was bought by a for-profit corporation, sparking protests amongst members and 'a somewhat lessened sense of community'.[59] The Couchsurfing platform, like SpareRoom, works through providing online profiles; the traveller and the local who find a good 'match' can then make arrangements. Neither guest nor host envisages a legal relationship; the arrangement is by nature precarious but can be categorised as intentional sharing.

A second variant is sofa surfing by young graduates who 'shuttle between friends' houses', unable to take on a tenancy due to a 'combination of

[55] https://homeshareuk.org/.

[56] '16 creepy ads from people on Craigslist who are offering "free" rooms', *Mirror.co.uk* (28 September 2016): www.mirror.co.uk/news/weird-news/16-creepy-ads-people-craigslist-8636382.

[57] www.couchsurfing.org.

[58] Harriet Line, 'Couchsurfing: would you sleep with a stranger?', *The Telegraph Travel* (21 August 2014).

[59] Belk (n 13 above) 9.

brutally high rents and a dearth of jobs', while others in the same situation 'pay "mates rates" for rooms in better-off pals' homes'.[60] The difficulties experienced by these sofa surfers in maintaining their jobs and also the strain of maintaining relationships with the friends whose goodwill they rely on, are easily imagined. A graduate working as a marketing executive for a start-up company said,

> I started splitting my time between my friend's house and my boyfriend's flatshare in Brixton. We'd talked a little previously about moving in together, but my situation definitely speeded up that process, which does make it a little less romantic.[61]

Both home and relationship are made more precarious by these pressures leading to enforced sharing, and there are many in the same situation.

Nonetheless, these mainly middle-class sofa surfers are usually already on an upward trajectory towards a better future. They have far more resources at their disposal than the homeless people whose sofa surfing makes them invisible to policymakers and ignored in official homelessness statistics.[62] This third variant of sofa surfing is often just a step in the downward spiral to street homelessness,[63] and provides an extremely precarious home. One in five survey respondents had resorted to this kind of accommodation in the past year; the major reason was family breakdown, in 11 per cent of cases involving domestic violence.[64] Homeless sofa surfers are likely to be imposing on friends and family members who themselves have limited space and few resources, and their presence as licensee may well jeopardise their host's tenancy agreement. Research suggests that in some cases, the relationship between the sofa surfer and their host may be 'abusive and exploitative', making the homeless person's situation even more precarious and potentially traumatic.[65] Particular groups: women, young people and minority ethnic and new immigrant households, seem more likely than others to adopt sofa surfing as a temporary solution to homelessness. It is unclear whether these groups are ignorant of alternative options such as shelters and hostels, or unwilling to use them.[66]

[60] Holly Thomas, 'Young, middle-class—and homeless: Meet the sofa-surfer generation', *Mail Online* (10 February 2013): www.dailymail.co.uk/home/you/article-2273809/Young-middle-class--homeless-Meet-sofa-surfer-generation.html#ixzz3cna2Auh5.

[61] Ibid.

[62] David Robinson, 'Hidden homelessness' in Susan Smith (ed), *International Encyclopaedia of Housing and Home* (Oxford, Elsevier, 2012).

[63] Suzanne Fitzpatrick, Glen Bramley and Sarah Johnsen, 'Pathways into Multiple Exclusion Homelessness in Seven UK Cities' (2013) 50 *Urban Studies* 148.

[64] Centrepoint 'Hidden homelessness revealed—new poll shows shocking numbers of sofa surfers' (Centrepoint, 4 December 2014): intranet.centrepoint.org.uk/news-events/news/2014/december/hidden-homelessness-revealed-new-poll-shows-shocking-numbers-of-sofa-surfers.

[65] Robinson (n 62 above) 370.

[66] Ibid, 369.

Housing associations have traditionally provided housing to groups at risk of homelessness, including supported housing in shared homes for disadvantaged groups. However, the recent policy turn to asset-based, market rent policies has had implications for these efforts to counter precarity. For example, the One Housing Group owns two large and now extremely valuable properties in Islington and in Kingston upon Thames. In the 1970s these were set up as shared housing projects for resident groups comprising both vulnerable people and others willing to provide support. In what have been described as 'London's last communes',[67] all residents shared the communal space and paid the same amount for bills and food; when vacancies arose rooms were offered to key workers (public sector employees providing an essential service such as nursing or teaching) and those on low incomes. The projects have been successful for decades. However, the housing association's assistant director of communications was recently quoted as saying

> these people are paying tuppence. We have a responsibility to look at this. We might fix up [the property in Islington] and refurbish it, make it into self-contained studio flats for people who have a right to be there [or] we might elect to sell it (Doward, 2015).

One resident faced with possible eviction said, 'I suppose I'd survive somehow. But for me, my life would be a quarter of what it was'. The new financial climate places responsibilities on housing associations, which makes residents' homes precarious because they apparently no longer have any 'right to be there'.[68]

The new regulatory and contractualised approach to providing services for disabled people has also affected Camphill Village Trust's long-established shared communities where 'people with learning disabilities, mental health problems and other special needs ... live, learn and work with others of all abilities in an atmosphere of mutual care and respect'.[69] In legal terms, Camphill's unsalaried volunteers (the residents without disabilities known as 'co-workers') were licensees. A recent inspection by the Care Quality Commission has brought about changes.[70] The co-workers are now treated as employees of the Trust and no longer offered licences to occupy shared accommodation, ending the Camphill model of a family household. The CEO of the Camphill Village Trust described this as

[67] Jamie Doward, '"We are a dying breed": two of London's last communes unite in fight against closure', *The Observer* (London, 7 June 2015).

[68] Ibid.

[69] See camphill.org.uk.

[70] Bob Rhodes and Richard Davies, 'Regulation: The unintentional destruction of intentional communities' (Sheffield, The Centre for Welfare Reform, 2014) www.centreforwelfarereform.org/uploads/attachment/415/regulation.pdf.

'a period of transition for CVT. We are working to align our values and achievements with the requirements of 21st century social care. Like other social care providers we exist in a time of economic austerity and regulatory scrutiny'.[71] This context produces values which emphasise the precarity of certain disadvantaged groups in society.

C. Sharing Space and Facilities Within and Around the Home

This particular form of sharing of property rights and space goes beyond household or family sharing, to a legally defined community within which space and facilities are shared. This section of the chapter will examine instances of this type of sharing provided by long leasehold tenure and housing co-operatives. My research suggests there are two distinct sharing models here: uninformed sharing of space and facilities with others, and genuinely intentional sharing in a community of choice. These models largely determine the extent to which homes are precarious.

Long leasehold is the most common, although not the only possible, legal framework for private housing developments in which space and facilities are held in common by the owners.[72] In leasehold sites, including for example blocks of flats or gated communities but also some houses on ordinary streets, a legal entity (which may be owned and controlled by the developer or successor in title, or transferred to the residents collectively) is the owner of the land. Residents have property rights to their home but also shared rights to the common property, which at some sites comprises only the roof and external and internal access ways, but at others includes extensive grounds and facilities. This is sharing in the sense of a one-off allocation of property rights and, frequently, uninformed sharing. Long leaseholds are 'pseudo-sharing' in Belk's terms.[73] Purchasers of long leaseholds consider themselves to be owner-occupiers and are often shocked to find that in law they are tenants.[74] Leaseholders' homes are made precarious by exploitative practices around service charges and ground rent.[75] If the owner defaults

[71] Ibid, 21.

[72] See Sarah Blandy, 'Legal Frameworks for Multi-owned Housing in England and Wales: Owners' Experiences' in Sarah Blandy, Ann Dupuis and Jennifer Dixon (eds), *Multi-owned Housing: Law, Power and Practice* (Aldershot, Ashgate, 2010).

[73] Belk (n 13 above) 11–12.

[74] Ian Cole and David Robinson, 'Owners yet Tenants: The Position of Leaseholders in Flats in England and Wales' (2000) 15 *Housing Studies* 595.

[75] The Homeowners Alliance asserts, based on their research, that 'freeholders use their positions of power to extort money from leaseholders in a number of ways': Homeowners Alliance, 'Homes Held Hostage—the rise and abuse of leasehold' (London, Homeowners Alliance, 2017): http://hoa.org.uk/catalogues/report-on-uk-leaseholder-system/index.html).

on either of these contractual payments, the lease (and therefore the home) could be subject to forfeiture.[76]

The developer of a multi-owned housing site may choose to set up a residents' management company and transfer the freehold to it; or residents may collectively purchase the freehold under the Leasehold Reform, Housing and Development Act 1993. Either route leads to leaseholders sharing the responsibility for and governance of the whole site.[77] Many people purchasing homes in multi-owned leasehold sites are not aware in advance of the combination of property rights, contractual obligations and self-governance that they are buying into when they sign legal documents which are complex, lengthy and non-negotiable. Unfortunately, this is a common experience across many jurisdictions.[78] Uninformed sharing then results from a lack of interest by leaseholders and a dearth of available information. The chair of a residents' association hoping to set up a company to purchase the freehold complained that 'there are always a number of people who just don't take any notice, aren't interested, you can't contact them'. A leaseholder in a site where the freehold was about to be transferred confessed that, 'I suppose to be honest, I'm not even that clear whether or not I have taken on any responsibility'.

Once a formally constituted residents' management company has acquired the freehold, tensions can develop between the owners. One described how 'the board members took a very hard line', sending formal letters to neighbours rather than attempting to resolve issues face to face. This officious approach had caused other board members to resign and had led to 'the destruction of any community spirit'. Such a divisive atmosphere causes homes to feel precarious, rather than residents sharing responsibilities for managing the site and being able to enjoy the common spaces together. By contrast, co-housing in leasehold sites potentially exemplifies intentional sharing, both in the sense of possession and use of a resource in common, and through participation and contribution to a common ideal. Co-housing is not a legal term but a set of principles governing 'intentional communities ... created and run by their residents. Each household has a self-contained, personal and private home but residents come together to manage their community, share activities, eat together'.[79] The concept of co-housing therefore centres around sharing: residents share a common house, some meals, and facilities such as a laundry room and grounds. They also share the task of collective governance through intensive meetings and discussions. In many

[76] Forfeiture can be exercised by 'peaceable re-entry', although it is advisable to obtain a court order: *Billson v Residential Apartments* [1992] 1 All ER 141.

[77] Blandy (n 72 above).

[78] Sarah Blandy, Ann Dupuis and Jennifer Dixon (eds), *Multi-owned Housing: Law, Power and Practice* (Aldershot, Ashgate, 2010).

[79] https://cohousing.org.uk/.

co-housing developments residents also cook, garden and carry out maintenance together, performing the values of 'equality, interdependence and reciprocity'[80] which are fundamental to intentional sharing.

Running a self-managed neighbourhood is a considerable time commitment, 'but it's countered by a sense of security. We are our own landlords'.[81] The style and effectiveness of communal decision-making and management determine how the communal spaces are shared and used, illustrated here by a co-housing leaseholder: 'There is a sort of collective responsibility … people go and clear it up after the kids have dropped litter … there is a perception that we own the common spaces together'. Over time, residents' social practices develop, some become written rules, subcommittees are formed and dispute resolution procedures are worked out and put into practice: 'I think as we live together longer and these things develop, you know what the rules are, what the unwritten rules are, what the conventions are'. Most co-housing communities also have procedures for vetting and induction of potential new residents, sending out detailed information packs about how the community works and the commitment that is expected, and inviting potential residents to share a communal meal. Such arrangements reduce the risk of tensions developing within the community, and guard against any lack of commitment to resolving difficulties together, thus making homes less precarious.

Around 20 co-housing projects have now been completed in the UK, and there are many more co-housing groups currently in development. Co-housing seems to be increasingly in the news.[82] Perhaps unsurprisingly therefore, the co-housing model is currently being adapted for profit by WeWork, which already provides shared office space on a membership basis (like the Uber taxi platform) and is now the eighth most valuable private company in the world.[83] It has identified 'millennials flocking to cities like New York and San Francisco at a time when rents … are hitting unprecedented highs',[84] as a lucrative market from which it intends to make over US$636m profit by 2018.[85] WeWork references kibbutzim and close-knit neighbourhoods as successful models. How does it compare with co-housing? A conventional 'strengths and weaknesses analysis' of

[80] Butler (n 1 above) 218.

[81] Harriet Sherwood, 'How to create happy communities through co-housing', *The Guardian* (London, 21 November 2014).

[82] See, for example, Rob Sharp, 'Affordable 13-bedroom home. Good Transport links. Would suit six families …' *The Independent Magazine* (London, 26 April 2014); and Sherwood (n 81 above).

[83] Carole Cadwalladr, 'Changing what we call home', *The Observer* (London, 10 January 2016).

[84] Michelle Cohen, 'WeWorks Communal Living Concept on Wall Street gets its First Residents' (*6sqft*, 13 January 2016) www.6sqft.com/residents-move-into-weworks-communal-living-concept-on-wall-street/.

[85] Cadwalladr (n 83 above) 21.

co-housing found that the benefits of affordability, safety, sustainability, and sociability, far outweigh the disadvantages, but raised concerns about ownership: 'Who owns the land and the houses? Who are the investors? What happens when community members die or decide to move away?'[86] WeWork plans to circumvent those issues by retaining control and ownership in its WeLive model, offering membership to residents rather than any property interest, making them more precarious.

While the 'real' co-housing movement challenges the assumptions of control, autonomy and exclusion associated with the tenure of home ownership, it has also been criticised for providing homes only for relatively affluent households. However, the newer co-housing sites are mainly urban, and are attracting interest and involvement from UK local authorities who see potential for a new form of affordable housing.[87] In order to challenge precarity and enable people on low incomes to become co-housing residents, LILAC ('low-impact living affordable community') uses an innovative variant of long leasehold.[88] The freehold of LILAC's land is owned by a Community Land Trust, a not-for-profit society that cannot sell its assets but must use them for the benefit of a defined geographical community.[89] The homes built on the land are owned by the LILAC Mutual Home Ownership Society, which is registered as a co-operative controlled by its members. The members are the residents; each has a 20-year renewable lease which 'gives the right to occupy a specified house or flat, and the right to democratically control the housing community in which they live'.[90]

Unlike the long leases offered at LILAC, most fully mutual co-operatives offer their residents either a tenancy or a licence to occupy. At one of my research sites, a radical housing co-operative committed to assisting destitute asylum seekers, residents described coming home to find that 'their' room was temporarily occupied by someone in greater need. This might be considered an extreme example of precarious housing, but the residents had discussed and chosen to use the co-operative's property to alleviate the precarity of others, in the full knowledge that it would diminish their individual rights. However, as with housing associations and trusts, even fully mutual housing co-operatives are not immune to changing economic conditions. In a 1988 parliamentary debate it was said that 'the nature of

[86] Towergate Insurance, 'Community 2.0: is co-housing the future of urban design?' (Maidstone, Towergate Insurance, undated): www.towergateinsurance.co.uk/commercial-property-insurance/is-cohousing-the-future).

[87] Sherwood (n 81 above).

[88] Paul Chatterton, *Low Impact Living: A Field Guide to Ecological, Affordable Community Building* (Abingdon, Routledge, 2015).

[89] Housing and Regeneration Act 2008.

[90] CDS Co-operatives, 'A consumer's guide to Mutual Home Ownership: A new way of owning a stake in your own home' (London, CDS, undated).

a co-operative [is that] the interests of landlord and tenants as a whole are in effect indivisible'.[91] Lord Hope quoted from this report in the case of *Berrisford v Mexfield Housing Co-operative Ltd*, but went on to say that 'at least so far as Mexfield is concerned, that happy state of affairs no longer exists ... financial pressures may cause the parties' interests to diverge to the detriment of the residential occupier',[92] making their home more precarious.

D. Shared Property Boundaries

In this type of sharing relationship affecting the home, the one-off allocation of property rights determines which homes adjoin each other. Boundaries are always shared, forming a connection between the resident of one home and the neighbours. In that sense, property boundaries represent enforced sharing and exemplify the precariousness this may generate. The fact that boundaries are permeable to nuisances such as noise and smell undermines the home as a place of security, privacy and refuge, as many tales of 'neighbours from hell' attest. For owner-occupiers, the surrounding neighbourhood is a potential risk to the home as it affects property values.[93] Obligingly, the British residential property website Zoopla assembles neighbourhood profiles: tenure breakdown, employment statistics, family types, residents' interests, and even what newspapers residents read,[94] for 'sharing' with prospective purchasers in their efforts to find a less precarious home.

Owners of neighbouring properties may disagree over the exact line of the boundary between them. In one disputed case that involved a small area of cobbled yard, the Court of Appeal recorded:

> There are too many calamitous neighbour disputes in the courts ... the case that cried out for compromise moves onwards and upwards to a conclusion that is disastrous for one of the parties, possibly for both. The extreme acrimony between these neighbours is nothing new.[95]

A wealthy homeowner can purchase extensive land and position their home at a distance from neighbouring properties, reducing the risk of direct disruption. However, longer boundaries are more difficult to protect, so ownership is performed through erecting deterrent boundaries around the home, symbolising control of space and property rights. Although burglary rates have continued to drop over the last 50 years, successive British

[91] HL Deb 3 November 1988, vol 501, col 395.
[92] *Berrisford v Mexfield Housing Co-operative Ltd* [2011] UKSC 52, at [81].
[93] Lee Anne Fennell, *The Unbounded Home: Property Values Beyond Property Lines* (New Haven CT, Yale University Press, 2009).
[94] www.zoopla.co.uk/.
[95] *Bradford v James* [2008] EWCA Civ 837, Mummery LJ at [1] & [2].

Crime Surveys have consistently indicated that fear of crime outstrips actual crime statistics. Anxiety itself makes the home feel insecure; huge amounts are spent on fortifying homes in an attempt to stave off this source of precariousness.[96]

V. PERFORMATIVITY, PARTICIPATION, PROTESTS AND PRECARITY

Discussion in this penultimate section of the chapter moves on to focus more closely on the third sense of sharing: collective participation and contribution. In her recent work, Butler has extended the idea of performativity to collective protests and demonstrations, asserting that these new politics of performativity embody the values of equality, interdependence and reciprocity.[97] Her statement that 'the opposite of precarity is not security, but, rather, the struggle for an egalitarian social and political order in which a livable interdependency becomes possible' is particularly relevant for this chapter.[98] A 'liveable interdependency' is modelled when people act together to organise and then participate in street demonstrations or occupations to protest against precarity.

Various housing campaigns span the social rented and the private rented sector, including: the Living Rent campaign;[99] Defend Council Housing;[100] Axe the Housing Act[101] (the Housing and Planning Act 2016, summarised above). Digital platforms enable such alliances to be formed, protests maintained and publicised; often social media are used to organise rapid action which effectively draws attention to housing injustices. These campaigning groups often combine forces, for example in protesting and making demands on local and national government following the fire at Grenfell Tower.[102]

The lobby group, Generation Rent, 'campaigns for professionally managed, secure, decent and affordable private rented homes in sustainable communities',[103] an aim which if achieved would remove much of the precarity from this sector. One such campaign concerned the New Era estate in London where nearly 100 tenant households were threatened with eviction by Westbrook Partners, the US investment company that owned the

[96] Rowland Atkinson and Sarah Blandy, *Domestic Fortress* (Manchester, Manchester University Press, 2016).

[97] Butler (n 1 above) 218.

[98] Ibid, 69.

[99] Living Rent Campaign, 'Homepage' (Living Rent) livingrent.org.uk.

[100] Defend Council Housing, 'Homepage' (DCH) www.defendcouncilhousing.org.uk/dch/.

[101] Axe The Housing Act, 'About' (Axe The Housing Act) www.axethehousingact.org.uk/about/.

[102] Danny Boyle, 'Grenfell Tower tensions could boil over as thousands set to attend "justice2" rally', *The Daily Telegraph* (London, 16 June 2017).

[103] Generation Rent, 'Homepage' (Generation Rent) www.generationrent.org/.

freehold and wanted a threefold increase in the rents. At the end of 2014, Westbrook Partners gave in to the protesters and sold the estate to Dolphin Living, a charitable foundation. Dolphin Living now plans to adopt rents fixed on a 'pay according to income' basis, rather similar to LILAC's rent structure. Dolphin's chief executive explained that 'there will be families with three children paying less for a big flat than a couple in a small flat'.[104] While this approach of prioritising the community interest over individual tenants is to be welcomed, Dolphin is imposing this sharing of the cost rather than the residents adopting it through informed choice. The homes of some New Era tenants seem about to become more precarious.

Focus E15 is another example of sharing as participation in anti-precarity protests, in this case focused on the effects of local authority regeneration policies for tenants in the social rented sector, and in particular Newham council which has earmarked the Carpenters Estate in London E15 for privatisation. The group has made common cause with other protesters. In April 2015 one of the group's leaders, Jasmin Stone, was arrested for re-occupying a council flat (not on the Carpenters Estate) from which the tenant had been evicted for rent arrears due to a reduction in her welfare benefits. The re-occupation was categorised as squatting, now a crime as previously discussed, but which may also constitute a shared protest against precarity. Stone's involvement in the protests has actually made her own position less precarious. She has been offered a five-year permanent tenancy by Newham council, who 'are bending over backwards to help me, and I know it's because of all the fuss caused by Focus E15'.[105]

Campaigners for the homeless set up protest camps in Manchester[106] and in Liverpool.[107] In Manchester, the campaign drew attention to the increase in rough sleepers, which meant that even the precarious accommodation offered by night shelters is overwhelmed by the numbers in need. One activist shared his experience of organising anti-fracking protest camps. The Liverpool protest was timed to coincide with the celebration of the shipping line Cunard's 175th anniversary. The empty shop doorways that are usually home to rough sleepers had been boarded over to make the problem invisible, but the camp placed 'the issue of homelessness firmly in the public eye'.[108]

[104] Robert Booth, 'New Era estate could means-test residents to set individual rents', *The Guardian* (London, 25 February 2015).
[105] Robert Booth, 'Focus E15 housing activist arrested on suspicion of squatting', *The Guardian* (London, 14 April 2015).
[106] Ciara Leeming, 'Manchester's homeless camp remains defiant', *The Big Issue North* (11–17 May 2015).
[107] K Brown, 'Activists camp by Liverpool Pier Head', *The Big Issue North*, 8–14 June 2015.
[108] Ibid.

Sharing campaigns, skills and expertise can strengthen and help publicise protests about the ways in which policies and practices create precarity for particular groups of occupiers, or in particular types of home.

Some forms of sharing housing are also performative enactments of this 'struggle for an egalitarian social and political order in which a livable interdependency becomes possible'.[109] A long-term housing co-operative resident explained that she was committed to this collective legal form because 'individual ownership of property leads inevitably to ... selfishness, self-interest and the gap between rich and poor'. LILAC's ethos and practice are based on a refusal to 'see housing as a commodity on which you speculate'.[110] Homes of this type epitomise intentional sharing, as well as the residents' commitment to participate in a way of life that models the possibility of a different approach to housing.

VI. CONCLUSIONS

Sharing has been used in this chapter as a lens for interrogating the idea of the precarious home. The continuum of sharing identified and applied here has shed light on the home's precariousness, and the precarity of different groups in relation to the home.

Clearly, the legal structures through which the tenure of the home is materialised are extremely important, for example the legislation that has created increasingly insecure forms of occupation in the social rented sector. Butler's distinction between precariousness and precarity has proved useful in identifying specific groups, for example the tenants of social housing providers governed by market-driven legislation and by regulatory regimes which embody funders' expectation that these landlords will adopt asset-based risk management. However, the degree of insecurity inherent in any particular tenure sector can be overridden by other risks associated with sharing the home, which make it more or less precarious than its tenure alone would indicate. It has been shown that the horizontal relationships between residents of the same accommodation, between neighbours, or between those collectively involved in governing their community, frequently matter more than the vertical relationship between landlord and tenant, or freeholder and leaseholder. In the case of shared property rights, for example in long leasehold multi-owned housing sites, a continuing commitment by residents to community self-government can significantly lessen precariousness. This echoes Belk's analysis of 'sharing in', which expands the domain of common property, as contrasted with 'sharing out' which preserves boundaries

[109] Butler (n 1 above) 69.
[110] Quoted in Sherwood (n 81 above).

between the individual and others.[111] However, as has been noted, sharing the home with anyone other than family challenges the powerful ideology of property as sovereign control over domestic territory, which is difficult to overcome.

Different meanings of sharing have been identified and examined in the current context of austerity policies. A trajectory towards intentional sharing (a deliberate and positive choice to share, on the basis of full information) is represented by the slowly growing co-housing movement, but the majority of sharing arrangements remain enforced (an unchosen response to external circumstances) and/or uninformed (sharing by choice, but without being aware of the implications).

Precariousness has been shown to be a subjective experience so, for example, a transient, insecure home may suit some residents at particular stages in their life or career cycle, while others would experience such instability as intolerably precarious. Notably, affluence can overcome insecurity associated with tenure, at the very highest end of the market. The ultra-wealthy often rent luxury homes (and therefore share property rights) in capital cities, exclusive resorts and tax havens, rejecting property ownership and its responsibilities.[112] It may be that some occupiers, although wanting to retain the right to leave on their own terms, are not seeking a home at all.[113]

This chapter has demonstrated that sharing is to some degree always intentional, although always tempered by the degree of choice available, which affects whether a particular home might be experienced as enforced sharing by one or more of the parties, for example in an intimate relationship or a full-nest household. Intention is also expressed through the performative and common practice of pre-vetting, whether meeting in person before becoming or taking on a lodger, the induction processes of co-housing groups, or putting your profile on an online flat-sharing platform. Online sharing has been highlighted as an important contemporary trend, enabling both the marketisation of sharing arrangements and the building of real and virtual communities to organise housing campaigns against precarity.

[111] Belk (n 13 above) 276.

[112] Jeremy Rifkin, *The Age of Access: The New Culture of Hypercapitalism, Where All of Life is a Paid-for Experience* (New York, Tarcher, 2000); Rowland Atkinson and Sarah Blandy, 'A picture of the floating World: grounding the secessionary affluence of the residential cruise liner' (2009) 41 *Antipode* 92.

[113] I am grateful to the anonymous reviewer for this thought-provoking insight.

3

Property, Well-being, and Home: Positive Psychology and Property Law's Foundations

NESTOR M DAVIDSON*

I. INTRODUCTION

PEOPLE ARE CONSTANTLY interacting with each other through the material stuff of the world, as well as through ideas and anything else that might theoretically constitute property. But once the state gets involved and those interactions carry legal consequences, we have to have some way of understanding the normative force of that intervention. Legal scholars have traditionally offered a familiar set of foundations that justify property law in terms of efficiency or utilitarianism, labour desert theory, reliance, or the moral obligations of community, among others.[1]

One prominent set of normative justifications for property law highlights the relationship between possessions and the self. Thus, for example, in the Hegelian view, elaborated by Margaret Radin in her work on personhood, property law should reflect the idea that the development of the individual as a moral being requires control over external resources.[2] Property scholars

* Albert A Walsh Professor of Real Estate, Land Use and Property Law, Fordham Law School. This chapter was prepared for the Onati International Institute for the Sociology of Law Workshop 'The Precarious Home: Socio-Legal Perspectives on the Home in Insecure Times', 25–26 June 2015. The author thanks Dillon Stern for his excellent research assistance.

[1] This cursory list mixes elements of moral and political philosophy with nominally instrumentalist accounts, but at root, these are all normative constructs in the exercise of justifying property rights. Moreover, while some theorists emphasise the normative and practical primacy of individual rationales, property pluralists properly understand that no one justificatory frame is—or, really, should be—overriding in a system as complex as property law. See Gregory S Alexander, 'Pluralism and Property' (2011) 80 *Fordham Law Review* 1017.

[2] Georg WF Hegel, *Philosophy of Right* (TM Knox (trans) 1942, [1821]) §§ 40–53; Margaret Jane Radin, *Contested Commodities* (Harvard University Press, 1996) 54–78; see also Jeremy Waldron, *The Right to Private Property* (Oxford, Clarendon Press, 1988) 351–60, 373–74.

have more recently invoked Aristotelian virtue ethics, with its assumption that people are inherently social beings, to emphasise the importance of property as a precursor for the development of human capacities necessary for flourishing and the corresponding obligations of the community to ensure a sufficient baseline for that flourishing.[3]

Because of their emphasis on identity and the self, these Hegelian and Aristotelian frameworks for property law render their psychological underpinnings particularly transparent. We understand the importance of property for personhood because of the intuitive strength of the role of possessions in everyday life. Likewise, the link between a foundation of material resources and the psychological space to flourish seems evident, as does the sense of community that Aristotelians draw on to justify a structure of property law that emphasises mutual obligation. However, almost *every* normative frame that scholars invoke to understand the why of property law draws force from underlying conceptions of human nature. Welfarism is grounded in rationalist assumptions about how people react to incentives. Reliance is predicated on how people experience what they perceive to be unfair change. Communitarian perspectives reflect strains of social psychological interconnection.[4]

If the normative force of property law relies on often unstated assumptions about human nature, moral justification becomes vulnerable to empirical dispute about those assumptions. If people are not fully rational, or decidedly bounded in their rationality, for example, welfarism requires a slew of potentially disabling qualifications.[5] If people experience tension between social obligation and their personal freedom, rather than constitutive of their self the moral valence of reciprocity becomes contested. Similar empirical questions about other property justifications are obvious.

What would it mean, then, to reverse the direction of the relationship between psychology and justification, to move more directly from what we understand in a concrete, empirical sense about human nature to how we

[3] Gregory S Alexander and Eduardo M Peñalver, *An Introduction to Property Theory* (Cambridge University Press, 2012) 80–101; Gregory S Alexander and Eduardo M Peñalver, 'Properties of Community' (2009) 10 *Theoretical Inquiries in Law* 127. This work explicitly imports into property scholarship the insights on human flourishing developed by Amartya Sen and Martha Nussbaum. See, eg, *ibid* at 136–37 (discussing Amartya Sen, *Commodities and Capabilities* (North-Holland Publisher, 1985); and Martha C Nussbaum, *Women and Human Development* (Cambridge University Press, 2000)).

[4] Although perhaps not as clear a psychological claim, Lockean labour theory is also grounded in the relationship between property and the self. Without ownership of the self, there would be no necessary causal nexus between labour and resulting ownership, although that truism says relatively little about individual state of mind. *Cf* Jeremy A Blumenthal, '"To Be Human": A Psychological Perspective on Property Law' (2009) 83 *Tulane Law Review* 609, 610.

[5] The endowment effect's confounding of Coasian bargaining is a well-known example of this. See Blumenthal, *ibid* at 634–37.

might construct property law? What would a property law predicated in the first instance on psychological insights look like? The resulting system might replicate a fair amount of what traditional normative theories yield, but psychological realism would foreground an empirical discourse on human nature and provide a possible corrective to under-examined moral intuitions. This is not to say that particular aspects of individual and social psychology are any less contested than elements of moral or political philosophy invoked by property scholars. But beginning with a more realistic foundation can ground these invocations in the realm of pragmatism.[6]

Bringing psychological realism to the fore, equally importantly, opens new possibilities for understanding the normative underpinnings for property. One promising set of possibilities that has not received sufficient attention among property scholars derives from positive psychology.[7] Positive psychology is a movement that seeks to turn the field away from dysfunction and pathology toward concrete determinants of individual and social well-being. A property law that incorporated the insights of this field would echo Hegelian and Aristotelian views of property's relationship to the self and community, but would be grounded in a clearer empirical understanding of individual flourishing and the institutions necessary to support that flourishing. Thus, personal experiences and strong interpersonal relationships have both been found to have a more meaningful and longer-lasting impact on psychological well-being than possessions,[8] which suggests a different valence for property's particular obligations.

The nature of the home provides a meaningful locus to explore this shift in emphasis. It is well recognised that psychological claims about the importance of home in property law appear to be over-stated in light of the

[6] As we will see in the course of this chapter, there is an existing literature on property and psychology that has provided important insights to specific debates in property law. See, eg, Blumenthal, *ibid* at 611 (arguing that 'property law—like all law—is based on assumptions about human behavior and cognition and emotion, assumptions that are empirically tractable'); D Benjamin Barros, 'Legal Questions for the Psychology of Home' (2009) 83 *Tulane Law Review* 645; Jonathan Remy Nash, 'Packaging Property: The Effect of Paradigmatic Framing of Property Rights' (2009) 83 *Tulane Law Review* 691; Stephanie M Stern, 'Residential Protectionism and the Legal Myth of Home' (2009) 107 *Michigan Law Review* 1094. This chapter approaches those contributions through the lens of justification and teases out how these psychological insights might inform a richer and more nuanced normative underpinning for property law. *Cf* Stern, above, at 1129 (arguing that 'legal theory and reform must move forward based on the best available evidence ... [and that if] psychological research proves [that assumptions are unwarranted], then an evidence-based approach not only encourages, but requires, further theoretical revision').

[7] There are a handful of glancing references to positive psychology in the property literature, see, eg, Stern, above (n 6), at 1120–21, but little systematic engagement. Legal scholars in other fields have been more active in explicitly drawing on positive psychology. See, eg, Clare Huntington, 'Happy Families? Translating Positive Psychology into Family Law' (2009) 16 *Virginia Journal of Social Policy & the Law* 385.

[8] See below text accompanying nn 28–32.

empirical evidence,[9] although that remains somewhat contested. Applying the insights of positive psychology would highlight the nature of home, less as a source of individual attachment to possessions per se, and more as a locus for positive experiences and a grounding for the development of social relationships. This might de-emphasise the importance of ownership to home and place greater weight on legal structures that foster the outcomes associated with well-being. Home, in this view, is a means to an end: less a font of individual identity as an object in itself and more a resource for what might connect and add meaning to people's lives.

This chapter argues, in short, that we can add to our existing normative understandings of property law's foundations a grounding generally in empirical psychology and more specifically in what has been shown in the research to support flourishing. This shifts the methodological emphasis of the exercise of justification towards realism, and adds important nuance to prescriptions for the structures of property law.

II. PSYCHOLOGY AS JUSTIFICATION: PROPERTY AND THE SELF

As noted, property as a *legal* construct inherently requires justification, and does so in two, interrelated, ways. First, at the most basic level, the question of why the state should intervene in private ordering to validate a person's claim to a given resource (your land, my car, her idea, etc) is ever-present, regardless of how one evaluates the resulting settlement. As the Legal Realists emphasised, the bargain represented by property law that any individual can call on the state to protect their claims against the world as a whole necessarily implicates a public choice between potential claimants.[10] That inevitable decision must have a normative foundation.

Intertwined with this foundational need for justification are more complex questions of the texture of the resulting system of property rights that likewise raise justificatory challenges. Should the state default to libertarian minimalism and its corresponding scope of seemingly absolute property rights? Or should the state pay more attention to the externalities that property use often generates and the reality that property is an interconnected and relational system? Such questions are endemic all the way down to the fine-grained details of doctrine and cannot be resolved without clear normative priors.

[9] Stephanie Stern has ably elaborated on the lack of empirical support for the psychological primacy of home as an argument for the special protection that home receives in property law. See generally Stern, above (n 6).

[10] Felix S Cohen, 'Dialogue on Private Property' (1954) 9 *Rutgers Law Review* 357, 374.

All of the many normative frames that property scholars have invoked are predicated, often without acknowledgment, on assumptions about human nature. The basic foundations of welfarist justifications of property law, for example, rely heavily on individually rationalist assumptions. Indeed, most basic first-generation law and economics claims about incentives are basically psychological arguments. Take the example of 'stability' as an overarching principle invoked to structure the conditions under which people will invest in property. One of the core arguments animating welfarist perspectives is that the system of property should valorise justifiable expectation and that state interventions that shift property rules once that expectation has crystalised should be minimised. This is an assertion about basic human nature: people will react to alterations in the existing pattern of entitlements by being 'demoralised' and will in turn invest less in property.[11]

In some justificatory frames, the psychological underpinnings seem closer to the surface. Two particularly prominent attempts have been made to set the normative terms of property law with reference to theories of the relationship between the self and property. The intuitive sense that we make ourselves in part through how we interact with our material possessions, forms a distinctive, underlying leitmotif for much of property law, with a number of intellectual roots that pair psychology and moral philosophy. As William James famously observed, in a comment that prefigured a literature on possession and identity in psychology, 'between what a man calls me and what he simply calls mine the line is difficult to draw.'[12]

A more philosophical perspective on the same idea comes to us through Hegel, for whom mastery of the external things of the world was not only

[11] See Frank I Michelman, 'Property, Utility, and Fairness: Comments on the Ethical Foundations of "Just Compensation" Law' (1967) 80 *Harvard Law Review* 1165, 1214 (describing demoralisation costs as both direct 'disutilities' from experiencing a property transition without compensation and the secondary shock that people feel 'disturbed by the thought that they themselves may be subjected to similar treatment on some other occasion.').

As seemingly natural as the idea that people will be upset when the rules of the game change may seem, there are counter-narratives about state responsiveness that can lead in very different doctrinal directions. There is a rich empirical literature that suggests that some people may be emotionally drawn to flexibility and when circumstances change in ways that necessitate a more active intervention by the state, it can be comforting to know that people will not be abandoned. See Nestor M Davidson, 'Property's Morale' (2011) 110 *Michigan Law Review* 437. This alternative psychological narrative yields decidedly different prescriptive outcomes, privileging intervention by the state rather than stoic neutrality.

[12] William James, *The Principles of Psychology* (Henry Holt & Company, 1890) 291. There is a literature that has developed within psychology elaborating on the self and property. See, eg, Leonard Bloom, 'People and Property: A Psychoanalytic View' in Floyd W Rudmin (ed), *To Have Possessions: A Handbook on Ownership and Property* (Cotre Madera, Select Press, 1991) 427; Daniel IA Cohen, 'On Property as Self' (1998) 26 *Journal of Psychiatry & Law* 3.

constitutive of self, but critical to moral development.[13] As Jeremy Waldron has translated this concept, the

> importance of property to individual wills is this: the actions that an individual performs on or with this object now may constrain or determine the actions that he can perform on or with it later. This is how an object can embody a will—by registering the effects of willing at one point in time and forcing an individual's willing to become consistent and stable over a period.[14]

From these Hegelian roots, Margaret Radin developed her conception of property and personhood, predicated on the idea that 'to be a person, an individual needs some control over resources in the external environment.'[15]

The prominence of property to individual moral identity finds an echo in Aristotelian conceptions of property as a foundation for human flourishing. As Gregory Alexander and Eduardo Peñalver have argued, the necessity to provide material resources to support human capabilities can justify certain institutions of property law. Alexander and Peñalver begin with the proposition in Aristotle that people are inherently social beings,[16] and that people exist in relations of mutual dependency.[17] To this, they further invoke the proposition from Thomas Aquinas that a mutual sense of humanity and respect for basic equality leads people to support the material conditions necessary for flourishing. And they conclude by drawing on Martha Nussbaum and Amartya Sen's work to argue that property law must be constructed to facilitate the acquisition of crucial capabilities.[18] No less than Hegelian justifications, this Aristotelian/Thomistic/capabilities theory is a psychological story. Asserting a moral claim from membership in a community reflects certain assumptions about the nature of mutual obligation that may or may not have an actual basis in how individuals experience community.

Each of these justificatory frames yields distinct positive claims about legal doctrine. Thus Radin's argument that what is normatively significant about property is that people form their identity through attachment to external objects means that law should prioritise the protection of 'personal' property—property that is constitutive of the self—over what she describes as 'fungible' property.[19] Likewise, a virtue ethics and flourishing view of capabilities yields prescriptions to temper property rights for the good of the community and to redistribute property to the extent necessary to support

[13] See Hegel, above (n 2), at 40–57.

[14] Waldron, above (n 2), at 373.

[15] Margaret Jane Radin, 'Property and Personhood' (1982) 34 *Stanford Law Review* 957, 957.

[16] See Alexander and Peñalver, above (n 3), at 80–81.

[17] *Ibid* at 83–84.

[18] *Ibid* at 89–90 (citing, eg, Sen, above (n 3), at 10–11; Nussbaum, above (n 3), at 50–55, 87–88).

[19] Radin, above (n 15).

minimum capabilities.[20] These conclusions, of course, reflect the psychological assumptions with which the frameworks begin: people constitute their identity through property and people are inherently social beings.

For any system of justification, leaping too quickly from intuitively appealing, but perhaps reductionist, assumptions about human nature, risks opening up critiques based on more complex understandings of actual psychological processes. Building a normative system without an explicit or deep engagement with the relevant underlying psychological predicates thus raises significant questions about the moral conclusions that follow. At the very least, sweeping past assumptions about human motivation, intrinsic intuitions, identity formation, and similar core questions of individual psychology render the structures built on those assumptions potentially vulnerable to empirical contest.

It is possible, however, to reverse the direction of the exercise and start with a more realistic picture of psychology before then moving to what might flow normatively from assumptions based on that picture. This would, metaphorically speaking, cut out the middle man and seek to ground the invocation of moral frames on a more empirical, nuanced foundation. Moral philosophy, of course, need not have any empirical basis in actual human nature to make strong claims about normative obligations. But the question for property theorists is not the abstract validity of Hegelian, Aristotelian, Kantian, utilitarian or any other perspective—it is rather how any of those theories are invoked to justify property's institutions.

This is not to argue that it is easy to derive first principles from psychology or that the exercise would be any less contested than the battles that property theorists currently fight on other grounds.[21] Complicating the argument that changing rules might make people hesitate to invest or to maintain their property can correspondingly complicate arguments for legal stability. That added layer of psychological realism will not necessarily tell you how precisely to balance stability against dynamism, or likewise how to mediate individualism and community obligation. But it will begin with a more realistic foundation than sweeping assumptions about human nature that too often go unquestioned.

[20] See Alexander and Peñalver, above (n 3), at 87 ('Our ability to flourish requires certain basic material goods and a communal infrastructure that themselves depend on contributions from all members of the relevant society.').

[21] Psychology raises suspicion for some property theorists because some of the empirical work done in the field can be invoked in a relatively reductionist way to support a narrow and absolutist conception of property. At least some of the literature attempting to translate empirical psychological insights does, indeed, lend itself to overly simplistic conclusions—that, for example, people have some kind of inherent possessive instinct that valorises exclusionary theories. But there are many countervailing veins in the psychological literature that suggest that systems of property rights that are more mutually interdependent have an equally valid foundation.

There are three potential advantages that can flow from reversing the direction of the psychological-normative valence.[22] First, beginning with psychological realism can ground critiques of our moral intuition in empirical understanding. Jeremy Blumenthal has argued that the intersection between psychological research and property can yield insights into lay perceptions that are important to property law because of the potential mismatch between lay intuitions and doctrine.[23] Empirical evidence of revealed behaviour is likewise critical to understand, Blumenthal asserts, because faulty psychological premises might undermine theoretical claims and require adjustment to comport with the behaviour of what Bruce Ackerman called the 'Ordinary Observer'.[24]

Blumenthal's thesis—that understanding the empirics of lay perception and behaviour can shed light on doctrine—is compelling, as far as it goes, but does not go nearly far enough in terms of crucial questions of primacy and justification. One can take Blumenthal as a starting point, but extend his insight more deeply to the basic structure of property law. It is not enough simply to observe that there might be some variance between what the psychological literature reveals and how property institutions are instantiated. That evidentiary base (and broader psychological literature not necessarily focused on property) can be used to interrogate the assumptions underlying basic justification.

A second advantage to explicitly recognising psychology as the first underpinning for normative claims about property is that doing so opens space for more complex mental states than the often monotonic assumptions about human nature that currently prevail without much interrogation. The basic welfarist incentive story, for example, can be complicated on a number of grounds.[25] It turns out that many people are motivated at least in part by an intrinsic comparative instinct. We can call it envy, or drive to outdo others, or some other label, but many people derive value not merely from the (theoretically) absolute or intrinsic value of an object

[22] Without wading too far into a complex set of issues, it is important to acknowledge that claims about psychology and human nature are to a great extent culturally contingent. Indeed, there is an emerging field of cultural psychology that explores the intersection between culture and psychological processes. See Darrin R Lehman et al, 'Psychology and Culture' (2004) 55 *Annual Review of Psychology* 689. What this means for present purposes is that claims of universal human nature—about property or otherwise—should be greeted with some measure of skepticism.

[23] See Blumenthal, above (n 4), at 623–24 (citing the example of popular outcry over the breadth of the 'public use' requirement for eminent domain).

[24] *Ibid* at 632–33; Bruce A Ackerman, *Private Property and the Constitution* (Yale University Press, 1977).

[25] For an earlier and still quite relevant discussion by a property scholar on this point, see Robert C Ellickson, 'Bringing Culture and Human Frailty to Rational Actors: A Critique of Classical Law and Economics' (1989) 65 *Chicago-Kent Law Review* 23.

or experience, but from the relative value in comparison with others.[26] If that is true—and there is a great deal of empirical basis for the claim—then many doctrinal arguments that assume a constant intrinsic motivation can be called into question. Similar layers can be added to other unstated assumptions that cut across the discourse.

There is, finally, a third advantage that can flow from prioritising psychology in the exercise of justifying property. Beyond simply problematising or complicating existing accounts, drawing on psychological research can also open new horizons. It is to one such example that we now turn.

III. POSITIVE PSYCHOLOGY AS A NEW FOUNDATION

If we accept that the empirics of individual psychology can form an alternative starting point for the exercise of justifying property rights, the literature on psychology can also fruitfully suggest new horizons to explore. One example of this can be found in the arena of positive psychology. Positive psychology is an evidence-based movement that explores signature personal strengths that foster healthy individuals and communities. The field traces back to the early work of humanist psychologists, notably Abraham Maslow, who coined the term,[27] but has taken on new prominence in the past two decades.[28]

As positive psychology's leading contemporary proponent, Martin Seligman, has succinctly summarised:

> The field of positive psychology at the subjective level is about valued subjective experiences: well-being, contentment, and satisfaction (in the past); hope and optimism (for the future); and flow and happiness (in the present). At the individual level, it is about positive individual traits: the capacity for love and vocation, courage, interpersonal skill, aesthetic sensibility, perseverance, forgiveness, originality, future mindedness, spirituality, high talent, and wisdom. At the

[26] The idea that property can be a way to establish relative status comes into the modern literature through Thorstein Veblen and 'conspicuous consumption.' See Thorstein Veblen, *The Theory of the Leisure Class*, Martha Banta (ed) (Oxford University Press, 2007 edn, [1899]). As Veblen argued, some people acquire property not so much (or at least not solely) for the value of that property standing in isolation, but in no small measure to attempt to signal superiority through objects of wealth. Over the intervening century plus, a large literature has expanded on the empirical foundation for relative value. See Nestor M Davidson, 'Property and Relative Status' (2009) 107 *Michigan Law Review* 757; see also Lior Jacob Strahilevitz, 'Absolute Preferences and Relative Preferences in Property Law' (2012) 160 *University of Pennsylvania Law Review* 2157.

[27] Abraham Maslow, *Motivation and Personality* (Harper & Row, 1954).

[28] See generally Corey LM Keyes and Jonathan Haidt (eds), *Flourishing: Positive Psychology and the Life Well-Lived* (APA, 2003).

> group level, it is about the civic virtues and the institutions that move individuals toward better citizenship: responsibility, nurturance, altruism, civility, moderation, tolerance, and work ethic.[29]

As it applies to an expanded foundation for evaluating moral intuitions about property, positive psychology gives us a different vocabulary and a largely untapped empirical knowledge base on which to draw.[30] There are two subsets of research into positive psychology that are particularly relevant to the exercise. First, consistent findings through a variety of research methodologies—recognising the risk of reductionism despite the strength of the evidence—have demonstrated that experiences are more important for individual well-being than the pursuit of material possessions.[31] Indeed, consumption can be a barrier to individual experience where there is a choice to be made about how people are going to invest their resources, time, and energy.

A second critical insight garnered from the field is the value of engagement and the importance of relationships to psychological health. As Clare Huntington has described it, a 'well-documented finding in positive psychology is that close interpersonal relationships are significantly correlated with subjective well-being and a host of desirable outcomes on a societal level, from greater civic engagement to thriving communities.'[32] And these two strands of the literature are connected, given that there is empirical evidence suggesting that what is most salient about the link between experiences and well-being, as compared to consumption and acquisition, is that experiences tend more often to be communal, whereas material possessions tend more often to be socially isolating.[33]

[29] Martin EP Seligman and Mihaly Csikszentmihalyi, 'Positive Psychology: An Introduction' (2000) 55 *American Psychologist* 5, 5. See also Huntington, above (n 7), at 390 (arguing that 'positive psychology is not the glib study of happiness but rather the study of what makes life worth living, which involves far more than fleeting, superficial happiness').

[30] To the extent that assumptions about psychology have been evident in the doctrine and the literature, they tend to reflect an emphasis on the more traditional, negative aspects of psychology.

[31] Darwin A Guevarra and Ryan T Howell, 'To Have in Order to Do: Exploring the Effects of Consuming Experiential Products on Well-being' (2014) 25 *Journal of Consumer Psychology* 1; Leaf Van Boven, 'Experientialism, Materialism, and the Pursuit of Happiness' (2005) 9 *Review of General Psychology* 132, 133; Leaf Van Boven and Thomas Gilovich, 'To do or to have: That is the question,' (2003) 85 *Journal of Personality & Social Psychology* 1193 (reviewing a broad array of evidence that experiences make people happier than consumption for the sake of consumption because life experiences 'are more open to positive reinterpretations, are a more meaningful part of one's identity, and contribute more to successful social relationships').

[32] Huntington, above (n 7), at 387 (citing, eg, Harry T Reis and Shelly L Gable, 'Toward a Positive Psychology of Relationships' in *Flourishing*, above (n 28)); David Myers, The Funds, Friends, and Faith of Happy People (2000) 55 *American Psychologist* 56).

[33] See Peter A Caprariello and Harry T Reis, 'To Do, To Have, or To Share? Valuing Experiences Over Material Possessions Depends on the Involvement of Others' (2013) 104 *Journal of Personality & Social Psychology* 199.

How, then, do these insights shed new light on moral intuitions about the connection between property and the self? At a high level of generality, positive psychology implies the centrality of subjective well-being as a normative goal, with individual and social structures that can support that goal. Positive psychology acknowledges the importance of responding to pathology (and much of psychology as a therapeutic field continues to give primacy to that), but proceeds on the argument that merely getting to a baseline lack of dysfunction is not enough. Across time and cultures, people desire meaning and fulfilment in their lives and focusing on flourishing has implications for social engagement, personal relationships, and individual life paths.[34]

Shifting from the macro-level to the institutional, this research suggests that property can be understood not only as an extension of the self—as the Hegelians would have it—but also as an indispensable component of how that self can best flourish. This does not translate easily into any simple dichotomy between personal and fungible property, to use Radin's terms. On the one hand, things—objects—appear not to make most people happy in comparison to experiences and relationships.[35] This might suggest contexts where less vigorous property rights might prevail, even for resources otherwise clearly constitutive of the self. Moreover, those who posit a hard divide between consumption and life satisfaction can too quickly gloss over the many ways in which the material world can serve as a platform for what we know fosters well-being.[36] People need resources or possession to access or enjoy many important formative personal experiences, from travel to culture to personal health. That said, a focus on material possessions can actually be a barrier to self-actualisation,[37] and positive psychology provides a basis for questioning the constitutive value of much of what Radin describes as 'personal'.[38]

The complications of the link between property and well-being that positive psychology introduces also have relevance to the Aristotelian invocation of human flourishing as a normative grounding for property.

[34] See Corey LM Keyes and Jonathan Haidt, 'Introduction: Human Flourishing—The Study of that which Makes Life Worthwhile' in *Flourishing*, above (n 28), at 3.

[35] See Stern, above (n 6), at 1121 ('An extensive body of research in social, health, evolutionary, and clinical psychology establishes that social relations—not possessions—are nonfungible, irreplaceable, and critical to human development.').

[36] *Cf* Elizabeth W Dunn et al, 'If Money Doesn't Make You Happy Then You Probably Aren't spending It Right' (2011) 21 *Journal of Consumer Psychology* 115 (discussing ways in which consumption can be directed toward enhancing well-being).

[37] See Van Boven and Gilovich, above (n 31), at 1200 (discussing research that shows that experiences contribute more and more favourably to self-actualising than the acquisition of possessions).

[38] Scholars have also critiqued personhood theory for paying insufficient attention to fetishization, *see*, eg, Stephen J Schnably, 'Property and Pragmatism: A Critique of Radin's Theory of Property and Personhood' (1993) 45 *Stanford Law Review* 347, although this is a fairly tangential critique in the main.

While the institutional and doctrinal conclusions this perspective yields can overlap in some respects with virtue ethics, at least in terms of the emphasis on well-being, positive psychology shifts the focus towards individual and micro-institutional determinants that tend somewhat to decentre property. In either approach, a baseline of material resources can be important, but positive psychology places greater emphasis on experiences and relationships. On the other hand, Aristotelian focus on capabilities resonates quite closely with much of what positive psychology has to say about individual development. As to the nature of people as social beings, there is a confluence around the value of relationships, but positive psychology understands the relational as contingent and as potentially subject to dysfunction as to fostering well-being.[39]

If the need of the community to foster individual capabilities engenders mutual responsibility for each member of the community as full and equal members, then the felt experience of individuals subject to that communal norm is important for that valence to resonate. The proposition that people are inherently social beings leads Aristotelians to assume moral obligation, but positive psychology highlights that the quality of relationships can be more or less meaningful and more or less correlated with subjective well-being. In light of that, the obligations of community in contexts where there is not a sufficiently positive basis for the relevant relationships can mean that the social nature of people actually undermines flourishing. It is also possible that community in the political sense may be felt as a derogation of more intimate relationships, where there is tension between the obligations owed to multiple communities.

A focus on 'capabilities' risks at times being a bit too much about lining up the right personal and social goods, with scholars debating which capabilities are necessary.[40] Positive psychology offers research about what, in fact, tends to provide people with more satisfying lives. As it turns out, the answer is mostly about relationships and a sense of meaningful contribution. This is consonant with much of what the Aristotelians assume about human nature as social, but suggests that positive relationships and communal engagement is a condition that itself must be fostered, not a pre-existing social reality.

[39] See Huntington, above (n 7), at 387 (discussing research showing the negative effects of bad relationships).

[40] See Gregory S Alexander, 'The Social-Obligation Norm in American Property Law' (2009) 94 *Cornell Law Review* 745, 764–65 (noting amongst Aristotelian and related social-obligation theorists the 'robust debate about exactly what capabilities are the crucial components of human flourishing').

IV. REVISITING HOME AS WHERE THE HEART IS

Given the focus of this volume, questions about the possible fragility of the home can provide a particularly 'thick' locus to study what a normative shift not only toward psychological empiricism but positive psychology might yield. Claims about the psychological importance of home—and the legal protections that should flow from that primacy—are well rehearsed in the literature. The psychological case for the primacy of home in law echoes Radin's intuitive understanding of the home as central to individual identity. As Ben Barros has summarised it, home 'is associated with a range of feelings related to a long-term tie to a physical location ... [including] feelings of rootedness and belonging [and] emotional warmth and personal comfort.'[41] And there does appear to be some support in the psychological literature for home as an important extension of self-conception,[42] notable perhaps most significantly in the resonance over dispossession.[43]

On the other hand, property scholars have significantly complicated the seemingly natural intuitive link between home and individual identity.[44] Stephanie Stern has undermined much of the rationale for the psychological centrality of home in the law. The empirical literature, Stern relates, indicates that 'personality characteristics, values, social roles, and one's body parts are the conceptual categories most closely linked with self', not possessions, however subjectively important.[45] And studies specifically about where people live show that as important as home can be, 'other items are more strongly linked to their sense of self', notably 'relatives, friends, and body organs' as well as a 'favorite vacation place, hair, and United States'.[46] Indeed, Stern notes, 'research indicates that residential real estate serves a

[41] D Benjamin Barros, 'Home as a Legal Concept' (2006) 46 *Santa Clara Law Review* 255, 277.

[42] See Helga Dittmar, *The Social Psychology of Material Possessions* (1992) 47, 113 (discussing the empirical psychological literature on possessions and identity and noting support for the link between home and the self).

[43] See Lorna Fox, 'Re-Possessing "Home": A Re-Analysis of Gender, Homeownership and Debtor Default for Feminist Legal Theory' (2008) 14 *William & Mary Journal of Women & Law* 423, 434 ('The impact of losing one's home on an individual occupier's quality of life, social and identity status, personal and family relationships, and for his or her emotional, psychological, and physical health and well-being have been well-established in housing and health literature.'); see also Lorna Fox O'Mahony, 'The Meaning of Home: From Theory to Practice' (2013) 5 *International Journal of Law in the Built Environment* 156.

[44] Jeremy Blumenthal helpfully noted the distinction between the psychological literature on ownership in the context of the home—much the focus of property scholars, not surprisingly—and connections with 'home' regardless of tenure type. See Blumenthal, above (n 4), at 618 (discussing Jerome Tognoli's typology of the psychology of home in terms of 'centrality, continuity, privacy, self-expression and personal identity, and social relationships').

[45] See Stern, above (n 6), 1111.

[46] *Ibid.*

primarily self-expressive, not self-constructive, function', with home most saliently expressing 'attitudes, values, personal history, ethnic identity, and self-perceived status', rather than self-identity.[47]

If positive psychology can reorient the normative question toward the foundations for well-being rather than the primacy of identify formation, or resilience in the face of adversity, two themes come naturally to the surface: Home as a locus for experience and home as a nexus of relationships. As to the first, the literature on property and relative status is particularly relevant here. Where home serves as a fraught symbol for a hedonic treadmill, then other psychological drives may distort the benefits of home for personal experiences and as a locus for relational meaning. If people are investing in home for self-expression, and much of that exercise is bound up in comparative consumption, then the conflict between possessions and experience as well as between possessions and relationships comes to the fore. Indeed, it is clear that, at least in the United States, the drive for comparative consumption has at times significantly distorted the market for homes and inspired people to invest more than they might if they prioritised what actually fosters well-being.[48]

Home, moreover, may have less to do with a given physical property per se and more with the associations that come from interpersonal connections and experiences. As Ben Barros has argued, the intuitive view of the importance of home to the self 'tends to overstate an individual's personal connection to a home in a particular location because many of the important personal values associated with a home are movable.'[49] People need secure attachment and a base from which to foster positive relationships, but community and connection may matter more than any particular four walls and roof.

The bottom line is that home matters, but perhaps for slightly different reasons than the law tends to acknowledge. Positive psychology reinforces the strain of doctrine that emphasises the relational and experiential aspects of home—home as a place of family, for example. That is not to minimise the Aristotelian insight that a minimum baseline of resources is critical—that without a home, questions about materialism, comparative consumption, and individual well-being are quite academic. But beyond the extreme, for the bulk of how the system of property approaches home, we need to understand that home is a means to a particular set of ends and perhaps temper the veneration that law has for home in that light.

[47] *Ibid* at 1113.

[48] See Kwan Ok Lee and Masaki Mori, 'Do Conspicuous Consumers Pay Higher Housing Premiums? Spatial and Temporal Variation in the United States' (2016) 44 *Real Estate Economics* 726.

[49] Barros, above (n 41), at 280.

V. CONCLUSION

Although not sufficiently acknowledged, common understandings of property law are suffused with assumptions about human nature and psychological processes. Most normative frames elide those assumptions and build a justificatory edifice without much psychological nuance. Beginning, instead, with the messy, but more realistic complexities of human nature would form a more solid foundation and a more subtle set of prescriptions.

Applying this to the example of positive psychology—with its focus on the empirical predicates for well-being—shows that reversing the direction can provide a different understanding of the relationship between individuals and their property. And positive psychology ultimately provides a new lens through which to interrogate the role of home and material possessions, an exercise that can resonate much more broadly across justifications for the institutions of property law.

Part II

Rental Security

4

The 'Affordable Alternative to Renting': Property Guardians and Legal Dimensions of Housing Precariousness

CAROLINE HUNTER AND JED MEERS*

I. INTRODUCTION

FOR THOSE LOOKING for a 'new affordable alternative to renting'[1] and something 'more adventurous' than what is provided by a local lettings agent, then maybe being a 'Property Guardian' is 'truly the exciting and cheaper alternative.'[2] A number of companies in the UK offer the opportunity to be a property guardian. These companies—which are principally property management firms—function by advertising spaces in otherwise vacant commercial or residential buildings, providing security to the owner (against, for instance, squatting or criminal damage) and 'quirky homes for low rent' for those with a 'flexible lifestyle'.[3] The (advertised) room prices are attractive, with 'rents starting at £35 per week including bills',[4] and example offerings include spaces in former fire stations,[5]

* York Law School, University of York, UK.

[1] Camelot Europe, 'Find Rooms to Let': uk.cameloteurope.com/8/0/rooms-to-let/find-rooms-to-let-from-only-40-per-week.html.

[2] Ibid.

[3] Graham Norwood, 'Property guardian schemes offer quirky homes at low rents. But not for long', *The Guardian* (10 January 2010): www.theguardian.com/money/2010/jan/10/property-guardian-schemes.

[4] Ad-Hoc Property, 'Property Guardians': www.adhocproperty.co.uk/property-guardians/.

[5] Ad-Hoc Property, 'Fire Station—Property 220': properties.adhocproperty.co.uk/living-space/in-and-around-newcastle/fire-station~220/.

museums,[6] churches and pubs,[7] in addition to otherwise unoccupied residential properties.

Heralded by its proponents as providing cheap accommodation for occupiers prepared to accept 'flexibility',[8] an 'exciting' and 'adventurous' alternative, increasingly the phenomenon is receiving critical attention: guardians have been described as an 'underclass of renters'[9] and the companies themselves as participating in 'the monetisation of the housing crisis.'[10] The uncertain rights, obligations, and security, associated with a perceived 'unsettled' lifestyle of 'generation rent',[11] has sufficient purchase in popular culture to form the focus of a UK sitcom—*Crashing*—based in a disused hospital inhabited by property guardians. When asked if they enjoy living under the scheme, one character sardonically responds: 'You're not allowed to have parties, cook meals, light candles, have sex, express emotion, claim any rights, argue if they want to throw you out with only two days' notice, or smoke. It's a riot.'[12]

The growth in property guardians may be seen as 'a form of unregulated, semi-formal housing in the context of the growing shift of many housing practices from marginal to mainstream.'[13] The phenomenon appears paradigmatic of the 'precarious home' outlined in the introduction to this collection. In this chapter we use the example of property guardians to examine the legal determinants of housing precarity, mirroring the work of Nicola Kountouris on the legal determinants of precariousness in work relations.[14]

[6] Henry Zientek 'Property guardians have moved into a Kirklees museum to keep squatters away', *The Huddersfield Daily Examiner* (5 July 2017): www.examiner.co.uk/news/property-guardians-moved-kirklees-museum-13284067.

[7] Ad-Hoc Property, 'House Sitters Bag Top Properties on Cheap': http://www.adhocproperty.co.uk/2014/07/from-churches-to-pubs-to-million-pound-homes-professionals-are-slashing-rents-by-house-sitting-vacant-properties/.

[8] Eg Joe Jervis, 'What housing can learn from profit-driven property guardians', *The Guardian* (3 February 2012) www.guardian.co.uk/housing-network/2012/feb/03/housing-profit-property-guardian-industry?INTCMP=SRCH.

[9] Lucas Amin and Margot Gibbs, 'The high price of cheap living: how the property guardianship dream soured' *The Guardian* (24 December 2015): www.theguardian.com/society/2015/dec/24/the-high-price-of-cheap-living-how-the-property-guardianship-dream-soured.

[10] Tom Zephyr, 'My real-life experience as a property guardian was anything but funny' (2016) *The Guardian* (18 January 2016): www.theguardian.com/housing-network/2016/jan/18/property-guardian-channel-4-crashing-generation-rent.

[11] Jennifer Hoolachan, Kim McKee, Tom Moore and Adriana Mihaela Soaita, '"Generation rent" and the ability to "settle down": economic and geographical variation in young people's housing transitions' (2017) 20 *Journal of Youth Studies* 63.

[12] George Kane [Director], 'Crashing' [Television broadcast] (Channel 4, 2016).

[13] Mara Ferreri, Gloria Dawson and Alexander Vasudevan 'Living precariously: property guardianship and the flexible city' (2016) 42 *Transactions of the Institute of British Geographers* 246–59.

[14] Nicola Kountouris, 'Legal Determinants of Precariousness in Personal Work Relations: A European Perspective' (2013) 34 *Comparative Labor Law & Policy Journal* 21.

The 'intersectionality of housing and labour markets' has been repeatedly emphasised by Hoolachan et al[15] and others,[16] but a similar approach to precariousness has not been explored in the housing context. Although property guardians might be considered 'untypical'[17] in housing law terms, our argument is that by focusing on the legal elements of property guardians we can identify the determinants that contribute to rendering housing relations inherently precarious.

Furthermore, the example of property guardians and their legal determinants allows us to explore the role of the state in both enhancing and limiting housing precariousness. Our argument is that the state has an ambivalent response to housing precarity. Lorey argues for an understanding of 'governmental precarization', namely: 'understanding precarization as *governmental* makes it possible to problematize the complex interactions between an instrument of governing and the modes of subjectivation, in their ambivalence between subjugation and self-empowerment.' (emphasis added)[18]

There is already evidence in the work of Ferreri et al[19] of the 'constitutively double-edged'[20] nature of the precarity of property guardians, setting flexibility against insecurity, choice against dependence, and innovativeness against legal uncertainty in the views of property guardians. However, our focus is on the state itself. How do the organs of the state—national and local governments—respond to the phenomenon?

With this approach in mind, the chapter is divided into four further sections. The section II below provides an overview of the property guardian phenomenon and the current (limited) evidence base on its extent and composition. Section III sets out the legal determinants of housing precarity under five headings: immigration; tenure/time; control; cost; and conditions. Section IV focuses of the role of authorities as a particular organ of the state. The section draws on survey data collected from Local Authorities on complaints made about property guardian companies, any associated regulatory, or other forms, of action they have taken, and a small case-study of Bristol. In Section V conclusions are drawn.

[15] Hoolachan et al (n 11 above) 64.

[16] See eg: Jill Morgan 'Housing and security in England and Wales: casualisation revisited' (2009) 1 *International Journal of Law in the Built Environment* 42; Hannah Fearn and Kevin Gulliver, *A New Deal for Tenants Scoping a Precariat Charter for Social Housing* (Human City Institute, 2015).

[17] See Kountouris (n 14 above) 21.

[18] Isabell Lorey, *State of Insecurity: Government of the Precarious* (Verso, 2015) 13.

[19] Ferreri (n 13 above).

[20] Louise Waite, 'A Place and Space for a Critical Geography of Precarity?' (2009) 3 *Geography Compass* 412, 418.

II. PROPERTY GUARDIANS: AN OVERVIEW

In order to provide some context for the analysis which follows, it is important to outline what is currently known about the extent and working practices of property guardian companies. This will be concise; there is a paucity of available evidence on the phenomenon. There are, however, three key issues worth outlining: (i) their business models, (ii) evidence on extent and geographical spread, and (iii) possible explanations for their increasing prominence.

Though increasingly encompassing a wider range of activity, the largest Property Guardian companies—most notably, Camelot Europe, Ad-Hoc, and Global Guardians—operate in a broadly similar fashion, adopting a model with its roots in The Netherlands.[21] Taking Camelot as an archetype, there are two sources of income: 'licence fees' received from those living in the properties, and management fees charged to the owners of the property.[22] These vary depending on the nature and condition of the property,[23] and the potential for 'licence fee' income, with guardian fees described as between '£30–£70' per week, and property management fees as between '£30–£80' per week.[24] According to Camelot Europe, the general principle is that 'property guardians pay a quarter of the going rate', while recognising that it is 'difficult to say what the going rate is for a fire station, for instance.'[25] Circumstantial evidence suggests, however, that rents have become far closer to market levels as property guardian companies have attained a higher profile with renters.[26]

The proposition, therefore, is a win-win scenario for owners of otherwise empty properties and those looking for (generally, inner city) accommodation. The presence of guardians 'discourages squatting and allows control over the premises without the need for security guarding costs' and exempts the property from business rates,[27] while those who 'prefer to live centrally but cannot afford significant rents'[28] have access to otherwise unavailable housing.

[21] Ferreri (n 13 above) 5.

[22] Ferreri (n 13 above).

[23] For instance, a common practice is the installation of temporary showering facilities or the provision of certain white goods for communal areas. As stated in the Estates Gazette, 'the guardian company can advise on the installation of self-contained shower pod, while the tea point in an office building could be a perfectly suitable kitchen area': see Samantha Baden, 'Property Guardian Angels', *The Estates Gazette* (July 2013) 93–95.

[24] Ibid.

[25] Ibid.

[26] See per Lord Beecham, HL Deb, 9 February 2016, vol 768, col 2219. See also Maya Oppenheim, 'I can't even afford to be a property guardian', *New Statesman* (27 July 2015): http://www.newstatesman.com/politics/2015/07/i-cant-even-afford-be-property-guardian.

[27] Emma Chadwick, 'Rise of the property guardians', *The Estates Gazette* (April 2015) 96–97.

[28] Ibid.

The growth of property guardians may be characterised as a response to two different phenomena. First in England there is a crisis of affordability of housing. This crisis is largely caused by a mismatch between demand and supply.[29] While the economic crisis of 2008 had some short-lived impact on house prices, it has not significantly improved the position. Indeed the economic crash has exacerbated the fall in the relative share of households owning their home and the growth in private renting.[30]

This is particularly true of 'generation rent' who are increasingly excluded from owner-occupation.[31] As the number of first-time buyers has declined, so too has the proportion of those under 34 who are owner-occupiers. In 1991, 67 per cent of the 25 to 34 age group were homeowners. By 2015–16, this had declined to 38 per cent.[32] This has forced many young people into the ever-expanding private rented market.[33]

A very different issue is that of empty properties and this provides the second element to the context of the growth of property guardians. The empty properties may be residential or commercial. They may be awaiting sale, demolition or refurbishment, but for whatever reason the owner prefers or has no choice but to keep the property empty.

It seems that some of the demand for the service of property guardians comes from local authorities with empty blocks of flats, care homes and even offices. Freedom of Information requests have established that within 33 London-based local authorities in 2016, there were a total of 966 guardians living in 205 properties;[34] notwithstanding the snapshot nature of the data, this suggests that the use of these companies by local councils is fairly widespread within the capital. Cuts to public services may have fuelled the use of these services.

So how widespread is the use of property guardians? There is no robust evidence available on total usage. Industry estimates suggest there are 25–30 property guardian companies in operation, with around 4,000 guardians currently in occupation.[35]

[29] K Barker, 'Review of Housing Supply: Final Report—recommendations' (HMSO, 2004).

[30] Peter A Kemp, 'Private Renting After the Global Financial Crisis' (2015) 30 *Housing Studies* 601, 613.

[31] Kim McKee 'Young People, Homeownership and Future Welfare' (2012) 27 *Housing Studies* 853; Hoolachan et al (n 11 above).

[32] See DCLG, 'English Housing Survey: Private rented sector, 2015-16' (DCLG, July 2017) www.gov.uk/government/uploads/system/uploads/attachment_data/file/627686/Private_rented_sector_report_2015-16.pdf.

[33] Karen O'Reilly and John Bone, 'No Place Called Home: The Causes and Social Consequences of the UK Housing "Bubble"' (2010) 61 *The British Journal of Sociology* 231.

[34] Thanks to Samir Jeraj for providing the authors with the raw data of his Freedom of Information request activity in the city.

[35] Charlotte England, 'Property guardians: a solution to the UK's housing crisis?', *The Guardian* (24 March 2015): www.theguardian.com/sustainable-business/2015/mar/24/property-guardians-housing-solution-opportunism.

The only other publically available source of data is the websites of the companies themselves. The authors operated a 'web-scrape' of advertised lettings information from the websites of the three largest property guardian companies operating in the UK—Ad-Hoc, Camelot Europe, and Global Guardians—in order to ascertain the numbers of rooms being advertised and their geographical location.[36] Of the data, collected fortnightly between March and May 2015, we found a real-time average of 357 available rooms advertised across the three companies at any given time. The locations of these properties were than mapped to provide an indication of the geographical spread or any particular pattern. There was, perhaps unsurprisingly, a cluster of advertised properties within central London,[37] then further clusters between Manchester and Liverpool (specifically the Warrington area), and in Birmingham. Importantly, there does not appear to be any association with the prevalence of empty properties within area (as ascertained through Council Tax and Business Rates Base Data), or—outside of the London context—rental prices.[38]

III. LEGAL DIMENSIONS OF PRECARIOUSNESS

Having provided a general overview of the property guardian phenomenon, this section now situates the practice within the legal dimensions of renting homes, particularly in the private rented sector. With this in mind, drawing on Kountouris' analysis of work relations, we focus on the legal 'dimensions and contexts' of precariousness and how these are created and applied to different circumstances.[39]

This has two key implications. First, it demonstrates the importance of not assessing the relative precariousness of atypical arrangements (in this case, property guardianship) with reference to those which are typical (such as assured shorthold tenancies[40]). The inherent, and some would argue, increasing,[41] precariousness of the latter negates their utility as a

[36] More details and interactive maps can be found online at: www.propertyguardianresearch.co.uk/maps.

[37] Ferreri et al (n 13 above), 7 also comment on the significance and uniqueness of London, but it is clearly a nationwide phenomenon.

[38] For more information, please see: www.propertyguardianresearch.co.uk/maps.

[39] Kountouris (n 14 above) 24.

[40] The assured shorthold tenancy under the Housing 1988 is the 'norm' for private renting in England.

[41] See the introductory chapter to this collection. On the UK position, see: Jill Morgan, 'The casualisation of housing' (1996) 18 *Journal of Social Welfare and Family Law* 445; Jill Morgan 'Housing and security in England and Wales: casualisation revisited' (2009) 1 *International Journal of Law in the Built Environment* 42 and Suzanne Fitzpatrick and Beth Watts (2017) 'Competing visions: security of tenure and the welfarisation of English social housing', Housing Studies On-line: http://dx.doi.org/10.1080/02673037.2017.1291916.

benchmark for comparison.[42] Rather, by focusing on property guardians we can illuminate how other legal arrangements are also becoming more precarious. Likewise, the focus should not be on distinct categories or terms of reference (such as 'illegal' or 'legal'), but instead on the 'fact and degree of exclusion occasioned by legal distinctions'[43]—in other words, the specific 'legal determinants of precariousness'[44] which arise in specific arrangements to compound precarity. Put simply, the focus here is on elements which can exacerbate precarity, not comparing precarious arrangements to even more precarious ones.

Our starting point is the idea of security; with a lack of security tending to greater precarity. Kemp[45] has argued that housing tenures, such as the private rented, are a form of institution. Each tenure has a different make-up of security, depending on a number of factors including the nature of legislation/regulation and policy settings.[46] Hulse and Milligan suggest that in rental tenures there is a distinction between *de jure*, *de facto* and perceptual security of tenure.[47]

> De jure security is embedded in property rights, the legal rules that enable owners to acquire, use and dispose of their property and lease arrangements over land/housing ... De facto security refers to occupation and use of property such that, over time, occupiers may acquire greater security and the risks of eviction become less. Perceptual security refers to security as seen and experienced by occupiers; thus people may think that they may lose their housing/land whether or not this happens or is even threatened, or they may feel secure in their occupation even if they do not have legal rights that are enforceable.

Despite their separation of *de jure* and *de facto* security, in fact many of the *de facto* factors are also legal (others are market and public policy factors), so legal factors arise in both. In this chapter we have used Hulse and Milligan's legal factors as the starting point for the legal determinants of housing precarity. They are: tenure/time; control; cost; and conditions. However, we have added immigration, which does not feature in Hulse and Milligan's account. As in the labour market, one's capacity to access rental housing in England is becoming more and more limited by immigration status.

Before turning to the determinants, there are two further points to make. The first of these is about the place of 'legal uncertainty'. This is something

[42] Kountouris (n 14 above) 25.

[43] Sarah Marsden, 'The New Precariousness: Temporary Migrants and the Law in Canada' (2012) 27 *Canadian Journal of Law and Society* 209, 210.

[44] Kountouris (n 14 above).

[45] Kemp (n 30 above) 602.

[46] Kath Hulse and Vivienne Milligan, 'Secure Occupancy: A New Framework for Analysing Security in Rental Housing' (2014) 29 *Housing Studies* 638.

[47] Ibid, 641, building on Jean-Louis van Gelder, 'What tenure security? The case for a tripartite view' (2010) 27 *Land Use Policy* 449.

more specific than the general uncertainty experienced in most situations or insecurity experienced as a 'condition' of precariousness.[48] Instead, the suggestion here is that the uncertainty over one's legal position—be it immigration status or the nature of their legal occupation of property—of both the individuals themselves and importantly those enforcing the law, can act to 'compound' precariousness.[49] The problems associated with legal uncertainty as an aggravating factor in precarious arrangements has been considered elsewhere, particularly with reference to the status of migrants, where often the inability to define their legal status is 'taken for granted'.[50] Zou argues these uncertainties (for instance, the vacuities of work-related restrictions) are a specific way in which the law can aggravate their situation due to: the 'enormous control' it provides to those managing their employment, their associated inability to make long-term plans, and the uncertainty of conduct it generates, where individuals cannot be sure whether their actions or their situation is lawful or not.[51] As will become apparent from the discussion below, this 'legal uncertainty' is prevalent within the specific case study of property guardians.

The second is 'organisational precariousness'.[52] It is argued here that this comprises two key ideas, which illustrate Hulse and Milligan's perceptual security and how it interacts with legal determinants. First, that control and experiences of precariousness are compounded when there is particularly acute dependence; in other words, where an individual lacks the capacity to choose or negotiate their circumstances.[53] This in turn can be compounded by legal arrangements, particularly with elasticity in obligations, with Kountouris suggesting that organisational precariousness emerges when:

> a particular legal regime tends to lean more towards the *jus dispositivum* end of the spectrum rather than the *jus cogens* end of the spectrum ... To put it in simpler terms, flexibility is not per se a determinant of organizational precariousness, as long as workers can exercise some degree of control over their flexible working lives, instead of being subject to their employers' whim.[54]

[48] See: William Daniel Vera Rojas, Monica Budowski and Christian Suter, 'Threats to Happiness: How Lower Middle Class Households Deal with Insecurity and Precariousness' in Mariano Rojas (ed), *Handbook of Happiness Research in Latin America* (Springer Netherlands, 2016) 231; and David Farrugia, 'Youth Homelessness, Reflexivity and Inequality in Late Modernity' in Farrugia, *Youth Homelessness in Late Modernity*, vol 1 (Springer Singapore, 2016) 17–38.

[49] Laurie Berg, *Migrant Rights at Work: Law's Precariousness at the Intersection of Immigration and Labour* (Routledge, 2015) 44.

[50] Ibid.

[51] Mimi Zou, 'Hyper-Dependence and Hyper-Precarity in Migrant Work Relations' in Tindara Addabbo and others (eds), *Labour And Social Rights. An Evolving Scenario* (Giappichelli Editore, 2015).

[52] Kountouris (n 14 above).

[53] Zou (n 51 above).

[54] Kountouris (n 14 above) 34.

This dimension addresses important arguments about the 'constitutively double-edged' nature of precariousness, where *objectively* precarious arrangements may be *subjectively* valued by an individual due to, for instance, their flexibility.[55] This is not necessarily problematic, indeed, the private rented sector, and other forms of housing which may be described as precariousness, can often offer flexibility and responsiveness not found in other tenures. It is important, however, to consider whether the individual is able to 'exercise some degree of control' over this flexibility, as opposed to it being mandated by the situation in which they find themselves.[56] As suggested by Lorey, precariousness can engender 'ambivalent productive moments, as they arise through techniques of self-government.'[57] Otherwise, dependency demands long-term security and predictability, and precariousness provides short-term unpredictability; the two consequently struggle to reconcile and the latter is compounded.[58]

A. Immigration

Kountouris notes that:

> [i]t is often ignored that one's immigration status plays a crucial role in determining whether she will be in a position to enter a secure and rewarding work contract or relation, or instead will be confined at the margins of the labor market, in an inherently precarious, and often undeclared work, relation.[59]

The same is true of the housing market. Access to ownership is tied to access to capital, leaving most immigrants to rented housing.

For over 20 years, access to social housing[60] in England has been limited by immigration status.[61] Despite the popular view, amounting to a moral panic, that immigrants have privileged access to social housing, the reality is the opposite.[62] Rather the evidence is that 'new immigrants and migrants are being revealed to encounter major problems accessing and maintaining accommodation and to be experiencing poor housing conditions, overcrowding and homelessness, as well as exploitation by landlords in the private rented sector.'[63]

[55] Waite (n 20 above) 418.
[56] Kountouris (n 14 above).
[57] Lorey (n 18 above).
[58] Zou (n 51 above).
[59] Kountouris (n 14 above) 27.
[60] ie provided by local authorities or not-for-profit landlords at less than market rents.
[61] Housing Act 1996, s. 160ZA and the Allocation of Housing and Homelessness (Eligibility) (England) Regulations 2006 (SI 2006/1294).
[62] David Robinson 'New immigrants and migrants in social housing in Britain: discursive themes and lived realities' (2010) 38 *Policy & Politics* 57.
[63] Ibid, 64.

For the private rented sector, the Immigration Act 2014 required private landlords to police the immigration status of any new tenant. To have the 'right to rent' a person must have the requisite qualifying status.[64] Further, an amendment of the Act in 2016 permits landlords to terminate an agreement if the occupiers are disqualified.[65] The scheme was rolled out nationally in October 2016, so it is difficult to know the effect of the Act.[66] However, one estate agent felt:[67]

> Some of the most vulnerable people in the private rented sector may be forced to turn to the black economy to find a place to live. Someone who is homeless, for instance, may not hold a passport or visa; and obtaining one may be difficult, not to say costly, for someone living on the streets or in temporary accommodation, so this policy could well bar many such people from ever getting back into secure, rented accommodation.

The broad application of the Immigration Act 2014 means that offering an agreement to a property guardian would be covered by the Act.[68] In any case, despite the flexibility offered by property guardian firms, they are not flexible about who they take. The Camelot website stated that applicants must have 'proof of income and … provide an employer and character reference.'[69] This may limit the number of migrants who can apply. While out of London our survey of local authorities revealed one case where: 'Some of the tenants were EU residents with poor English and they did not know they were "Guardians".' Ferreri et al's work on property guardians indicates that in London the guardians were largely middle-class, university-educated, and often working in the creative industries.[70]

Accordingly, it seems likely that property guardianship does not and will not provide for the hyper-precarious migrant described by Lewis et al.[71] The stratified rights they note in immigration law may not be as inherent in housing, but can be seen developing. For migrants a further layer of

[64] Immigration Act 2014, s. 22.

[65] Immigration Act 2014, s. 33D.

[66] Although see: Claire Brickell, Tom Bucke, Jonathan Burchell, Miriam Davidson, Ewan Kennedy, Rebecca Linley and Andrew Zurawan, 'Evaluation of the Right to Rent scheme. Full evaluation report of phase one' (Research Report 83, Migration and Border Analysis, Home Office Science, October 2015): https://www.gov.uk/government/uploads/system/uploads/attachment_data/file/468934/horr83.pdf.

[67] Quoted in Hilary Osborne, 'Landlords "don't understand right to rent immigration"', *The Guardian* (1 Febuary 2016): www.theguardian.com/money/2016/feb/01/landlords-do-not-understand-rules-immigration-checks-association.

[68] See the Immigration Act 2014, s. 20.

[69] Camelot Europe, 'Guardian FAQs': uk.cameloteurope.com/frequently-asked-questions/guardian-faqs.

[70] Ferreri (n 14 above).

[71] Hannah Lewis, Pete Dwyer, Stuart Hodkinson and Louise Waite 'Hyper-precarious lives: Migrants, work and forced labour in the Global North' (2015) 39 *Progress in Human Geography* 580.

hyper-precarious housing, below property guardianship, is documented by Environmental Health News.[72] This documents the 'letting' of a disused fireplace showroom—similar to many of the buildings occupied by property guardians. When it was inspected by EHOs, they found 107 people living in just 32 rooms. The occupiers, largely Romanian migrants working on farms, were sharing three kitchens, six toilets and six showers. Their housing status is not recorded, but the response of the local authority was to close the premises under the Housing Act 2004, making the occupants homeless.

B. Tenure/Time

For Hulse and Milligan the length of a rental contract and its termination arrangements make up the *de jure* elements of security.[73] In English law it can be seen to be made up of a number of elements which when aggregated may lead to greater or lesser security for the occupier. At its simplest and providing least protection, some legal security may simply prevent eviction except in accordance with the contractual (or common law) requirements as to notice and termination of the tenancy. One step up from this, the law may impose a minimum period of notice which is longer than the contractual one. It may impose a requirement that a court order is obtained prior to any eviction. Thus, as in employment,[74] there is a strong temporal element in any relationship between an occupier and land owner.

Greater levels of security move beyond the contractual agreement between the landlord and tenant and limit the *basis* on which the landlord can evict the tenant. In these circumstances, notwithstanding that the contractual period of the tenancy may have come to an end or the contract makes a different provision, the landlord can only get permission to evict from the court on limited grounds. These may include fault on the part of the tenant (eg rent arrears or damage to the property) or need on the part of the landlord (eg to live in the property to redevelop it). Such security has usually been accompanied by rent control in order to prevent landlords simply pricing tenants out of properties.

These different levels can be mapped against the current legal provision for private tenants, but before doing so it is worth understanding how the

[72] Tom Wall, 'Borderlands: A special investigation into migrant worker housing' *Shorthand Social* (4 May 2016): social.shorthand.com/_tomwall/3yM1xsWekY/borderlands; Consider also the Government's clamp down on 'Beds in Sheds' in 2012: DCLG, 'Announcement: Major clampdown launched on "beds in sheds"' (DCLG, 31 August 2012): www.gov.uk/government/news/major-clampdown-launched-on-beds-in-sheds.

[73] Hulse and Milligan (n 46 above).

[74] See Kountouris (n 14 above).

current legal settlement contrasts with that which preceded it. The current legal position was largely established in 1988, when the then Conservative government passed the Housing Act 1988 and effectively deregulated the previous system which had offered a high degree of security to tenants. The pre-1988 position, which had existed from the mid-1960s, included rent control and quite severely limited grounds on which possession could be obtained (Rent Act 1977). Indeed in 1982, Honore concluded that the Rent Act 1977 provided 'those who could not afford to buy their homes with a substitute for home ownership, a right to remain in occupation for at least a lifetime and often more.'[75] This can be seen as the high-water mark of rights for private rented tenants.

One of the limitations of the Rent Act was the large number of exemptions, which had encouraged the use of agreements which fell outside the Act, as landlords attempted to circumvent the rent and security rules. Principal amongst these was the licence agreement. English landlord and tenant law has always differentiated between tenancies (which create an interest in land) and licences which are purely contractual. The Rent Act only applied to tenancies and not to licences. This led to a series of court cases where the boundaries between a tenancy and a licence were established by the courts. This culminated in two House of Lords decisions in the mid- and late-1980s: *Street v Mountford*[76] and *AG Securities v Vaughan; Antoniades v Villiers.*[77] The cases sought to subordinate the actual documents to the legal question, ie whether the three elements of a tenancy—exclusive possession, payment and term—were evidenced by the facts on the ground.[78]

The Housing Act 1988 essentially removed the need for landlords to use devices such as the licence as rents were set by the market, and the length of the tenancy, subject to a minimum six-month period, was a matter for agreement. However, the requirement of property guardianship is such that even this limited security is too great. In order to ensure the property owner can take back the property without complications guardian companies have sought to use licences, for their greater flexibility.

The Ad-hoc website is typical:

> Ad Hoc operates through licence agreements between it and our 'Property Guardians'. This means that Property Guardians do not have the same rights as

[75] Anthony Honore, *The Quest for Security: Employees, Tenants, Wives* (Stevens, 1982) 37.

[76] *Street v Mountford* [1985] AC 809, HL.

[77] *AG Securities v Vaughan; Antoniades v Villiers* [1990] 1 AC 417, HL.

[78] Andrew Arden, Martin Partington and Caroline Hunter, *Arden & Partington on Housing Law* (Loose-leaf: Sweet & Maxwell), paras 2-06, 2-07. See particularly Lord Templeman's warning about 'the judge awarding mark for drafting' in *Street v Mountford* [1985] AC 809.

> tenants. You are required to give us 14 days' notice to terminate your contract. Ad Hoc will provide you with 28 days' notice if we need to terminate your contract.[79]

Thus they clearly are drawing on the position established in *AG Securities v Vaughan; Antoniades v Villiers*. The importance of this is shown in the Camelot website, which boasts:[80]

> The main condition for guaranteeing the flexibility of the Property Guardian concept is to make sure that the legal agreement between the client, Camelot and the Guardian is watertight. The proxies and license are updated continuously by lawyers specialising in property law.[81]

Furthermore they (or their bailiffs) use the case law to underline their rights against occupiers when giving notice to leave the property:[82]

> We would bring to your attention the case of Street v Mountford. Whilst it is arguable that exclusive possession could be found, if in the absence of a fixed term of the agreement would fail to satisfy the 'tenancy test'. Alternatively please see in Gray v Taylor [1998] 1 WLR 1093.
>
> ... This right under Common Law is set out in Halsbury's Laws of England (Volume 97 (2010) 5th Edition).

There is a paradox here. Legally the licence limits the certainty of the guardian in terms of the right to remain in the property. But the legal terrain is not that 'watertight'; it is difficult to be so confident about the lease/licence distinction as every case will turn on its facts and the application of the law to them by a judge. In order to preserve the uncertainty for the occupier the property guardian companies sell guaranteed flexibility through creating legal certainty in their websites and documents. This limits the chances of the occupier challenging the agreement.

However, this certainty is a chimera, as was demonstrated in the County Court decision of *Camelot Property Management Ltd v Roynon*,[83] where the judge found the 'licence agreement' in fact created an assured shorthold tenancy. Nonetheless, property guardian firms continue to use licences and the guardians continue to be in a position of uncertainty.

[79] Ad-Hoc Property, 'Property Guardians—Frequently Asked Questions': www.adhocproperty.co.uk/property-guardians/faqs/.

[80] Camelot Europe, 'Reliable Legal Structure': uk.cameloteurope.com/property-guardians/reliable-legal-structure.

[81] For one of the changes that has happened to the occupier agreement is that they offer 28 days' notice rather than 14 which was common in 2012 in response to the Protection for Eviction Act 1977, s. 3: see Giles Peaker, 'We eat ham and jam and spam a lot' (*Nearly Legal: Housing Law News and Comment*, 26 September 2016): nearlylegal.co.uk/2016/09/eat-ham-jam-spam-lot/.

[82] For the full notice see ibid, where it is described as a 'farrago of nonsense'.

[83] *Camelot Property Management Ltd v Roynon*, judgment of 24 February 2017, Claim No: C01BS354. The judgment is available at: 431bj62hscf91kqmgj258yg6-wpengine.netdna-ssl.com/wp-content/uploads/2017/02/CamelotvRoyon.pdf.

C. Control

The licence/tenancy distinction is an important determinant of the rights of the occupier. As summarised by Arden et al,

> there can be no tenancy unless the occupier takes possession of the premises in question, and that possession is exclusive ... [W]hat it means is that the tenant has the right to exclude all others from the premises, including the landlord.[84]

The use of a licence allows for a greater organisational control over the property and occupier than would be the case if a tenancy were offered.

Most guardian firms impose additional limitations about conduct and can be far more intrusive in terms of monitoring behaviour (one aspect that indicates these are genuine licences). In 2015 the Camelot website noted that they carry out unannounced monthly inspections; further 'Guardians are only allowed two guests each at any one time, and cannot under any circumstances hold a party in the property.'[85] This sort of limitation seems normal for guardians, as Barbara Speed writes:[86]

> Even if you make it past the checks, there are a fair few rules to contend with. No pets, no parties, no smoking, no candles ... Oh, and you can't leave the property for more than 24 hours without explicit permission. Most agencies also carry out unannounced inspections at least once a month. Until recently, several also had clauses in their contracts forbidding guardians to speak to the press; as far as we can tell, this is no longer the case.
>
> The rules highlight the big catch with property guardianship: even its strongest advocate would admit that the exchange is, essentially, reduced rents (sorry, we mean fees) for reduced rights.

Rules are enforced through unannounced inspections, warning cards, threatening e-mails and fines.[87] For one of the property guardians interviewed by Ferreri et al, this created an 'aura of fear where you always have to be afraid that they are going to get you, somehow, that you are going to do something that is prohibited by the licence agreement' (Piero).

For Guy Standing[88] the 'precariat lives with anxiety—chronic insecurity associated ... with teetering on the edge, knowing that one mistake or one piece of bad luck could tip the balance between modest dignity and being a bag lady ...' The legal control in the agreements for property guardians indicates how housing precarity adds to this anxiety.

[84] Andrew Arden et al (n 78 above), para 2-05.

[85] The website has since been updated, and is more circumspect.

[86] Barbara Speed, 'Central London properties, minus the sky-high rents. But what's the catch' (Citymetric, 5 August 2014): www.citymetric.com/politics/central-london-properties-minus-sky-high-rents-what-s-catch; see also Ferreri et al (n 13 above) 10.

[87] Ferreri et al (n 13 above) 10.

[88] Guy Standing, *The Precariat: The New Dangerous Class* (Bloomsbury Academic. 2011) p. 20.

D. Costs

In employment 'income precariousness' is a

> multidimensional legal determinant that strikes, in many ways, at the heart of the problem of precarious work. A person's working life can easily be affected by all other legal determinants of precariousness, but the availability of a steady and decent income can still allow that person to live a fulfilling and dignified existence.[89]

One form of legal protection for employees is the minimum wage. Similarly rent control has in the past played a role providing protection of private tenants, in terms of protecting their standard of life. As noted above, that protection ended in the Housing Act 1988.

One of the attractions of property guardianship is the lower cost. Accordingly, it might be seen as helping to provide more affordable housing. However, there are elements that illustrate that costs of housing are not just about the rent. For example, guardians are generally asked to pay a deposit of at least £350 (£600 in London). This deposit is said to be refundable, but it is not clear from the website of property guardian companies in what circumstances it might not be. Given that the scheme operates outside the usual legal provision of an assured shorthold tenancy, there is no suggestion that it will be protected through the tenancy deposit legislation[90] and there is some anecdotal evidence of problems. Further, other fees are levied: for example a relocation fee to move into new property[91] and for a fire pack and administration fee to move in.[92] Although it may seem a form of housing with less 'income precariousness'[93] than the high cost of the private rented market, some of that is hidden in the lack of legal rights.

E. Conditions

The final element of the legal determinants is control of property standards. This takes a number of legal forms in England. Some are rights given directly to the occupier. The most important example of this is the Landlord and Tenant Act 1985, section 11 which implies a term into all short-term tenancy agreements that the landlord is responsible repairs to the structure, exterior and utilities serving a property. It is a feature of this legislation that it applies to tenancies and not to licences, as with tenure, taking guardians out of the certain legal framework.

[89] See Kountouris (n 14 above), 32.
[90] Housing Act 2004.
[91] Ad-Hoc Property (n 79 above).
[92] Camelot Europe, 'Reliable Legal Structure' (n 80 above).
[93] See Kountouris (n 14 above).

Residential property standards are also enforced by local authorities. Authorities are given a range of powers in the Housing Act 2004. In relation to the Housing Act 2004 ('the 2004 Act') two key Parts may potentially come into play: first Part 1, which contains the provisions relating to housing standards; and secondly Part 2, which relates to the licensing of houses in multiple occupation ('HMOs'). As Burridge and Ormandy[94] show, each Part has a separate history. Part 1 was a deliberate move from early methods of regulating 'unfit' housing to a risk-based approach. On the other hand, the regulation of HMOs continues to follow the 'traditional model' of specifying standards.

Part 1 applies to 'residential premises'.[95] Taking the definition it seems likely that any building occupied by guardians will fall within it.[96] If this is so then, under Part 1 local authorities will have powers and in some cases the duty to take action if the premises are hazardous. There are 29 different hazards identified by the 2004 Act and the relevant regulations, including, damp and mould, excess cold, lack of adequate facilities for food preparation, inadequate provision of facilities to maintain good personal hygiene. If deemed hazardous because of their poor state of repair, the authority could serve a prohibition order[97] preventing any occupation and thus defeating the whole point of the guardianship.

It is also likely that the management company will be the person having control for the purposes of Part 2, depending on the nature of the licence agreement with the property owner. The obligations in Part 2 will come into play if the premises are of three or more storeys and contain five or more guardians.[98] It will also come into play if the local authority has designated an area in which other houses in multiple occupation require licensing. In either case, certain mandatory conditions will apply as to gas, electrical and smoke safety, and local authorities may also require facilities such as bathrooms and completion of repairs before a property is licensed. Given these requirements, what do the guardian firms say about conditions in their buildings? Guardians of London[99] states in answer

[94] Roger Burridge and David Ormandy, 'Health and safety at home: private and public responsibility for unsatisfactory housing conditions' (2007) 34 *Journal of Law and Society* 544.

[95] Housing Act 2004, s. 1(4).

[96] See Caroline Hunter and Giles Peaker, 'Who Guards the Guardians?' (2013) 16 *Journal of Housing Law* 13.

[97] See 2004 Act s. 20.

[98] See 2004 Act, s. 55 and Licensing of Houses in Multiple Occupation (Prescribed Descriptions) (England) Order 2006 (SI 2006/371).

[99] See Guardians of London, 'Frequently Asked Questions': guardiansoflondon.com/faqs/. (Interestingly this is almost the exact same wording as on the Camelot site in 2015).

to the question: 'What condition does a property need to be in to qualify for temporary protection?'

> General property requirements are:
>
> — The property is wind and water tight.
> — The property is not vandalised or derelict.
> — Basic facilities are in place; electricity and water.
>
> For a small start-up fee we frequently install basic wheel-in, wheel-out shower pod units, which mean we can provide temporary washing facilities—these washing facilities have been approved by English Heritage. The guardians provide their own kitchen equipment including microwaves and portable kitchen hobs that are no greater than 13 amps for fire safety reasons.

There is no mention of the property meeting the standards laid down in the Housing Act 2004. The Guardians of London FAQ's for property owner continues:

> Q. It's too derelict, it's not suitable.
>
> Ideally, the property needs to be water tight and wind tight but we can recommend accredited maintenance teams who can very easily and economically bring a property to the minimum H&S and environmental requirements in order for it to be habitable.
>
> Our guardians are very flexible and you'll be surprised at how little is required to enable guardians to move in.

Nor is their reference to 'minimum … requirements' a reference to the standards required for HMOs. In order for an HMO to be licensed there will usually be a requirement of a minimum provision of cooking and bathroom facilities as well as stringent fire safety requirements. There is a reference to fire safety particularly by reference to the fact that 'Unlike other Guardian companies, we include a full property H&S and Fire Risk Assessment.' It is not clear how extensive this is, as there is also reference to minimum habitable standards, above.

Without extensive inspection of properties offered it is difficult to know what standards are usually met in guardian properties. However, it seems safe to conclude that they are likely to be at the lower end of compliance and, as will be discussed below, there is some evidence that local authorities find that there is a failure to meet standards set out in the Housing Act 2004.

IV. THE LOCAL AUTHORITY RESPONSE

In this penultimate section we consider the response to property guardians by the state, in particular local authorities. As set out above, they have duties and powers in terms of housing standards. At the same time there is evidence that local authorities use property guardian firms for buildings they own.

This potential clash is evidenced in Bristol, where property guardians were occupying a number of otherwise empty buildings, including an elderly persons' home. One of the residents was served a notice to quit in May 2016; he refused to leave and, as noted above, the County Court found him to be a tenant.[100] In the light of the 'scandal' the council pledged to 'investigate fully'.[101] At least two of the properties required licences but it took two years for even one to have an application made.

Even when Camelot did apply for an HMO licence for Broomhill, in October 2015, it took Bristol City Council more than a year to actually issue one. A council spokesman said:

> A number of factors have affected the time it took to issue the licence over this period, including the possibility of the property being demolished and the agreement between Camelot and Property Services coming to an end and not being renewed.[102]

In June of 2017 the Council decided to initiate a 'managed withdrawal from these arrangements. There'll be no new ones. Of the ones we've already got, we'll be giving notice to end the contracts on buildings we can do something with straight away.'[103]

As the Bristol experience illustrates, the use of legal duties and powers by local authorities can be problematic. In order to find out more about whether local authorities have encountered issues relating to property guardians, an on-line survey was set up. We wanted to find out if the same legal requirements were being applied to property guardian buildings as to other homes. The survey was promoted to local authority staff (primarily environmental health officers) working in private rented sector teams through the Institute of Environmental Health and RH Environmental's Housing Professionals Forum. A total of 33 responses were received from across England.

The number of responses to the survey does not allow for any significant quantitative analysis. The responses came from all the regions of the country, save the north east. Fourteen of the 33 respondents had received direct complaints about guardian premises, with issues raised including: fire

[100] *Camelot Property Management Ltd v Roynon*, judgment of 24 February 2017, Claim No: C01BS354.

[101] Tristan Cork, 'Scandal of Bristol City Council's empty nursing homes being rented out "illegally"', *Bristol Post* (22 December 2016): www.bristolpost.co.uk/news/bristol-news/scandal-bristol-city-councils-empty-6655.

[102] Ibid.

[103] Councillor Paul Smith, quoted in Triston Cork, 'Bristol council to become first in UK to ban property guardian companies after six months of scandal around empty buildings', *Bristol Post* (17 June 2017): www.bristolpost.co.uk/news/bristol-news/bristol-council-become-first-uk-117026.

hazards, disrepair, vermin, lack of facilities, 'unfair terms' and inadequate heating. In most cases where there had been a complaint the local authority had inspected, sometimes requiring the assistance of other organisations in their assessment—particularly the fire authority or other council departments such as building control (for instance, to assess the adequacy of fire precautions). Generally, the authority was able to negotiate some improvement, but some had resorted to legal notices and requirements to licence, with a particular dependence on identifying the property as an HMO.

What emerges from the comments is some frustration and uncertainty about the legal position. The fact that the occupiers are not tenants is frequently part of an argument that there is no legal protection in relation to standards:

> [Having referred to a particular case involving empty properties belonging to a housing trust which was persuaded to make improvement to avoid negative publicity] However, some of the other property being managed by the guardianship company are privately owned e.g. ex-nursing homes and the owners are not as easily swayed by our arguments as they have been told the guardians have no tenancy rights.

> The company responsible for creating the guardianship were unaware of the legislation relating to EH, HMO and planning and believed that the fact that the occupants were guardians (not tenants) and their occupation was transient, that the legislation did not apply. They believed their responsibilities for safety etc were discharged by providing a 'tenant pack' which included a battery smoke alarm.

This in turn leads to uncertainty about what legal action the local authority can take: 'Not had the approaches [requiring application for a licence] tested but aware that there are problems with HMO definition. No action taken more recently due to uncertainty of how to act.'

This may be evidence of the arbitrary approach to HMOs that Burridge and Ormandy discuss.[104] That certainly stems from the temporal limit of the guardians' rights. 'There is anxiety that the licence the Guardians are on [has a] 14 days' notice period so any intervention by the authorities will simply result in the Guardians becoming homeless.' In one instance it was reported that once the property owner became aware of the legal position the properties were taken out of guardianship:

> Camelot briefly let out individual floors in an office block to rent paying tenants … I visited the accommodation and declared it to be an HMO due to shared bathrooms. I took the Fire Officer with me who discovered severe fire safety deficiencies. Upon contacting the owner of the building he did not realise how it all worked and that he had responsibility for maintenance and the tenants. The premises were vacated and taken out of Camelot management.

[104] Burridge and Ormandy (n 94 above) 564.

The disordered and uncertain approach to the enforcement of what are—in terms of their substantive design—minimum standards and requirements for the provision of settled housing, demonstrates firms using legal uncertainty to try to limit the use of state power. Further there is fragmentation of power: owners of the properties themselves may not be aware of the extent of the practices of the management company; local authorities may be reliant on informal mechanisms or forms of negotiation to respond, and approaches may require action spread across multiple departments or agencies with different interests or priorities:

> Coordination of depts and agencies proved effective, as did exposing the problem to the landowner in this case.
>
> The big issue for me was the sham licence; for Planning and Environmental Health it was the mass letting of a large site (a former hospital) without any regard to planning or environmental health law. Perhaps the biggest scandal was that the head landlord, which knew all about what the guardianship company was doing, is a registered social landlord, a housing charity.

These problems align with both the structural difficulties inherent in responses to precarisation by the state, with the act of enforcement and regulation being fragmented, and also with the 'normalisation of the precarious.'[105] Indeed, a response from one participant at a London local authority stated that: 'It is my understanding that the Council continues to track down and challenge the guardianship model, in terms of HMO and wider Housing Act 2004 requirements, protection from eviction and planning use.'

Data received from FOI requests[106] on the use of property guardian companies by local authorities demonstrates that this same authority utilises such schemes, having spent nearly £70,000 on associated fees since 2014. As in Bristol, the same authority attempting to enforce regulation on a property guardian property, while at the same time utilising their services, demonstrates the Janus-faced nature of the state to housing precarity. We would suggest that different elements of the legal determinants have different traction. The element of tenure/time has little traction and the use of licences to ensure control of the return of property is appealing to local authorities. On the other hand, the duties in terms of condition of housing still exercises authorities, but it is sometimes the use of legal uncertainty by the property guardian firms which leaves them floundering.

[105] Lorey (n 18 above).

[106] Thanks to Samir Jeraj for providing the authors with the raw data of his extensive Freedom of Information request activity in the city.

V. CONCLUSIONS

As the Introduction to this collection demonstrates, precarity in housing has many elements. However, the legal security of occupiers must play an important role. This chapter has used the example of property guardians to explore the legal determinants of this element of housing precarity. By focusing in on these five elements—immigration status, tenure/time; control; cost; and conditions we have sought to illuminate the elements which can exacerbate precarity, rather than comparing precarious arrangements to even more precarious ones.

What emerges for property guardians is a mixed picture; the loss of security through lesser tenure/time, control and conditions being most strongly evident. Furthermore we have argued that two intersecting dimensions of precariousness—'organisational precariousness' and 'legal uncertainty'—can be useful in highlighting how the legal dimensions can compound precariousness. These two elements have received particular attention within the literature on the precarious status of legal migrants[107] and on the difficulties associated with increasingly precarious employment;[108] the case study of the property guardianship phenomenon demonstrates their application here.

First, though 'legal uncertainty' may sound a trite descriptor of precariousness, it can act as an important compounding element. In a similar fashion to how the in-determinability of a migrant's legal status can compound both their own situation and complicate the task of those governing it,[109] uncertainty as to the legal position of 'property guardians' and the correct enforcement practices, can act as a distinct compounding element.

Secondly, and linked to this first issue, the dimension of 'organisational precariousness' often employed to analyse precarious employment practices,[110] can aid the understanding of the property guardian phenomena too. This is in two ways: by accounting for the problems caused by acute dependence and the lack of choice in compounding precarious arrangements, and by focusing attention on the fragmented power relations between individuals and organisations in the governing of these phenomena.

In legal terms the picture is one where one party attempts to strip back security to an absolute minimum for these occupiers. It is asserted that there is no more than a contractual right to a period of usually four weeks' notice, at which point all rights terminate. Firms seem to suggest that this also

[107] For instance, see Zou (n 51 above).
[108] Kountouris (n 14 above).
[109] For instance, see Zou (n 51 above).
[110] For instance, see Kountouris (n 14 above).

enables the legal requirements as to property standards to be avoided. The legality of this has yet to be tested and there are reasons to doubt whether it is as clear cut as suggested by the property guardian firms. This problematic position further underscores the problems inherent in regulatory responses to 'precariousness' within housing contexts; minimum standards, so often articulated as a means for providing an adequate 'floor' to these unpredictable practices, are not always effectively enforced or their application clearly delineated.

As to the state response to the phenomenon of property guardians, it is clear that it is unconcerned with the tenure/time dimension, as illustrated by local authorities using property guardians firms for their own empty properties or at a national level in a different way stripping away that dimension for tenants.[111] The position in terms of conditions is more ambivalent.

[111] See Morgan, and Fitzpatrick and Watts (n 41 above) and Chris Bevan and Emma Laurie, 'The Housing and Planning Act 2016: Rewarding the Aspiration of Homeownership?' (2017) 80 *Modern Law Review* 661. Also on Australia, Brendan Edgeworth, Chapter five of this volume.

5

Public Housing Insecurity in New South Wales: An Historical Overview (1971–2014)

BRENDAN EDGEWORTH*

I. INTRODUCTION

THIS CHAPTER LOOKS at the changing levels of legal protection afforded tenants in the State of New South Wales in the field of public housing. Public housing is defined in this context as housing provided by the State to disadvantaged members of the community. The approach adopted is a socio-legal one, focusing on the shifting legal regimes over the period from 1971 to 2014, as well as the changes in the pattern of provision of public housing attendant on the legal developments. The picture that emerges is one of a markedly increasing propensity over time for termination of tenancies by the State landlord, and a much more vigorous policing of tenants' obligations. The corresponding increase in the precariousness of public housing tenants is of particular concern given that tenants in this position have very few options for any kind of satisfactory housing once they have been evicted, as they are relegated to an increasingly unaffordable, and therefore inaccessible, private tenancy market. The fate of public housing tenants therefore provides especially sharp evidence of the increasing precarisation of rights to the home. The data examined below also sheds light on wider policies adopted in the sphere of public housing by State authorities over the last three decades. These policies display a more intrusive approach to managing and governing public tenants alongside a far more stringent regime of regulation of entitlement to public housing. The net effect has been to introduce an historically unprecedented level of insecurity for public housing tenants. And although the chapter focuses in

* Professor, School of Law, University of New South Wales, Sydney. I would like to thank Wendy Finnegan for research assistance.

detail on the position in New South Wales, comparable trends are evident in other jurisdictions, so this study may be seen to reflect a broader shift in policy.[1]

II. PUBLIC HOUSING IN NEW SOUTH WALES—A BRIEF HISTORY

The system of public housing provision in Australia developed rather more slowly than in other advanced industrialised democracies. The abundance of land, a relatively benign climate and an underdeveloped welfare state all combined to render the provision of housing by the state for the disadvantaged a very low political priority.[2] Non-owner occupancy in urban centres was overwhelmingly in the form of tenancies granted by private landlords. And the form of legal regulation of leases was determined by market forces, with minimal security of tenure for tenants in a system based essentially on freedom of contract principles.

During the Second World War, a completely new set of policies was introduced. The Federal Government, under its war powers, and as part of the war effort, enacted legislation that provided security of tenure for tenants, alongside a comprehensive system of rent control. Landlords were prevented from terminating tenancies except for just cause, and rent was determined by ability to pay. The States with the largest populations, New South Wales and Victoria, enacted similar legislation after the war. In part, this was to offer protection to the families of returning soldiers. But it extended to tenants generally in the immediate aftermath of the conflict. To supplement the tight regulation of the private rental market, States (pursuant to Commonwealth–State Housing Agreements) began to set aside funds for public housing. In New South Wales, a modest building programme commenced in the 1950s, which accelerated over time, reaching the 100,000 properties mark covering approximately five per cent of the population by the 1970s.[3] The 2014 figure stood at 146,600 properties, housing almost five per cent of the population.[4]

[1] See generally, Kevin Bell, 'Protecting Public Housing Tenants in Australia from Forced Eviction: The Fundamental Importance of the Human Right to Adequate Housing and Home' (2013) 39 *Monash University Law Review* 1.

[2] For a general historical overview, see Chris Martin, 'Government-Housing: Governing Crime and Disorder in Public Housing in New South Wales' (PhD thesis, University of Sydney, 2010) especially Part 2.

[3] New South Wales Government, 'History of Public Housing in New South Wales': www.housing.nsw.gov.au/about-us/history-of-public-housing-in-nsw.

[4] NSW Government, 'Six monthly social housing waiting list released' (*Family & Community Services*, 23 October 2014): www.facs.nsw.gov.au/about_us/media_releases/media_release_archive/gabrielle-upton/six-monthly-social-housing-waiting-list-released.

Moreover, the current landscape of public provision of housing for poor people has changed: where once only public housing operated, that is to say, housing exclusively owned and managed by the State, now a mosaic of 'social housing' subsists. The provision of subsidised housing now represents a threefold mix of a) public housing owned by the State of New South Wales, b) community housing owned by not-for-profit entities or leased from the State, and c) Aboriginal Housing, owned by Aboriginal corporations or other organisations, or similarly leased from the State. Over the last decade, community housing has grown substantially as successive governments have sought to enlist community groups and organisations into the leasing of property to disadvantaged groups, by means of subleasing or transferring some public housing stock.[5] This chapter will focus primarily on public housing.

III. FROM 'COMMAND AND CONTROL' TO 'FREE' MARKET TO 'SOFT' REGULATION

The protective regime of secure tenancies introduced in the post-war period[6] as noted above was consistent with a general process of historically generous welfare state provision of security across housing, employment and welfare of the post-war years up to the 1970s in advanced Western societies.[7] But amid complaints, particularly from landlords, that this framework was causing an investment flight from housing, the legislative framework was progressively pared back in New South Wales from the late 1960s onwards. In consequence, by the 1980s only a fraction of protected tenancies remained, the vast majority of residential tenants now covered once more by the former, market-based insecurity of tenure system. This regressive trend towards free market principles in residential tenancy law in turn led to a counter-movement, as reflected in the 1975 Federal Government-commissioned Sackville Report on Law and Poverty.[8] The Report recommended many changes to tenancy law, which fell into two broad categories. First, a set of 'consumer protection'-type reforms were

[5] Michael Nancarrow, 'Between the Market and the State: The Regulatory Reform of Community Housing in New South Wales' (Phd Thesis, University of New South Wales, 2010), ch 1; New South Wales Government (n 3 above). By 2013, community housing represented 17.9% of all housing stock (25,973 dwellings out of 145,248), and growing: NSW Government, New South Wales Land and Housing Corporation: Annual Report (NSW Land and Housing Corporation, 2012–13), 7.

[6] Landlord and Tenant (Amendment) Act 1948 (NSW), s 61.

[7] See generally, Ross Cranston, *The Legal Foundations of the Welfare State* (London, Weidenfeld and Nicolson, 1985); Gosta Esping-Andersen, *The Three Worlds of Welfare Capitalism* (Cambridge, Polity, 1990).

[8] Commission of Inquiry into Poverty: Law and Poverty in Australia, 'Second Main Report' (Australian Government Publishing Service (AGPS), Canberra, October 1975).

proposed to offer greater safeguards to tenants in respect to notice, condition of premises, and bonds. Secondly, and most relevantly for this chapter, the Report recommended reform legislation to establish specialist tenancy tribunals to deal with disputes. They were intended to afford parties, but particularly tenants, cheap, speedy and efficient justice. The Report was influential on legislatures across Australia with the result that from the late 1980s onward, most of its recommendations had been implemented in all jurisdictions.[9]

Yet for all the rhetoric about protecting tenants in the Report and the ensuing parliamentary debates, the legislation did not go so far as to restore the security of tenure conferred by the post-war legislation as recommended by the Report. Instead, a statutory compromise eventuated, leading to residential tenancies being not so much 'protected' as 'regulated'. The highly interventionist, 'command and control'[10] regulation of terminations and the rent control provisions of the former regime were replaced by an enhanced set of procedural rules, and an expanded range of duties on landlords, for instance in relation to notice periods and standards of premises. To counterbalance the gains by tenants, landlords were guaranteed rights to regain possession at the end of the contractually agreed term; and rents were market-based, irrespective of the tenant's income. In the circumstances, it would be tempting to see the reforms as a hollow victory for tenants. But such a conclusion would be too simplistic. Tenants have benefited in a number of respects from the new phase of protection, as Tribunal data over the period clearly reveal. For instance, a longitudinal study conducted some years ago showed that tenants are active, regular, and frequently successful litigants under the new regime.[11] However, the insecurity remains; and the most recent legislation introduced in New South Wales in 2010, which tenant advocacy groups unsuccessfully urged the government to pass with enhanced security protection, replicates the insecurities of its predecessor.[12] Significantly, this legislation applies to both public and private tenancies. In consequence, public tenants have no greater formal legal security of tenure than tenants in the private sector, and as we shall see below, fare poorly under the newer, informal regime. The evidence appears to offer firm support in the housing

[9] Brendan Edgeworth, 'Residential Tenancies Law 40 Years After the Sackville Report: A Multi-level Snapshot' in Andrea Durbach, Brendan Edgeworth, Vicki and Sentas, *Law and Poverty in Australia: 40 Years After the Poverty Commission* (Leichhardt, Federation Press, 2017) pp 119–33; Adrian Bradbrook, 'Residential Tenancies: The Second Stage of Reforms' (1995) 20 *Sydney Law Review* 402.

[10] On 'command and control' regulation, see generally Ian Ayres and John Braithwaite, *Responsive Regulation* (Oxford, Oxford University Press, 1992).

[11] This study is part of a much wider research exercise into residential tenancy disputes in a part of Sydney over a 43-year period culminating in 2014: see, for example, Brendan Edgeworth, 'Access to Justice in Courts and Tribunals Compared—Residential Tenancy Disputes in Sydney (1971–2004)' (2008) 27 *Civil Justice Quarterly* 151–80.

[12] Residential Tenancies Act 2010 (NSW).

context for what Isabell Lorey refers to as 'governmental precarization', namely 'the complex interactions between an instrument of governing and the modes of subjectivation'.[13]

IV. PUBLIC HOUSING DISPUTES BEFORE THE COURT AND THEN THE TRIBUNAL

To better understand the changing legal landscape of public housing, the legal rules need to be examined in the context of their application in practice, specifically in the role played by the landlord in disputes with tenants.[14] The specific geographical area covered is the Eastern and South Eastern Suburbs of Sydney. During roughly the first half of this period, from January 1971 until October 1989, Waverley Local Court had almost exclusive jurisdiction over residential tenancy matters.[15] Later, from 30 October 1989, when the Residential Tenancies Act 1987 (NSW) came into effect, jurisdiction over these disputes was transferred to the Residential Tenancies Tribunal, since 2001 re-constituted and enlarged to become the Consumer, Trader and Tenancy Tribunal.[16] Later still, this Tribunal was absorbed into a larger entity, the New South Wales Civil and Administrative Tribunal (NCAT) in 2014, although the procedural law relating to residential tenancies has remained largely the same since 1989. That is to say, the rules of evidence do not apply, legal representation is in general not allowed, and costs are only awarded in exceptional cases.

The duration of the period under examination allows a comparison of the extent to which the present tribunal-based regime—a form of 'alternative dispute resolution'—delivers a better quality of justice than the formal courts do, and if so, how far and how effectively. Other effects of the Tribunal can also be examined. 'Quality of justice' in this context means the capacity to resolve disputes according to law to the satisfaction of the parties. This approach allows a direct comparison to be drawn between the position of public housing tenants before and after the introduction of the Tribunal, but also compares the position of public and private tenants since that date to see if the introduction of the Tribunal has played a role in any divergences in outcomes for these very different cohorts. It is frequently argued that alternative forms of dispute resolution provide a more economic and efficient means of resolving disputes without the need for a judicial decision.

[13] Isabell Lorey, *State of Insecurity: Government of the Precarious* (London, Verso, 2015) 13.

[14] See Edgeworth (n 11 above).

[15] In exceptional cases parties could apply to the Supreme Court to have such matters heard. Statistically, these numbers are so small as to be insignificant.

[16] Residential Tenancies Act 1987 (NSW). Also, in exceptional circumstances applications to the courts are possible, generally on points of law, but the numbers are very small.

It also provides an accessible process for disadvantaged sections of the community, who are more likely to need such access. This was very much the thinking behind the reforms introduced from the late 1970s onwards in most Australian jurisdictions, an example, historically, of the latest 'third wave' of access to justice, succeeding the earlier waves of legal aid and public interest law as welfare states sought to widen access to justice to all citizens.[17]

But is the introduction of tribunals a real advance on the formal courts? Do they dispense justice more widely and more effectively than courts do, and if so, who are the main beneficiaries? Do different groups fare better or worse under the Tribunal system, particularly from the perspective of security of tenure? This chapter attempts to provide some answers to these questions by comparing the position of public housing tenants before and after the introduction of the Tribunal. This is of particular significance as it relates to one of the most disadvantaged groups in Australian society, in respect of the basic human right to housing and shelter.

V. METHODOLOGY

This study utilises data sets first, from the Australian Bureau of Statistics, secondly, from Waverley Local Court, and thirdly, from NCAT, to compare access to and outcomes from the two regimes spanning the period from 1971 to 2014. The census population data from the Australian Bureau of Statistics have been analysed to provide a broader picture of five-yearly trends in residential tenure for New South Wales generally, and the Waverley area specifically is also presented between 1971 and 2014. Such changes and shifts in the tenure categories over this time period will provide a background context to any fluctuations in the number of disputes over the same period. The period chosen for examination allows for a long-term view of the extent, or lack, of security of tenure for public housing tenants, how it might have fluctuated, and whether there are any broad patterns that have emerged.

The area chosen for examination—the Eastern and South Eastern suburbs of Sydney—covers the exact geographical jurisdiction of Waverley Court, the local court responsible for hearing tenancy matters up until 1989.[18] A direct comparison between the Court and Tribunal data was possible because the Tribunal keeps data accessible by postcode, so the exact number

[17] Mauro Cappelletti (ed), *Access to Justice and the Welfare State* (Alphen aan den Rijn, Sijthoff, 1981); Mauro Cappelletti, 'Alternative Dispute Resolution Processes within the World-wide Access to Justice Movement' (1993) 56 *Modern Law Review* 282–96; Christine Parker, *Just Lawyers, Regulation and Access to Justice* (Oxford, Oxford University Press, 1999), ch 2; Hazel Genn, 'Tribunals and Informal Justice' (1993) 56 *Modern Law Review* 393–411.

[18] Postcodes: 2021, 2022, 2023, 2024, 2025, 2026, 2027, 2028, 2029, 2030, 2031, 2033, 2034, 2035 and 2036.

of social housing tenancies in the same set of postcodes over which Waverley Court had jurisdiction could be identified. The area will be referred to as the 'Waverley area'.

VI. TENANCIES IN THE WAVERLEY AREA—GENERAL FEATURES

The tenure landscape across the Waverley Court area differs in some respects from the general picture across the state of New South Wales. First, within the Waverley area there are suburbs with residents with highly diverse levels of income: there are large numbers of social welfare recipients residing in public housing in some suburbs (generally the southern half), with significant numbers of high-income tenants renting privately in others (generally the northern half). Importantly for this study, however, Waverley's proportion of public housing tenure is not significantly dissimilar to that of New South Wales as a whole. Figure 1 shows the general picture. The very low level of public housing as a proportion of the total housing stock by international comparison reflects the general pattern across Australia historically: both in Waverley and nationally, public housing stands at less than five per cent of total stock.

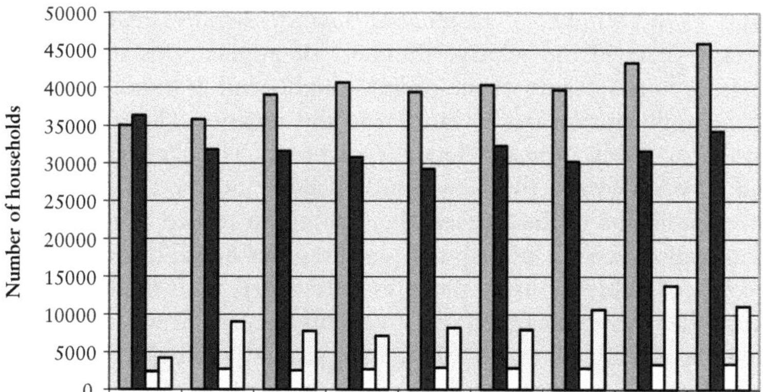

	1971	1976	1981	1986	1991	1996	2001	2006	2011
Owner/purchaser	35060	35848	39108	40725	39518	40374	39766	43304	45880
Private tenant	36395	31808	31605	30824	29220	32303	30241	31653	34339
Housing authority tenant	2411	2732	2553	2751	2951	2901	2862	3420	3444
Other/not stated	4228	9024	7777	7181	8253	8002	10707	13820	11142

Census Year

Figure 1: Waverley Area: all households by tenure type[19]

[19] Source: Census of Population and Housing 1976–2001 Selected housing characteristics for Waverley Court jurisdiction and NSW. Notes: 1) 1991, 1996 and 2001 Censuses include

VII. WAVERLEY LOCAL COURT AND THE TRIBUNAL COMPARED: FINDINGS

As noted above, for the period under consideration (1971–89), tenancies under both former legal regimes, namely the Landlord and Tenant Act 1899 (NSW), covering largely unregulated residential tenancies, and the Landlord and Tenant (Amendment) Act 1948 (NSW), with security of tenure and rent control, were heard by Waverley Local Court. By section 5 of the Landlord and Tenant (Amendment) Act 1948 (NSW), the State of New South Wales as landlord was not bound by the Act. Accordingly, public housing tenants were in a somewhat anomalous legal position: while they were granted tenancies that were in practice 'secure' by virtue of the State's obligations under the Housing Act 2001 (NSW), which required it to provide housing to qualifying disadvantaged citizens, the tenancies were in the form of common law weekly periodic tenancies. This meant that in order to terminate a tenancy, all the Corporation was required to do legally was to serve the appropriate notice. Their formal legal rights were therefore extremely fragile: the lease could be terminated by a week's notice, putting them in a worse position than most tenants in the private sector.[20]

Once identified, the public housing matters appearing before Waverley Court (and later the Tribunal) were scrutinised to extract the following data: 1) the number of residential tenancy disputes reaching the Tribunal in that year; 2) the relative numbers of applications made by landlords/ tenants; 3) the nature of the orders sought, and granted; and a comparison of the application rates of landlords and tenants. The Court records show details of public housing tenancy disputes. The Department of Housing, and its predecessor, the New South Wales Housing Commission, were the only applicants in these cases, there being no record of tenants being other than respondents. The Tribunal on the other hand, did not originally keep records of public housing disputes until 2001, with the exception of 1991, when the Tribunal carried out a one-off survey. However, detailed records are now available back to 2005, and are analysed below in Figures 3–5.

As Figure 2 shows, public housing applications to Waverley Court represent a tiny proportion of the total throughout the period 1971–89.[21]

visitor only and unclassifiable households; 2) Other/not stated includes 'rented—landlord not stated' for 1976–2011 censuses.

[20] Bell (n 1 above), 96; Adrian Bradbrook, 'Poverty and the Residential Landlord-Tenant Relationship' (Australian Government Publishing Service, 1975).

[21] The numbers in Figure 2 are consistent with early reports of the position in New South Wales as a whole: see Commission of Inquiry into Poverty: Law and Poverty in Australia, 'Second Main Report' (Canberra, Australian Government Publishing Service (AGPS), October 1975) p 99 which found that there were only 21 cases recorded in the whole of New South Wales for the period 1973–74.

From a total of 6775 tenancy disputes heard between 1971 and 1989, only 151 were public housing tenancies, representing just 2.2 per cent of all applicants to the Court. In relative terms, the rate of applications from the State as landlord was significantly less than that of landlords in the private sector: over the period, public tenancies amounted to between 7.5 and 10 per cent of all tenancies in the area, yet applications averaged only a quarter of that figure. In numerical terms also they were very small: for 13 of the years shown, public housing applicants numbered fewer than 10 per year, peaking to 23 and 20 over 1985–86. In contrast, other tenancies leapt to highs of 625–636 in the same two years. The figures reflect a significant measure of housing security for public housing tenants, notwithstanding the fragility of their position in law, typically in their status as weekly tenants, as noted above.

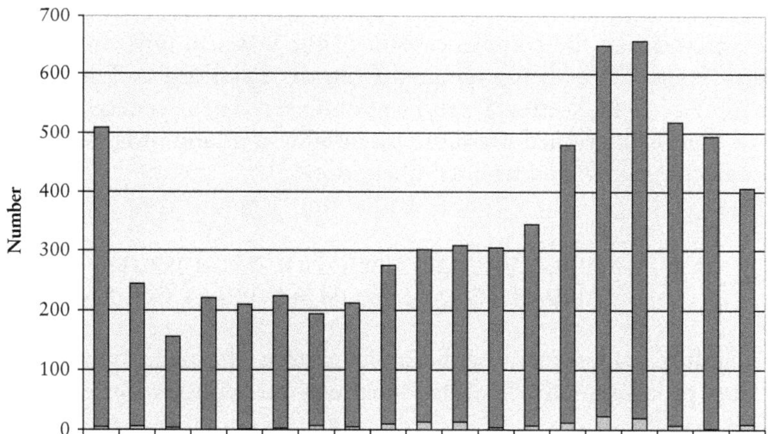

	1971	1972	1973	1974	1975	1976	1977	1978	1979	1980	1981	1982	1983	1984	1985	1986	1987	1988	1989
All other tenancies	504	238	152	221	209	221	187	207	265	288	295	300	338	467	625	636	512	492	397
Public housing tenancies	5	6	4	0	1	3	7	5	10	13	13	4	7	12	23	20	7	2	9

Figure 2: Tenancy Disputes, Waverley Local Court 1971–89[22]

The clear spike in private tenancy matters in 1985–86 may well be explained by the leap in mortgage interest rates, which were uncapped at the time,

[22] Source: Waverley Local Court data 1971–89. The figure of 484 for 1989 is made up of 403 actual matters for January–October and a notional figure of 81 for November and December extrapolated from the figures earlier in the year because the Tribunal came into operation on 30 October 1989.

rising immediately from 13.5 per cent to up to 17 per cent within a very short time, with dramatic effects on housing investment. This may be a possible explanation for the comparative spike—roughly double—of the numbers of public housing tenancy terminations at the time, as an acute increase in demand for public tenancies unfolded.[23]

One further notable feature of the litigation recorded in the Waverley Court files is the uniformity of the matters considered by the Court. First, only landlords, private and public, ever featured as applicants to the Court. There was no evidence in the records of a tenant, either public or private, commencing an action against a landlord for breach of a term of a tenancy agreement. It might be argued that the obligations of landlords under the former were very limited, as defined by the parties. But this point can be countered by the typical practice of the parties to sign what was known as 'a section 5A' standard form lease for residential lettings.[24] This lease imposed a general duty of repair on the landlord by reference to the standard of the premises at the commencement of the lease. In any event, the State of New South Wales was exempted from the Landlord and Tenant (Amendment) Act 1948 (section 5), and was obliged to keep premises in good repair. The Court functioned therefore essentially as a landlords' forum enforcing landlords' rights, and tenants' obligations.[25]

VIII. TYPES OF PUBLIC HOUSING DISPUTES AND OUTCOMES FROM WAVERLEY COURT

Excluding dismissed or withdrawn matters, the main outcome from the Court process for the State landlord was for repossession of the premises. This was the case even where the court files reveal that the reason for the landlord originally going to court was because of rent arrears. The Court was simply not deployed to recoup these monies, even though it had a small claims jurisdiction, and Court data for the period under consideration reveal that many small claims debts were sought in respect of other matters such as breach of contract. A number of reasons may explain this fact.

[23] Another factor may have been a change in taxation policy of the Federal government in 1985 to remove tax exemptions on investment residential property: see Mike Seccombe, 'Negative Gearing Bonanza', *The Saturday Paper* (2 May 2015) 1.

[24] The 'section 5A lease' refers to s 5A Landlord and Tenant (Amendment) Act 1948 (NSW) which allowed premises to be 'decontrolled' under certain circumstances. The s 5A lease was accordingly free from the tight regulatory framework of the Act.

[25] As acknowledged in regard to residential tenancies generally in Australia at the time by the Sackville Report: 'Commission of Inquiry into Poverty: Law and Poverty in Australia, 'Second Main Report', (Canberra, Australian Government Publishing Service (AGPS), October 1975) ch 3.

In many instances, tenants would be impecunious, and so would be judgment-proof: any order in favour of the landlord would be worthless. Also, the granting of the possession order may have been used as the blunt instrument to pressure tenants into paying up any outstanding arrears; the files do not reveal whether the Commission actually took possession of the premises.

Another feature of the litigation was that tenants mostly did not defend the action, and when they did, were usually without legal representation, while landlords were usually represented if they proceeded with the matter. For instance, in 75 per cent or 113 of public housing cases, the landlord was represented and the tenant was absent. In those instances when the Commission proceeded with the matter, it was successful in almost all matters. By comparison, public housing tenants personally defended matters in only 12 per cent of cases and had representation in a further eight per cent of cases. In 4.6 per cent, or seven matters, neither party turned up to court.

Even in those small number of matters where the tenant either defended the matter or was represented (30 out of a total of 151), the most common result was still an order and warrant of possession (13 cases), followed by dismissal/ withdrawal and orders for payment of rent arrears. This suggests that the process was a simple one: the landlord had only to demonstrate that the notice to quit had been served, and that the appropriate notice period had expired in order to be entitled to possession. The Court retained no discretion to suspend the order for possession, or to attach terms to the order. Despite the wide range of obligations contained in the leases, the only matter the court considered, and typically ordered, was the landlord's right to repossession of the premises. These figures suggest the one-dimensional nature of the disputes landscape. Nonetheless, given the overall numbers of public housing tenancies in the Waverley area at the time, the number of tenants whose leases were terminated was very low. As Figure 3 shows, even the second-highest instance of disputes appearing before the court in 1986 meant that there was one dispute for every 137 tenancies. Anecdotal evidence suggests that the Commission in general at the time predominantly sought to negotiate resolution of disputes, and showed considerable flexibility in doing so.[26] Overall the picture is of a low level of formal disputes, and a very small number of terminations over that 19-year period, indicating genuinely high levels of de facto security of tenure for residents.[27]

[26] Interview: Robert Mowbray, Tenants' Advice and Caseworker over the period, 9 May 2014.

[27] For the distinction between de facto and de jure security, see Kath Hulse and Vivienne Milligan, 'Secure Occupancy: A New Framework for Analysing Security in Rental Housing' (2014) 29 *Housing Studies* 638.

IX. TENANCY TRIBUNALS AND PUBLIC HOUSING DISPUTES (1989–2014)

The establishment of a specialised Residential Tenancies Tribunal in New South Wales on 30 October 1989 extended to public housing tenancy disputes, which since that time have been almost exclusively dealt with in that forum. Despite the changes in the name and structure of the Tribunal,[28] the procedural law has remained essentially the same up to the present time. The most striking feature of the landscape of disputes under the Tribunal is how very different from a quantitative perspective it is from the court-based system.[29] In 1990, the first full year after the introduction of the Tribunal,

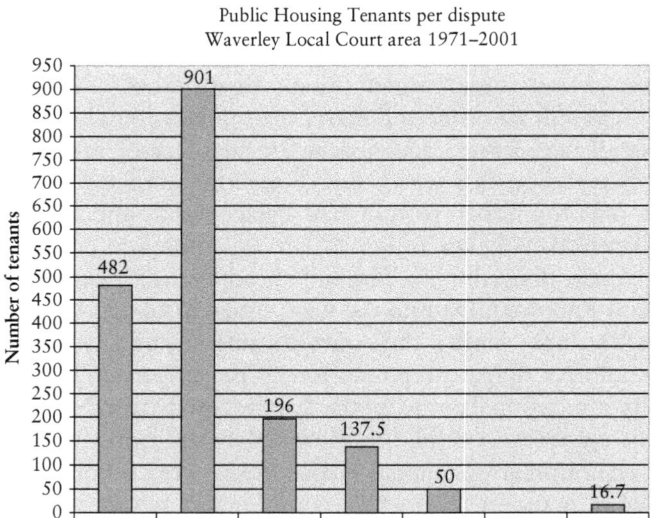

	1971	1976	1981	1986	1991	1996	2001/03
Tenants per dispute	482	901	196	137.5	50		16.7

Figure 3: Ratio of Disputes to Tenancies (Public Housing)[30]

[28] The Tribunal has operated under a number of different names over the period considered, specifically the Residential Tenancies Tribunal (from 1989–96), the Consumer, Trade and Tenancy Tribunal (1996–2013) and now New South Wales Civil and Administrative Tribunal (NCAT) (2014).

[29] For completeness, it should be noted that the disputes landscape is a little more complex than the account here suggests by virtue of the transfer of all rental bond disputes to the Consumer Claims Tribunal (CCT) in 1977 by the enactment of the Landlord and Tenant (Rental Bonds) Act 1977 (NSW). In consequence, from 1977 until 1989 the total of residential tenancy disputes was the sum of bond disputes at the CCT, and all others at the court. From 1989 all disputes are heard by the Tribunal, including bonds: see s 83(3) Residential Tenancies Act 1987 (NSW), and now New South Wales Civil and Administrative Tribunal Act 2014 (NSW).

[30] Source: Australian Bureau of Statistics, Census of Population and Housing 1976–2001, Selected housing characteristics for Waverley jurisdiction and NSW; Waverley Local Court data (1971–89) and Consumer, Trader and Tenancy Tribunal (1990–2004).

the number of applications generally to it from landlords and tenants in the Waverley local area had already almost tripled the number to the Court recorded in the previous year, jumping from 484 in 1989 to 1358 in 1990. Unfortunately, it is not known what proportion of these were public housing tenancies. However, a one-off survey of public housing tenancy disputes by the landlord, the Department of Housing (the Department) in 1991 provides a State-wide picture of applications brought to the Tribunal.[31] In 1991 the Department lodged 2253 applications with the Tribunal and of these, 43 per cent resulted in orders for possession, a further 21 per cent were orders to pay arrears of rent, and 12.5 per cent were orders to cease breaches. 22.6 per cent were either withdrawn or dismissed. Of the 978 possession orders granted, only 155 were carried through to execution, comprising 7 per cent of all cases brought to the Tribunal by the Department of Housing in 1991. A further 714 of orders for possession were not proceeded with due to new tenancy agreements being negotiated or tenants' compliance with conditions imposed by the Tribunal. Based on the State-wide figure of 2253 applications in public housing disputes recorded by the Tribunal in 1991, which comprised 2 per cent of the New South Wales population of public housing tenancies in 1991 (112,572), an extrapolation can be made to reach an estimated figure for the Waverley area.

Assuming that the rate of applications in Waverley did not differ significantly from the State-wide rate of two per cent in 1991, it can be estimated that from 2951 public housing tenancies in the Waverley area there would be roughly 60 disputes in that year. As Figure 3 shows, this represents approximately one dispute for every 50 social housing tenancies. While this may not appear to be a large number, it is significantly higher than the rates of disputes in earlier census years, all of which were before the introduction of the Tribunal. One clear consequence for public housing tenants, therefore, from the very earliest years of the Tribunal, was that it proved to be a mechanism availed of far more frequently than the Court to enforce tenant obligations. Only five years earlier, for instance, the ratio of disputes to public housing tenancies was 1:137.5, so the leap represented by the Tribunal numbers was almost threefold. Therefore the Tribunal appears to have quickly become a very efficient mechanism for the landlord both to compel performance of obligations as well as terminating agreements.

X. TERMINATIONS BY DEPARTMENT OF HOUSING: 2003–04 AND 2005–14

This acceleration of the use of the Tribunal by the Department, with consequential increases in the number of terminations of tenancies is particularly

[31] Residential Tenancies Tribunal, 'Residential Tenancies Update' (NSW Department of Housing, 1993) 1–2.

noticeable if figures for the years after 2002 are examined, when the Tribunal began to keep more systematic data of private and public housing disputes. Data provided by the Tribunal show that by mid-2004, the numbers for the Waverley area had increased dramatically from the 1991 figures. During the 2003–04 financial year, from a total of 1,996 orders made by the Tribunal, 171 or 8.5 per cent were public housing cases brought by the Department.[32] Just over one-third (59) of orders in these matters related to payment of money or rental bond, while a quarter (42) required some kind of action or obligation on the part of the tenant in order to maintain the tenancy. One in nine orders (19) was for termination of the tenancy. A further 19 per cent were withdrawn by the applicant (Department of Housing) and 9 per cent were dismissed by the Tribunal, resulting in no orders being made on these applications. Only 16 per cent of orders made were by mutual consent between the Department and the tenant. As Figure 3 above shows, in the 12 years since the previous year for which public housing data is available (1991), an almost threefold increase in disputes in the Tribunal is evident, from approximately 60 to 171 disputes, or one dispute for every 50 tenancies to one for every 16.7 in 2003–04.

By the following calendar year of 2005, the rate of orders made by the Tribunal in favour of the Department of Housing had almost tripled to

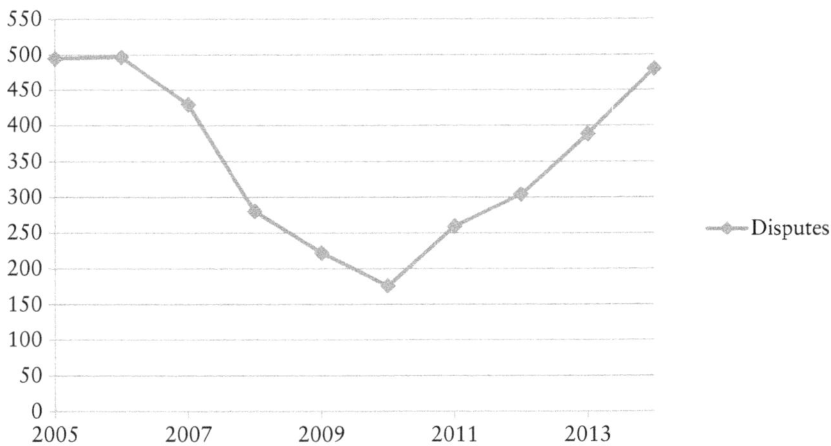

Figure 4: Public Housing Tenancy Disputes, 2005–14[33]

[32] Consumer, Trader and Tenancy Tribunal data for Waverley area provided on 6 December 2006 (on file with author).

[33] Source: NCAT, April 2015 (on file with author).

495 comprising 17 per cent of the total.[34] This substantial leap in disputes was maintained in 2006, but then a steady decline back to the 2003–04 figure is evident before the numbers climb again to 480 in 2014, as Figure 4 shows. The overall picture, however, is a dramatic increase in the deployment of the Tribunal by the Department[35] when compared with the Court.

XI. RANGE OF MATTERS CONSIDERED BY THE COURT AND THE TRIBUNAL

Another significant change since the introduction of the Tribunal is that a far wider range of matters has become the subject of disputes, such as the landlords' rights to compensation for abandonment of the premises, for unpaid rent and water charges, and performance orders, such as requiring tenants to keep premises in repair, or not to cause nuisance or disturbance to neighbours. This position provides a stark contrast with the solitary concern of Waverley Local Court to determine whether or not the landlord was entitled to possession.

The figures in Figure 5 clearly demonstrate the extent to which Department of Housing as landlord has benefited from access to the Tribunal in respect of this range of obligations. Perhaps the most notable feature of the litigation is that the lowest figures relate to 'no result', indicating that once the matter reaches the Tribunal, an order will be forthcoming unless the applicant elects to withdraw: less than six per cent of matters over the decade fell into this category. The next most significant category is that of termination, as this order has the most profound impact on tenants. As noted above in Figure 3, where terminations were ordered on average eight times per year for the period 1971–89 (and on average 12 times per year in the decade to 1989), the average jumps to 29 over the decade to 2014, with a peak of 55 in 2014, seven times the average before the Court. This represents a dramatic increase in insecurity of tenure for public housing tenants in recent years, particularly given the generally static numbers of public housing tenancies in the Waverley area over that period of time.[36] Whereas under the former regime the likelihood of a tenant ever being evicted from public housing was extremely rare (one in every 369 tenancies on average

[34] Source: NCAT, April 2015 (on file with author). For a brief summary of these figures by reference to the Poverty Commission's recommendations, see Brendan Edgeworth, 'Residential Tenancies Law 40 Years After the Sackville Report: A Multi-level Snapshot' (n 9 above) 130–32.

[35] The Department of Housing became 'Housing NSW' in 2008. For simplicity, and because the landlord was known at the Department of Housing for the bulk of the period under consideration, I will refer to it as 'the Department'.

[36] See Figure 1 and NSW Government, New South Wales Land and Housing Corporation: Annual Report (NSW Land and Housing Corporation, 2012–13) 7.

over the 19-year period, one in 246 during the 1980s), it ranges from one in every 54 tenancies in 2014 to one in every 295 in 2010, with an average of one in every 102 tenancies over the period.

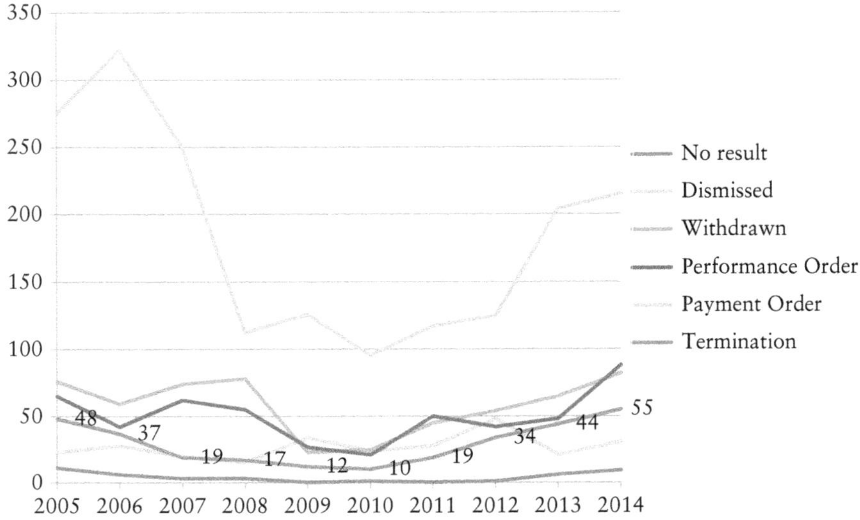

Figure 5: Tribunal Outcomes for Department of Housing[37]

Figure 5 also demonstrates the extent to which the Tribunal has provided the Department with a range of forms of redress not limited to the termination of tenancy agreements and repossession that predominated as the *modus operandi* under the Court system. It shows the spread of matters before the Tribunal including the substantial and growing rate of orders requiring payment by the public housing tenant. Throughout the decade-long period, the most frequent tribunal application by the Department concerned payments in the form of outstanding rent, water usage or other charges. This is to be contrasted with the invariant practice under the Court regime where only repossession orders were sought: matters relating to the actual payment of rent arrears were either not pursued at all, or were dealt with informally, or punitively by termination as a remedy of last resort where rent remained unpaid. When seen alongside the significant numbers of performance orders also made by the Tribunal, such as orders to refrain from doing certain things such as causing nuisance or annoyance to neighbours, or causing damage to the property, or keeping the property in a satisfactory state of cleanliness, the data show how comprehensively effective the Tribunal has

[37] Source: NCAT, April 2015 (on file with author).

become for the Department in their objective to compel tenants to meet in full their obligations. Moreover, these more intensive practices of regulating tenants contribute to the growing precariousness of tenure: failure to comply with orders to rectify breaches in turn can prove to be the trigger for termination of the tenancy.

An additional significant feature of the processing of these disputes is the overwhelming success attained by the Department. Orders in the Department's favour (termination, payment and performance orders) tend to outnumber unsuccessful applications (dismissed, withdrawn and no result) by a ratio ranging from 3:1 to 5:1 over the decade (2005–14).[38]

A further perspective on the extent to which public housing tenancies have become more precarious is by comparing the ratio of such disputes to numbers of private tenancies in the Waverley area. In 2014, for example, there were 894 applications to the Tribunal from private landlords, seeking redress against their tenants. By contrast, the number of applications from the Department was 436.[39] Public housing landlord applications are therefore 49 per cent of private landlord applications, yet public housing tenancies represent no more than 10 per cent of private housing tenancies in the Waverley local area.[40] It follows that the public landlord is roughly five more times as likely to bring an action against a tenant as a private landlord. This indicates that even though there is a striking increase in litigation in the domain of tenancies generally with the introduction of the Tribunal, it is much more acutely evident in the case of public housing tenancies.

What might explain the growing recourse by the Department to the Tribunal in this way, in contrast to its sparing use of the Court before 1990? One obvious answer is that the procedures of the Tribunal, without rules of evidence and rights to legal representation, in addition to the speed of processes and relatively low cost for applicants, makes it at least as easy for landlords to access as the tenants for whom it was originally designed. In the case of the public housing landlord, it has the additional advantage of being a repeat player, and is therefore better able to deploy its familiarity with the tribunal's operations to its advantage. The repeat player factor has been observed frequently in research into the day-to-day workings of the formal

[38] New South Wales Civil and Administrative Tribunal, 'Applications and Orders' (NCAT, April 2015) (on file with author). These findings are consistent with state-wide analysis and the Tribunal's general data: see Chris Martin (n 2 above) ch 6; Chris Martin, 'Contracts and Conduct: Using Tenancy Law to Govern Crime and Disorder in Public Housing in New South Wales' (2015) 5 *Property Law Review* 81.

[39] Source: NCAT, ibid (on file with author).

[40] See Figure 1 above. This figure is somewhat smaller than elsewhere in New South Wales, as the overall public to private tenancy ratio approximates 5:1. See also, 'Commission of Inquiry into Poverty: Law and Poverty in Australia' (n 25 above) p 94.

courts; but research also indicates that this factor is also present in the case of forums that dispense informal justice.[41]

The Tribunal has therefore proved to be a very effective mechanism for redress for landlords in general where tenants are in breach of terms of the agreement, offering far cheaper, quicker and more efficient procedures than the Court ever could. The speed of the Tribunal's processes mean that remedies can be ordered promptly before they are likely in practice to be unrecoverable. For example, on average over the period examined, in excess of 75 per cent of applications are finalised within 28 days. A corollary of this finding, of course, is that tenants now walk a precarious regulatory tightrope that was not in existence before 30 October 1989. Any breach, such as missing a rental payment date, gives the landlord a right to make an application to the tribunal. In turn, a termination order may be made before an impoverished tenant is able to organise remedial action. Under the Tribunal, a tightened regime of obligation governs landlord–tenant relations, and as the termination numbers attest, it is one that is increasingly deployed by landlords generally to police tenant compliance. Moreover, the scope for strategic behaviour on the part of tenants (and landlords) is correspondingly reduced.

But even acknowledging the Tribunal's appeal for landlords of all kinds, this consideration alone does not explain why the public housing landlord has made significantly disproportionate use of the Tribunal to terminate tenancies since its establishment, when compared with private landlords. To answer this question requires examining the broader context of the provision of public housing over the last couple of decades.

XII. MORE STRINGENT ELIGIBILITY FOR, AND INSECURITY OF, PUBLIC HOUSING

The Tribunal data considered above, indicating an increasing regulatory and even punitive approach to tenants by the Department of Housing, needs to be seen as part of a much wider strategy of managing the entire stock of housing at the Department's disposal. Since the late 1990s, an increasingly intrusive approach to regulating this cohort of tenants was adopted as official policy. The State government introduced a number of highly restrictive approaches. As we have seen, increasing resort to the Tribunal to manage tenants was one. Secondly, in 2002 the government introduced the concept of renewable or 'probationary tenancies' that had the effect of making a

[41] Carrie Menkel-Meadow, 'Do the "Haves" Come out Ahead in Alternative Justice Systems?: Repeat Players and ADR' (1999) 15 *Ohio State Journal for Dispute Resolution* 19–61. This point will be discussed further below.

group of public tenants' tenure more precarious. Thirdly, around the same time the government came to see public housing tenants, particularly given that such tenants were commonly housed with others in large 'estates', as part of a wider problem of public order and particularly drug addiction and supply, so began to enforce tenancy obligations more intensively. Fourthly, and relatedly, a policy of 'acceptable behaviour agreements' was proposed in 2004 to activate heightened responsibilities towards neighbours to make housing estates into more viable and livable communities. In combination, this cluster of practices has produced an increasingly dense governance of public housing in general and tenants in particular. Moreover, their aim is expressly to make public housing a 'pathway' to other forms of housing, rather than it to provide security of tenure for those who most need it.[42]

In the case of probationary tenancies, in 2002 the Department introduced the fixed-term tenancy, with a right of renewal. The right of renewal was dependent on good behaviour; that is to say, compliance by the tenant (and, importantly, his or her family) with the terms of the agreement. This new tenancy represented a significant change in policy. The previous practice was to grant tenants continuing tenancies from the commencement of their tenancy. The new policy also significantly weakened the legal position of tenants. By contrast, ever since the New South Wales Supreme Court's decision in 1994 in *Nicholson v NSW Land and Housing Corporation*,[43] the Department had been prevented on administrative law grounds from terminating tenancy agreements without first providing tenants with the reasons for termination. But under the 2002 regime, the net effect was to render the public housing tenants' rights to remain in occupation increasingly vulnerable. The contemporary precarisation of life in other social spheres had come to infect the housing sector intended to provide a lasting safety net for the most disadvantaged citizens.[44] To the extent that the Department now had unfettered discretion to choose whether or not to renew the tenancy, the power to determine continuance of occupation shifted from the Tribunal to the Department.[45] The criteria for renewal were whether the tenant had complied with their obligations under the agreement, and the extent to which they had done so would determine the duration of the next fixed term (from one to ten years), or whether one would be offered at all.

[42] Family and Community Services, 'Social Housing in New South Wales: A Discussion Paper for Input and Comment' (NSW Government, 2014) 38.

[43] *Nicholson v NSW Land and Housing Corporation* [1992] NSW Supreme Court 30027 (unreported, Badgery-Parker J, 24 December 1991).

[44] Lorey (n 13 above).

[45] NSW Department of Housing 'Policy EST0020A: Renewable Tenancies' (NSW Government, 2005); NSW Department of Housing, 'Future Directions in Social Housing: fact sheet no 2—renewable tenancies' (Sydney, NSWDOH, 2002); Chris Martin, 'Government-Housing: Governing Crime and Disorder in Public Housing in New South Wales' (n 2 above).

This policy could only apply to new tenancies: current tenants were in occupation pursuant to continuing contracts that could not be changed without their consent. From November 2002 virtually all new tenancies were in the form of renewable tenancies. Then, in 2004, legislation was introduced to give the Department power to convert any current continuing tenancy agreement to a renewable one. By section 14A of the Residential Tenancies Act 1987 (NSW), the Department of Housing could 'declare' a tenancy agreement to be renewable.[46] The State government offered as its reason for doing so the need to tackle 'anti-social behaviour' in public housing. This provision was accompanied by new provisions that allowed the Department to require tenants to enter into 'acceptable behaviour agreements'. As of 2014, close to 40 per cent of tenancies are renewable,[47] and under the Residential Tenancies Act 2010 (NSW), these provisions were revised to allow eligibility assessments to be one further ground of termination of agreements, whether continuing or fixed-term, in an entirely new Part 7 of the statute.

By a new section 35A(1) of the 1987 Act the Department of Housing could 'by notice in writing ... request the tenant give a written undertaking ... not to engage in specified anti-social behaviour.' The term 'anti-social behaviour' was given a non-exhaustive meaning, including 'emission of excessive noise, littering, dumping of cars, vandalism and defacing of property' and not just by tenants but all 'lawful occupants' such as partners, children or extended family (section 35A(6)). Failing or refusing to enter into such an agreement is grounds for automatic termination of the agreement (section 64I).[48] The introduction of these policies may explain the apparent drop in applications and orders for terminations and other remedies in the years 2008–12 shown in Figure 5 above, as the Department focused on these rather different mechanisms for regulating tenant behaviour.

In the event, the recent practice of the Department to offer renewable tenancy agreements has been to dispense with requirements for good behaviour. Instead, the new focus of renewal is whether the tenant remains eligible for public housing by reference to recognised categories of need. Issues of compliance with obligations are therefore now returned to the Tribunal, which may also explain the recent rise in Tribunal applications and orders against tenants. As for the acceptable behaviour agreements, they appear to have become a dead letter with no available evidence that they have ever been used by the Department. This suggests that the Department has had no need for them, the same objectives possibly being adequately met by

[46] See now Residential Tenancies Act 2010 (NSW), s 142.
[47] Family and Community Services (n 42 above) 25.
[48] See now Residential Tenancies Act 2010 (NSW), s 138.

the other policies, including the effectiveness of the process of Tribunal applications.[49]

XIII. CONCLUSION

The appropriate role and scope of alternative dispute resolution (ADR) within the legal system has been the focus of many recent studies. Descriptively, a number have charted an explosion of ADR over the last couple of decades.[50] Prescriptively, this development has been welcomed by many as providing space for litigants by removing the obstacles of cost, time or excessive formality typical of the courts.[51] Some scholars have viewed this development as opening a space for 'restorative justice'[52] for the reason that negotiated resolution tends to affirm relationships rather than fracturing them further, as adjudication routinely does; and that it is often far more effective at delivering justice in the sense of restoring parties to a status quo than the more cumbersome, costly and hazardous process of court resolution.

On the other hand, counterbalancing the largely affirmative literature extolling ADR's rule of law-enhancing qualities, are the studies that focus on 'litigation explosions',[53] and related analyses that focus on the excessive amount of legal regulation, or the unfolding 'juridification' evident in contemporary advanced societies.[54] These studies seek to offer general accounts of how ballooning rates of litigation in society represent a largely undesirable and unhealthy development in the regulation of social life.

The data detailed above reveals a very different aspect of the spread of ADR, not reducible to one single logic. In the case of the State landlord

[49] Chris Martin, 'Government-Housing: Governing Crime and Disorder in Public Housing in New South Wales' (n 2 above) ch 6.

[50] Hilary Astor and Christine Chinkin, *Dispute Resolution in Australia* (2nd edn, Sydney, Butterworths, 2002); Erhard Blankenburg, 'The Infrastructure for Avoiding Civil Litigation: Comparing Cultures of Legal Behaviour in the Netherlands and West Germany' (1994) 28 *Law and Society Review* 789–808; Erhard Blankenburg, 'Access to Justice and Alternatives to Courts: European Procedural Justice Compared' (1995) 14 *Civil Justice Quarterly* 176–89; John Braithwaite, *Restorative Justice and Responsive Regulation* (Oxford, Oxford University Press, 2002).

[51] Gordon Woodman, 'The Alternative Law of Alternative Dispute Resolution' (1991) 32 *Les Cahiers de Droit* 3; Hazel Genn, *Mediation in Action: Resolving Court Disputes Without Trial* (London, Calouste Gulbenkian Foundation, 1999); Hazel Genn, *Paths to Justice: What People Do and Think About Going to Law* (Oxford, Hart, 1999).

[52] Heather Strang and John Braithwaite (eds), *Restorative Justice and Civil Society* (Melbourne, Cambridge University Press, 2001).

[53] Marc Galanter, 'The Day After the Litigation Explosion' (1986) 46 *Maryland Law Review* 3.

[54] See generally, Gunther Teubner (ed), *Juridification of Social Spheres* (Berlin, de Gruyter, 1997); and in particular, Martin Partington, 'The Juridification of Social Welfare in Britain' in the same volume, pp 419–38.

of public housing in New South Wales, the dominant 'benefit' of the Tribunal-based process is one that substantially enhances its power over tenants when compared with the court-based regime. The Tribunal's more informal mechanisms for dispute resolution, far from reducing the impact of law on the resolution of conflict, actually increase it. Under formal, costly court-based processes, only the tip of the pyramid of disputes was subjected to the scrutiny of law. The data shows public housing tenants to be now increasingly vulnerable to termination of their rights to their homes. In the apparently more tenant-tolerant, former court-based regime, termination was a last resort and an extremely rare mechanism for enforcing tenant obligations. By contrast, its successor Tribunal appears to facilitate a very different policy, namely the routine eviction of significantly greater numbers of tenants under a fast-track procedural regime. This policy is accompanied by a much more vigorous cost-recovery stance whereby tenants are summoned in very large numbers before the Tribunal to pay off arrears, frequently at risk of subsequent termination in the case of default. In this context, a policy of saving tenancies in the interest of tenant security, if at all possible, has been supplanted by a far more selective one, where tenants walk a compliance tightrope, as the public housing system is marked by an increasing proportion of temporary, short-term tenancies. The litigation strategy of the State landlord is consonant with its parallel legislative message of strictly rationing tenancies by imposing an array of novel statutory restrictions and obligations.

One further consequence of this development is that the sense of community within housing estates is being eroded as a more transient population, less likely to establish long and lasting connections to their neighbours or the location, move in, and are at a later stage, moved out. In this changed, 'pathway'-defined, rather than 'security'-defined, public housing system, it is likely that the Tribunal's role will remain a central tool in the State landlord's armoury as long as it sticks with a housing policy that emphasises recycling of tenancies among, rather than security of tenure for, many of the most disadvantaged citizens in society. At a deeper level, the changed fate of public housing tenants reflects transformations of the local welfare state, which mirror comparable changes in many welfare states over the last three decades.[55] The post-war social rights mantra of 'cradle to the grave' security has been replaced by the notion of welfare housing as highly provisional, limited to only the most seriously disadvantaged, and increasingly precarious.

[55] See generally, Christopher Pierson, *Beyond the Welfare State? The New Political Economy of Welfare* (Cambridge, Polity, 1991); Gosta Esping Andersen (ed), *Welfare States in Transition: National Adaptations in Global Economies* (London, Sage, 1996). For an analysis of parallel trends in England and Wales, see eg: Jill Morgan, 'Housing and security in England and Wales: casualisation revisited' (2009) 1 *International Journal of Law in the Built Environment* 42.

6

The Tenant's Home and the Landlord's Property—The Polish Struggle to Achieve a Balance of Rights

MAGDALENA HABDAS*

I. INTRODUCTION

IN THE ERA of increased mobility of citizens, residential leases are becoming increasingly important in satisfying the housing needs of households. The past credit crunch has caused many banks to introduce stringent requirements for mortgage credit that not all households can meet. In addition, market stagnation is forcing citizens to relocate in order to secure a job. One should also acknowledge that various social and economic phenomena have caused the precarisation of many aspects of life, including employment (labour) relations,[1] financial stability of individuals, as well as the security of home.[2] Lorey points out that neoliberal work and life is characterised by the requirement to work more, earn less, be constantly flexible

* Dept. of Private and Private International Law, Faculty of Law and Administration, University of Silesia, Katowice.

[1] See Carl-Ulrik Schierup and Martin Bak Jørgensen (eds), *Politics of Precarity: Migrant Conditions, Struggles and Experiences* (Leiden, Brill, 2017), particularly Ronaldo Munkc, 'Globalisation, Labour and the "Precariat": Old Wine in New Bottles?', pp 78–98.

[2] See Nicole Cook, Aidan Davison and Louise Crabtree (eds), *Housing and Home Unbound: Intersections in economics, environment and politics in Australia* (New York, Routledge, 2016), particularly Fiona Allon and Jean Parker, 'Liquid Housing Wealth in an Era of Financialisation', pp 56–71; also see Sarah Nield, 'Mortgages and the Credit Crunch: Cause and Effect' in Lyria Bennett Moses, Brendan Edgeworth and Cathleen Sherry, *Property and Security Selectes Essays* (Sydney, Thomson Reuters/Lawbook Co, Sydney, 2010) 127–48 and Sarah Nield, 'Borrowers as consumers: new notions of unconscionability for domestic borrowers' in Mel Kenny. James Devenney and Lorna Fox O'Mahony (eds), *Unconscionability in European Private Financial Transactions. Protecting the Vulnerable* (Cambridge, Cambridge University Press, 2010) 184–204.

and willing to further develop. This denotes that individuals face precarious employment and indebtedness which reflect the political and economic regime of precarisation.[3] This regime brings about not only cultural and academic consequences, but manifests itself in real life, particularly in the context of securing and maintaining a home.

It must come as no surprise that precarisation leads to the lack or the reduction of financial stability. This causes an increasing number of persons to be interested in leasing as opposed to buying a place to call home. Residential leases are an important segment of the real estate market as well as an essential instrument for securing a home for those who cannot afford to buy it. When the price of land becomes an economic barrier for buying a place to live, legal institutions that enable one to use the property of another must provide an economically viable and a socially beneficial alternative.[4]

Unfortunately, in Central and Eastern European countries that experienced a wave of public housing privatisation after the transition to a market economy, the lease remains an underappreciated legal instrument that is not properly utilised to satisfy the interests of both the landlord and the tenant, the state and local authorities, and the society as such. In the former socialist countries, the private rental market is underdeveloped and owner-occupation seems to be the preferred option. Simultaneously, the development of the real estate market and other economic phenomena have caused a significant increase in the prices of real estate, making it difficult for many to enter the owner-occupier market. Consequently, the development of the private rental market is indispensable; however it cannot occur without a proper legal framework. When one considers the inherent tension between: the landlord and the tenant, the notion of property as an asset or an investment and the notion of home, the economic and the personal attachment to premises,[5] it becomes obvious that precarisation of the home will occur if a proper balance is not struck between the interests of the landlord and the interests of the tenant.

In the light of the above, the purpose of this chapter is to examine the state of the Polish residential rental market in the context of the precarisation of home exacerbated by the political choices that are being made by the state. It is necessary to show that economic and political choices influence

[3] See Isabell Lorey, 'Precarisation, Indebtedness, Giving Time. Interlacing Lines across Maria Eichhorn's 5 Weeks, 25 Days, 175 Hours' in Katie Guggenheim and Polly Staple (eds), *Maria Eichhorn 5 Weeks, 25 Days, 175 Hours* (London, Chisenhale Gallery, 2016) 39, 41–42.

[4] Susan Bright, Nicholas Hopkins and Nicholas Macklam, 'Owning Part but Losing All: Using Human Rights to Protect Home Ownership' in Nicholas Hopkins (ed), *Modern Studies in Property Law: Volume 7* (Bloomsbury Publishing, 2013) 15–16.

[5] Chris Bevan, 'Challenging "Home" as a concept in Modern Property Law: Lessons from the Supreme Court Post—Stack and Jones' in Warren Barr (ed), *Modern Studies in Property Law: Volume 8* (Hart Publishing, 2015) 196–97.

decisions concerning the law and thus shape the legal framework of tenancy law,[6] simultaneously determining the level of home precarisation. In the first part of the chapter the economic situation and state housing policies' influence on the market and citizens' ability to satisfy their housing needs are considered. In the second part of the chapter the problem of balancing landlord and tenant rights is shown in relation to rents and rent increases, as this issue has generated many controversies after the shift to a market economy in the 1990s.[7] It has also been the object of numerous European Court of Human Rights (ECtHR) judgments where the state's housing policies are contrasted with its obligation to protect property (article 1 Protocol 1 to the European Convention on Human Rights and Fundamental Freedoms—ECHR) but also to protect the home (article 8 ECHR). The conclusions show that the lack of long-term housing policies, promoting only owner-occupation, and disregarding the need to strike a balance between the general and the individual interest have hampered the development of the residential market and have left many housing issues unresolved, thus increasing the precarisation of home.

II. THE HOUSING SITUATION IN POLAND

In order to give a very general idea of living standards in Poland, it may be useful to note that 45.2 per cent of households live in single family, detached houses and 40.1 per cent live in multifamily houses (apartment blocks); however these numbers are very different when one compares the situation in cities and in rural areas. In the cities, 59.4 per cent of households live in multifamily houses, while in the countryside this type of accommodation accounts for only 4.1 per cent. In rural areas the situation is opposite to that described in the cities, as 82.8 per cent of households live in single family, detached houses.[8]

In Poland the predominant form of tenure concerning homes has always been private owner-occupation.[9] According to the Central Statistical Office of Poland almost 82 per cent of households are owner-occupiers of their

[6] This unique interdependence between hosing policies and tenancy law is the object of the project: Tenancy Law and Housing Policy in Multi-level Europe (project funded from the European Union's Seventh Framework Programme for research, technological development and demonstration under grant agreement no 290694. This chapter was prepared and presented as a part of that project and its dissemination strategy.

[7] For reasons of space, this chapter will not focus on evictions and repossessions, which of course is another important dimension of precarisation. See Hunter and Meers, Chapter four above, for a framework to considered tenancies.

[8] Central Statistical Office, *Living conditions of families in Poland* (Warsaw, Statistical Information and Elaborations, 2014) 51–52.

[9] Alistair C Blunt and Alina Muzioł-Węcławowicz, 'Improved Management of the Existing Stock—the Case of Poland' (1998) 5 *Housing Studies* 697, 697.

homes and out of this figure 10.9 per cent are homes encumbered by a mortgage.[10] These numbers include not only the right of ownership but also the cooperative proprietary right to a unit which, technically speaking, is a limited real property right within a housing cooperative. The right is, however, transferrable *inter vivos* and *mortis causa*, may have its own register (the equivalent of a land register), and may be encumbered by a mortgage;[11] therefore, for statistical purposes holders of this cooperative right have also been classified as owner-occupiers. In a slightly earlier study of the Central Statistical Office of Poland it was indicated that physical persons are owner-occupiers of 64.1 per cent of homes, whereas holders of the cooperative proprietary right to a unit who are in possession of the unit amount to 15.4 per cent.[12] The above numbers show that approximately 17 to 20 per cent of households rely on renting to satisfy their housing needs.

In comparison with the EU-28 average the share of owner-occupation in Poland is rather high and the share of leases is quite low. According to Eurostat data, 70.6 per cent of persons in the EU-28 lived in owner-occupied dwellings, whereas renting accounted for 29.4 per cent (18.5 per cent were tenants with a market price rent, and 10.9 per cent tenants in reduced-rent or free accommodation).[13]

Although Poland has a high level of home ownership, it does suffer from an acute scarcity of dwellings. The problem is rooted in various historical as well as contemporary economic and political problems which require careful programming and genuine political attention if they are to be solved in a satisfactory manner.[14] Soon after the transition to a market economy it was noted that as of 1994 the shortage of dwellings was approximately equal to 1.6 million and that at the rate of construction achieved in 1993 it would take at least 18 years to erect the required number of dwellings (units/flats).[15] The situation was further exacerbated by the fact that the

[10] Central Statistical Office, 'Living Conditions of Families in Poland' (Statistical Information and Elaborations, 2014) 52–53.

[11] See also Magdalena Habdas, 'Property and Trust Law Poland', *International Encyclopaedia of Laws* (Alphen aan den Rijn, Kluwer Law International, 2015) 142–45.

[12] Central Statistical Office, 'Mieszkania: Narodowy Spis Powszechny Ludności i Mieszkań 2011' ['Housing: National Census of Population and Housing 2011'] (Warsaw, Statistical Information and Elaborations, 2013) 25.

[13] More than half of the population in each EU Member State lived in owner-occupied dwellings in 2012, but the range was very wide, starting with 53.2% in Germany and ending with 96.6% in Romania: 'Housing Statistics' (Eurostat, last edited 22 June 2017): ec.europa.eu/eurostat/statistics-explained/index.php/Housing_statistics.

[14] For a historical account of the development of the Polish housing market and law in Poland see: Grzegorz Panek, 'National Report for Poland, TENLAW: Tenancy Law and Housing Policy in Multi-level Europe' (European Commission, 2014), points 1 and 5, available at: www.tenlaw.uni-bremen.de/reports/PolandReport_09052014.pdf.

[15] Oleg Kapliński and Tomasz Thiel, 'Evaluation of multi-family housing systems in Poland' (1995) 13 *Construction Management and Economics* 291, 291–92.

economic transformation was not accompanied by a developed housing policy. The number of units per 1000 persons nationwide amounted to 283 in 1988 and to 297.6 in 1995, whereas in Western Europe this was as high as 400.[16] Throughout the 1990s housing construction was well below the population's needs[17] due to high inflation and the lack of developed market institutions and legal regulations. Additionally, mortgage financing did not develop on a significant scale until after the year 2000.[18] According to OECD studies, in 2002 the housing shortage, which reflects the difference between the number of households and the number of available dwellings, still amounted to almost a million units.[19]

Unfortunately, despite many political promises to achieve on a yearly basis an increased construction rate of dwellings, Poland is currently last in Europe when it comes to the size of its housing stock. In 2013, just like in 2011 and 2012, Poland had the lowest housing stock per 1,000 citizens, which was almost 25 per cent below the European average, the latter amounting to 475.9 apartments per 1,000 citizens.[20] In 2013 it was estimated that the Polish housing stock was on average equal to 348.5 apartments per 1000 inhabitants, however in the cities this was 384.9 and in the rural areas this was 291.7.[21] This housing shortage has further ramifications concerning living conditions. In 2012 the percentage of persons between the ages of 25–34 who continued to live with at least one of their parents was 43.4 per cent while the EU-27 average was only 28.2 per cent.[22] Although this may be partly the effect of tradition and culture, to a large extent it is the result of economic difficulties also connected with the labour market and unemployment rates. Additionally, in Poland the average home contains one room per person, while the OECD average is 1.6 rooms per person. This is one of the lowest rates in the OECD.

In Poland, housing affordability, defined by the number of the annual gross salaries required to buy a standard-sized new dwelling (70 m^2) is low: it takes 7.4 years to acquire such a dwelling. In countries with

[16] Blunt and Muzioł-Węcławowicz (n 9 above) 698.

[17] See Panek (n 14 above) 6–9.

[18] Jacek Łaszek, 'Recent Developments in the Housing Market in Poland' (2011) *Housing Finance International* 6, 7.

[19] OECD, *OECD Economic Surveys: Poland* (Paris, OECD Publishing, 2008) 108.

[20] Diana Rádl Rogerova et al, *Property index. Overview of European Residential Markets European housing 2013*, 3rd edn (Czech Republic, Deloitte Real Estate, 2014) 7.

[21] Alina Muzioł-Węcławowicz, 'Poland: Old Problems and New Dilemmas' in József Hegedus, Martin Lux and Nóra Teller (eds), *Social Housing in Transition Countries* (New York/London, Routledge, 2013) 195.

[22] Central Statistical Office, 'Europejskie badanie dochodów i warunków życia (EU-SILC) w 2012 r' ['European research on income and living conditions (EU-SILC) in 2012'] (Statistical Information and Elaborations, 31 January 2014) available at: http://stat.gov.pl/obszary-tematyczne/warunki-zycia/dochody-wydatki-i-warunki-zycia-ludnosci/warunki-zycia-rodzin-w-polsce,13,1.html.

affordable own housing (eg Denmark, Germany and Portugal) this figure is 2–3.5 years, whereas in countries with relatively affordable own housing (eg Belgium, The Netherlands, Ireland, Spain and Austria) this ranges from 3.6 to 5.6 years.[23] The above, combined with the shortage of rental flats and the fact that mortgage lending has been substantially reduced, clearly indicates that bridging the existing housing gap in Poland will not be easy. In 2012 the number of mortgage loans granted to physical persons was 15 per cent lower than in 2011, while their aggregate value was seven times lower than their value in 2011.[24]

III. THE PROBLEMATIC RENTAL MARKET

The shortage concerning dwellings for sale as well as for rent predominantly influences large cities and well-developed labour regions of Poland. More than 215,000 rental apartments are needed out of which 125,000 are required for rentals with public (social) renting, entrusted to local authorities.[25] The severe underdevelopment of the rental market has been found to contribute to persistent disparities in regional unemployment and to significantly obstruct labour mobility.[26] In fact, persons who are willing to move in order to secure a job are more likely to simply emigrate from Poland, because it is easier for them to rent a dwelling for a reasonable rent abroad than it is to do so in a Polish city where employment may be found. The private housing sector offers virtually no flats for rental due to the extensive protection of the tenant and the resulting risk to the flat owner.[27] The flats that are available in the private sector have market rents (which must offset the increased risk to the landlord) that are too high when compared to average monthly salaries. Thus, precarisation of employment coupled with an underdeveloped private rental sector leads to the precarisation of home, however surprisingly, not because the tenant is unprotected, but because the landlord is under-protected and not willing to risk entering the private rental market, or willing only to enter it unofficially, without observing the full extent of tenant protection.[28]

Although after the transition to a market economy the governmental housing policies contained declarations of creating legal and economic conditions for the development of a rental market, including rentals for

[23] Rogerova et al, (n 20 above) 13.

[24] Instytut Rozwoju Miast, 'Informacje o mieszkalnictwie. Wyniki Monitoringu za 2012r.' ['Information on housing. Monitoring results for 2012'] (Kraków, IRM, 2013) 89.

[25] Muzioł-Węcławowicz (n 21 above) 195.

[26] OECD (n 19 above) 107.

[27] Łaszek (n 18 above) 6.

[28] *cf* Carla Jacqueline Huisman, 'A silent shift? The precarisation of the Dutch rental housing market' (2016) 31 *Journal of Housing and the Built Environment* 93, 97–98.

low-income households, support was in fact directed to the acquisition of privately owned dwellings.[29] Following the 1990s reforms, all post-communist countries introduced large-scale privatisation of publicly owned housing stock, often at prices that were a fraction of the dwellings' market value, thus in theory creating quantitative conditions for the creation of a private rental sector.[30] Unfortunately, the process of rapid privatisation had a number of drawbacks, although it is difficult to imagine it having been prevented at the time. All social forces strongly advocated privatisation and even today it remains a very popular, although short-term, plan to achieve greater political support.[31] In fact, Polish politicians perceive and present privatisation as the market approach to housing.[32]

Meanwhile, the large-scale privatisation of the public housing stock residualised the social rental sector which houses the most vulnerable social groups. Moreover, privatisation had a regressive social effect, because financial gains were the greatest only for the wealthier households, while the low-income ones were unable to buy their dwellings even at discount prices. Politicians recognised the need for social housing only after privatisation and/or restitution to previous owners had already taken place but were unable to prepare alternative plans to cater for social housing.[33] Simultaneously, extensive tenant protection quickly stigmatised the already shallow private rental market and led to many landlord and tenant problems connected with regulated rents, and the difficulty to terminate the lease and to evict the tenant.[34] Professional landlords, whether private or public/social are thus presently non-existent in Poland. The former fear the excessive tenant protection, insecurity of rent revenues and the associated increased business risk. This causes private, foreign investors who successfully operate on the Polish real estate market, to abstain from investing in the residential rental market.[35] The public/social landlords additionally face problems of inadequate financial support from the central budget, needed for capital investment to either build or renovate the existing housing stock, particularly when in Poland central government funding for this purpose is scarce, rare and incidental.

[29] Łaszek (n 18 above) 7.

[30] Martin Lux et al, 'Housing Restitution and Privatisation: Both Catalysts and Obstacles to the Formation of Private Rental Housing in the Czech Republic and Estonia' (2012) 2 *International Journal of Housing Policy* 137, 137–38.

[31] József Hegedus, 'The Transformation of the Social Housing Sector in Eastern Europe. A conceptual Framework' in József Hegedus, Martin Lux and Nóra Teller (eds), *Social Housing in Transition Countries* (New York/London, Routledge, 2013) 13.

[32] Muzioł-Węcławowicz (n 21 above) 206.

[33] Hegedus (n 31 above) 13, 24.

[34] See also Lux et al (n 30 above) 148–49.

[35] Polski Związek Firm Deweloperskich, 'Sytuacja mieszkaniowa w Polsce 2012. Raport' ['The Housing Situation in Poland 2012. A report'] (PZFD, 2012): docplayer.pl/1895933-Raport-sytuacja-mieszkaniowa-w-polsce-2012.html.

Although the Polish Constitution (PC)[36] of 2 April 1997[37] specifies in article 75 section 1 that public authorities shall pursue policies conducive to satisfying the housing needs of citizens, in particular combating homelessness, promoting the development of low-income housing and supporting activities aimed at acquisition of a home by each citizen, the task has in fact been delegated to local governments. According to article 6 section 1 of the Act of 8 March 1990 on the commune self-governments,[38] the commune (the lowest tier of the three-tier system of self-government in Poland) is responsible for all public tasks of a local character which have not been entrusted to other authorities. This provision must be read in conjunction with article 4 section 1 of the Act of 21 June 2001 on the protection of tenants, consideration of the housing stock of the commune, and the amendment of the civil code (TPA)[39] where it is stipulated that creating conditions conducive to satisfying the housing needs of the commune is the commune's own task. In particular, the commune is obliged to provide social and substitute dwellings as well as satisfy the housing needs of low-income households (article 4 section 1 TPA). Essentially this denotes that the commune is responsible for carrying out as well as financing this task.

Consequently, the central government does not provide any grants to the commune, but only runs certain policy programmes which are meant to assist the commune in performing the above tasks. Unfortunately all of these programmes (the social renting housing programme, the thermal modernisation programme,[40] the social housing subsidy programme) are short- rather than long-term, and have very limited budgets. In fact, only the social renting housing programme and the thermal modernisation programme lasted long enough to bring about some visible results.[41]

The social renting housing programme requires more explanation. Established in 1996, it is oriented at constructing and maintaining rental apartments for families who have a stable income not exceeding a defined level, but who cannot afford to buy their own home. The programme introduced a new housing operator on the market, namely the Social Housing Association (SHA) that usually took the form of a limited liability company and was frequently set up by various communes, with preferential loans from a National Housing Fund established for this purpose. The rents in SHA buildings are cost rents, which cover maintenance and repair costs,

[36] English, German, French and Russian translations of the Polish Constitution are available on the following website: www.sejm.gov.pl/prawo/konst/konst.htm.
[37] Journal of Statutes 1997, No. 78, item 483, as amended.
[38] Consolidated version: Journal of Statutes 2013, item 594, 1318 as amended.
[39] Consolidated version: Journal of Statutes 2014, item 150.
[40] See Panek (n 14 above) 49–50.
[41] Muzioł-Węcławowicz (n 21 above) 207.

but also a repayment of the preferential loan from the fund.[42] In order to secure a lease, however, the prospective tenant is obliged to cover a part of the construction costs (up to 30 per cent), which confirms that SHA social rentals are not addressed to the lowest income households.[43] In 2013 it was estimated that SHA have constructed 92,066 units which, compared to the existing local government (the commune) housing stock equal to 934,863 units, may be unimpressive.[44] Studies have shown that the overall assessment of SHA homes by their inhabitants is positive and that despite not actually owning the flats, the tenants do feel at home. They view their lease as a stable, long-term instrument that affords them certainty of occupation.[45]

It seemed that the social renting housing programme had run its course, when the National Housing Fund, as a result of highly controversial, political decisions, was dissolved in 2009 and its assets were merged with those of the state National Economy Bank. The latter, however, did not receive adequate funding to continue the previous activity of the fund and required additional legislation to be enacted if the programme was to continue in one shape or another.[46] The matter remained unresolved, but the situation had been made even more obscure by introducing in 2011 the possibility for the tenant to purchase the SHA unit,[47] the idea being explained by the fact that tenants participated in unit construction costs by making an initial financial contribution.[48] Thus the main reasoning behind rental flats in SHA buildings, whereby it was assumed that households who can afford to buy or rent on the free market should move out and not diminish the availability of the social rental stock, seems to have been abandoned as politicians have once again perceived privatisation and home ownership as the only answer to satisfying the housing needs of the population. Nevertheless, practice has shown that the purchase price of an SHA unit is unattractive to tenants, who seem to have expected massive reductions in purchase prices, like those

[42] See Martin Lux, 'Social Housing in the Czech Republic, Poland and Slovakia' (2001) 1 *European Journal of Housing Policy* 189, 200–201.

[43] Panek (n 14 above) 46.

[44] Central Statistical Office, 'Gospodarka mieszkaniowa w 2013 r. Informacje i opracowania statystyczne' ['Housing management in 2013. Statistical information and analyses'] (Warsaw, GUS, 2014) 17.

[45] Maciej Kowalewski, 'Poczucie Własności Mieszkania Lokatorów Towarzystw Budownictwa Społecznego /Tenants of Social Housing Associations and Their Sense of Ownership of Flats' (2009) 3 *Ruch Prawniczy, Ekonomiczny i Socjologiczny* 197, 210–11.

[46] Muzioł-Węcławowicz (n 21 above) 205–6; Panek (n 14 above) 42.

[47] See Marlena Jankowska and Miroslaw Pawełczyk, 'Wykup mieszkań budowanych przez TBS' ['Buyout of the Dwellings Built by Housing Association'] (2011) 4 *Świat Nieruchomości* 49–53.

[48] J Hegudus correctly noted that the dependence of the SHA on the central budget and the pressure from the tenants to eventually privatise the apartments made the long-term sustainability of the programme uncertain, see Hegedus (n 31 above) 13.

employed in the communal and cooperative housing stocks during privatisation processes.[49]

Several years after discontinuation of the SHA programme, at the end of 2015 the government renewed the initiative through the National Economy Bank, which will grant preferential credits for the next 10 years. The cost rents in SHA housing must not exceed five per cent of the flat's reconstruction value annually (previously four per cent) and the initial payment by the prospective tenant to secure the lease must not exceed 25 per cent of the flat's construction costs (previously 30 per cent). It is planned that at least 30,000 new rental flats with controlled rent levels will be erected.

The above show that Poland, like many other Central European Countries, requires a greater differentiation among legally and economically accessible forms of satisfying housing needs, since ownership remains the prevailing option and the rental market is underdeveloped, risky to private landlords and too costly for self-governments. This lack of differentiation contributes to the precarisation of home, as there is less choice and opportunity to satisfy one's housing needs, as well as fewer options to adjust the housing arrangement to the changing financial resources (often caused by precarisation of employment) and social needs of an individual or a family. The government is still devoting most of its efforts to programmes supporting the acquisition of home ownership, thus focusing only on young persons who have a chance of obtaining a loan, and promoting their early dependence on long-term loans which impede their mobility. The needs of lower-income groups or those who need greater mobility to find employment are still disregarded.[50]

Interestingly, the effects of the various housing policies implemented in Poland may in fact stimulate gentrification instead of promoting a healthy tenant mix within buildings. The lowest income households rely almost exclusively on municipal/commune housing, only middle-income households had access to SHA rental flats, and higher income households are to satisfy their housing needs in the private rental sector and the ownership sector. This may cause serious social segregation problems that may prove difficult to solve in future years.[51] It is also a result of housing policies which had a narrow scope, unclear objectives and were badly targeted.[52]

[49] Panek (n 14 above) 45.

[50] This phenomenon is not characteristic only of Central and Eastern Europe, but may increasingly be observed also in Western Europe, see Warren Barr, 'The Big Society and Social Housing: Never the Twain Shall Meet?' in Nicholas Hopkins (ed), *Modern Studies in Property Law: Volume 7* (Bloomsbury Publishing, 2013) 39, 42; Huisman (n 28 above) 102.

[51] Lux (n 42 above) 207.

[52] Jozsef Hegedus and Ivan Tosics, 'Rent Reform—Issues for the Countries of Eastern Europe and the Newly Independent States' (1998) 5 *Housing Studies* 657, 665; OECD (n 19 above) 107–8.

IV. THE POST-COMMUNIST LEGACY OF REGULATED RENTS

The development of the rental market must be supported by adequate legal provisions which properly balance the rights of the landlord and the tenant of a residential unit. Although there are numerous detailed issues which may be examined in this context, the most fundamental one, particularly for post-communist countries of Central and Eastern Europe, concerns the level of payable rents. The evolution that Poland has undergone in an effort to remove regulated rents from the private rental sector is worth considering, as it reflects the difficulty of devising a system that protects the interests of both the private landlords and the tenants. In the process of introducing necessary changes in tenancy law, the Polish legislator did not avoid serious mistakes, which were the object of important judgments of the Polish Constitutional Tribunal as well as of the ECtHR.

It must be noted that during the communist era (1945–90) rents were to be kept at an artificially low level, both to prove that the centrally planned economy was able to satisfy the housing needs of the citizens but also to show that housing expenditure was only a small percentage of a person's monthly income.[53] The relevant legal provisions came into force as early as 1945 and focused not only on regulating rents but also on allocating dwellings to tenants, through administrative decisions, both in publicly and in privately owned buildings.[54] It was not until 1988 that private owners regained the right to freely rent their dwellings and not have the tenant selected and brought into possession by public authorities; however the right could only be exercised with respect to units that tenants had willingly vacated. Stringent restrictions on terminating leases by landlords and calculating rents were still applied to those tenants whose leases continued to run. Needless to say, regulated rents were excessively low and did not come close to the expenses owners had to bear with respect to the maintenance and repair of buildings, thus causing the latter to fall into disrepair.[55]

After the 1990 reforms, owners of buildings with rental flats had great expectations regarding the new Leases of Residential Units and Housing Benefits Act 1994 (LRU),[56] hoping that regulated rents would no longer apply to privately owned rental flats. At first sight the LRU in article 25 did

[53] Blunt and Muzioł-Węcławowicz (above n 9) at 698; Hegedus and Tosics (n 52 above) 658, 661.

[54] For a historical evolution of the legal regulations concerning the housing market see Panek (n 14 above) 65–89.

[55] Janina Panowicz-Lipska, 'Najem' ['Leases'] in Janina Panowicz-Lipska (ed), *System Prawa Prywatnego. Tom 8. Prawo zobowiązań—część szczegółowa* [*The System of Private Law. Vol. 8. The law of obligations—the nominate contracts part*] (Warszawa, CH Beck, 2011) 73.

[56] Act of 2 July 1994, Journal of Statutes 1994, no. 105, item 509.

limit the application of regulated rents only to the housing stock of local governments (ie the commune) as well as of: the state, state juridical persons and other not-for-profit juridical persons (eg housing cooperatives). Upon closer inspection, however, it was clear that regulated rents found a much wider application, since according to article 56 LRU they also applied to all leases created on the basis of administrative decisions or other types of public allocation of dwellings, even when the leased dwellings were owned by private persons.[57] In article 56 section 2 LRU it was further specified that regulated rents in dwellings owned by private, physical persons were to be freed after 31 December 2004, but in dwellings owned by private, juridical persons no such time-limit was introduced (article 57 LRU).[58] Moreover, all fixed-term leases created on the basis of administrative decisions or other types of public allocation of dwellings were transformed into open ended leases upon the entry into force of LRU, which meant that terminating the lease was very difficult for the landlord and limited to particular situations indicated in LRU. This left little scope to introduce freely negotiated rents, that could apply only to newly concluded leases in the very limited, vacant private housing stock.[59]

The exact level of regulated rents was to be determined by each commune; however it could not annually exceed three per cent of the unit's reconstruction value (article 25 section 2 LRU). It was assumed that rents at three per cent of the unit's reconstruction value annually would cover the complete costs of necessary maintenance and repairs of buildings (the so-called cost rent). The problem was that it specified the highest permitted level of controlled rent, but not the lowest one. In particular, the commune was not obliged to ensure that regulated rents set below the admissible three per cent did in fact cover the costs of maintenance and repairs (this was not a factor listed in article 26 LRU). Consequently, private owners stuck with tenants from the previous political era had to charge regulated rents that were far from the level of cost rents, even though from 1995 onwards regulated rents did increase significantly when compared to the pre-1995 levels.[60]

The situation was excessively onerous for private owners who were burdened with various public law obligations to maintain their buildings in a safe and habitable condition but were deprived of an adequate rental

[57] Wojciech Chrościelewski and Jan Pawel Tarno, 'Elementy administracyjno-prawne najmu lokali mieszkalnych oraz dodatki mieszkaniowe' ['Administrative elements of residential leases and housing benefits'] (1995) 9 *Samorząd Terytorialny* 62, 66.

[58] See Malgorzata Podrecka, 'Ograniczenia zasady swobody umów w ustawie o najmie lokali mieszkalnych i dodatkach mieszkaniowych' ['Restrictions on the freedom of contracting in the act on leases of residential dwellings and housing benefits'] (1996) 1 *Przegląd Sądowy* 21, 21 et seq.

[59] Zbigniew Radwański and Jamoma Panowicz-Lipska, *Zobowiązania—część szczególowa* [*The law of obligations—the nominate contracts part*] (Warszawa, CH Beck, 1996) 122–23.

[60] See also Hegedus and Tosics (n 52 above) 663–66.

income. In effect the Polish Constitutional Tribunal was faced with the dilemma of deciding whether article 56 section 2 LRU, in connection with articles 25 and 26 LRU, violated the PC provisions concerning the protection of ownership.[61]

The Constitutional Tribunal in an extensive justification to its judgment of 2000,[62] noted that most communes set the levels of regulated rents at an average of 1.3 per cent of the unit's reconstruction value annually and thus ensured covering only about 60 per cent of the costs of upkeep of residential buildings. The remaining costs not covered by rental income had to be borne by private owners exclusively. Therefore regulated rents were being enforced solely at their expense. Moreover, such rents applied to approximately 600,000 dwellings in privately owned buildings, so the scale of the phenomenon was significant. The Constitutional Tribunal continued to explain that the need to protect tenants by regulating rents within the 10-year period specified in LRU (until the end of 2004) was justified by the fact that an immediate adjustment of rents to market levels would leave many without a home and cause great social harm; however this in itself did not denote that the costs of protecting the tenants should be borne solely by private owners of residential buildings. The Constitutional Tribunal held that article 56 section 2 LRU, in connection with articles 25 and 26 LRU, violated article 64 section 3 PC as well as article 1 Protocol 1 ECHR. The loss of its binding force, effectively meaning that private housing stock will not be subject to regulated rents, was postponed until 11 July 2001 in order to give the legislator time to introduce solutions compatible with articles 21, 64 section 3, and 31 section 3 PC, as well with article 75 section 2 PC, where it is stipulated that the protection of the rights of tenants shall be established by statute.

V. INTRODUCING PROVISIONS ON INCREASES OF REGULATED AND MARKET RENTS

The solutions that were aimed at executing the requirements set out by the Constitutional Tribunal in the 2000 judgment were introduced in the TPA, which superseded the LRU; however provisions on the admissible levels of rent in the private housing stock remained controversial. Firstly, since according to article 56 section 2 LRU, regulated rents in the private housing stock were to apply until the end of 2004, the legislator wished to protect tenants from arbitrary and unlimited increases in rent after the entry into

[61] Article 21 PC: The Republic of Poland protects ownership and the right to inherit (s. 1). Expropriation is allowed only for public purposes and with just compensation (s. 2).

[62] P11/98, OTK 2000/1/3.

force of the Constitutional Tribunal's judgment on 11 July 2001. Therefore in article 28 section 2 TPA it was decided that regulated rents in leases concluded before the entry into force of TPA (on 21 June 2001) could not be increased above three per cent of the unit's reconstruction value annually before 31 December 2004. This meant that from 1 January 2005 all rents in the private housing stock would be freely negotiated market rents; however, this would apply only to new leases concluded after that date. It must also be noted that excessively high rents may be opposed by the tenant on the basis of general civil code provisions on the creation and performance of contracts.

Rents in the public sector are now referred to as limited rents, because they are no longer subject to the requirement of not exceeding three per cent of the unit's reconstruction value, but should be consistent with the commune's policy (which takes the form of a resolution) on rent levels (article 8 TPA). These policies should differentiate rent levels, taking into account at least the following factors: the building's location, the dwelling's location within the building, the building's state of repair, the available facilities and installed equipment available in the building and in the dwelling (article 7 section 1). However, rent levels for the so-called social dwellings cannot exceed half of the lowest level of rent within a given commune's housing stock (article 23 section 4 TPA).

Rents in SHA buildings are also limited because they are calculated so that the aggregate of rental incomes in the Association covers maintenance and repair costs of the building, as well as the repayment of the preferential loan utilised for the building's construction. In any event, the rent cannot exceed in a single year four or five per cent of the unit's reconstruction value (article 28 of the Act of 26 October on particular forms of supporting residential construction).[63]

Secondly, when TPA entered into force in 2001, a separate provision (article 9 section 3 TPA) regulated the possibility to review and raise rents. This provision was of paramount importance, as it concerned sitting tenants who paid rents not exceeding the mentioned three per cent of the unit's reconstruction value annually. Rent reviews could not be effected more often than once every six months and the rise could not exceed levels calculated with reference to three factors, namely: the level of inflation, the unit's reconstruction value, and the rent that was actually being paid. In practice this denoted that raising rents to at least the cost level would take an unreasonable amount of time, because the starting point of increases was the very low regulated rents, and inflation levels were also steadily falling.[64] It was calculated that at the rate permitted by TPA, obtaining cost rents from

[63] Consolidated version: Journal of Statutes 2000, no. 98, item 1070 as amended.
[64] Panowicz-Lipska (n 55 above) 108–9.

tenants who were still within the regulated rent regime could take up from 100–200 years(!).[65] Similarly, landlords who were able to conclude new leases with market rents would not be able to sustain a fair yield, because the allowed increases in rents were too low to maintain a satisfactory level of yield.[66]

It was only a question of time before the Constitutional Tribunal was faced with an application by the Polish Human Rights Defender (Ombudsman) who questioned the constitutionality of article 9 section 3 TPA in relation to the requirement that limitation of property rights had to be proportional to the goal that was to be achieved (article 31 section 3 PC). In a judgment of 2002[67] the Constitutional Tribunal noted that article 9 section 3 TPA was unconstitutional as it introduced restrictions so onerous for landlords that they could not be reconciled with the proportionality principle required for restrictions of property rights. In addition, it was emphasised that the unfavourable conditions for increasing rents effectively meant that even after the conclusion of the 10-year protective period of tenants with regulated rents (end of 2004), the landlord could not attain a cost rent for the property in his/her lifetime, because rent increases would be made from the very low level of regulated rent and at a very low rate, particularly with steadily decreasing inflation rates.

Consequently, for the majority of landlords abolishing regulated rents in 2001 occurred only on paper, as tenancies created in the previous political and economic system continued and could not be easily terminated, and rises in rent were so limited that not even cost rents could be attained. Furthermore, the Constitutional Tribunal noted that the legislator was allowing an unwarranted discrimination among landlords, because those with regulated rent tenants were in a worse situation than those with newly concluded leases. This compelled the Constitutional Tribunal to conclude that there was an unconstitutional limitation of property rights, and article 9 section 3 TPA lost its binding force on 10 October 2002. Consequently, tenants with regulated rents faced rent reviews, which until the end of 2004 could not increase the rent above three per cent annually of the dwelling's reconstruction value (article 28 section 2 TPA), but allowed landlords to at least collect a cost rent.

New regulations concerning rent increases were enacted on 12 and 22 December 2004[68] and entered into force on 1 January 2005. The rule

[65] Krzytof Dybowski, 'Ustawa o ochronie praw lokatorów na tle wcześniejszych uregulowań' ['The Act on the protection of tenants' rights in the context of previous regulations'] (2001) 11 *Państwo I Prawo* 52, 59.

[66] Miroslaw Nazar, 'Ochrona praw lokatorów. Cz. I' ['The protection of rights of tenants. Part one'] (2001) 19 *Monitor Prawniczy* 960, 966.

[67] K 48/01, OTK-A 2002/5/62.

[68] Journal of Statutes 2004, no. 281, items 2783 and 2786.

that rents cannot be reviewed more often than once every six months was maintained; however, a new solution was adopted concerning the level of admissible rent increases. For rents exceeding three per cent annually of the dwelling's reconstruction value, the increase could not raise the rent by more than 10 per cent annually of the rent paid before the rent review (article 9 section 1 TPA). The same rule applied if as a result of the rise, the reviewed rent would exceed the mentioned three per cent (article 9 section 1a TPA). However, if rent increases did not raise the rent to the mentioned level of three per cent, they could exceed 10 per cent of the rent paid before the review.

These new restrictions in rent increases were questioned by the General Prosecutor who made an application to the Constitutional Tribunal, claiming that article 9 sections 1 and 1a violated provisions of the Polish Constitution which ensured the protection of proprietary rights and allowed their limitation only if the proportionality rule was observed (article 31 section 3, article 64 sections 1 and 2 PC). Among other issues, the General Prosecutor emphasised that restrictions on rent increases arbitrarily limited proprietary rights of landlords and in fact did not achieve a socially justified aim. The protection of tenants from excessive rent increases was not aimed at those tenants who in fact had financial difficulties, but encompassed all tenants regardless of their financial status. The application was supported in its entirety by the Polish Association of Real Estate Owners, which also pointed out that the introduced mechanisms of calculating rent increases were completely removed from economic and financial realities of the market.

In its judgment of 2005[69] the Constitutional Tribunal explained that the public allocation of dwellings prevalent for almost 40 years before the shift to a market economy had brought about a serious pathology on the rental market. Reversing its negative effects would require a careful balancing of the rights of tenants and landlords; however the latter have been consistently neglected by the Polish legislator. The Tribunal stipulated that managing the housing market is a difficult task because of the inherent social aspect; however, neither a completely market-driven policy nor a restrictive rental policy within the private sector, were acceptable solutions. It was noted that rent levels and their increases are of particular importance because they often determine whether the proprietary rights of landlords and the housing rights of tenants are adequately protected. The evolution of provisions on the protection of tenants demonstrate that the legislator, although moving in the right direction, unnecessarily continued various forms of rent or rent review restrictions, which were subsequently held to be unconstitutional by the Constitutional Tribunal.

[69] K 4/05, OTK-A 2005/4/37.

However, in the present situation an additional factor required consideration, as based on the development of tenant protection provisions, citizens had the right to be convinced that from 1 January 2005 onwards (the end of the tenants' 10-year transition period, first stipulated in the 1994 LRU) rents and their reviews would be subject to the freedom of contract. Meanwhile, provisions introduced at that time created new restrictions preventing regulated rents from being adjusted to market level. This violated the principle of the democratic state ruled by law and implementing the principles of social justice (article 2 PC). Finally, the Constitutional Tribunal made reference to case law of the European Court of Human Rights (ECtHR), namely *Mellacher and Others v Austria*;[70] *Hutten-Czapska v Poland*,[71] where it was emphasised that control mechanisms would amount to the violation of article 1 Protocol 1 of the European Convention on Human Rights if the entire or substantial burden of achieving social housing policies were placed on landlords.

Another Constitutional Tribunal judgment was issued in 2006[72] and further provisions of the TPA concerning rent reviews were held to be unconstitutional and lost their binding force. Their unconstitutionality was in part due to their obscurity, leading to their various application by courts and subsequently to legal uncertainty. In part it was also due to the fact that the objectives and conditions for introducing provisions on rent reviews set out in the Constitutional Tribunal judgment from the previous year had again not been adequately reflected in the legislation.

Currently, after years of struggling to remove restrictions on rent levels that were unnecessary and inconsistent with both the PC and the ECHR, rent increases are subject to the following control mechanism. Firstly, according to article 9 section 1b TPA, rent increases cannot be introduced more often than once every six months. Secondly, the notice should be made in writing at least three months in advance, at the end of a calendar month (article 8a sections 1 and 2). Finally, an increase of the yearly rent above three per cent annually of the dwelling's reconstruction value must be justified by conditions set out in article 8a section 4a TPA. These conditions are defined as situations in which the owner's profits from rent do not cover the costs of maintaining the dwelling, as well as the return of capital and the return on capital. If the above are not being achieved, the landlord may increase the rent so that with respect to the recovery of capital he receives annually no more than 1.5 per cent return of the capital invested to construct or purchase a dwelling or no more than 10 per cent return of capital on an investment permanently upgrading the dwelling and increasing its use value.

[70] *Mellacher and Others v Austria*, Application nos. 10522/83; 11011/84; 11070/84.
[71] *Hutten-Czapska v Poland*, Application no. 35014/97 (ECtHR, 19 June 2006).
[72] K 33/05, OTK-A 2006/5/57.

In addition, the landlord is entitled to a fair return on capital, for which the legislator does not provide a particular percentage rate (article 8a section 4b TPA), so in cases of disputes this is decided depending on the facts of a given case.[73] In any event, a rent increase is always justified if its yearly rate does not exceed the yearly rate of inflation announced for the previous year (article 8a section 4e).

A tenant may demand that the landlord presents a calculation of the rent increase in writing (article 8a section 4 sentence 2), which entails explaining and mathematically showing how the new level of rent was determined.[74] Tenants dissatisfied with the rent increase may bring an action to court demanding a decision on whether the increase is or is not justified; however the burden of proving that an increase was made in accordance with the above TPA rules is placed on the landlord (article 8a section 5, point 2 TPA).

The above regulation on rent increases has been in force since 1 January 2007 and it seems that the legislator has finally managed not to violate the proprietary interests of landlords and at the same afford tenants predictable and justified rent increases that may be reviewed by courts. The proportionality principle has been observed and the Constitutional Tribunal has concluded in a judgment of 2012[75] that rent increases connected with TPA rates of return of and on capital are consistent with the PC.[76] Consequently, the requirements indicated by the Constitutional Tribunal in its previous judgments (see above) have been properly accounted for in legislation.[77]

VI. ECTHR EVALUATION OF TENANCY LAW RESTRICTIONS

The development of Polish tenancy law after the 1990s reforms was a long process, during which, as has been shown above with respect to rents, the legislator had great difficulty in attaining a balanced protection of the rights of tenants as well as of the owners. The need to achieve a proper balance

[73] Katarzyna Zdun-Załęska, *Ustawa o ochronie praw lokatorów, mieszkaniowym zasobie gminy I o zmianie kodeksu cywilnego. Komentarz* [*The act on the protection of tenants, the residential housing stock and the amendment of the civil code. A Commentary*] (Warszawa, Lexis Nexis, 2014) 88.

[74] See Supreme Court resolution of 5 February 2010, III CZP 130/09, OSNC 2010/7-8/109; Malgorzata Łoboz, 'Umowne formy korzystania z nieruchomości—najwazniejsze umowy' ['Contractual forms of using real estate—the most relevant contracts'] in Barbara Baran (ed), *Nieruchomości. Zagadnienia prawne I zarząd* (Warszawa, Wolters Kluwer, 2014) 294.

[75] SK 25/09, OTK-A 2012/1/1.

[76] Adam Doliwa, *Najem lokali. Komentarz* ['*Leases of units. A commentary*'] (Warszawa, CH Beck 2014) 276.

[77] See Karolina Wyrwińska, 'Komentarz do zmiany art 8a ustawy o ochronie praw lokatorów, mieszkaniowym zasobie gminy i zmiany kodeksu cywilnego' ['Commentary to the amendment of art. 8a of the act on the protection of tenants, the residential housing stock and the amendment of the civil code'] (LEX Publishing House, 2007).

and protection of rights was furthered by the fact that in 1991 Poland joined the Council of Europe and on that same day signed the ECHR.

Consequently, the Polish legislator was not only faced with the task of removing the remnants of the previous political system from the law but also had to reflect the standards of human rights protection guarded by the Council of Europe through the ECHR. It is not surprising that with the collapse of Soviet domination over Central and Easter European countries and the subsequent membership of these countries in the Council of Europe, the ECtHR experienced a new wave of applications.[78] These included ones submitted by Polish citizens who had difficulty in regaining possession of their immovables or at least securing a justified income from their ownership, due to sitting tenants, regulated rents, restricted rent increases and multiple requirements concerning evictions.[79] Simultaneously, access to the ECtHR denoted a real possibility to execute the newly binding human rights standards of international law, because all aggrieved citizens gained direct access to the Court. They were able to obtain a verdict resolving an individual case and providing a concrete outcome that had to be executed by the country violating the ECHR.[80]

With respect to Polish tenancy law, in *Schrimer v Poland*[81] the ECtHR explained that the lengthy process of relaxing the restrictive regulations of residential leases which had been in force for a period of almost 50 years was a very difficult transition and posed many challenges for attaining a balance of rights. Nevertheless, despite the enormity of the task, the legislator cannot be held exempt from obligations derived from the ECHR and its Protocols.[82] Although the control of use of property is quite common in the field of housing due to its social and economic implications, a fair balance between the general interest of the community and the requirements of protecting fundamental rights of an individual must be achieved.[83] The Court concluded that the legislator while drafting LRU put too much emphasis

[78] See Ed Bates, *The Evolution of the European Convention on Human Rights—from its Inception to the Creation of a Permanent Court of Human Rights* (Oxford, Oxford University Press 2010) 445 et seq.

[79] See also Jan Sztombka, 'Eksmisja z lokalu mieszkalnego na tle ustawy o najmie lokali mieszkalnych i dodatkach mieszkaniowych' ['Eviction from a dwelling on the basis of the act on leases of residential units and housing benefits'] (1996) 6 *Przegląd Sądowy* 3, 3 et seq; Z Merchel, 'Praktyczna realizacja orzeczeń sądowych o eksmisji po wejściu w życie ustawy o najmie lokali i o dodatkach mieszkaniowych' ['Practical implementation of court judgments on eviction after the entry into force of the act on leases of residential units and housing benefits'] (1996) 16 *Problemy Egzekucji Sądowej* 53, 53 et seq; Zenon Knypl, 'Eksmisja. Aktualny stan prawny' ['Eviction. The contemporary legal status'] (2001) 14 *Problemy Egzekucji* 5, 5 et seq.

[80] Malgorzata Bednarek, *Prawo do mieszkania w konstytucji i ustawodawstwie* [*The right to housing in the constitution and legislation*] (Warszawa, Wolters Kluwer, 2007) 59.

[81] *Schrimer v Poland*, Application no. 68880/01 (21 September 2004), (2005) 40 EHRR 47.

[82] Ibid, [38].

[83] Ibid, [34]–[35].

on the rights of tenants while almost completely overlooking those of the owners.[84] As a consequence, owners had to bear an individual and excessive burden that disrupted the aforementioned balance, and thus article 1 Protocol 1 ECHR had been violated.

In the case mentioned above the applicants complained about the interference with the right of peaceful enjoyment of possessions, because as landlords they were unable to evict a tenant from their building under the LRU regulations, although an alternative flat was offered to the tenant. Polish courts relied on a very literal interpretation of the provisions in force, requiring the landlords to be owners of the offered, alternative flat. The landlords held a lesser right, which was a right in rem, effective *erga omnes*, unlimited in time, hereditary, and transferrable, so in essence it was not very different from ownership and unquestionably offered the tenant security of accommodation. Polish courts refused to issue an eviction order, but the ECtHR questioned the literal, although completely legal, interpretation of LRU, pointing out that it placed an excessive burden on the applicants. The excessiveness was caused not only by the fact that the tenant remained in the flat, but also by the fact that the tenant was entitled to continue paying a regulated rent and his tenancy was automatically transformed into an open ended lease when LRU came into force.

It is important to emphasise that in cases concerning the violation of article 1 Protocol 1 ECHR, it is not unusual for the ECtHR to find that the law in force has been correctly applied by national courts and that the questioned provision does not in itself violate the Convention. Frequently it is the lack of proportionality between the employed means and the aim to be realised that results in a violation of the ECHR. This proportionality requirement has perhaps been most clearly characterised in *James and Others v United Kingdom*.[85]

Since a fair balance must be achieved between the general interest and the protection of an individual's fundamental rights, judgments of the ECtHR should be viewed from an individual, case-specific perspective, because proportionality must always be assessed *in casu*.[86]

The case of *Mellacher and Others v Austria*[87] is an example of the fact that rent-control mechanisms imposed by the state are not always classified as violations of the ECHR. In this case, tenants of the applicants benefitted from the possibility to demand a reduction of previously set, freely negotiated rents. Their requests to decrease rent resulted from new legislation (the Rent Act 1981) which set fixed rent limits per square meter and

[84] Ibid, [43].

[85] *James and Others v United Kingdom*, Application no. 8793/79 (21 February 1986) A Series no 98.

[86] Bednarek (n 80 above) 67.

[87] *Mellacher and Others v Austria* (n 70).

could also be applied to leases concluded before its entry into force. The Government explained that the reason for introducing new legislation was to reduce great disparities in rent levels among equivalent apartments, decrease property speculation, and make apartments more available to less affluent members of the society. In addition, maximum rents were also meant as an incentive to modernise and improve old apartments thus enabling the owners to charge higher levels of maximum rents.[88]

The ECtHR held that article 1 Protocol 1 ECHR does not preclude the legislature from interfering with existing contracts, if the aim of the interference and the proportionality of the interference satisfy the conditions resulting from the mentioned provision.[89] The ECtHR did not find that there had been a violation of article 1 Protocol 1 ECHR because the aims to be achieved were focused on striking a fair balance between the general interests of the community and the individual interests of landlords (owners of property). The means were assessed to be proportional to the identified aims, particularly since rents were not decreased automatically but only upon the request of the tenant who had to file a special application to a public authority. The maximum rents were set in a manner which allowed owners to cover the maintenance costs of apartments. The lower the standard of the apartment, the lower were its maintenance costs and thus rents should be set accordingly.[90] The above position was adopted by the ECtHR despite the fact that the Mellacher applicants under the new legislation were receiving rent that was only 17.6 per cent of the previously negotiated contract rent. It seems that the Court agreed that the previous high rent levels were socially unacceptable, particularly for low standard apartments, like the ones owned by the applicants.

In a more recent case of *Bitto and Others v Slovakia*[91] the applicants complained of continued rent regulation in flats that were restored to them after the 1990s reforms. The problem consisted of the fact that flats restored to the owners had sitting tenants who continued to pay regulated rents, whose tenancies were practically impossible to terminate and who were the only ones entitled to buy the flat in case of its sale. The regulated rents received by landlords were not high enough to cover maintenance costs and were considerably lower than rents for similar flats to which rent control did not apply.[92] Although the Slovakian Government intended this to be a temporary situation and initially planned to bring rents up to the level which covered the landlord's costs as in 1995, these promises were not fulfilled.

[88] Ibid, [47].
[89] Ibid, [50].
[90] Ibid, [53], [55].
[91] *Bitto and Others v Slovakia*, Application no. 30255/09 (judgment of 28 January 2014, became final on 28 April 2014).
[92] Ibid, [12], [13], [18].

The applicants alleged violation of article 1 (second paragraph) Protocol 1 ECHR (control of use of the property).

The ECtHR examined whether the interference with property was lawful, pursued a legitimate aim in the general interest, and struck a fair balance. Unsurprisingly, the Court did find that the Government pursued a legitimate, social policy aim concerning housing, however there were visible shortcomings in implementing programmes that were to abolish the rent regulation scheme. In particular, rent increases of regulated rent were also controlled and landlords could not cover maintenance costs or receive a fair profit. As a consequence, the Court noted that the Government was obliged not only to protect the social interests of the tenants, who had to be given time to adjust to the new market situation, but also to protect private property rights, including those that had been restored to their previous holders. The continuing rent regulation did not fulfil these objectives. The social and financial burden of the transformation period was in fact placed on only one social group, ie the landlords, and therefore a fair balance between the general interest of the community and the property rights of the applicants was not achieved.[93]

Similar findings were made by the ECtHR in the case of *Anthony Aquilina v Malta*.[94] The applicant complained that restrictions on rent levels, increases of rent, and the possibility to terminate a lease that were introduced in 1979 and applied to leases concluded in market conditions before that time violated article 1 Protocol 1 ECHR. The new law deprived owners of a realistic possibility of resuming possession of property (the practical impossibility to terminate a lease) and of raising rent in accordance with market conditions.[95] Although the stringent tenancy law was subsequently liberalised in 1995, it applied only to newly concluded leases. The 2009 and 2010 amendments of tenancy law were intended to remove some restrictions applicable to the pre-1995 leases, however their interpretation and application to many of these leases was legally questionable and difficult to implement in practice.

The ECtHR confirmed the wide margin of appreciation given to state legislatures when deciding on implementing a social policy, particularly one connected with housing. However, in the present case it seems that the court was not entirely convinced that there had been a legitimate social aim in the first place. The Court noted that even if this was so in 1979, three decades later those aims might no longer be justified by the existent social situation.[96] In conclusion the Court held that a fair balance between the

[93] Ibid, [113]–[116].
[94] *Anthony Aquilina v Malta*, Application no. 3851/12 (judgment of 11 December 2014).
[95] Ibid, [30].
[96] Ibid, [56]–[57].

general interest and the protection of individual property rights had not been struck, particularly when one took into account the joint effect of controlled rent, uncertainty as to the possibility of recovering possession, lack of procedural safeguards in the application of law and finally the changed social situation, which showed not only the significant increase of living standards of Maltese residents but also many vacancies in rental flats.[97]

VII. THE *HUTTEN-CZAPSKA* v *POLAND* PILOT JUDGMENT

A pivotal case for Polish tenancy law was the case of *Hutten-Czapska v Poland*,[98] which was initially lodged with the European Commission of Human Rights on December 1994. The applicant was a French national of Polish origin who owned a house and a plot of land in Gdynia, a city located on the coast in the North of Poland. The application concerned restrictive tenancy laws discussed above.

The facts of the case were representative of the situation of the vast majority of private landlords in Poland. During World War II, Ms Hutten-Czapska's house was occupied by the German army and from May 1945 by the Soviet Army. In that same year a first-floor flat was allocated to a tenant through an administrative decision. In 1975 the ground-floor flat was allocated to a tenant through an administrative decision on the basis of a lease for an unfixed period of time. A third flat in the house was also appointed a tenant. In 1998, the lease of the first-floor flat was held to be acquired by the relative of the initial tenant. In 1990 the management of the house was restored to the applicant by the Mayor of Gdynia. Shortly after that date the applicant instigated court procedures to evict the tenants and relocate them to municipal flats as well as to receive compensation for being deprived of her property since the end of WWII. After completing the court procedures before Polish courts, in the final judgment it was declared that the 1994 LRU did not place any obligation on the municipality to remove tenants from private houses and relocate them to municipal buildings. In addition the court held that the defendant municipality could not be held liable for laws that were in force in the period after WWII until the 1990s. The applicant also instigated administrative proceedings in which it was found that some of the administrative decisions before 1990 concerning the allocation of tenants were in fact unlawful, however due to the lapse of time they could not be annulled or the administrative proceedings could not be reopened. Two flats in the applicant's house became vacant in 2003 and 2004 respectively, while the last flat was vacated in 2006.

[97] Ibid, [66]–[67].
[98] *Hutten-Czapska v Poland*, Application no. 35014/97, Grand Chamber judgment of 19 June 2006, 2006-VIII GC.

The first ECtHR judgment in the case was delivered in 2005.[99] The Court observed that it was competent to consider only the period from 10 October 1994, ie the date Poland ratified Protocol No 1 of ECHR.[100] The court noted that the rent-control scheme in Poland was a result of many historical events and the resulting, acute shortage of dwellings. Initially implemented legislation was to protect tenants in the transition period from state-controlled rent to a fully negotiated contractual rent. This legislation was therefore viewed as having a legitimate aim in the general interest.[101]

However, when assessing the impact of the rent-control scheme on the applicant's right of property and the three different laws applicable, namely: the 1994 LRU, the 2001 TPA and its December 2004 amendments (see above), the Court found that there was a systemic problem in the Polish legislation. Its malfunctioning was connected with the continuing restrictions on rent increases which made it impossible for private landlords to even cover the costs of property maintenance. These structural deficiencies of the law had continued despite Polish Constitutional Tribunal judgments (see above) in which the legislator was, time and time again, made aware of the necessity to strike a balance between the rights of tenants and landlords/ owners of property. Consequently, the ECtHR held that there had been a violation of article 1 Protocol 1 ECHR because the authorities had imposed a disproportionate and excessive burden on the applicant, which could not be justified by any legitimate interest of the community.

In addition, the Court recognised that the case had far-reaching consequences, as according to information supplied by the Government, there were approximately 100,000 landlords affected by the restrictive tenancy law that was complained of by the applicant, and between 600,000 and 900,000 tenants in Poland have taken advantage of the intense protection of tenants.[102] For this reason, the Court decided that due to the identified, continuing deficiencies of the legal system which violate the ECHR and its Protocols it was not sufficient to merely resolve the case with respect to the applicant, particularly since potentially hundreds of 'clone' cases might be brought before the ECtHR. The Court decided to resort to article 46 ECHR, having already set a precedent of delivering the so-called pilot judgment[103] in *Broniowski v Poland*,[104] and obliged Poland to definitely end the systemic

[99] *Hutten-Czapska v Poland*, Application no. 35014/97 (ECtHR, 22 February 2005), [2005] 19 BHRC 373.

[100] *Hutten-Czapska v Poland* (n 99 above) [140].

[101] Ibid, [160].

[102] Ibid, [141].

[103] See Philip Leach, 'Tackling systemic human rights violations—the role of Pilot Judgments' in *Pilot Judgment Procedure in the European Court of Human Rights and the Future Development of Human Rights' Standards and Procedures. Third Informal Seminar for Government Agents and Other Institutions* (Warsawa, Kontrast, 2009) 23 et seq.

[104] *Broniowski v Poland*, Application no. 31443/96, ECtHR judgment of 22 June 2004, ECHR 2004-V, [2004] ECHR 274.

violation of the ECHR. Poland was to adopt appropriate legal or other measures, which will allow landlords to collect a reasonable level of rent or will provide them with other reimbursement mechanisms which mitigate the consequences of regulated rents and restricted rent increases. Poland was thus specifically required to take general measurers necessary to achieve compliance of its law with the ECHR, which confirmed the significant role of the ECtHR in securing the proper and actual implementation of human rights.[105]

Upon the request of the Polish Government the case was referred to the Grand Chamber. The Grand Chamber meticulously analysed the historical development of housing policies and tenancy law in Poland, the relevant legal provisions, as well as the Polish Constitutional Tribunal judgments relating to tenant protection law and its incompatibility with the Polish Constitution and the ECHR. It confirmed the findings of the Chamber that rent-control mechanisms linked with other defective provisions of tenancy law produced an unacceptable violation of the ECHR, and the Polish Government was unable to prove that landlords were supported by subsidies or that other ways to offset their costs of property maintenance not covered by rent levels were made available to them. Moreover it was also emphasised that the rule of law and the citizens' confidence in the state had been jeopardised, as the promised end of regulated rents by 2005 was in fact substituted by restrictions on rent increases which effectively maintained low levels of controlled rents.[106]

The Grand Chamber also rejected the Polish Government's objection to the application of the pilot judgment procedure and pointed out that, contrary to what the Polish Government was arguing, the Constitutional Tribunal (CT) judgment of 19 April 2005 was not in itself enough to bring Polish legislation in line with Convention standards.[107] The final holding of the Grand Chamber coincided with the one of the Chamber and a violation of article 1 Protocol 1 ECHR was identified. In addition, Poland was obliged to remove the systemic violation by implementing adequate legislation and/or other measures, and a settlement was agreed in 2008.

As has already been noted, regulated rents were always intended to be a temporary measure necessary in the transition period and were to be abolished after the 10-year tenants' protection period (on 1 January 2005). In reality this was not the case and it coincided with the ECtHR judgment of 2005 in the *Hutten-Czapska* case. P Styczeń, the Deputy Polish Minister of Infrastructure in the years 2008–2013, pointed out that had the rent

[105] Christian Tomuschat, *Human Rights: Between Idealism and Realism* (Oxford, Oxford University Press, 2014) 291–92.

[106] *Broniowski v Poland* (n 104 above) [223]–[225].

[107] Ibid, [237].

restrictions been effectively removed in 2005 as promised, it is very probable that Poland's temporary measures would have been assessed as justified and proportionate to the goal that was to be achieved. However, due to misconceived political decisions to continue the protection of tenants at the sole expense of private landlords (a fact pointed out by the Polish CT in its numerous judgments mentioned in this chapter) Poland was held to be liable not only for the post 1 January 2005 violations, but also for ones during the 10-year transition period.[108]

The above makes it plausible to conclude that the ECtHR pilot case greatly influenced the shape of Polish tenancy law and accelerated its compliance with the ECHR. Judging from earlier endeavours of the Polish legislator, it could have taken a number of years and judgments of the CT before a solution that afforded protection to both tenants and private landlords was adopted in the TPA. It seems that politicians found it easier to place the burden of the reform on private landlords rather than to find a fair and balanced solution. The latter was risky from a political point of view, as there were more tenants which continued to benefit from the old regime than there were landlords.

VIII. CONCLUSIONS

This chapter focused on two distinct, but interconnected issues, namely: the housing situation in Poland and the unnecessarily difficult and lengthy road to enacting laws which protect tenants but do not violate the property interests of landlords. Its aim was to consider these issues in the context of precarisation of home, as it was argued that the lack of a long-term housing policy has resulted in the reluctance to implement fair and balanced tenancy laws, thus limiting the application of this instrument on the housing market. In order to avoid the cost of providing social housing and other alternatives to owner-occupation it was easier for the government to place the social and financial burden on landlords, claiming that it was a necessary measure in the transition period of the 1990s. In effect, enacted legal provisions on tenancy law, in particular on rent levels and rent reviews, violated not only the national constitution but also the ECHR. For many years this stigmatised the private rental sector, often leading to the conclusion of informal contracts which greatly undermined the tenant's security. Precarisation of home occurred because stigmatising the residential lease effectively

[108] Pitor Styczeń, 'Polish experience of the pilot procedurę and implementation of the judgment in the case of Hutten-Czapska against Poland—an example of specific non-compensatory redress' in *Pilot Judgment Procedure in the European Court of Human Rights and the Future Development of Human Rights' Standards and Procedures. Third Informal Seminar for Government Agents and Other Institutions* (Warsaw, Kontrast, 2009) 82.

eliminated it as a flexible instrument of satisfying housing needs. A policy of intense state intervention and overregulation in the interest of only the tenant paradoxically harmed prospective tenants by reducing the choice on the market and the access to residential leases. The incorrect application of the principles of the rule of law and the social state, unsurprisingly have led to undesirable consequences in one of the most socially sensitive areas—namely housing.[109]

It seems that if it were not for the *Hutten-Czapska* case, the Polish legislator would have continued to place an excessive burden on landlords for still some time, as this was easier than to tackle the question of a long-term, sustainable housing policy that caters for all social groups, including ones with low incomes. Unfortunately, as shown in sections II and III above, such a policy is still missing and apart from owner-occupation, political actors have no other suggestions on how to fill the housing gap, although the revival of the SHA programme is a welcomed improvement. Promoting ownership of homes for everyone is a very poignant political idea; however after the financial crisis and considering the difficulties in the labour market (precarisation of employment), advocating long-term loans to purchase dwellings, usually too small to fulfil households' needs, is not a socially responsible solution. Conversely, it encourages the precarisation of home by depriving citizens of necessary flexibility and choice on the housing market. It is a classic example of placing all eggs in one basket, instead of developing accessible, various ways of satisfying the housing needs of different social groups, limiting precarisation of home by offering more solutions that may be employed by various persons in varying circumstances.

Although the housing situation is unique in each country, most EU Member States face the same challenges, which include problems of renewing the housing stock, providing social housing, helping disadvantaged groups to enter the housing market and preventing social segregation in housing. It is important to remember that only long-term housing policies based on an in-depth understanding of economic and social factors enable drafting tenancy laws that satisfy the interests of both tenants and landlords and reduce the precarisation of home. The Polish example shows that the unwillingness to understand the housing market leads to political shortcuts that are reflected in legislation. The latter is subject to the scrutiny of the Constitutional Tribunal and the ECtHR, but it is little consolation to the aggrieved parties to find out after years of legal struggles that the legislator has made a wrong choice. Above all, in the long run it is not a strategy that will benefit the landlord, the tenant, or society.

[109] See Hamri Mostert, 'Landlessness, housing and the rule of law' in Hanri Mostert and Marius Johannes de Waal, *Essays in Honour of CG van der Merwe* (Lexis Nexis, Durban/Johannesburg/Cape Town, 2011) 78–79.

Part III

The Home and Governmental Precarisation

7

Law and the Precarious Home: A Case Study of Thermal Inefficiency in English Homes

HELEN CARR*

I. INTRODUCTION

ENGLISH HOMES APPEAR to be peculiarly susceptible to the characteristic cold and damp of the local climate.[1] This porousness to the weather impacts disproportionately on the poor and the vulnerable, and it has consequences. Annually, in England, there are around 25,000 deaths during December to March which exceed the average number over the rest of the year (described as excess winter deaths).[2] The energy inefficiency of English homes is a major factor in fuel poverty and, because domestic energy consumption accounts for about 27 per cent of England's carbon emissions, unless it is significantly reduced, England will fail to meet the 80 per cent reduction in 1990s emission levels by 2050 to which it is legally committed.[3] More recently the problem of inadequate thermal

* Kent Law School University of Kent. Email: h.p.carr@kent.ac.uk. The author is grateful for the comments of Nick Pisca and Professor Dave Cowan on earlier versions of this chapter.

[1] The chapter focuses on the regulation of thermal comfort in residential property in England rather than Britain, in recognition of the increasing divergence between housing law, poverty law and social policy in Scotland, Wales and England since the devolution settlements of 1999. See K McKee, J Muir, T Moore, 'Housing policy in the UK: the importance of spatial nuance' (2017) 32 *Housing Studies* 60.

[2] Office of National Statistics, Statistical Bulletin: *Excess winter mortality in England and Wales: 2015/16* (provisional) and 2014/15 (final), Published 23 November 2016: www.ons.gov.uk/peoplepopulationandcommunity/birthsdeathsandmarriages/deaths/bulletins/excesswintermortalityinenglandandwales/2015to2016provisionaland2014to2015final#main-points.

[3] The Climate Change Act 2008. See also the House of Commons Communities and Local Government Committee, *Existing Housing and Climate Change* (2007–08, HC 431-1); also see Department of Energy and Climate Change, *United Kingdom Housing Energy Factfile* (London, DECC, 2013). For further discussion of carbon emissions and poor quality housing see: John Hills, *Fuel Poverty Review Final Report: Getting the measure of fuel poverty (Case Report 72)* (London, DECC, 2012).

comfort has intensified; there is increasing evidence, particularly in England's urban areas, of the letting of accommodation not designed for human habitation either to the young temporary workers who take up property guardianship[4] or to the hyper-precarious undocumented migrant,[5] accommodated, for instance in 'beds in sheds'. There is one further twist, just as much a consequence of the contemporary intensification of urban living as the degradation of private rental accommodation, the problem of excess heat in the home, which it is suggested, might lead to a further 7000 excess deaths a year by the 2050s.[6]

The long-standing and serious nature of the thermal inefficiency of English housing—the excess winter death figures are the fourth worst in Europe and out of line with other northern European countries,[7] and at least 2.3 million households are currently estimated to be in fuel poverty[8]—together with its contemporary shifts, makes it a productive site from which to respond to Ettlinger's call to resist accounts of 'precarity' which seek to locate it within particular political projects and time frames and instead develop a more expansive view of precarity over time and across space.[9] The focus of this chapter therefore has a broader historical narrative, the slow, contested and highly contingent emergence of thermal inefficiency as a housing problem.

The chapter draws on the work of Jacobs *et al* who suggest that traditional accounts of housing are limited, presenting housing problems as self-evident and therefore minimising the role of power.[10] Their alternative is to problematise 'the historical processes whereby social problems emerge and develop their own life histories'.[11] They suggest that

> for a housing concern to become a problem demanding a policy response it will often ... entail a combination of adverse material circumstances experienced by people alongside a coalition of interest groups who are able to articulate concerns as a policy problem that will be taken seriously by decision-makers.[12]

[4] See Caroline Hunter and Jed Meers, 'The "Affordable Alternative to Renting": Property Guardians and Legal Dimensions of Precariousness' (Chapter four of this volume); Mara Ferreri, Gloria Dawson and Alexander Vasudevan, 'Living precariously: property guardianship and the flexible city' (2016) 42 *Transactions of the Institute of British Geographers* 153.

[5] Hannah Lewis, Peter Dwyer, Stuart Hodkinson and Louise Waite, 'Hyper-precarious lives: Migrants, work and forced labour in the Global North' (2015) 39 *Progress in Human Geography* 580.

[6] Committee on climate change, *Managing climate risks to well-being and the economy Adaptation Sub-Committee Progress Report* (2014): www.theccc.org.uk.

[7] JD Healy, 'Excess winter mortality in Europe: a cross country analysis identifying key risk factors' (2003) 57 *Journal of Epidemiology Community Health* 784.

[8] Department of Energy and Climate Change *Annual Fuel Poverty Statistics Report* (London, DECC, 2015).

[9] Nancy Ettlinger, 'Precarity Unbound' (2007) 32 *Alternatives* 319.

[10] Keith Jacobs, Jim Kemeny and Tony Manzi, 'Power, Discursive Space and Institutional Practices in the Construction of Housing Problems' (2003) 18 *Housing Studies* 429.

[11] ibid 430.

[12] ibid 432.

Their claim is that interrogating these factors serves to 'illuminate the interest and power dynamics that underlie housing problem formulation and give voice to alternative solutions'.[13]

I apply this approach to the emergence of thermal inefficiency as a housing 'problem'. I argue that thermal inefficiency provides an important case study of the construction of housing problems for a number of reasons. First, it is an endemic problem with serious consequences. Second, it is closely related to poverty, which means it becomes entangled in the long-standing tensions within English social policy between redistribution and disciplining fecklessness. Finally, its contingent emergence reveals significant power struggles with other areas of economic and social policy. Two areas in particular have proved important. First, the problematisation of domestic energy supplies and the slow move from the UK's domestic energy being supplied by publicly owned, monopoly-based industries to fully privatised provision. Second is the periodic encouragement of speedy house building in response to the chronic shortage of housing which appears to have been endemic in England since the urbanisation which followed the industrial revolution.

The chapter is divided into three further sections: Section II explores more fully the relationship between the problem of inadequate thermal comfort and precarity, both physical and ontological. Section III focuses on regulation and thermal efficiency, as it explains the privatisation of domestic energy supplies and the emergence of fuel poverty as critical drivers in the problematisation of thermal inefficiency. Section IV considers governmental techniques to increase housebuilding and homeownership, as well as critically evaluating a number of legal initiatives, such as building regulations which are designed to reduce thermal inefficiency.

II. THERMAL INEFFICIENCY AND PRECARITY

Medical evidence makes clear that everyone who lives in cold housing has a dramatically increased risk of cardio-vascular and respiratory morbidity, and winter mortality is particularly increased for the elderly.[14] Dampness is also exacerbated by cold housing. The most recent English Housing Survey reports that around one million English homes are affected by damp, predominantly condensation and mould growth, with homes in the private rented sector being disproportionately affected.[15] Although the impact of

[13] ibid 443.

[14] The Marmot Review Team, *The Health Effects of Cold Housing and Fuel Poverty* (London, Friends of the Earth, 2011).

[15] Department of Communities and Local Government, *English Housing Survey: Housing Stock Report 2008* (London, DCLG, 2010) 32.

damp on health is contested, the consensus of scientific opinion confirms that there is a significant association between damp housing and asthma and other respiratory problems, and provides some evidence of other health consequences.[16]

Cold and damp conditions are not the only cause of thermal precarity. Overheating in the home also has a significant physiological impact upon the body and can pose a risk to life.[17] During the 10-day heat wave in England in August 2003, when temperatures reached 37–38 °C in some areas, it is estimated that there were more than 2000 excess deaths, with mortality rates in London increasing by 42 per cent.

Of course, whilst all human bodies share vulnerability to extremes of temperature, as Lorey points out, this, 'shared precariousness is hierarchized and judged'.[18] There are two interlinked factors that increase vulnerability. First the physical condition of the occupiers, so the sick, the disabled, the young and the old are at greater risk, most particularly those who are confined to the home or who are socially isolated.[19] Second, the problem of cold homes is exacerbated when the people who live there cannot afford to heat them adequately, a phenomenon described as 'fuel poverty', a particular articulation of poverty which is discussed more fully below. Nor is vulnerability to thermal inefficiency evenly distributed. Statistics indicate that people living in buildings constructed with solid walls have a higher prevalence of fuel poverty compared to those living in buildings with cavity walls, people living in older and larger buildings have higher levels than people living in new-builds and smaller dwellings, and households with no boiler or a non-condensing boiler have higher levels compared to those with condensing boilers.[20] The level and depth of fuel poverty is also greater for households not connected to the gas grid which means that rural areas suffer particularly from fuel poverty. There are regional differences because of differences in the age of the housing stock, climatic conditions and relative income levels. The North East, Yorkshire and the Humber, West Midlands and the South West of England have the highest proportion of households in fuel poverty compared to the East and South East. Tenure also has an

[16] See for instance WJ Fisk, EA Eliseeva and MJ Mendell, 'Association of residential dampness and mold with respiratory tract infections and bronchitis: a meta-analysis' (2010) 9 *Environmental Health* 72; World Health Organization, *Guidelines for Indoor Air Quality: Dampness and Mould* (Copenhagen, WHO, 2009).

[17] Zero Carbon Hub, *Overheating in homes: An introduction for planners, designers and property owners* (Milton Keynes, Zero Caron Hub, 2017): http://www.zerocarbonhub.org/sites/default/files/resources/reports/Overheating_in_Homes.

[18] Isabell Lorey, *State of Insecurity Government of the Precarious* 2015 (Verso, 2015).

[19] Eric Klineberg, *Heat Wave: A Social Autopsy of Disaster in Chicago* (Chicago, University of Chicago Press, 2002) and see Ed Kirton-Darling, Chapter nine of this volume.

[20] Department of Energy and Climate Change, *Annual Fuel Poverty Statistics 2016* (Statistical Release, National Statistics, DECC, 2016).

impact; households living in private rented houses have the highest prevalence of fuel poverty whereas owner-occupied households have the lowest, although when owner-occupiers do suffer from fuel poverty, their fuel poverty is most acute.[21] Even within one tower block, thermal inefficiency can vary enormously, dependent upon, for instance, a flat's exposure to prevailing winds, the number of external walls, proximity to rubbish chutes, etc.[22]

Being cold makes people live differently. Qualitative research demonstrates the different ways in which 'precarious lives are segmented'.[23] Cold homes, for instance, increase social isolation. The Fuel Poverty Review interim report found that in the winter, householders

> would try to avoid leaving the house and getting cold, because they knew they would find it difficult to warm up again once they returned home. However, this does not appear to lead to social activities occurring within the home instead: 26 per cent of those reporting that their home was 'much colder' than desired also reported that they did not feel able to invite friends or family to their home.[24]

There are other behavioural changes. Ambrose's research into the experiences of energy inefficiency in the private rented sector in Hackney, London and Rotherham Yorkshire describes tenants

> keeping warm by routinely wearing coats and multiple layers inside the home, keeping blankets in the main living areas and spending extra time in bed or outside of the home ... It was also common practice to heat the home for very short periods in order to save money and to simply endure the cold thereafter.[25]

Other strategies to manage thermal comfort make clear that the ways in which people 'shun ideas of victimhood in favour of imaginaries of resourcefulness and expediency under adverse circumstance'[26] are not limited to a new 'precariat' shaped by neoliberal sensibilities. For instance prepayment meters that work to exacerbate fuel poverty because of high tariffs can be appreciated as this extract from Ambrose *et al* demonstrates,

> 'Yeah I like it, it were like that when I moved in but I didn't change in, I like to see where I am and see when I'm getting down to a few pounds and I can just pop some more on, that's not a problem.' (Sarah, Rotherham)[27]

[21] ibid 44.

[22] See Katie Bates, Laura Lane and Anne Power, *High Rise Hope The social implications of energy efficiency retrofit in large multi-storey blocks (Case Report 75)* (London, Centre for Analysis of Social Exclusion, London School of Economics, 2012).

[23] Lorey (n 18 above).

[24] John Hills, *Fuel Poverty Review Interim Report* (London, Centre for Analysis of Social Exclusion, London School of Economics, 2011).

[25] Aimee Ambrose, Lindsey McCarthy and James Pinder, *Energy (In)Efficiency: what tenants expect and endure in private rented housing* (Centre for Regional Economic and Social Research, 2016).

[26] Ferreri *et al* (n 4 above) 11.

[27] Ambrose *et al* (n 25 above) 20.

The researchers also note how in Rotherham in particular, 'a clear sense of stoicism was detectable with multiple references to the old maxim of "putting on another jumper"'.[28] Low expectations of keeping warm and the normalisation of discomfort combined with a pragmatic 'common sense' approach to problem-solving appear to be long-standing strategies in connection with fuel poverty.

Precarity consequent upon thermal inefficiency cannot be reduced to a straightforward binary divide, or summarised as a phenomenon experienced by the young and the urban. The chapter now turns to consider the first governmental power struggle I focus on, the struggle between the privatisation of domestic energy, which has had outcomes for the costs of energy, and the management of thermal efficiency.

III. FROM KEEPING HOME FIRES BURNING TO THE PRIVATISATION OF DOMESTIC ENERGY SUPPLIES

Foucault's definition of governmentality as, 'tactics of government that make possible the continual definition and redefinition of what is within the competence of the state',[29] is a reminder that there are shifts over time in the problems that are considered to be a proper concern of government. If we imagine a map of the governmental landscape of the working-class English home produced at the turn of the twentieth century, then energy supply and energy efficiency would be at the periphery of that map, if they featured at all. Central would be public health, sanitation, overcrowding, poverty and an overarching concern with the morality of occupiers.[30] Geographical, historical and socio-economic circumstances explain this marginalisation.[31] The climate is relatively mild, suggesting that thermal efficiency need not be a priority. Another factor is that from the middle of the nineteenth century, there was a plentiful and affordable supply of coal.[32] This meant that most

[28] ibid 17.

[29] Michel Foucault, 'Governmentality' in Graham Burchell, Colin Gordon and Peter Miller (eds), *The Foucault Effect: Studies in Governmentality* (Chicago, University of Chicago Press, 1991) 103.

[30] See for example Thomas Osborne, 'Security and vitality: drains, liberalism and power in the nineteenth century' in Andrew Barry, Thomas Osborne and Nikolas Rose (eds), *Foucault and Political Reason: Liberalism, Neo-liberalism and Rationalities of Government* (London, UCL Press, 1996) 99–122; David Cowan and Morag McDermont, *Regulating Social Housing: Governing Decline* (Abingdon, Routledge Cavendish, 2006).

[31] See Joan Rudge, 'Coal Fires, fresh air and the hardy British: a historical view of domestic energy efficiency and thermal comfort in Britain' (2012) 49 *Energy Policy* 6.

[32] Muthesius explains that: 'The total output of coal rose from about 10 million tons in 1790 to 240 million in 1900. Prices fluctuated and varied greatly from area to area, 15s to £1 5s a ton in London, 10s in a coal area. Miners received around 12 tons per annum free, and each house could store about two tons at a time.' S Muthesius, *The English Terraced House* (New Haven CT, Yale University Press, 1982) 51.

houses from Victorian times until the middle of the twentieth century, when concern about air pollution led to the passage of the Clean Air Act 1956, could heat their houses cheaply using open coal fires. These were not necessarily effective or efficient. At the turn of the twentieth century, Notter and Firth in the then leading work on public hygiene, noted:

> Long established custom and prejudice have caused open fires to be the means of heating nine-tenths of the houses in England, notwithstanding the fact that they are really the most costly and imperfect means of heating, as evidenced by the fact that they only render available 13 per cent of the total heat capable of being yielded by coal or coke and only 6 per cent of that by wood, the rest being lost in the air or escaping as unconsumed carbon up the chimney.[33]

Despite this, they conclude that, 'on account of the cheerful light which they emit, and the ventilation which they ensure, open fires will always be preferred as the pleasantest and healthiest form of heating'.[34]

In the 1970s domestic energy supply became of increasing government concern. The first reason was the international crisis caused by oil price rises, first in 1973–74 and then again in 1979.[35] Pearson and Watson explain how

> The first oil shock had raised the status of energy policy in the UK and in governments worldwide. It led the UK government to establish the Department of Energy and the OECD states to set up the International Energy Agency.[36]

The second reason was the election of Margaret Thatcher in 1979 with an agenda that included privatisation and 'rolling back' the state.[37] Pearson and Watson suggest that Lawson's speech to the British Institute of Energy Economics Cambridge conference in June 1982 encapsulates the changed approach.[38] No longer was government's role to plan the production of energy.[39] Instead, the task was to 'set a framework which will ensure that the market operates with a minimum of distortion and energy is produced and consumed efficiently.'[40]

The third reason was the coal industry. For the Conservative government, the power of the National Union of Mineworkers to 'hold the country to ransom' had to be broken, and it ensured, through various strategies, that the national strike of 1985–86 would fail. There were other problems.

[33] James Notter and Robert Firth, *The Theory and Practice of Hygiene* (London, Churchill, 1908) 206.

[34] ibid.

[35] Peter Pearson and Jim Watson, *UK Energy Policy 1980–2010: A History and Lessons to be Learnt* (London, Parliamentary Group for Energy Policies, 2012).

[36] ibid.

[37] Jamie Peck and Adam Tickell, 'Neoliberalizing Space' (2002) 34 *Antipode* 380.

[38] Pearson and Watson (n 35 above).

[39] This had been its role since the nationalisation of energy supply in 1947.

[40] Dieter Helm, *The New Energy Paradigm* (Oxford, Oxford University Press, 2007) 20.

As Pearson and Watson point out, by 1980, the industry was increasingly dependent on the demand for electricity because it had lost its market in gas production and most of its sales in the industrial and domestic markets. The costs of deep mining justified the closure of a number of pits and it was extremely vulnerable to increasingly available cheap imports of coal.

The defeat of the coal miners cleared the way for privatisation and competition. The gas industry was initially privatised in 1986, a fully competitive market coming into force in mid-1997. An electricity market was slowly opened to full competition by May 1999. What was left of the coal industry (24 pits were closed in 1985, 16 the following year and a further 35 before 1990) was privatised in 1994, allowing increased competition from new producer companies. The purpose of the privatisations was to modernise domestic energy supplies, increasing efficiency through competition, bringing about lower prices, technological advances and an increased international role for the companies.[41] Privatisation was crucial to the emergence of thermal inefficiency as a housing problem because domestic fuel became increasingly unaffordable for the poor.

A. The Market and Poverty

Although energy prices fell immediately following privatisation, from 2002 to 2012 household energy spending increased by 55 per cent, far exceeding inflation.[42] Privatisation does not explain all of the increase, but government decisions about liberalisation of the market played a significant part.[43] Government imagined that competition between providers would protect consumers, but this strategy has failed.[44] There is overwhelming evidence that customers do not switch between providers. In 2016 the Competition and Markets Authority estimated that, as a result, consumers had overpaid by £2 billion in 2015. There is a particular twist to the privatisation story; statistics indicate that the poor pay proportionally more. The poorest fifth of households in the UK spent 11 per cent of their income on energy in 2012, up from eight per cent in 2002 whilst the richest fifth spent just three per cent in 2012, up from two per cent in 2002. Retired households

[41] Department of Trade and Industry, 'The Social Effects of Energy Liberalisation: The UK Experience' (Launching a Common European Energy Market, Lisbon, 5–6 June 2000) available at: www.wto.org/english/tratop_e/serv_e/symp_mar02_uk_social_effects_energy_lib_e.pdf.

[42] Office of National Statistics, *Household Energy Spending in the UK 2002–2012* (London, ONS, 3 March 2014).

[43] See the Competition and Markets Authority, 'Energy Market Investigation Final report 2016' (London, CMA, 2016).

[44] ibid. Since writing this chapter the government has announced proposals for legislation to place price limits on standard variable tariffs.

also spend a greater percentage of their income on household fuel than non-retired households. Social exclusion explains these spending disparities. Prepayment meters are a more expensive way of buying energy than buying on a standard tariff paid for by direct debit but are often the only way that people with poor credit history can obtain energy. Discounted tariffs are available to those who purchase via online accounts, but those categorised as fuel poor are also disproportionately on the wrong side of the digital divide. Whilst there is some competition between suppliers, switching suppliers to achieve the best deals requires, yet again, internet access and a good credit record. The ability of private tenants to obtain a good deal is particularly limited. Although a landlord cannot prevent a tenant from switching provider, he or she can insist on the tenant switching back at the end of the tenancy and that switch back can incur financial penalties. The Competition and Market Authority reported that 35 per cent of those whose household incomes were above £36,000 had switched supplier in the last three years, compared with 20 per cent of those whose household incomes were below £18,000, and 32 per cent of those with degree level qualifications had switched in the last three years compared with 18 per cent of those with no qualifications.[45] The problems experienced by the poor in relation to the costs of energy have led to an increasing concern with fuel poverty. In the next section I consider the emergence of fuel poverty as a (highly contested) housing problem and its relationship with thermal inefficiency.

B. A Brief Genealogy of Fuel Poverty

Fuel poverty, argued to be distinct from other forms of poverty because of its causes and effects,[46] became a campaigning issue in England during the 1970s and 1980s. Campaigning gained a new urgency from the time of domestic energy privatisation. Governments seem to have been particularly resistant to claims that fuel poverty was an appropriate field for intervention,[47] although there was clearly greater sympathy towards the demands of the fuel poverty campaigners following the election of New Labour in 1997. The charity, National Energy Action, records a timeline of interventions into fuel poverty and energy efficiency. In remarkable parallels with the trajectory of the sanitation and other social movements of the nineteenth century, the timeline records efforts to establish a common

[45] CMA (n 43 above) 449.

[46] John Hills, *Fuel poverty: the problem and its measurement. (Case Report 69)* (London, DECC, 2011).

[47] Boardman notes how Conservative governments prior to 1997 dismissed fuel poverty as a recognisable problem. Brenda Boardman, *Fixing Fuel Poverty: Challenges and Solutions* (London, Earthscan, 2010).

language about and a scientific and expert understanding of the risks from cold homes in the 1980s, followed by initially small (insulation grants) but increasingly significant concessions (universal winter fuel payments to all over 60 year olds[48]) from government during the 1990s, and a growing foothold in parliamentary politics from the mid-1990s, finally culminating in legislation, the Warm Homes and Energy Conservation Act 2000. From the advent of the global financial crisis of 2008 and particularly following the defeat of New Labour in 2010, the status of fuel poverty has become more contested. Nonetheless in 2010, Boardman, one of the leading scholars and architects of fuel poverty, felt able to assert that now, 'fuel poverty is politically accepted as a real problem'.[49]

The Warm Homes and Energy Conservation Act 2000 was considered a significant achievement by fuel poverty campaigners. It contained a statutory obligation on government to publish a fuel poverty strategy which was to include a target date for the ending of fuel poverty no later than 15 years from its publication. But even following that legislation fuel poverty's status as a 'real' problem was not certain. It took the threat of judicial review from Friends of the Earth and other environmental campaigners to persuade it to set a target date of 2016 for the ending of all fuel poverty.[50] Government reluctance seems to have been based upon the lack of clarity of what exactly fuel poverty was. Boardman had provided a definition in 1991.[51] For her, fuel poverty was a condition experienced by any household which spent more than 10 per cent of its income on fuel. She explains that the origins of the definition came from 1988 data, which indicated that

> household average expenditure on energy use was 5% of the weekly budget, and the 30% of households with the lowest income did indeed spend 10%. The figure of 10% was therefore in some sense 'affordable' for the poorest households. It was what they were spending, although they were often cold as well.[52]

Boardman's definition established a norm of expenditure on fuel, and pushed government towards accepting a responsibility to put people in a position to achieve that norm, enabling them to avoid fuel poverty if they allocate their finances responsibly. For Boardman, the poor energy efficiency of English housing was an important dimension of fuel poverty, one which enabled her to articulate a compelling case for intervention.

> The fuel poor, like anyone else in poverty, rarely have access to sources of capital, so this expenditure [on improved energy efficiency] has to be funded through some other medium. The energy efficiency of the homes of the fuel poor indicate, in a very real sense, the extent to which society is concerned about fuel poverty.[53]

[48] From 2010 eligibility became linked to the State Pension Age.
[49] Boardman (n 47 above) 21.
[50] ibid 13.
[51] ibid 21.
[52] ibid 23.
[53] ibid 125.

There are two points to note here about the characteristics of fuel poverty. First it makes homes of the poor into places where occupiers are required to be disciplined about their use of energy and,

> to calculate for themselves, to translate their activities into financial terms, to seek to maximize productivity for a given income, to cut out waste, to restructure activities that were not cost effective, to choose between priorities in terms of their relative costs and benefits, to become more or less like a financial manager of their own professional activities.[54]

Secondly, it has spatial dimensions; government has to acquire knowledge of the energy efficiency of the homes of the poor. The statistical vehicle for acquiring knowledge of the energy efficiency of dwellings is Standard Assessment Procedure (SAP), a methodology developed by the Building Research Establishment in the early 1990s. It works by assessing how much energy a dwelling will consume when delivering a defined level of comfort and service provision.[55] The assessment is based on standardised assumptions for occupancy and behaviour. This enables a like-for-like comparison of dwelling performance and facilitates the determination of fuel costs and emissions of carbon dioxide (CO_2). But there is a problem. The SAP's assumptions are that houses are warm with good supplies of hot water, adequately lit and neither under- nor over-occupied. These assumptions are problematic for poorer people's housing, so government knowledge of poor people's homes is flawed. This means when assessing the effect of energy-efficiency improvements,

> the energy, money and carbon savings will be less, sometimes substantially less, in practice. It is useful to be able to compare properties on a like-for-like basis, but the failure of energy savings to materialize can cause policy uncertainty and confusion.[56]

There is a further problem. When energy-efficiency improvements to poor people's homes fail to generate reduced consumption, which is likely as they are probably under-consuming energy, the worry is that the poor will be criticised for their profligacy.

Whilst New Labour had problems understanding fuel poverty, for the coalition government which was elected in 2010, there was another problem. Boardman's definition meant that fuel poverty would increase as fuel prices increased, posing difficulties for a government which saw fuel prices as beyond its control. In 2011 the government commissioned John Hills of the LSE to review the definition. His conclusions, that a more nuanced

[54] Nikolas Rose, *Powers of Freedom* (Cambridge, Cambridge University Press, 1999) 152.
[55] See for further information on SAP: DECC, *The Government's Standard Assessment Procedure for Energy Rating of Dwellings 2012* (Watford, BRE 2014).
[56] Boardman (n 47 above) 127.

definition of fuel poverty was required, were accepted.[57] A household in England is now considered to be fuel poor, and therefore the target of intervention, if it has higher than typical energy costs and would be left with a disposable income below the poverty line if it spent the required money to meet those costs.

The new definition is justified by its proponents for several reasons. It makes clear that fuel poverty is distinct from general poverty. It ensures that households who have low energy bills because they limit their energy bills by keeping their homes cold are included within the scope of fuel poverty. It enables the measurement of the level, ie the extent, of fuel poverty, as well as its depth, the amount by which someone's income would have to be increased in order to lift them out of fuel poverty. But as Middlemiss points out, the Low Income High Costs (LIHC), as the measurement is referred to, represents a significant shift in fuel poverty politics, one which obfuscates the links between poverty and fuel poverty, ignores the impact of the high costs of energy and entrenches the belief that only the most vulnerable are worthy of assistance.[58] The effect of redefining fuel poverty has been instantaneous. Two million households previously considered to be fuel poor no longer are, removing them at a stroke from the possibility of government assistance.[59] It does something else as well, whilst energy inefficiency was an important factor in Boardman's definition, its role is transformed by LIHC. The result of the new definition is that eliminating fuel poverty is now virtually indistinguishable from the requirement to improve energy efficiency.

The redefinition of fuel poverty was accompanied by the abandonment of the aspiration to abolish it by 2016. The Department of Energy and Climate Change publication which explained the move to LIHC, also announced a new policy truth, 'fuel poverty is a challenge of both scale and complexity. It is not a problem that can be eradicated in any meaningful way, certainly not by 2016 and not in any short time horizon'.[60] This new 'truth' is strongly related to the government's commitment to the liberalisation of the energy market. The primary remedy appears to be assisting the poor to engage more fully with the market, rather than questioning the fairness

[57] For a full discussion see: John Hills, *Getting the Measure of Fuel Poverty: Final Report of the Fuel Poverty Review, Case Report 72* (London, Centre for Analysis of Social Exclusion, 2012).

[58] Lucie Middlemiss, 'A critical analysis of the new politics of fuel poverty in England' (2016) 37 *Critical Social Policy* 425.

[59] Carbon Brief, 'How a Definition Change Lifts Households out of Fuel Poverty': www.carbonbrief.org/how-a-definition-change-lifts-households-out-of-fuel-poverty.

[60] Department of Energy and Climate Change, *Fuel Poverty: A Framework for Future Action* (Cmd 8673, 2011).

of market solutions for the poor or indeed introducing subsidies.[61] There is a new fuel poverty target—ensuring that as many fuel poor homes as is reasonably practicable achieve a minimum energy efficiency rating of Band C, by 2030.[62] The banding system is derived from the energy rating system of consumer white goods which ranges from A–G, where A is most efficient and G least efficient, and the rating is based on annual CO_2 emissions per unit floor area. By any standards the new fuel poverty target represents very limited aspirations and does little to eradicate poverty.

At this point I turn to the second of the governmental priorities which have impacted upon the contingent status of thermal inefficiency as a housing problem: government interventions designed to encourage house-building and homeownership to alleviate housing shortages.

IV. GOVERNING THROUGH HOUSE BUILDING AND PROPERTY OWNERSHIP

Returning to the notion of a governmental map of English housing, one major and persistent feature of that map has been the need to encourage, or at least not inhibit house building. England has suffered periodically from severe housing shortages from the onset of industrialisation and urbanisation in the late eighteenth century. There was a massive private house building boom in the nineteenth century, which, for the middle classes, was a time of housing independence and even extravagance, and the creation of the Victorian ideal of the private sanctity of the home.[63] The reality for the poor was more problematic. In general, the poor rented rooms in the housing abandoned by the middle classes, ensuring high profits for landlords. The speculative building which characterised England's housing boom had little interest in working-class housing, so that even when working-class housing was built, standards were skimped on to ensure profitability.[64] Interestingly the ample ventilation, which was the inevitable result of poorly constructed houses, was necessary in order to disperse the fumes produced by coal fires and was regarded as a virtue by public health reformers, who were convinced that a lack of ventilation, as well as filth, was a significant cause of the diseases that were endemic in the Victorian slums.[65]

[61] See Professor Martin Cave's minority dissenting report to the Competition and Market Authority report arguing that 'The harm which is presently inflicted on households in this market (£2 billion in 2015, or an average of £75 for every British household) is very severe'. He proposed a wider price cap remedy on all Standard Variable Tariffs. CMA Final Report (n 43 above) 1415–17.

[62] Fuel Poverty (England) Regulations 2014.

[63] Muthesius (n 32 above).

[64] Rudge (n 31 above).

[65] ibid.

England's early housing boom has had long-term consequences, resulting in one of the oldest housing stocks in the world, with 20 per cent of its housing stock pre-dating 1919 and 85 per cent pre-dating 1990.[66] Retro-fitting this housing so that it is thermally efficient when it was initially poor quality and designed to be reliant on open fires for heating, was always going to be problematic.

The failure of speculative building to provide for the poor stimulated first, philanthropic responses to the problem of working-class housing, and then the growth of council housing, built by municipal government for rent to the working classes. The quality of council housing was initially better than equivalent private provision, but the pressures of housing shortages, particularly following the Second World War (in 1942 the Ministry of Housing estimated that an additional 1,350,000 houses were necessary to replace bombed and deteriorated houses, to clear the slums and to cater for the expected growth in population[67]) meant that speed and economy would always be political priorities. Two particular types of building—non-traditional, industrialised system-built housing such as Airey housing, and tower blocks constructed from large panel systems—each designed to provide a rapid and economical response to housing shortages, caused problems of thermal efficiency. Poor construction and design meant that the homes had limited resistance to the weather, were prone to condensation and expensive to heat.[68]

The lack of resources available to ensure proper maintenance of council and housing association property was, in part and for a short time, addressed by New Labour's Decent Homes Initiative launched in 2000. The aim was to bring all social housing into decent condition, and increase the proportion of private rental housing in decent condition by 2010. The standard of decency to be achieved had four elements, housing had to meet the statutory minimum fitness standard, be in reasonable repair, have the benefit of modern facilities and services and, importantly for this chapter, housing had to provide a reasonable degree of thermal comfort.[69] £4 billion worth of improvements meant that the thermal efficiency of social housing dramatically improved. There was an increase in SAP ratings from 48 in 1996 to 58 in 2004 and between 2001 and 2006 there was a 31 per cent reduction in the number of homes failing the thermal comfort element of

[66] Department of Communities and Local Government, *English Housing Survey: Housing Stock Report 2008* (London, DCLG, 2010).

[67] P Malpass, *Housing and the Welfare State* (Basingstoke, Palgrave Macmillan, 2005) 589–606.

[68] For an explanation see Keith Ross, *Non-traditional housing in the UK—a brief review* (London, The Council of Mortgage Lenders, 2002).

[69] See: Helen Carr, 'The Right to Buy, the Leaseholder, and the Impoverishment of Ownership' (2011) 38 *Journal of Law and Society* 519.

the decent homes standard, with 470,000 homes benefitting from energy efficiency improvements.[70] By the end of the programme, almost half (48 per cent) of dwellings in the social rented sector had an energy efficiency rating of A–C, compared with 26 per cent in the private rented sector and 24 per cent of owner-occupied homes.[71]

By the time of the Decent Homes Initiative, however, social house building was virtually at a standstill. From the election of Margaret Thatcher and the implementation of the 'Right to Buy' in the Housing Act 1980, council house building declined rapidly and although there was some building by housing associations, the government positioned the private market as the prime source of housing supply. Whilst house building for the working classes has always been caught up in disciplinary technologies—both philanthropists and local government aimed to improve those they housed—the shift to the market marked a shift in the moral template. Social housing and its providers became culpable for the dependency and passivity that were deemed to be characteristic of its tenants. In contrast, homeownership, as Cowan and McDermont put it, provides 'a key method of governing individuals, working through their freedom. It prevents the descent to pauperism, as well as providing stability, responsibility, thrift, health, wealth and an example to others.'[72]

Moreover there is an assumption that, whatever its form and however it is extended, homeownership conveys its inherent qualities to all who acquire its status.[73] But this is a flawed assumption. Marginal homeownership may well mean living in a home you cannot afford to maintain or heat. It should also be noted that the decline in social housing provision has forced many into the private rented sector, the least thermally efficient housing in England.

Just as in Victorian times, house builders have shown limited interest in building affordable homes and the issue of inadequate housing supply once again dominates housing governance. Sajid Javed, the Secretary of State for Communities and Local Government, made this clear in the foreword to the recently published White Paper, *Fixing the broken housing market*, 'This country doesn't have enough homes. That's not a personal opinion or a political calculation. It's a simple statement of fact.'[74]

[70] Department of the Environment, Food, and Rural Affairs, *Climate Change: The UK Programme 2006* (Cmd 6764, 2006).

[71] Department of Communities and Local Government (n 66 above).

[72] David Cowan and Morag McDermont, *Regulating Social Housing: Governing Decline* (Abingdon, Routledge Cavendish, 2006) 165. See also Kirton-Darling (Chapter nine of this volume).

[73] Carr (n 69 above).

[74] Department for Communities and Local Government, *Fixing our Broken Housing Market* (Cm 9352, 2017) 7.

There are two points to be made. The first is that, whilst the White Paper includes a nod to the growing significance of the private rented sector, the emphasis is on providing homes for ownership rather than rental, as part of the continuing story of homeownership as the best protection against insecurity. Secondly the preferred solution is building new homes, with no evidence of any commitment to refurbish and improve existing housing stock, which is where the problem of energy inefficiency is primarily located.

The White Paper contains some discussion of energy standards, but it is limited and expressed as contingent upon maintaining the supply of affordable housing. The emphasis on the need to increase the quantity of housing, in effect works to marginalise quality in general and energy efficiency in particular.

Nonetheless the energy efficiency of new built housing has improved remarkably. In 2008 the House of Commons Committee on Energy Efficiency and Existing Housing Stock noted 'that a home built today is likely to be 40 per cent more energy efficient than one built just five years ago, and up to six times more efficient than the substantial proportion of Victorian housing in the stock'.[75] The major driver for improvement has been building regulations which have imposed increasingly stringent demands for energy efficiency on new houses, particularly since the Kyoto protocol—the first international agreement which committed industrialised countries to the reduction of carbon emissions—came into force in 2005.

A. Building Regulations

The history of building regulations is tied to the emergence of cities. There was evidence of building codes, for instance, in the Babylonian Empire.[76] London and other English cities developed systems of building regulations from the Middle Ages, primarily as a means of protecting urban environments from potentially catastrophic risks such as fire, and to prevent nuisances. Regulations were intensified during Victorian times, when requirements for drainage, light and ventilation were imposed, largely in response to public health concerns.[77] Building regulation remained local until the mid-1960s when, following the passing of the Public Health Act 1961, a national scheme was implemented in 1966. The insulation requirements introduced in the original regulations were designed to prevent condensation. They were only increased to provide for energy efficiency following the international fuel crisis of 1973.[78]

[75] Department of Communities and Local Government (n 67 above) 5.

[76] See the History of Building Codes: Buyer's Choice, 'History of Building Codes' (2017): www.buyerschoiceinspections.com/history-of-building-codes.

[77] Rudge (n 31 above).

[78] Rudge (n 31 above) 8.

The Building Act 1984 provides for current regulations. The Act moved from prescriptive regulation to an outcome-based system, and introduced, in Schedule 1 of the Act, Part L, which relates to energy efficiency. Originally it required builders to make reasonable provision for the conservation of fuel and power and provided guidance on compliance. Since then there has been a gradual escalation of requirements; double glazing became a requirement when installing new or replacement windows in 2002 and condensing boilers required when replacing gas boilers from 2005. In 2003 the UK government adopted the Buildings Energy Performance Directive, which required EU Member States to use a whole-building calculation method for assessing the carbon emissions of new buildings, and in 2006, following implementation of the Kyoto agreement, the UK government determined that from 2016 all new homes would be zero carbon homes. The plan was that, over the next 10 years, successive building regulations would move incrementally towards that target. As a result, significant changes were introduced in the 2006 iteration of building regulations; SAP (discussed above) was adopted as the measure of thermal efficiency for the EU directive, and requirements were imposed which would improve the energy efficiency of new homes by 20 per cent compared with 2002 standards. In 2013 building regulations provided for a further six per cent improvement. However, by this date, government enthusiasm had begun to wane; energy efficiency had to compete with the policy commitment to reducing the regulatory burden. The requirements were less ambitious than had originally been planned and the proposal, that up-to-date energy efficiency requirements would be imposed on the entirety of a dwelling when extensions to homes were carried out, was abandoned, to avoid penalising 'hard working families'.[79] The Code for Sustainable Homes, a voluntary code designed as a driver for change to Building Regulations was abandoned as part of the review of housing standards. In 2015 the 2006 commitment for zero carbon new homes by 2016 was also abandoned, as part of a Treasury-led drive to improve national productivity, including the productivity of house builders.[80] The House of Lords attempted to provide an alternative to the zero carbon requirement through an amendment to the Housing and Planning Bill in 2016. This would have imposed a carbon compliance standard but the House of Commons rejected the amendment because of the alleged impact it would have on the building of new homes. The government promised it would review energy performance requirements under the Building Regulations, a promise repeated in the White Paper. Not only has this not materialised, the concern is that once Britain leaves the European Union there will only be weak external drivers towards improving energy efficiency in domestic

[79] HL Deb, 30 July 2013, vol 651, col 165.

[80] Department for Business, Innovation, and Skills, *Fixing the Foundations: Creating a More Prosperous Nation* (Cm 9098, 2015).

buildings and there is little evidence of much domestic commitment to the project of increased energy efficiency when so much priority is being given to removing any barrier, real or perceived, to the construction of new houses.

Some limitations to Building Regulations should also be noted. They only impact upon new homes, or extensions to existing homes, so the vast majority of English homes are unaffected. The energy efficiency requirements for non-residential buildings are less stringent than for residential buildings, and small outbuildings are exempt. This means that some of England's most precarious homes, the non-domestic buildings occupied by property guardians[81] and those outbuildings and garages which are being used to provide 'beds in sheds' fall outside of regulation. One further point needs to be made about Building Regulations. They have been blamed for the new phenomenon of *over*heating homes, which the Zero Carbon Hub estimates could, in the future, affect up to 20 per cent of England's housing stock.[82] However, as the Zero Carbon Hub points out, it is not only improved energy conservation which has led to this outcome. Climate change, resulting in more frequent and more intense heatwaves, continued construction in cities, particularly of flats and single aspect dwellings and the proliferation of technology in homes, have all contributed to the problem. Nor is it only new properties which have a tendency to overheat. The Zero Carbon Hub notes that dwellings built around the 1960s as well as small top-floor purpose-built flats appear to be considerably more prone to overheating. There are relatively simple solutions to the problem of overheated homes such as ensuring windows can be opened and providing external shading to windows so, although it may be appropriate to provide greater nuance to the requirement that buildings be airtight, thoughtful construction and retrofitting of homes should resolve any problems.

B. Energy Labelling

In terms of existing homes, the current government appears most enthusiastic about energy efficiency measures which can be delivered by a consumerist model. Energy labelling of dwellings, required by Europe as part of the Buildings Energy Performance Directive referred to above, has been in force since 2007. The scheme requires that a building's energy performance is certified at the completion of construction or when a property is sold or rented. The idea is that consumers will be able to take into account the information provided when making decisions about purchase or rental.

[81] See Hunter and Meers, Chapter four in this volume.

[82] Zero Carbon Hub, *Overheating in Homes—The Big Picture 2015* (London, Zero Carbon Hub 2015).

Whilst the extent to which house purchasing decisions will be influenced by this information is debatable, there is an even greater problem in expecting tenants to behave like rational consumers. Because of high demand for rental properties, tenants are rarely in a position to act upon energy efficiency information and there is little incentive for landlords to spend money to increase energy efficiency when this appears to have limited impact on rental levels. The government has therefore implemented further measures. From April 2016, tenants have been able to require landlords to consent to energy efficiency improvements, although they will have to bear the cost of carrying out those improvements themselves, making it unlikely that the provisions will have much effect whilst the assured shorthold tenancy regime remains in force because it provides tenants with very limited security.[83] Such consumer-based solutions are augmented by more prescriptive provisions. From April 2018 a landlord will not be able to rent out a residential property which falls below energy efficiency band E, and from April 2020 will not be able to continue to let out such a property, without carrying out prescribed improvement works.[84] Government estimates suggest that this will benefit around I million private rental homes.[85] In general campaigners have welcomed the reforms, but would like them strengthened so that the minimum requirement was band D.[86] It is also worth reflecting that it has taken more than 130 years since the original requirement that homes be fit for human habitation was enacted in the Housing of the Working Classes Act 1885,[87] to reach this very minimum level of energy efficiency requirement for rental homes.

V. CONCLUSION

Thermal inefficiency makes homes and lives precarious because of its impact upon individual health and wellbeing and its impact upon the planet. Despite the potentially catastrophic consequences of thermally inefficient homes, however, my account demonstrates that the status of thermal

[83] See s. 21, Housing Act 1988.

[84] See the Energy Act 2011 and Energy Efficiency (Private Rented Property) (England and Wales) Regulations 2015.

[85] See Department of Energy and Climate Change, *Renters and landlords to enjoy warmer properties and cheaper bills* (5 February 2015): www.gov.uk/government/news/renters-and-landlords-to-enjoy-warmer-properties-and-cheaper-bills.

[86] See Friends of the Earth, *Minimum Standards of Energy Efficiency for Private Rented Homes* (June 2011): https://www.foe.co.uk/sites/default/files/downloads/private_rented_homes.pdf.

[87] (48 & 49 Vict. c. 72). The provision, which remains in force as s. 8 of the Landlord and Tenant Act 1985, has been rendered largely ineffective because of failures to update the rent levels relating to the provision since 1957.

inefficiency as a housing problem is highly contested. It has had to compete with other more powerful agendas, such as the privatisation of domestic energy supplies and the privileging of house building and homeownership. It has been caught up with fuel poverty, a housing problem which for a short period of time captured the policymakers' imagination, but has now been folded into the problem of thermal inefficiency, demonstrating contemporary reluctance to respond to poverty of any sort with meaningful strategies. The contested status of thermal inefficiency has had other consequences: the solutions that government is prepared to promote are based upon consumerist protections, which are unconvincing in a failing housing market.

For Jacobs *et al* a social constructionist approach is important because of the possibilities it provides for alternative and more progressive solutions. Because of the power dynamics within which thermal inefficiency as a housing problem is captured it is difficult to see alternative solutions without dramatic shifts in policy agendas, shifts which would ensure a more holistic approach to housing policy and which would prioritise lived experience in the home as opposed to housing as a financial asset. Perhaps that is the most valuable outcome of a critical, if inevitably partial, history of a social problem, the realisation that homes will continue to be precarious until such shifts happen.

8

Governing Risk and Uncertainty: Financialisation and the Regulatory Framework of Housing Associations

RICHARD GOULDING*

I. INTRODUCTION

ENGLISH HOUSING ASSOCIATIONS are private registered providers of social housing, subsidised by the government and regulated by the Homes and Communities Agency (HCA), a non-departmental body that combines the functions of both a funder and a regulator. The HCA—and its predecessor organisation prior to 2008, the Housing Corporation—has been crucial to the development of the sector as it has become the primary conduit for social housing in the UK, enabling associations to register and bid for grants while establishing performance and reporting standards.[1] Since the Housing Act 1988 associations have also combined grants with private borrowing in order to develop and acquire housing, with recent years seeing larger associations increasingly diversify into more commercial products such as market sale and rented housing, while bond markets have become an important source of finance.[2] Austerity policies implemented since 2010 have cut funding and weakened the security of social housing tenants, raising concerns over the move to a more commercial footing in the sector that undermines its traditional welfare functions.[3]

* School of Law, University of Sheffield

[1] David Cowan and Morag McDermont, *Regulating Social Housing: Governing Decline* (Oxford, Routledge-Cavendish, 2006).

[2] Andrew Heywood, 'Investing in Affordable Housing: An analysis of the affordable housing sector' (The Housing Finance Corporation, 2016).

[3] Tony Manzi and Nicky Morrison, 'Risk, Commercialism and Social Purpose: Repositioning the English Housing Association Sector' (2017) *Urban Studies*. Published online 2 May 2017.

The risks and uncertainties of this environment also imply a more precarious environment for the homes of social housing tenants. This chapter explores the extent to which the restructuring of social housing in the aftermath of the financial crisis is reshaping the precariousness of home, focusing on the case of housing associations, as the main conduit for the provision of new subsidised social housing within England. Precariousness is understood here not as the absence of security but, following Butler, the uncertainty generated through the shared vulnerability of social relations.[4] The home, for example, can be subject to precariousness due to the mutual dependencies of voluntary or involuntary sharing, or the obligations placed on it through a financial agreement.[5] Precarity, by contrast, can be understood as the hierarchical distribution of precariousness through society.[6] A mortgage agreement, for example, can insure a bank against the uncertainties of lending by giving it a security interest in the home of a borrower. While this enables a mortgagor to access credit for a house, providing the security of homeownership, this comes at the expense of the precarity of repossession for a homeowner if they cannot keep up with repayments.

To explore these issues, I draw on policy documents, housing and financial sector reports, and qualitative fieldwork data collected over the course of PhD research over 12 months from Spring 2015 to Spring 2016. Original data used here is sourced from a wider sample of 20 semi-structured elite interviews averaging one hour in length with actors involved in shaping housing policy, including social housing executives, policymakers, auditors, solicitors, treasury consultants, valuers, fund managers, and officers from representative sectoral bodies. Interviews have been analysed according to themes of precariousness, commercialisation, and how risks and uncertainties are understood by the actors involved in shaping the sector, and the precarisation effect this may have for tenants.

The remainder of the chapter is structured as follows. In section II, I establish my analytical framework, arguing that the transfer of risks and uncertainties has been crucial to the financialisation of aspects of the welfare state such as social housing providers. In section III, I argue that the shift to private finance since the 1980s has led to the creation of risks which undermine the security of tenants.[7] This has been a process mediated by legal and regulatory frameworks that have sought to minimise risks through the governance of associations: however, with the regulatory stability this provides enabling associations to borrow at rates lower than they could otherwise expect.[8] In section IV, I argue that austerity has undermined this

[4] Judith Butler and Athena Athanasiou, *Dispossession: the performative in the political* (Cambridge, Polity, 2013) 20.

[5] See Sarah Blandy, Chapter two of this volume.

[6] Butler and Athanasiou (n 4 above).

[7] Cowan and McDermont (n 3 above).

[8] Heywood (n 2 above).

model, however. Funding cuts and a diminished ability of the regulator to govern the stability of associations have resulted in an increase in the sector's precariousness,[9] as it becomes more exposed to ongoing financial and real estate volatility.[10] Drawing on original fieldwork data, in the section V, I argue that faced with this diminished capacity, regulatory emphasis has switched to ensuring resilience in the face of crisis rather than preventing instability, in accordance with a wider entrenchment of business logics in the sector and normalising insecurity as a tool of governance.[11] These developments in turn create the risk of greater precarity being passed down to current and prospective tenants in social housing, through the raised potential for more exclusionary lettings policies and exposure to greater risks in the event of a disaster such as a provider insolvency.

II. FINANCIALISATION, RISK AND UNCERTAINTY

A broad and contested term, financialisation has received increasing academic debate over the past 15 years. The concept has been used to focus attention on numerous overlapping aspects of the spread of financial relations and institutions in contemporary society. These include increased profit-making through financial channels and corporate reorganisation,[12] the growing influence of the financial sector on international political economy since the 1970s,[13] and the spread of financial logics and metrics such as credit and debt relations as a form of governance in daily life.[14] This chapter attempts to gain analytical purchase on financialisation by using the example of English housing associations to build on literature that views financialisation not as the presence or importance of financial relations such as capital markets,[15] but as the spread of financial logics and calculus into other areas of social life.[16]

[9] Butler and Athanasiou (n 4 above).

[10] Rodrigo Fernandez and Manuel Aalbers, 'Financialisation and Housing: between globalisation and varieties of capitalism' (2016) 20 *Competition and Change* 71.

[11] Isabell Lorey, *State of Insecurity: government of the precarious* (London, Verso, 2015).

[12] Greta Krippner, 'The financialization of the American economy' (2005) 3 *Socio-economic Review* 173; Ismail Ertürk, Julie Froud, Sukhdev Johal, Adam Leaver and Karel Williams (eds), *Financialisation at Work: Key Texts and Commentary* (London, Routledge, 2008).

[13] Gerald Epstein, *Financialisation and the World Economy* (Cheltenham, Edward Elgar, 2005); Costas Lapavitsas, *Profiting without Producing: How finance exploits us all* (London, Verso, 2013).

[14] Randy Martin, *Financialization of Daily Life* (Philadelphia, Temple University Press, 2002); Paul Langley, *The Everyday Life of Global Finance: saving and borrowing in Anglo-America* (Oxford, Oxford University Press, 2008).

[15] Epstein (n 13 above).

[16] Dick Bryan and Michael Rafferty, 'Financial Derivatives as Social Policy Beyond Crisis (2014) 48 *Sociology* 887; Emma Dowling, 'In the Wake of Austerity: Social Impact Bonds and the Financialisation of the Welfare State in Britain' (2017) 22 *New Political Economy* 294.

Outsourcing and marketisation within social housing are not themselves new, but build on over four decades of neoliberalisation in which the state has actively extended market relations through other areas of social activity.[17] Finance has played a structural role in enabling these processes, allowing capital to be levered in upfront to acquire and operate services in areas such as health, housing, or infrastructure, while receiving long-term interest payments in return.[18] A common justification for such policies is that they pass risks onto the private sector, with companies receiving payments in exchange for accepting the risks of meeting service delivery and value-for-money targets, with extra costs—such as raising finance privately rather than through government borrowing—being offset by efficiencies achieved through greater market discipline.[19]

As argued by Froud[20] in an analysis of the use of private finance in delivering public services however, this is a justification that conflates risk and uncertainty, two concepts with very different implications for profitability. Uncertainty acts as a limit to what is knowable, given circumstances where there are no scientific grounds for predicting future events. In contrast, risk as understood and put into practice by private sector actors is a probabilistic concept, grounded in practices such as cost–benefit analysis that attempt to provide actionable grounds for making the future knowable.[21] Attempts to identify and transfer risk to the private sector change the nature of services and projects that can be delivered, however, as contracts and other legal criteria are used to lock-in the costs and levels of service that the private sector can be expected to deliver.[22] This removal of uncertainty through contract design in turn creates risks and costs for the state, with the private sector's limited flexibility in delivering services restricting the state's much greater ability to react to the contingency of future events when attempting to fulfil policy goals.[23]

While Froud's analysis specifically focuses on public-private partnerships such as the Private Finance Initiative (PFI), this need to manage risks and uncertainties when services are divested from the state can be applicable to issues such as housing association financialisation, where the private borrowing by housing associations drives commercial pressures on

[17] Jamie Peck and Adam Tickell, 'Neoliberalising Space' (2002) 34 *Antipode* 380.

[18] Dexter Whitfield, *Public Services or Corporate Welfare: Rethinking the Nation State in the Global Economy* (London, Pluto Press, 2001); Allyson Pollock, *NHS plc: The privatisation of our healthcare* (Verso, 2004); Ewald Engelen et al, *After the Great Complacence: Financial crisis and the politics of reform* (Oxford, Oxford University Press, 2011).

[19] Whitfield (n 18 above).

[20] Julie Froud, 'The Private Finance Initiative: Risk, uncertainty and the state' (2003) 28 *Accounting, Organisations and Society* 567.

[21] Ibid 573.

[22] Ibid 580.

[23] Ibid 587.

them to maintain payments to lenders or risk default. In this respect, the financialisation of welfare services such as social housing can therefore be characterised not just by an increase in the size of the financial sector,[24] but the extension of financial metrics and logics into other areas of social life through a broader process of commodification, including the production and transfer of risks.[25] As opposed to characterisations of privatisation or neoliberalisation that view financialisation as a form of deregulation and the shrinking of the state in favour of the free market, this is a process that is deeply mediated by legal and regulatory frameworks.[26] These delimit outcomes and assign risks in order to ensure that the private sector can profitably deliver its expected services or recover interest rates from financing them.[27] Fiscal retrenchment through austerity policies can open up new opportunities for this financialisation, a process that often involves costs that are passed downward to be managed by the social reproduction of service users.[28] How precarities arising from these processes in the financialisation of housing associations have been managed and distributed is the question which the remainder of the chapter now considers.

III. GOVERNING RISKS AND PRECARIOUSNESS WITHIN SOCIAL HOUSING FINANCE

A diverse sector, English housing associations consist of over 1,500 providers and range in size from small and specialist organisations to large and increasingly commercialised property management companies that operate many tens of thousands of homes.[29] Over 95 per cent of the sector's stock is concentrated among roughly 300 providers that own over 1,000 homes each however, and these form the focus of policy attention and regulatory oversight.[30] Associations are still largely non-profit in that they do not distribute profits to shareholders, but they operate in order to generate surpluses, are exposed to development risk, and issue private sector assured tenancies, although of a much more secure form than assured shorthold tenancies available in the private rented sector.[31] Although 85 per cent of

[24] Epstein (n 13 above).

[25] Bryan and Rafferty (n 16 above).

[26] Manuel B Aalbers, 'Regulated Deregulation' in Simon Springer, Kean Birch, Julie MacLeavy (eds), *The Handbook of Neoliberalism* (London, Routledge, 2016).

[27] Phillip O'Neill, 'The financialisation of infrastructure: the role of categorisation and property relations' (2013) 6 *Cambridge Journal of Regions, Economy and Society* 441.

[28] Dowling (n 16 above).

[29] Homes and Communities Agency, '2016 Global Accounts of Housing Providers' (HCA, 2017).

[30] Ibid 1.

[31] David Hughes and Stuart Lowe, *Social housing law and policy* (London, Butterworths, 1995).

the sector's income still derives from 'general needs' social housing lets, since the 1980s many associations have built low-cost products for owner occupation such as shared ownership.[32] The last 10 years have nonetheless seen increasing commercial diversification among larger providers into market sale and rental, alongside other areas such as care accommodation and student housing, as larger providers have been able to exploit their assets in order to become prominent developers in addition to their functions as social landlords.[33]

Prominent voices within the sector are keen to portray an image of commercial acumen as a means to achieving communal goals, with representative bodies such as the National Housing Federation (NHF) operating promotional campaigns under slogans such as 'In Business for Neighbourhoods'. The role of the state has nonetheless been vital for the sector's growth, acknowledged by NHF head, David Orr in his presentation of the sector as 'the most successful public–private partnership in the history of our economy'.[34] The relationship with the regulator has been of crucial importance to the sector's development, the regulator being a non-departmental body acting on behalf of the government in a role originally fulfilled by the Housing Corporation until its abolition in 2008 and replacement with the Homes and Communities Agency (HCA) as successor.[35] For most of this period funding and regulatory functions have been combined under a single body, with the exception of the short-lived Tenant Services Authority from 2008–12, that was intended to act as a separate regulator until its intended abolition was announced in 2010 by the incoming Cameron government before finally being closed in 2012.[36]

The containment of risk and uncertainty can be seen in the opening up of housing associations to private finance. From the Housing Act 1988 associations have also combined public grants with private finance, replacing an earlier funding system made up of grants and government loans in which the state assumed development risk by paying for costs at the end of a completed project.[37] The Act reformed the grant system by ensuring providers would be paid at the beginning of a project, formally passing development risk and recorded debts from the Treasury onto associations while expecting

[32] Homes and Communities Agency. '2015 Global Accounts of Housing Providers' (HCA, 2016) 3.

[33] Heywood (n 2 above).

[34] Helia Ebrahimi, 'Why Are Housing Associations Failing to Build Enough Homes? (*Channel 4 News*, 23 July 2015): www.channel4.com/news/housing-associations-homes-property-bob-blackman-david-orr.

[35] Morag McDermont, *Governing independence and expertise: the business of housing associations*. (Oxford, Hart Publishing, 2010).

[36] Homes and Communities Agency, 'The Regulatory Framework for Social Housing in England from 2012' (HCA, 2012).

[37] Hughes and Lowe (n 31 above).

them to top up grants through private loans.[38] The logic of this was to reduce the exposure of the state to the uncertainties of the development process, avoiding having to 'shell out' for unexpected costs. This in turn created the policy problem of how to induce financial institutions to lend to the sector however, with lenders expecting low risks if they were to enable associations to borrow at affordable rates.

An important way in which this was achieved has been through the transfer of risks onto tenants, exposing them to greater precariousness through a reduction in their security of tenure, with the Housing Act 1988 creating a new private sector 'Assured Tenancy' for housing association tenants.[39] Although stronger than assured shorthold tenancies in the private rented sector proper, assured tenancies have weaker protections against court-ordered evictions in the event of rent arrears than secure tenancies still used in council housing.[40] The 1988 Act also lifted associations out of the statutory 'Fair Rent' system of rent control, leading to a sharp rise in rents throughout the early 1990s that led to concerns and debates over affordability between the regulator and representative bodies such as the NHF.[41] The state continued to share risk in this system through the social security system however, with a rise in housing benefit payments to cover the rent increases passing part of the cost onto the public as well as renters.[42] This shift to private finance acted as a major driver of a more commercial sector, encouraging rounds of consolidation and the spread of market-simulating accounting and valuation techniques; this early wave of financialisation was characterised by providers facing new requirements to manage their assets as collateral and secure more debt.[43]

IV. DE-RISKING LENDING THROUGH THE USE OF STOCK AS COLLATERAL

Financialisation has further been de-risked for lenders via associations using stock as collateral in order to secure loans against their assets, introducing a further source of precariousness into the homes of social housing tenants.[44] In the event of a provider becoming insolvent or otherwise in breach of a

38 Ibid.

39 Norman Ginsburg 'The Housing Act 1988 and its policy context: A critical commentary' (1989) 9 *Critical Social Policy* 56.

40 David Cowan, *Housing Law and Policy* (Cambridge, Cambridge University Press, 2011).

41 Hughes and Lowe (n 31 above).

42 ibid.

43 Michael Pryke and Christine Whitehead, 'The provision of private finance for social housing: An outline of recent developments in funding existing housing associations in England' (1993) 8 *Housing Studies* 274.

44 Heywood (n 2 above).

loan agreement, this meant that the lender could legally repossess the home of a tenant if it had a charge attached to it, bringing that home out of the regulated social housing sector. A tenant would be likely in such a situation to keep the protection of their tenancy agreement, ensuring some security, but would lose the rent level protection that comes with being in the social housing sector.[45] Unless housing benefit were to cover their rent, then this could expose tenants in a repossessed property to the risk of rent hikes and possible eviction. Both tenants and providers were therefore exposed to the risk of greater precarity, with a default also making it likely that lenders would charge much higher rates on the borrowing of the sector as a whole. Although an unmanaged insolvency is yet to occur and it is uncertain what action the state would take given the potential costs, it has nevertheless enabled lenders to attain a position of power within the sector's governance, given the willingness of lenders to provide capital essential for housing associations to access money for development and refurbishment.[46]

Lending to the sector up to the 2008 financial crisis was largely dominated by a small number of high street banks, with just five holding 85 per cent of the sector's debt in 2008.[47] Associations prefer to borrow on fixed-rate terms for long 25-year periods that enable them to embed certainty into their business plans. This is not ideal for banks, who raise cash to fund their loans on an ongoing basis from money markets with unpredictable interest rate fluctuations, but an implicit expectation of stability due to the sector's regulatory governance helped de-risk the sector from the perspective of lenders and provide them with reassurance that they would get their money back.[48] This stability was bolstered through indirect subsidies to the sector in the form of housing benefit, a means-tested social security payment intended to partly cover rental costs, which was paid directly to landlords rather than tenants, providing assurance against arrears.[49] Financialisation in associations from the late 1980s therefore depended heavily on the sector's relation to the state as mediated through the regulatory framework, with ratings agencies classifying them as analogous to public sector organisations despite their independent existence as privately owned property companies, though ones run on a not-for-profit basis.[50]

Development of the regulatory governance of housing associations has been a process in which the regulator, providers and lenders and their

[45] Fieldwork interview with senior housing policymaker (Summer 2015).

[46] Cowan and McDermont (n 1 above).

[47] Tenant Services Authority, 'Private Finance Strategy' (TSA, 2009).

[48] Peter Williams, 'Private Finance for a Social Purpose: Mortgage Lenders and Housing Associations Within the UK' (June 2003) *Housing Finance International* 9.

[49] Hughes and Lowe (n 31).

[50] TradeRisks, 'Social Housing Bonds' (TradeRisks, 2012); Moody's Investors Service, 'Rating Methodology: English Housing Associations' (Moody's Investors Service, 2013).

respective representative bodies have all taken active roles in negotiating and defining the sector's identity through shaping standards and practices, such as audit and account formats that can be readily understood and used by lenders.[51] In the development of this framework however, the retention by lenders of their power to access security has been a major determining factor in the sector's development, due to the serious consequences if social housing stock is repossessed. Although this power has not yet been used, lenders have actively defended their rights against the government; a potential infringement of this ability in draft bills of the Housing Act 1996 prompted a capital strike by lenders until the offending provisions were struck out.[52] Repossession of housing association stock is not necessarily an option they would wish to take given the chance of reputational damage and the risk that it would not cover costs, but this power nonetheless provides protection against uncertainty, an example of how financialisation in public services such as social housing can rest on legal powers to mediate and pass on risk.

The rights of lenders to take possession of collateral from an association in default have been a fundamental power minimising the inherent uncertainty of lending, acting as a key enabler of financialisation even if it is a power that has never been activated. Liberalisation in the consents regime governing stock disposals has enabled greater freedom for associations in asset management and the use of their stock as collateral, associated with auditing and accounting practices that have taught them to think of their stock as assets. Although operational and development risk was formally passed to associations throughout this period, the state still played an implicit role in acting as a backstop to the sector, with risk to lenders minimised through the assumption that the government would act to guarantee the debts of the sector in the event of a crisis.[53] Managing the regulation of the sector with an eye to lenders has been a constant focus of the regulator, even leading to criticism by select committee MPs in 2013 when it emerged that the HCA was reluctant to officially downgrade the viability ratings of housing associations in the fear that it might trigger a repricing of debt by creditors.[54] How austerity has the potential to increase the precariousness of this model and generate the potential for greater precarity among providers and tenants is the question to which this chapter will now turn.

[51] Morag McDermont, 'Territorializing Regulation: A Case Study of "Social Housing" in England' (2007) 32 *Law and Social Inquiry* 373.

[52] Christine Whitehead and Peter Williams, 'Development and Change: Private Finance for Social Housing in the UK.' (A Background Paper for the LSE London Finance Seminar, London, LSE, 2009).

[53] Heywood (n 2 above).

[54] Communities and Local Government Select Committee, *The Work of the Regulation Committee of the Homes and Communities Agency: Second Report of 2013–14* (2013–14, HC 310).

V. PRECARITY AND UNCERTAINTY UNDER AUSTERITY URBANISM

The financial crisis devastated the balance sheets of many banks, raising their cost of funds and causing many of the loans they had made to housing associations prior to 2008 to become unprofitable.[55] Although banks scaled back lending, associations were able to sustain access to capital through the bond markets, with institutional investors such as pension funds and insurance companies hunting for safe long-term assets with which to offset their own liabilities in the context of a global slump and weak growth.[56] Lending through the bond markets can be attractive for associations in that it offers long-term fixed-rate debt on the 25-year timescales they require, although bonds are less flexible and setting up deals requires assembling a more complex and daunting range of different organisations.[57] Large associations are able to participate in their own bond issues, while smaller providers pool resources through aggregator companies such as The Housing Finance Corporation, a non-profit entity founded by the government in the 1980s.[58] Lenders can also be wary of associations taking on greater levels of commercialisation by expanding beyond core social housing services into areas such as market sale or rent, given the greater exposures to risk this brings, troubling their status as safe and reliable assets.[59]

Austerity policies imposed since 2010 potentially undermine this stability through means such as welfare cuts, reduced grants and funding regimes predicated on a greater reliance on commercial income. Social housing tenants disproportionately rely on benefits to cover their incomes and have been hit hard by welfare retrenchment, with sanctions becoming a *de facto* routine part of the benefits system and spending reductions and more restrictive criteria aimed at groups such as people in receipt of disability benefits who are disproportionately represented in social housing.[60] Overall planned welfare reforms come to a £19 billion spending reduction if fully implemented, with likely effects being to intensify spatial concentrations of deprivation while increasing the possibility of rent arrears.[61] Specific housing benefit cuts such as the politically-named 'bedroom tax' that deducts payments if social housing tenants are deemed to have one or more spare

[55] Ibid 35.

[56] International Monetary Fund, 'Safe Assets: Financial System Cornerstone?' (IMF, 2012).

[57] Andy Taylor, 'Coping with Financial Cuts: Keeping the Core Business on Track' (Barclays Corporate, 10 May 2011).

[58] Heywood (n 2 above).

[59] Thomas Wainwright and Graham Manville, 'Financialisation and the Third Sector: Innovation in social housing bond markets' (2017) 49 *Environment and Planning A* 819.

[60] Christina Beatty, Mike Foden, Lindsey McCarthy and Kesia Reeve, 'Benefit Sanctions and Homelessness: a scoping report' (Centre for Regional Economic and Social Research, March 2015).

[61] Christina Beatty and Steve Fothergill, 'The Local and Regional Impact of the UK's Welfare Reforms' (2014) 7 *Cambridge Journal of Regions, Economy and Society* 63.

bedrooms have garnered particular controversy,[62] while the proposed rolling of existing benefits into a single 'Universal Credit' may increase the risk of arrears through paying housing benefit to tenants rather than directly to landlords.[63] Cumulatively these have the potential to increase displacement, with one quantitative study from the regional city of Leeds indicating greater housing precarity and moves from social housing into the private rented sector, associated with housing benefit cuts.[64]

This increase in the precarity of tenants was accompanied by a reduction in their security however, changes that have the potential to place their relationship with housing associations on a more commercial footing.[65] Precariousness has been increased through the Localism Act 2011's removal of the statutory underpinnings by which associations were obliged to grant so-called 'lifetime' tenures, although the actual uptake of 'fixed-term' tenancies by associations beyond probationary periods for new tenants has so far been patchy and uneven.[66] Grant funding has been reduced as a proportion of new developments, with remaining subsidies largely made available for shared ownership products and a new form of 'affordable rent' tenure that can be offered at up to 80 per cent of market rent, intended to shift the weight of finance onto the rental streams of providers rather than grants from central government.[67] At the same time, regulatory powers over tenant standards have been downgraded since 2012, with grounds for intervention by the regulator subject to a highly stringent 'serious detriment' test that would require the possibility of occurrence of major harms before the HCA would step in.[68] Although the impact of these reforms is necessarily long term, they have the potential to change the relation between providers and tenants, cementing the final residualisation of the tenure and converting it into an 'ambulance service' for the most vulnerable as it becomes less and less likely to be able to act as a tenure that can provide secure, long-term housing.[69]

[62] Helen Carr and David Cowan, 'The Social Tenant, the Law and the UK's Politics of Austerity' (2011) 5 *Oñati Socio-legal Series* 73.

[63] Anne Power, Bert Provan, Eileen Herden and Nicola Serle, 'The Impact of Welfare Reform on Social Landlords and Tenants' (Joseph Rowntree Foundation, 2014).

[64] Stuart Hodkinson, Andy Turner and Chris Essen, 'Exploring the Impacts and Implications of a Changing UK Welfare State under Digitalisation and Austerity: the Case of Leeds. Final Report, Pilot Study on Welfare and Austerity for the RCUK Digital Economy 'Communities and Culture' Network +' (University of Leeds, 2016).

[65] Power et al (n 63 above).

[66] Elizabeth Parkin and Wendy Wilson, 'Social Housing: the end of "lifetime" tenancies in England?' (Briefing Paper 07173, House of Commons Library, 2016).

[67] Stuart Hodkinson and Glyn Robbins, 'The Return of Class War Conservatism? Housing policy under the UK Coalition government' (2013) 33 *Critical Social Policy* 57.

[68] Homes and Communities Agency, 'The Regulatory Framework for Social Housing in England from 2012' (n 36 above).

[69] Hodkinson and Robbins (n 67 above); Suzanne Fitzpatrick and Hal Pawson, 'Ending Security of Tenure for Social Renters: Transitioning to 'ambulance service' social housing?' (2014) 29 *Housing Studies* 597.

The unexpected re-election of the Conservatives with a full working majority in 2015 brought a range of new measures into the sector that have the potential to undermine the perceived stability that associations have so far relied on in dealing with lenders, however. Among these has been the planned extension of the Right to Buy to housing association tenants, a controversial measure still undergoing trials that is likely to undermine the asset base of providers if implemented, even though they will be compensated for sales.[70] An annual one per cent rent cut between 2016 and 2020 has also been imposed through the Welfare Reform and Work Act 2016 in order to bring down housing expenditure, a move likely to have a huge cumulative impact on association business plans through undermining their income streams.[71] The vote for the UK to leave the European Union is likely to have further effects on the sector, given the possibility of economic turbulence and political upheaval, though any full assessment of the impacts at this time is speculative and beyond the scope of this chapter.

As argued above, this stability provided by the legal and regulatory system has been a vital mediator of financialisation within housing associations, acting to insulate lenders from the risks of insolvency, while the preservation of the ability of lenders to take charge of their collateral has acted as a major hedge against uncertainty. In exploring how this is reshaped under austerity in a post-financial context of greater volatility, the next section of this chapter draws on fieldwork data with social housing stakeholders generated over 12 months between 2015 and 2016 immediately prior to and in the aftermath of the Conservative re-election. Grounded in semi-structured interviews with key stakeholders such as accountants, policymakers, consultants and association executives, the following explores the extent to which any precarities arising from this situation are passed on to providers and, ultimately, tenants.

VI. GOVERNING PRECARIOUSNESS IN A 'POST-CRISIS' CONTEXT

By undermining public subsidy and opening up housing associations to further commercial pressures, austerity generates new risks and uncertainties within social housing that have to be managed in order for financialisation to continue in the aftermath of the financial crisis. This section argues that in governing enhanced precariousness, the regulatory framework is adapting to a form comparable to the managed precarity outlined by Lorey,[72] enacted

[70] National Housing Federation, 'An Offer to Extend Right to Buy Discounts to Housing Association Tenants' (NHF, 2015).

[71] Nick Billingham, 'Social Landlords in the Firing Line: Rent reduction and the Welfare Reform and Work Bill 2015' (2015) 18 *Journal of Housing Law* 106.

[72] Lorey (n 11 above).

less through the granting or withholding of collective security, and more by the normalisation of precariousness as part of a wider retrenchment of neoliberalisation. For the Homes and Communities Agency (HCA) 'poor governance' is recognised as 'a leading indicator of financial weakness',[73] and recent emphasis has been on improving the ability of associations to act in a crisis through measures such as stress testing, asset and liability registers, and greater skills requirements on boards. These are intended to enable quick response in a crisis, identifying the circumstances that would break a provider's cash flow and its implications for the stricken association's stock, while developer associations liable to these risks are intended to have governing board members with the requisite expertise to handle the situation.[74]

In governing this precariousness however, I argue there has been a shift in regulatory emphasis in how the sector's orientation to future uncertainty is managed through the entrenchment of commercial approaches that redistribute risks from lenders onto providers and tenants. This in turn leads to greater precarity in the present, as greater numbers of people risk exclusion and displacement from social housing through these practices. As pointed out by Langley,[75] measures such as stress testing have a performative aspect, in that they attempt to 'manage the financial future in the present'[76] by dealing with the uncertainty of crisis events that cannot be predicted through probabilistic risk calculations, shaping actions now through anticipation of future events. Prior to the financial crisis for example, financialisation was often discursively legitimised on the grounds that it enabled the accurate pricing and trading of exposures to risk for market participants, an assumption undermined by the credit crunch and the failure to account for systemic risk.[77] Managing the uncertainties of this new situation has been a significant legacy of financialisation in a 'post-crisis' context, with consequences for how any precarity the shift to finance generates is transferred to groups such as social housing tenants.

In particular, I argue that the weakened power of the regulator in a context of heightened uncertainty has manifested itself in a shift in regulatory and legal emphasis toward preparedness for the next crisis, rather than trying to prevent associations experiencing the impacts of crisis. In his analysis of stress testing in the financial sector, Langley[78] draws on the typology

[73] Homes and Communities Agency, 'Regulating the Standards' (HCA, 2016) 8.
[74] Ibid.
[75] Langley, *The Everyday Life of Global Finance: saving and borrowing in Anglo-America* (n 14 above).
[76] Ibid 68.
[77] Randy Martin, Michael Rafferty and Dick Bryan, 'Financialisation, Risk and Labour' (2008) 12 *Competition and Change* 120.
[78] Langley, *The Everyday Life of Global Finance: saving and borrowing in Anglo-America* (n 14 above).

by Anderson[79] of three strategies for coping with future uncertainty. These include preventing an identified threat through *precaution*, taking action on the basis of indeterminate threats through *pre-emption*, and attempting to anticipate disaster through *preparedness*. For Langley, new regulatory frameworks in the aftermath of the financial crisis have entailed a greater shift to preparedness as a strategy, with a heightened need for market actors to demonstrate resilience in the face of unpredictable but nevertheless feasible threats, such as another market crash. Within social housing, as the regulator experiences diminished resources under austerity while associations have come to rely on more commercial sources of income, it has faced a policy problem of how to manage the risk exposure of creditors in such a way as to continue to induce them to lend. Returning to the earlier point made by Froud[80] in section II of this chapter however, the removal of uncertainties for lenders has resulted in both the continued exposure of the state to the consequences of provider failure, restricting its future policy options, while intensifying the precarity experienced by tenants as associations are encouraged to adopt more commercial approaches.

A. Precariousness and the Precautionary Insolvency Regime in the Governance of Housing Associations

Recent years have increased the precariousness of the operating environment for associations, with measures such as the imposed one per cent annual rent cut coming alongside a greater push for associations to commercialise and the greater size and complexity of many providers within the sector.[81] This is a potential problem for the perceived stability of associations that has hitherto underpinned lending to the sector however, which has so far relied on an implicit assumption that government and regulatory support would continue to ensure that no association would collapse. This perception among lenders has been undermined by government actions since the election such as the rent cut and right to buy expansion, leading to an erosion of trust in the sector's stability as illustrated by the following quote from a financial consultant to the sector:

> There's been a very beneficial willing suspension of disbelief on the part of investors, the HCA and the government. There is no guarantee but let's pretend there is, sort of thing, and very right. It's £60bn of private finance on very good terms

[79] Ben Anderson, 'Preemption, precaution, preparedness: Anticipatory action and future geographies' (2010) 34 *Progress in Human Geography* 777.

[80] Froud (n 20 above).

[81] Trowers & Hamlins, 'Quarterly Housing Update: Housing and Planning Act 2016 edition' (Trowers & Hamlins, 2016).

that's been arranged on that, and government action has at a stroke more or less destroyed that. *(Financial consultant)*[82]

The increased precarity of lenders in this more precarious context is further illustrated by the introduction of a new insolvency regime under the Housing and Planning Act 2016, following on from recommendations in the Altair report that was commissioned to investigate the near collapse of Cosmopolitan.[83] Previously the regulator in the event of an insolvency would have to secure the agreement of all creditors for a moratorium period of 28 days while it attempted to engineer a rescue in order to prevent social housing stock from being repossessed, most likely a merger with another, larger association.[84] Alongside extending its scope to all assets owned by an association, not just its social housing assets, the new insolvency regime contains a crucial innovation through enabling the regulator to apply for a court appointed administrator to oversee a stricken housing association. A court appointed administrator would have a 12-month period to oversee proposals and attempt to rescue the provider as a going concern or otherwise govern the disposal of its assets, a more feasible time period with which to work with.[85] This may be considered an example of precautionary action, given the identified threat of needing to deal with an insolvency, but, as argued below, this turn to the courts also suggests a new and potentially more adversarial relation between associations and the regulator, in view of the perceived greater likelihood of default.

The involvement of the courts sparked concern among lenders over issues such as the power of the administrator to withhold interest rates. This led to a burst of lobbying that ensured that the wording of the legislation explicitly prioritised the achievement of a solution in the best interest of creditors over the goal of ensuring that social housing stock that may be effected remained within the housing association sector, though the need to rescue a provider as a going concern continued to be the primary priority in statute.[86] Reassurance of lenders in this case can therefore be seen to have come through the transfer of precarity downward onto housing association tenants, who now have fewer legal rights against having their homes repossessed from the social housing sector in the event that their landlord becomes bankrupt. This nevertheless gave comfort to lenders, although the turn to the courts and the beefed up regime nevertheless left creditors feeling less certain over

[82] PhD fieldwork data (Spring 2016).

[83] Altair Consulting, 'Cosmopolitan Housing Group: lessons learned' (Altair Consulting, 17 June 2014) altairltd.co.uk/2014/06/cosmopolitan-housing-group-lessons-learned/.

[84] Trowers & Hamlins (n 81 above).

[85] Ibid.

[86] Stephen O'Grady and Jack Isaacs, 'The New Special Administrations Regime for Social Housing Providers in England' (*Out-Law*, 8 September 2016): www.out-law.com/en/articles/2016/september/the-new-special-administration-regime-for-social-housing-providers-in-england/.

protecting their loan interests, as this subsequent quote from the consultant referenced above indicates:

> I think the HCA has managed to satisfy most lenders with the wording around the primary function of administration would be to protect first charge lenders and housing tenants, and that's given comfort to most lenders, but I think there's still a few that are very concerned about that change and the uncertainty that adds to in terms of existing and new lending. *(Financial consultant)*[87]

Although this new regime acts as an infringement on the formal rights of lenders compared to the previous moratorium process, the change in process to a court appointed administrator represents a deeper underlying shift in the relationship between lenders and the regulator. As pointed out by Veitch,[88] drawing on Loughlin,[89] in the former's analysis of how legal forms structure who can be made accountable for collective harms, the translation of political conflicts into 'justiciable' legal terms can transform normative understandings, shifting policy disputes into 'dispute over competing rights claims that can be adjudicated by courts'.[90] It is possible therefore that the shift to a court appointed administrator process may be a reflection of a declining authority of the regulator to reconcile the interests of creditors, particularly given the increased range and complexity of lenders via the recent turn to bond markets. While this is a topic that requires further research, it could indicate an important new source of precariousness within the housing association sector if the relation between lenders and the regulator is increasingly framed as an adversarial one of competing rights claims legally enforceable by the state, rather than being governed by less formal and more mutual understandings.

B. Managed Precarity and the 'Preparedness' of Housing Associations

Responding to this greater precariousness has been important for the regulation of housing associations, with the need to maintain the willingness of creditors to lend to the sector in an environment where the regulator has fewer resources and the primary attraction of housing associations as safe assets needs to be maintained to attract institutional finance. The near collapse of Cosmopolitan Housing Group in 2013 due to failed student housing developments—an association with complex financial arrangements poorly

[87] PhD fieldwork data (Spring 2016).

[88] Scott Veitch, *Law and Irresponsibility: On the legitimation of human suffering* (Oxford, Routledge-Cavendish, 2007).

[89] Martin Loughlin, *Sword and Scales: An Examination of the Relationship between Law and Politics* (Oxford, Hart Publishing, 2000).

[90] Veitch (n 88 above) 83.

understood by its governing board that exposed its social housing stock to liabilities in its commercial developments—represented a major crisis for this model, however. Unmanaged failure in one association would likely raise the cost of finance for the sector as a whole, damaging their reputation as safe and stable assets. Ensuring that such a failure does not happen has been a major priority for the regulator, as indicated by this following quote from a solicitor in a law firm that advises the sector:

> Cosmopolitan slightly shocked the world, and I think in a way that's why the HCA post-Cosmopolitan have been very, very, very, very, very keen to make all their registered providers understand that this was a really serious, a really serious thing. And I think almost, because it happened at a time when the private investors, the institutional investors were just beginning to go into the market, and all of a sudden all the things they feared most were happening. *(Solicitor)*[91]

Ensuring that the housing association sector as governed by its regulatory framework can demonstrate that another Cosmopolitan either does not happen or could be managed effectively without risking the money of creditors has therefore been a major priority for the HCA. This precariousness of housing associations in the event of such a crisis, given a less favourable policy context and the possibility of further housing market upheaval, remains a major concern for the regulator even given the current high surpluses and seeming robustness enjoyed by many associations, as indicated by this quote from a senior housing policymaker:

> What is worrying is that even in this relatively benign period where welfare reform has rolled out slowly, the housing market has been pretty buoyant, and interest rates have been at all-time lows …
>
> … which has led to the higher surpluses, but even in that very benign period we've had quite a number of associations getting into trouble. *(Senior housing policymaker)*[92]

Although the regulator retains powers over setting standards in governance and viability and value for money that impact on how associations are perceived by lenders, austerity has reduced the funding available for it to intervene to ensure the security of providers in the event of a major crisis, such as another property market crash.[93] The recent imposition of regulatory liberalisation in the Housing and Planning Act 2016 additionally removes tools such as the ability to withhold consent for the use of social housing stock in index-linked finance deals such as those involved in

[91] PhD fieldwork data (Summer 2015).
[92] PhD fieldwork data (Summer 2015).
[93] Interview with a senior housing policymaker (Summer 2015).

the Cosmopolitan debacle, further limiting the direct scope for intervention by the regulator and placing the sector as a whole into a more precarious position. Within this context, an emphasis on increasing the sector's crisis management capacity through means such as stress testing, asset and liability registers and greater skills requirements for boards can be viewed as instituting greater preparedness in the event of a harsher future environment, making associations more resilient in the face of volatility.

C. Commercialisation and the Transfer of Risk onto Tenants and the Public

The emphasis on preparedness raises the issue, however, of the implications of regulating insecurity as a tool of governance highlighted by Lorey,[94] including the transfer of risk and precarity onto others within social housing such as tenants, in a post-financial crisis context where the future has become subject to greater uncertainty.[95] Associations now have a greater expectation for resilience, but this may also further embed financialisation that may further entrench precariousness within contemporary UK cities, making associations structurally dependent on acting more in accordance with commercial practices, for example in dealing with rent arrears. This is reflected in the changing stance of the regulator, which has shifted to a more permissive stance with respect to evictions, given the need for associations to reduce their own uncertainty over their incomes, as indicated by the following quote from a solicitor advising the sector:

> Until relatively recently the HCA's policy was that they shouldn't evict people just on the basis of rent arrears. There normally had to be some other compelling reason why. But I think now housing associations are saying they have committed to a business plan, we cannot—I mean, don't get me wrong, they will do all they possibly can to help somebody, but at the end of the day they cannot risk too great arrears. *(Solicitor)*[96]

In addition to a greater chance of evictions there is also the possibility of a changing tenant profile, as social housing becomes more exclusionary for people impacted by welfare reform. Cuts to housing benefit and other support, alongside the planned move toward universal credit paid directly to the tenant rather than the social landlord, are likely to make rental streams less secure. The recovery from the financial crisis has been precarious for many on low incomes, and although mass unemployment seen in previous

[94] Lorey (n 11 above).

[95] Paul Langley, 'Anticipating uncertainty, reviving risk? On the stress testing of finance in crisis' (2013) 42 *Economy and Society* 51.

[96] PhD fieldwork data (Summer 2015).

recessions has not occurred, real wage growth in the UK has been poor and its labour market is increasingly characterised by 'flexible', precarious and temporary work.[97] As a result welfare reform has the potential to impact a broad range of tenants who move in and out of employment, resulting in the potential for more associations to explicitly include affordability criteria when deciding who to house, as indicated by the quote below from a housing association executive in a northern city:

> The thing is most of the people we rehouse are on zero hours contracts or part-time employment, fairly insecure employment, so even when you house people and they are in employment, chances are a few months later they're not going to be. So will we therefore start to vet our tenants based on incomes and ability to pay, whereas in the past it's been, our lettings policies have been based on need pretty much. It's a big change. *(Housing association executive)*[98]

As implied in this quote the extent to which associations adopt this remains a matter of debate within the housing association sector itself, given the significance of moving from a needs-based lettings system to one where the ability to pay takes a greater role. This indicates attitudinal and cultural shifts play a role in the extent to which associations adopt commercial values and metrics, indicating that financialisation is not a mechanical process but one that has to be actively negotiated and internalised through the organisational identity of associations.[99] Although the regulator may not directly prescribe these measures, it nonetheless can enable these attitudinal reforms within the sector through taking a less prescriptive stance toward lettings policies. This is indicated by the highlighted portion of this quote from a senior housing policymaker familiar with the regulatory framework in regards to greater commercial pressures driving associations in an 'upmarket' direction:

> There will be I guess some pressures that could be construed as driving housing associations upmarket. But equally they're very alive to that risk and they have to, <u>that's one for them to balance rather than for us to balance.</u> We don't tell associations what business model they ought to have, but we are conscious that they would be faced with those kinds of dilemma. And it's their job to work out how they best meet their usually charitable objectives. *(Senior housing policymaker)*[100]

Here can be seen how the enactment of financialisation has resulted in a transference of risk onto tenants as mediated by the regulatory framework,

[97] Jeremy Green and Scott Lavery, 'The Regressive Recovery: Distribution, inequality and state power in Britain's post-crisis political economy' (2015) 20 *New Political Economy* 894.

[98] PhD fieldwork data (Autumn 2015).

[99] See also Manzi and Morrison (n 3 above).

[100] PhD fieldwork data (Summer 2015).

with a greater permissiveness toward commercialisation as a means of negotiating a more precarious housing context. The cost of this is likely to be greater precarity for tenants, as more find themselves excluded from social housing in the future as associations are pressured in a more commercial direction.

Recalling the distinction by Froud[101] between risk and uncertainty however, the contingencies and uncertainties of future events mean that the state still bears some of the risks of this transition. A genuine unmanaged insolvency and the collapse of a provider with its stock repossessed by lenders would likely be politically disastrous to a government that still requires housing associations in order to meet housing policy criteria. Pushing associations too far in a commercial direction if they are perceived as unready to meet these risks may result in lenders ultimately withdrawing from the sector, leaving the government with the possibility of having to take responsibility for both the sector's £60 billion debts and the £40 billion in public grants the government has historically invested in it. The ambiguities of this are indicated in the following quote from an auditor in reference to the contestation between lenders and the Conservative Finance Minister of the time, George Osborne:

> The funders are saying that if you push too far we'll see it as more risky, and then the government's got to think about where that funding will come from. The worst thing they want is that funding comes back onto them, into public, and … they'll ease off them. He does not want all that debt, George Osborne, does he? Coming back onto public books. *(Auditor)*[102]

The entrenchment of financialisation in the more precarious context since the financial crisis therefore indicates the continued need for state intervention and support if the welfare state is to continue to be a source of profitable accumulation for financial actors. Financialisation can therefore be seen here not to be a matter of deregulation or the retreat of the state provision in favour of the market,[103] but a process that requires the ongoing mediation of legal and regulatory frameworks to manage risks and uncertainties within a more precarious housing context.

VII. CONCLUSION

Financialisation of welfare services is often justified through the transference of risk to the private sector in exchange for the assumed benefits of

101 Froud (n 20 above).
102 PhD fieldwork data (Spring 2016).
103 Aalbers (n 26 above).

market efficiency. This rests on a conflation between risk and uncertainty however,[104] as private actors need to be insulated from the uncertainties and contingencies of social delivery, a process often mediated through legal and regulatory frameworks that see risks re-appear through their transfer back to service users and ultimately the state. These can have consequences for the imposition of greater precarity on service users, as risks are passed from lenders to providers to welfare state recipients. Although associations operate independently and are still largely not-for-profit actors, the shift to private finance since the late 1980s has brought greater commercialisation into the sector that is likely to be exacerbated by current austerity policies that have increased the precariousness of the sector.

Although financialisation has continued in the aftermath of a the financial crisis, an operating environment characterised by greater risk has led to a weakening of the regulator in its relationship with a changing profile of lenders, as indicated by the shift toward the courts in the process for dealing with the potential insolvency of a provider. Weakened regulatory powers have led to a renewed emphasis on resilience among associations in light of the greater precariousness they are subject to, indicating how preparedness in the face of uncertainty is becoming a more important mode of governance in the aftermath of the financial crisis.[105] In associations this has also led to a greater emphasis on commercialisation and regulatory permissiveness toward more restrictive lettings policies, potentially increasing the precarity of social housing tenants through the exclusion of greater numbers of people from the sector. Financialisation has therefore been able to persist in the aftermath of the financial crisis, but at the cost of a rescaling of risks downwards, passed progressively from lenders, to providers, to low-income renters living within a more precarious housing system.

[104] Froud (n 20 above).

[105] Langley, 'Anticipating uncertainty, reviving risk? On the stress testing of finance in crisis' (n 95 above).

9

Safe and Sound: Precariousness, Compartmentation and Death at Home

EDWARD KIRTON-DARLING*

I. INTRODUCTION

IMMEDIATELY PRIOR TO final submissions for this book, the horrific fire at Grenfell Tower in west London broke out. It is too early to be able to draw proper conclusions about what caused that horrible fire on the night of 14 June 2017, but it appears many of the issues which may have contributed were foreshadowed in 2009 in the fire at Lakanal House also in London. This chapter focuses on that earlier disaster, and on the ways in which the Right to Buy—a policy allowing social tenants to purchase council properties—emerges in accounts of the deaths of six people at Lakanal House. Analysing the law and the response to that fire, it engages with the question of what death at home tells us about the contemporary governance of precarious life. I explore competing strategies of governance of precarious life and argue, drawing on Lorey,[1] that some of these strategies are deployed to precarise the residents of the high rise block, but that other competing approaches are also evident. In particular, I argue that the approach of central government is revealed as a deliberate deployment of narratives of ownership to provide a deregulated space, while local government frames the lease and the leaseholder as an obstruction, undermining its responsibility to keep high rise homes safe from fire.

Examining the legal technicalities, this chapter tests the hegemony of the model which Lorey proposes by undertaking a detailed situated analysis

* Contact Details Edward Kirton-Darling, Lecturer in Law, Kent Law School, University of Kent, ek276@kent.ac.uk. I would like to thank Helen Carr, Nick Piska and David Cowan for their reflections on this chapter as well as Jo Pearman for her help preparing the piece for publication. Any mistakes are my own.

[1] Isabell Lorey, *State of Insecurity: Government of the Precarious* (London, Verso, 2015).

of specific aspects of the general accounts of precariousness developed in Butler and Lorey's work. My discussion confirms the strength of these accounts, but also demonstrates that Lorey's framework fails to capture the continuing power of narratives of safety in modes of governance, and additionally highlights the importance of an engagement with context and space in such discussions.

The chapter is in five main sections; it opens with my account of scholarship on precarious life (section II) before I move to set out the background context on the Right to Buy in leasehold properties (section III). I then discuss the fire at Lakanal House (section IV), and in sections V and VI, I analyse the responses of central and local government to the fire. In my conclusion (section VII) I consider the future in the light of the Grenfell Tower fire.

II. GOVERNMENTAL PRECARISATION AND THE DISRUPTION OF SAFETY

Death is central to scholarship on precariousness. Precariousness, for Judith Butler, is inherent to a life lived with others; it is 'coextensive with birth'.[2] Living in a complex society means that a life is dependent on, sustained by, and vulnerable to the activities of anonymous others, rendering impossible claims of absolute control and protection. Therefore instead of focusing on an inevitably absent security, Butler's scholarship explores the differential value given to life and the role of death and grief in exposing contemporary precariousness. For Butler, bereavement is fundamental to a discussion of the ways in which the value of life relates to the apprehension of precarious life. Building on a discussion of the conflicting emotions she felt in the wake of the September 11 attacks[3] and work by Barthes and Derrida, she argues that the value of life only appears when the loss of life will be grieved: 'Without grievability, there is no life, or, rather, there is something living that is other than life. Instead "there is a life that will never have been lived," sustained by no regard, no testimony, and ungrieved when lost.'[4]

My focus is on inquests in this chapter because in England and Wales the responsibility to investigate sudden death and to produce an official public account of that death generally falls on the inquest system.[5] This ancient

[2] Judith Butler, *Frames of War: When is life grievable?* (London, Verso, 2010) 14.

[3] Judith Butler, *Precarious Life: the powers of mourning and violence* (London, Verso, 2004).

[4] Butler 2010 (n 2) 15.

[5] See Part 1, Coroners and Justice Act 2009 and associated secondary legislation, potentially acting alongside the criminal justice system. Although in some cases, as with Grenfell Tower, a public inquiry (potentially under the 2005 Inquiries Act) can also be held, which may supplant the inquest.

forum has undergone a contemporary renewal through human rights jurisprudence and recent legislative reform focused on a greater role for the bereaved, more contextual narrative conclusions, and greater emphasis on the prevention of future deaths.[6] It is a jurisdiction in which the Coroner is charged with curating a space which draws these narratives together,[7] and as such the inquest plays a critical role in exposing, in Butler's terms, who 'counts'. It is a place which reveals who is capable of being grieved—or conversely who, in Razack's terms, is framed as impossible to protect because their death was inescapable, because they were, in some sense, already dead.[8] Razack's work highlights the way in which deaths in marginalised communities—in her case, First Nation Canadians—are detached from the structural violence and injustice in which they occur. I return to reflect on this and the relationship of grievability and precariousness in my conclusion.

Lorey takes Butler's account of social precariousness as her starting point and focuses on the distribution of precariousness and its shifting role in governance.[9] She distinguishes between three categories: precariousness, which is Butler's condition of living a shared life with others; precarity—an orientation examining ordering and the production of hierarchy in precariousness (the ways in which some life is protected and some is not); and governmental (neoliberal) precarisation. She argues that liberal governmentality was legitimised through precarity—the protection of some, and the construction of dangerous others—while neoliberal governance relies on the removal of the safe/precarious distinction, such that 'insecurity becomes a normalised mode of governing.'[10] She therefore calls for attention on the ways in which precarisation is the contemporary mode of governing; destabilising, repressive but also ambivalently productive, a method which is based on engendering as much insecurity as possible before it leads to insurrection. 'Managing this threshold is what makes up the art of governing today.'[11] In her account, the withdrawal of the state from promises of

[6] In particular post-Human Rights Act 1998 case law linked to Article 2 European Convention on Human Rights (ECHR), the Coroners and Justice Act 2009, and the Coroners (Inquest) Rules and (Investigation) Regulations 2013.

[7] See eg G Tait and B Carpenter, 'Suicide and the therapeutic Coroner: Inquests, governance and the grieving family' (2013) 2 *International Journal for Crime, Justice and Social Democracy* 92–104; and B Carpenter, G Tait, N Stobbs and M Barnes, 'When Coroners care too much: Therapeutic jurisprudence and suicide findings' (2015) 24 *Journal of Judicial Administration* 172.

[8] See SH Razack, 'Timely deaths: Medicalizing the deaths of Aboriginal people in police custody' (2011) 9 *Law, Culture and the Humanities* 352; also see SH Razack, *Dying from Improvement: Inquests and Inquiries into Indigenous Deaths in Custody* (Toronto, University of Toronto Press, 2015).

[9] Lorey (n 1 above).

[10] Ibid 65.

[11] Ibid 2.

protection is a move away from a national 'normal' constructed through opposition to a deviant 'other'. Instead governance now operates through the regulation of 'a tolerable balance between diverse normalities'.[12] In this approach to governance, individuals are supposed to 'arrange their lives on the basis of a repeatedly lowered minimum of safeguarding'[13] and collective mechanisms which endeavour to create security and safety are diminished while the individual is fêted above all else. In modern Britain, perhaps the most visible material paradigm of this shift from the collective to the individual is the policy I turn to examine next: the Right to Buy.

III. THE RIGHT TO BUY AND PRECARISATION

Now closely associated with Margaret Thatcher's personal legacy, the Right to Buy is 'arguably one of the most iconic and significant applications of neoliberal policy worldwide'.[14] However, the basic policy—a right for local authority tenants to compulsorily purchase their home from the council—had first been mooted in 1947[15] and a version had been included in the January 1974 Conservative manifesto.[16] Prior to the 1980 Housing Act, there was a discretion to sell to tenants if approved by the Housing Minister, but despite a general consent issued by then Housing Minister Harold Macmillan in 1952, relatively few properties were sold until Conservative controlled councils in the 1960s in Birmingham, London and Manchester piloted widespread sales and, as Davies shows, made the idea politically viable. Taking up the idea, the Thatcher government swiftly passed the 1980 Act, marking a 'decisive turning point'[17] in post-war housing policy, rolling out a policy of compulsion, legislating for generous discounts for council tenants, and heralding the start of three decades of deregulation and privatisation of housing provision.[18]

Jones and Murie put total Right to Buy sales across the UK from 1979 to 2003 at 2.78 million,[19] and since then sales have continued, with an average

[12] Ibid 70.

[13] Ibid 71.

[14] Stuart Hodkinson, Paul Watt, and Gerry Mooney, 'Introduction: Neoliberal housing policy–time for a critical re-appraisal' (2013) 33 *Critical Social Policy* 3, 4.

[15] Aled Davies, '"Right to Buy": The Development of a Conservative Housing Policy, 1945–1980' (2013) 27 *Contemporary British History* 421.

[16] Colin Jones and Alan Murie, *The right to buy: Analysis and evaluation of a housing policy* (Oxford Blackwell Publishing, RICS Research, 2006) 27.

[17] Hodkinson, Watt, Mooney (n 14 above) 6.

[18] Including the 1988 Housing Act which deregulated private sector renting, and large-scale stock transfers from councils to arms-length bodies.

[19] Jones and Murie (n 16 above) 55.

over the period 2013–16 of approximately 16,000 per year in England.[20] Most dramatically, from a peak of 32 per cent in 1979 and 1980,[21] by 2016 local authority housing accounted for only 6.8 per cent of dwellings in the UK (although a further 10 per cent of dwellings were housing association properties).[22]

In his account of the development of the Right to Buy before 1980, Davies demonstrates the philosophical foundations for the policy, highlighting a Conservative Party research paper from 1953 entitled 'The Ownership of Property' which argued that the Party should seek to make property owning available to as wide a group as possible, being 'just as concerned to spread responsibility as to spread wealth.'[23] Unpicking this explicit underpinning emphasis on responsibility, Hunter and Blandy analyse the way in which the financial risks created by the Right to Buy act as a tool of responsibilisation. They argue that courts and local authorities have sought to move risk onto the shoulders of the Right to Buy purchaser, while central government has sought to ameliorate risk for owners: 'despite Government rhetoric which emphasises the benefits of the Right to Buy and ignores the risks, the courts ... have agreed with local authorities' allocation of risk to the individuals exercising the Right to Buy.'[24] As they show,

> the history of change to the Right to Buy legislation over the 1980s and 1990s shows governments acting to minimise risks to purchasers as they become apparent. Ultimately the courts refused to interpret these as providing a complete safety net to the Right to Buy purchasers.[25]

The outcome is that to advance a policy of responsibility and autonomy, central government intervened to protect their newly created class of owners from the responsibility and autonomy which otherwise might attach themselves to their status.

These developments must be read in the context of a tension between central government advocates of the policy and local government resistance to the depletion of their stock, and also in the context of a wider neoliberal agenda, including financialisation of housing.[26] However, at the same

[20] Department for Communities and Local Government, 'Live Tables on Social Housing Sales Table 671': www.gov.uk/government/statistical-data-sets/live-tables-on-social-housing-sales#right-to-buy-sales.

[21] Jones and Murie (n 16 above) 52.

[22] 'In England, at March 2016, making up the 23.7 million dwellings were 14.8 million owner occupied, 4.8 million private rented, 2.4 million rented from private registered providers (housing association) and 1.6 million rented from local authorities'—see Department for Communities and Local Government, 'Dwelling Stock Estimates 2016' (London, DCLG 2016).

[23] Quoted in Davies (n 15 above) 424.

[24] Sarah Blandy and Caroline Hunter. 'The Right to Buy: Examination of an exercise in allocating, shifting and re-branding risks' (2013) 33 *Critical Social Policy* 17, 25.

[25] Ibid 28.

[26] See discussion in D'Adda, Delgarda and Sala, Chapter fourteen of this volume.

time, it is essential to attend to the local distinctions which condition, shape and subvert the development of such global trends.[27] In this context, it is critical to acknowledge the particular issues which attach to management of Right to Buy properties in high rise blocks, in which residents of such blocks may now have neighbours with a range of tenures, including social tenants, leaseholders (either former council tenants who have exercised the Right to Buy or assignees of the lease who have purchased from the original owner), or private sector tenants of those leaseholders.[28] Jones and Murie note that 'selling flats has created severe management problems and management has generally become more complex and expensive',[29] as leaseholders are often not well informed about their obligations, there is a high turnover of leaseholders, and in London in particular, there are more flats which are let in the private sector.[30] In relation to financial risks for leaseholders, such blocks—unlike those in the private sector—have not generally had sinking funds or provision for major works built into their service charge costs,[31] which means owners are far more likely to be served with large bills for refurbishment. The impact is that such leaseholders are likely to be resistant to major works (which creates further management problems for the freeholder who retains responsibility for the overall fabric of the building) and, potentially having bought their home with a large discount and with little ready access to capital, may be particularly financially vulnerable, as Carr has argued. She demonstrates the problematic nature of a simplistic framing in which the Right to Buy transformed supplicant social tenants into property-owning responsible citizens.[32] In her detailed analysis of the conditional nature of Right to Buy ownership, she notes that New Labour initiatives to improve social housing resulted in 'extraordinary'[33] service charge demands on Right to Buy leaseholders, with a consequent high risk of impoverishment. Furthermore, her analysis of the nature of the ownership of those same leaseholders highlights the limited autonomy of the Right to Buy leaseholder, and the vulnerable and marginal nature of their ownership.

Drawing together this analysis with Lorey's taxonomy, the Right to Buy leaseholder is revealed as a paradigm of the citizen subjected to governmental precarisation, with the prioritisation of the productive ambivalence

[27] W Larner, 'Neoliberalism?' (2003) 21 *Environment and Planning D: Society and Space* 509.

[28] For a critical appraisal of the use of tenure in the management of social housing see: See Cowan and McDermott, *Regulating Social Housing: Governing Decline* (Abingdon, Routledge, 2006).

[29] Ibid 170.

[30] Jones and Murie (n 16 above), See discussion in Chapters seven and nine of this volume.

[31] Ibid 159.

[32] H Carr, 'The Right to Buy, the Leaseholder and the Impoverishment of Ownership' (2011) 38 *Journal of Law and Society* 519.

[33] Ibid 521.

of individual opportunity over collective responses to precarity framed by conceptions of housing need. It is an example of central government's management of widening precariousness—moving from a collective safety net to individual responsibility, and only intervening (as Hunter and Blandy demonstrate) when a crisis threatens a revolt.[34] Critically, the policy offered the illusion of security to social tenants while destabilising both the individual—subjected to the tension between a discourse of owner-occupier autonomy and the reality of a conditional mode of ownership—and the landlord, a local authority trapped between public-law-type responsibilities towards their social tenants and private law restrictions on their relationship with long leaseholders.

This chapter will develop this analysis by examining the fire at Lakanal House. An analysis of the fire and the investigations into the deaths it caused adds two aspects to the discussion set out above. Firstly, building on Hunter and Blandy and Carr, the discussion of Lakanal House demonstrates that risk in this context is not just financial, as vulnerability is founded here on not simply destitution, but on risks to life arising out of the fabric of the home and the space it occupies. It therefore highlights the need for an approach to precariousness which attends to the governance of these spaces,[35] of recognition of the distinctive role of space and the nature of high rise blocks, and the ways in which regulation of those blocks acts to protect or precarise. Secondly, that regulation reveals the complex interaction of modes of governance, and calls Lorey's shift from liberal to neoliberal forms of governance into question by demonstrating the continuing power of exclusionary safety. At the same time my analysis problematises that approach to governance, highlighting that the impact of keeping some safe and passing on risk to others is a passing on of risk to everyone sharing the space of the high rise building. And as the responses outlined below demonstrate, this is not an example in which central government has so far stepped in to ameliorate risk on behalf of anyone—leaseholders, social tenants, private tenants, or local authorities.

IV. THE FIRE AT LAKANAL HOUSE

Lakanal House in Camberwell, South London, a 15-storey Brutalist block of flats comprising 98 homes, was completed in 1960. It was owned and

[34] On which, see for example, the powers and duties in the Housing Act 1985 Part XVI in relation to defective properties sold under the Right to Buy, on which also see *Berry v Newport Borough Council* (2001) 33 HLR 19.

[35] On which, see Mara Ferreri, Gloria Dawson, and Alexander Vasudevan, 'Living precariously: property guardianship and the flexible city' (2017) 42 *Transactions of the Institute of British Geographers* 246.

managed by London Borough of Southwark ('Southwark'), and by 2009, it included a mixture of residents, including tenants of Southwark, leaseholders who had purchased flats under the Right to Buy (or who had bought from previous Right to Buy purchasers), and tenants of some of those leaseholders. Similarly to Grenfell Tower, it had undergone a recent refurbishment, including the removal of old asbestos insulation and a new exterior cladding added in 2006–07.

On 3 July 2009, a fire started in Flat 65. In the resulting blaze, three women and three children died: Dayana Francisquini and her daughter Thais and son Felipe; Helen Udoaka and her 20-day-old daughter Michelle; and Catherine Hickman. Lakanal House was designed so that each two-bedroom property in the building was built as a maisonette over two floors, with the kitchen and lounge on the upper level of the individual unit, and the bedrooms and bathrooms on the access level. Catherine Hickman was in the lounge of Flat 79 when the fire from Flat 65 spread upwards through the panels under the bedroom windows in her flat. In the findings into her death the jury found serious failures on the part of Southwark, including that panels under the window were required to be of limited combustibility,[36] and that asbestos removal and replacement with composite panels had a significant impact on the fire resistance of the external wall of Lakanal House. The fire warped the window frames, the curtains in the bedroom set alight, and the fire spread rapidly throughout the flat. According to the jury, Catherine Hickman was overcome by heat, smoke and later flames, and died in the lounge of Flat 79.

After the fire had spread to Flat 79, it also spread to Flats 37 and 53 and smoke spread around much of the rest of the building. Dayana Francisquini, Thais and Felipe Cervi, and Helen and Michelle Udoaka were sheltering together in the bathroom of Flat 81 when they were all overcome by the smoke. The jury found that they died from the smoke which was able to spread due to a serious failure of compartmentation. As the guidance on fire risk assessment highlights in its discussion of fire in high rise properties, compartmentation is the central feature of approaches to fire regulation in such buildings: 'In blocks of flats, each flat is designed to be a fire-resisting "box". It is important to maintain the integrity of this compartment, particularly when building work and alterations take place.'[37] In Lakanal House however, doors, panels and other parts of properties failed to offer sufficient resistance to the spreading fire; there were interconnecting ducts between bathrooms and a lack of adequate fire stopping around pipework.

[36] Known as Class 0, see Building Regulations Approved document B of 2010 vol 2.

[37] 'Fire safety in purpose-built blocks of flats', *Local Government Association*, May 2012, p 18: https://www.local.gov.uk/sites/default/files/documents/fire-safety-purpose-built-04b.pdf.

The jury found that a fire risk assessment might have identified the features which contributed to all six deaths, and that there were numerous opportunities during the refurbishment in 2006–07 to consider whether the level of fire protection was adequate. During the fire itself, all six acted on advice to 'stay put' from the fire brigade, and the inquest found that there were possibilities for escape, but that they were not aware of escape routes. Furthermore, the inquest found that insufficient efforts had been made to locate and rescue all six, and that confusion about the layout of the building had hampered the work of firefighters.

Following the inquest's conclusion on 28 March 2013, using her power under Rule 43 of the Coroners Rules 1984, the Coroner sent four letters; to Southwark, to the Department for Communities and Local Government (DCLG), to the Fire Sector Federation, and to the London Fire Brigade.[38] Prior to reforms in 2013[39] the legislation gave power to a Coroner to send reports about the circumstances of the deaths to anyone who has power to take some action, if the evidence in the inquest gave rise to a concern that circumstances creating a risk of other deaths will occur or continue to exist, and if the Coroner believed that some action should be taken to prevent future deaths. The letter to the Fire Sector Federation focused on training of fire risk assessors, while the letter to the London Fire Brigade set out issues about advice to residents, familiarisation of fire crews with the layouts of high rise buildings, and in relation to operational management of fire crews. My analysis focuses on the letters and responses to Southwark and the DCLG, and analyses these through Lorey's framework—focusing first on governmental precarisation, and then the deployment of precarity.

V. GOVERNING THROUGH PRECARISATION—THE APPROACH OF THE DCLG

Flat 79 in Lakanal House had been bought from Southwark under the Right to Buy scheme, and then subsequently sold on the open market. Ms Hickman was a private sector tenant of an assignee of that lease, and had rented the property with her boyfriend.

In addition to the criticisms around the exterior panelling and the response during the fire itself, the jury found that internal modifications to Flat 79 made more than a minimal contribution to Ms Hickman's death. The modifications included the removal of a staircase wall, which facilitated

[38] All the letters and responses are available, along with the verdicts by the jury into the six deaths (known as Inquisitions): www.lambeth.gov.uk/elections-and-council/lakanal-house-coroner-inquest.

[39] Which changed the power to a duty, and brought the requirement into primary legislation for the first time—see the Prevention of Future Death report under the Coroners and Justice Act 2009, Schedule 5, para 7.

the spread of smoke up the internal staircase into the lounge. The modifications had been undertaken by the leaseholder, and had been approved by Southwark as the freeholder, but with a recommendation that they be checked for fire safety by Southwark's Building Design Services. This check did not take place.

In relation to this modification, the Coroner's letters of 28 March 2013 to the DCLG noted that

> there remains uncertainty about the scope of inspection for fire risk assessment purposes which should be undertaken in high rise residential buildings. Evidence was adduced which indicated that inspection of the interior of flats or maisonettes in high rise buildings was necessary to enable an assessor to identify possible breaches of the compartment which have the potential to impact on the fire safety of the resident or others.

The Coroner proposed that clear guidance be put in place to assist authorities responsible for undertaking inspections.

The DCLG's (undated) letter was received by the Coroner on 20 May 2013. It stated that following the fire, they had worked with the Local Government Association and had funded the development of detailed national guidance. This guidance was published in the summer of 2011, and according to the DCLG, 'takes a practical approach to ensuring that those responsible for the safety of residents and others in purpose built blocks can take a comprehensive and pragmatic approach to managing risk effectively …'.[40]

The letter from the Secretary of State, Eric Pickles, goes on to state that feedback on the guidance has been very positive and it addresses the issues raised by the Coroner, but that further revisions might be made (to date, no further revisions have been published). Importantly, the letter pointedly ignores the fact that the Coroner had stated that her concerns were expressed 'notwithstanding publication of your Department's 2006 guide (Fire Safety Risk, sleeping accommodation) and of the Local Government Association's August 2011 guide.'[41] Critically, on the evidence heard by the Coroner, two years after the new guidance was published, uncertainty remained. The specific contents of that guidance are revealing, and an analysis of it explains why uncertainty might—quite reasonably—continue to exist amongst local authorities.

A. Deliberate Uncertainty and the Fire Safety Guidance

The guidance, 132 pages plus seven Appendices, acknowledges in its Introduction that there has been confusion over the scope of legislation in

[40] Letter from Eric Pickles to Lakanal House Coroner (20 May 2013).

[41] Letter from Coroner to the DCLG (28 March 2013).

relation to fire safety in purpose-built blocks of flats, and in particular how much control can be exercised over the insides of flats in such blocks, and states it aims to provide tailored guidance for housing providers and enforcing authorities.[42] It states explicitly that it applies irrespective of tenure, and uses the term 'resident' to cover all who live within the building (paragraph 3.9 page 13). However, in relation to the law governing fire safety in blocks of flats (Part C of the guidance) and in relation to fire risk assessment (Part D), it does acknowledge that differences in tenure may affect the way in which the local authority deals with fire safety. In some of its discussion of those differences, it overstates the autonomy of leaseholders—reaffirming the perceived lack of control of freeholders—and fails to give clear guidance to local authorities on the ability to inspect for modifications.

The guidance sets out the relevant legislative powers in Part C. It states that once a block of flats has been occupied, the control of fire safety falls under in the Housing Act 2004 and the Regulatory Reform (Fire Safety) Order 2005. While this is not incorrect, this framing reveals some of the underlying ideologies and tensions in relation to the Right to Buy flat, from the perspective of both local and central government. From a local government perspective, the leaseholder appears in the guidance as an obstacle to be overcome, not a citizen to be engaged with—it is telling, for example, that the Appendices include a case study of a 'three-storey leasehold block with uncooperative leaseholders.' There is no suggestion in the guidance that a freeholder might start by asking permission from a resident to enter to check for modifications. Clearly, a leaseholder focused solely on the possible costs of rectification might conceivably resist such a request, but this is not automatically the case, and it is also conceivable that a private tenant of that leaseholder might be more willing to permit access to a freeholder who was seeking to protect both their neighbours and themselves from fire.

The guidance also reflects a central and local government perspective[43] which emphasises the individual autonomy of the Right to Buy leaseholders, their ability to control their property and exclude unwanted entry, and so is founded on an assumption that the leaseholder has the legitimate right to restrict unwanted state interference. Part of this approach is seen in the presumption that the Right to Buy lease will not include a right of entry to check for modifications which might impact on the fire safety of the whole building. As a result, the lease itself is side-lined, and the possibility of the lease—and the covenants within it—acting as a potential tool for managing fire safety is excluded. For example, this lease might include the power to

[42] See Local Government Association, *Fire Safety in Purpose-Built Blocks of Flats* (London, LGA, 2012) Introduction, pp 2–3.

[43] While the Guidance is published by the Local Government Association, it was published at a time when both the LGA and central government were under the control of the same political party, and was also approved by the responsible Conservative Secretary of State (Eric Pickles).

enter properties on 48 hours' notice to inspect for modifications or necessary repairs (as, for example, in the case of a sample RTB lease produced by the Leasehold Advisory Service).[44] In some of the discussion in the guidance, it does implicitly acknowledge that some leases might include such a right, but failing to put the terms of the lease at the front of its discussion about how to manage fire risk means that no-one reading the guidance would go first to the lease as an enabling mechanism to respond to possible fire hazards.[45] For example, after outlining the statutory powers of entry, it discusses some common issues with the relationship between common parts and internal parts and states that in

> many existing leasehold flats, the responsibility for maintenance of the flat entrance doors rests with the residents ... In new leases, ideally the freeholder should retain control over all flat entrance doors.[46]

This is undoubtedly a sensible piece of advice in relation to the issues potentially caused by demised front doors in high rise blocks, but it is revealing that the guidance does not suggest that all new leases include the power of entry as set out in the sample Right to Buy lease. It does not consider and dismiss this; it is as if it were not within the frame of the possible approaches to Right to Buy properties. The governing presumption of the guidance is that the leasehold property is necessarily a space which remains out of reach of the freeholder, unless the exceptional circumstances arise where statute compels some action be taken.

The guidance suggests that these possible options lie within two pieces of legislation, the Housing Act 2004 (the 2004 Act—discussed by Carr in detail in Chapter seven in this volume), and the Fire Safety (Regulatory Reform) Order 2005 (the 2005 Order). The 2005 Order was a deregulatory piece of legislation which shifted responsibility away from fire authorities and 'introduced a self-compliance risk-based system, with primary responsibility imposed on employers, occupiers and owners of premises'.[47] Camiss and Manchester's empirical work suggests that, as a result, authorities have much less liaison and engagement with controllers of premises than under the previous legal regime.[48] Critically, the 2005 Order relates to common parts and gives no power of entry to private premises. In contrast, the 2004

[44] See Clause 3(5), The Leasehold Advisory Service, 'The Right to Buy Sample Lease': www.lease-advice.org.uk/documents/Sample_RTB_lease.pdf; and see advice from LEASE which describes this as a 'typical Local Council lease' p 4: www.lease-advice.org.uk/documents/Right_to_Buy.pdf.

[45] Furthermore, there is no reference to the possibility of taking action to enter leasehold properties and deal with potential issues using an action for breach of covenant.

[46] LGA (n 42 above) 40.

[47] Steven Cammiss and Colin Manchester. 'Application process and Decision-Making under the Licensing Act 2003.' (2011): www.lra.le.ac.uk/bitstream/2381/10017/2/2011_4_WebJCLI.pdf.

[48] Ibid.

Act gives power of entry to leasehold premises to check for hazards, and so the only way the guidance suggests that action to check for internal modifications is possible is via the Housing Health and Safety Rating System (HHSRS) under the 2004 Act.[49] In relation to discussion about when this might arise, the guidance merely notes that a local authority must have some reason to suspect that a hazard may exist.

Importantly, as the guidance does acknowledge, there is necessarily an overlap between the 2004 Act and the 2005 Order, as the division between individual flats and common parts is critical in maintaining compartmentation and protecting the common areas. As such, borders between flats and the common areas become key regulatory sites, and, in relation to front doors demised to the leaseholder, the guidance suggests that 'use of powers under the [2004] Act may be a more appropriate and better defined route to achieving compliance with the [2005 Order]' than treating the leaseholder as if they were persons with control over the common parts of premises and therefore responsible for ensuring the adequacy of the fire safety arrangements. From the perspective of a local authority charged with responding to this complexity, this appears a pragmatic approach, but it also amounts to a desire to emphasise the leaseholder/common parts distinction—to maintain the artificial boundaries between spheres of control.

While some such modifications such as front doors might at least be assessed without entering the property, others—such as the removal of the internal wall in Flat 79—can only be checked in a fire assessment which includes consideration of the internal features of the flat. The requirement to carry out a fire assessment is set out in the 2005 Order, and details of how to carry out a fire risk assessment are set out in Part D of the guidance. It is here that the guidance gives its most astonishing advice. It outlines four different kinds of risk assessment: Types one and two which involve inspection of common parts: and Types three and four which involve internal inspections. Type four involves internal destructive inspections, which the guidance states is the most comprehensive approach but would usually only be carried out in limited circumstances, so it is a Type three (non-destructive) risk assessment which is the most common type of internal assessment. In the discussion of a Type three assessment, which involves consideration of 'the arrangements for means of escape and fire detection [including] the fire resistance of doors to rooms' it states:

> A Type 3 fire risk assessment may sometimes be appropriate for rented flats if there is reason to suspect serious risk to residents in the event of a fire in their flats. (This might be, for example, because of the age of the block or reason for suspicion of widespread, unauthorised material alterations). This type of fire risk assessment will not be possible in the case of long leasehold flats, as there is normally no right of access for freeholders.[50]

[49] Discussed in detail in Carr in Chapter seven in this volume.
[50] LGA (n 42 above) 46.

It is not difficult to see why this guidance might confuse local authorities, who might reasonably wonder why the power of entry under the 2004 Act could not be used in such an instance if they had suspicion of widespread, material alterations. The guidance notes in an earlier section that the risk assessment under the 2005 Order should not be confused with the assessment of hazards under the 2004 Act, but it is not immediately obvious why an officer who had gained entry using their power to assess hazards could not subsequently complete a fire risk assessment based on the information they had gained during their visit or pass the information on to a fire risk assessor.

However, more fundamentally, while the guidance again acknowledges that there may sometimes be a lease-based right of access for freeholders but 'normally' there isn't, it states without condition that this kind of assessment will not be possible (rather than concluding it 'may' not be possible and they should check the lease for example). It is here that the guidance mostly clearly reveals its ideological underpinnings, emphasising the autonomy and privacy of the leaseholder and their inviolable space, which is only to be invaded in the most exceptional of circumstances. Critically, it generates ambivalence and confusion about the scope for such intervention, as highlighted by the Coroner in her letter. Contrary to the assertion of the DCLG in their response—that the guidance 'provides advice on when accessing individual flats for the purpose of inspecting the effectiveness of compartmentation and other fire safety measures should be considered'—the guidance does little but restate the statutory language in relation to the 2004 Act and is silent on what Southwark regards as a lacuna in the law—the lack of a statutory power of entry where no suspicion of a hazard has arisen.

Read in this way, the approach is revealed as a strategy deliberately premised on individualised precarisation, in which the state's role in protecting life is residualised, with the marginalisation or de-legitimation of possible collective responses to the risks presented by the complexity of intermingled life. In such strategies—ignoring the realities of messy everyday existence—governance is oriented towards the compartmentation of both properties and lives, and where such compartments are inevitably occasionally breached, any intervention undertaken is limited, exceptional and part of public law powers and duties; it is not part of the routine management of high rise life.

B. Southwark and the Mundane Reality

In contrast, the approach of Southwark is focused on that mundane reality. The Coroner had suggested that they do more in relation to fire inspection, and they responded to state that the lack of a right of access to Right to Buy flats meant they could not properly inspect such flats internally. Importantly, while they were aware of the modifications to Flat 79, and so might reasonably be said to have had reason to suspect a hazard might exist, the annual property check they rolled out could not be applied to properties where they had no reason to suspect a possible hazard might exist. Their check, which included checking for fire safety issues including modifications and 'any lifestyle issues',

> only applies to the council's tenanted properties and the council does not currently have a right of access to check the internal layout of leasehold properties without the owner's consent. This access issue is particularly important when the council is seeking to ensure the safety of all of its properties.
>
> [This is from the letter from Southwark to the Coroner for Lakanal House, 23 May 2013, page 5 of the letter]

Their response goes on to anticipate the response from the DCLG, stating that this issue is of national significance, and subject to the response from the DCLG and 'further exploration of the legal basis for inspection of all council properties … the council will continue with its current strategy.' (Southwark letter, page 5). The letter does not make any reference to potential rights of entry under the 2004 Act, using breach of covenant as a route to entry, or simply asking permission to enter. Similarly, later in the letter, the possibility of retrofitting sprinklers is ruled out in part because of access issues with Right to Buy properties, with the council noting that

> the effectiveness of a sprinkler system would be undermined if it was not installed to all individual properties in a block as it would leave parts of blocks unprotected, in some cases up to 50 per cent of the block.[51]

No suggestion is made that sprinklers could be offered to leaseholders, or that they could work with leaseholders to discuss prevention options, and throughout Right to Buy leaseholders are framed as a barrier to Southwark's public law duty to manage the risk of fire in all their properties.

On the issue of access for inspections the responses thus entirely fail to engage with each other, and in their refusal to hear each other, they re-expose the long-standing conflict between a central government which promotes Right to Buy, and a local government pulled between sufferance of and opposition to the policy. They also illustrate Lorey's account of a shift in modes of governance from liberal to neoliberal responses to precariousness. Analysed through this framework, the approach of Southwark appears as a collective net of security to those who fall within their control while the Right to Buy leaseholder is constructed as a dangerous outsider. Precarity—the hierarchisation of the precariousness of those governed—is thus central to their approach (as I will discuss further in the following section).

[51] Letter from LB Southwark to the Coroner (23 May 2013) 5.

In contrast, the approach of the DCLG relies on a widespread precarisation of residents of high rise blocks.

Despite the clear direction from the Coroner that there continued to be a lack of clarity around inspection, supported by the response from Southwark, the response of the DCLG rejected any claim of state responsibility for collective endeavours to manage precariousness caused by fire. Instead the DCLG—in line with the Right to Buy responsibilisation agenda—prioritised individual autonomy and responsibility. In a block of flats like Lakanal House, and perhaps at Grenfell Tower, such an approach amounts to a policy of collectively instituted insecurity, as the insecurity created by such a policy will not apply solely to residents in Right to Buy properties, but all those in the building, as discussed further below. The strategy adopted by DCLG of deregulation and the deliberately generated lacuna in enforcement powers is thus an individual instance of neoliberal precarisation through governance. What the fire at Lakanal House failed to do—and where Grenfell Tower may yet prove different—was provoke wider insurrection in relation to these strategies.

However, the fire did provoke some reassessment of the physical safety of some properties, as some local authorities undertook reassessments of social housing stock (although again, as Grenfell Tower demonstrates, this work does not appear to have dealt with all the issues raised by the Lakanal fire). This reassessment focused on communal parts of these properties, and reaffirms Carr's analysis of the vulnerability of the leaseholder and potential impoverishment caused by the purchase of a Right to Buy flat. The costs of such work fell in part on leaseholders, and where a local authority deemed urgent work necessary, leaseholders were obliged to pay, even if—as in one case—the work was to take place in a building which was scheduled for demolition in the near future.[52] Unlike those identified by Hunter and Blandy, this financial risk was not ameliorated by central government, and reconfirms the precarisation of Right to Buy leaseholders; individual citizen-stakeholders, financially responsible for the upkeep of the building in which they sit, who otherwise act to dismantle the collective security of that building (an unmaking of collective security which is enthusiastically supported by national government, and uncritically, albeit reluctantly, accepted by local government).

VI. GOVERNING THROUGH PRECARITY—THE APPROACH OF SOUTHWARK

The approach of Southwark, as signalled above in their response in relation to fire risk assessments, was to focus their attention on who they had

[52] *London Borough Southwark v Robinson*, 23/6/2014, FTTPC Case Ref: LON/00BE/LSC/OO10.

a responsibility to protect, and who fell outside that responsibility. This is most clearly demonstrated through their approach to the Coroner's concerns in relation to training.

The Coroner suggested that in future, Southwark should demonstrate the safety features of flats for new residents, and consider additional ways of disseminating information, including affixing notices inside each flat of what to do in the event of a fire.[53] In response, Southwark confirmed they would roll out fire training for all new tenants, and existing residents would receive an information pack. In relation to fire safety notices, they did not propose to do this, taking into account increased information and signage in communal areas, the information pack they would be giving out, and also 'considering we cannot do so in dwellings sold under the right to buy … without the owner's consent'.[54] The leaseholder is again constructed as presenting an insurmountable obstruction (the response does not explain why, for example, leaseholders could not be offered the *option* of a fire safety notice for the inside of their flat). In addition, the differential treatment of residents and tenants means that new leaseholders would not be given training (or, presumably, a new information pack) on fire safety, while new public tenants will, including training in relation to safe exit routes. In addition—and of particular importance given the high turnover of such residents—new private tenants in leasehold properties will not be given training or, unless their landlord does so, an information pack. The only reference to residents rather than tenants is a statement by Southwark that, in particular complex buildings, they would consider making a referral to the fire safety team to provide demonstrations to residents. As with the fire assessments, the leaseholder and their tenant, are framed as outsiders who cannot be given (or perhaps should not be given) the same level of protection as the public tenant.

The strength of this narrative and of these approaches to governance highlights the continuing power of Lorey's account of liberal governmentality and the creation of precarity. Furthermore, just as the fires at Lakanal House and Grenfell Tower are vivid reminders of the social nature of precariousness—that life is dependent on and vulnerable to the actions of others—they demonstrate that mechanisms of protection built on differentiation and exclusion are a chimera. The fire demonstrates the failure of a liberal governmentality built on constructing safe subjects and dangerous others, as fire does not distinguish between tenure types, and the actions of those exposed to fire are inherently interlinked. Residents who are unaware of safety measures make all those in the block more vulnerable, as escape routes can be blocked or congested by those who do not know escape procedures. They are likely to seek assistance from others in the face of danger,

[53] Letter from Coroner to LB Southwark (23 March 2013).
[54] Ibid 5.

gathering together as Helen Udoka, Dayana Francisquini and their children had done in Dayana's flat. Such security as is possible in such a situation is necessarily collective, and cannot be exclusive to those of a particular tenure. Compartmentation and different approaches dependent on ownership cannot address the ways in which individuals live their lives together in a common space, frustrating endeavours to include/exclude or to individually precarise, and potentially inadvertently or deliberately resisting or subverting those strategies of governance. An engagement with space, and the shared spaces in which subjects live, is therefore critical in unpicking relationships between precarious life and governance.

VII. CONCLUSION

In her introduction to Lorey's book *State of Insecurity*, Judith Butler states that precarity has become a hegemonic mode of being governed, and that only an engagement with precariousness in its general form demonstrates this.[55] For Lorey, it is specifically governmental precarisation that is the rule,[56] as government is no longer legitimised by a Hobbesian promise of protection and security but instead operates through the maximum possible insecurity 'promoted by proclaiming the alleged absence of alternatives.'[57]

As well as building on the important insights from both Lorey and Butler in their work on precariousness, this chapter has sought to test aspects of their arguments. In particular, in drilling down into the detail in my case study and drawing out the techniques of governmental precarisation and the role of precarity in relation to the fire, I have sought to show that the Butlerian general account risks glossing over important nuance, including the importance of unpicking 'the state' and the critical role of space, while Lorey's emphasis on the hegemony of governmental precarisation misses the ways in which liberal protection continues to exist as a strategy of governance.

Lorey argues that 'the state is not withdrawing from all formerly fundamental institutions of safeguarding. In neoliberalism, however, safeguarding no longer needs the extent of the liberal welfare-state techniques of protection.'[58] Instead the state limits itself to policing and military safeguarding. However, the contrasting approaches of Southwark and the DCLG in my account highlight that contradictory modes of governance emanating from the state continue to exist alongside each other. Central government strategy, revealed once again in the DCLG's deliberately engineered lacuna,

[55] Lorey (n 1) vii.
[56] Ibid 1.
[57] Ibid 2.
[58] Ibid 64.

constructs the Right to Buy leaseholder as an isolated investor, an owner and builder of capital to be protected from overweening bureaucracy. In Lorey's terms, the high rise Right to Buy leaseholder is self-precarised, their ownership equivalent to other citizen-owners in the abstract, but in reality, as Carr shows, qualitatively different to others with stakes in property. The account points towards one of Lorey's key concerns—the role of self-governance in neoliberal governance—but for reasons of space, development of those themes will need to take place in another paper. What my analysis does suggest is that the status of the Right to Buy leaseholder, a complex blending of freedom and insecurity, in an economicised home, is an archetypal subject of governmental precarisation.

However, my case study also reveals the continued power of a liberal form of governmentality, albeit in a radically changed form. The normality of Southwark's tenants is disrupted by the presence of the Right to Buy other; an uncontrolled, uncontrollable outsider who undermines collective immunity. Importantly, they are a dangerous outsider whose presence is central to the aims of other parts of the state, complicating the progression from liberal to neoliberal governance which Lorey proposes and suggesting the need to examine the ways in which different aspects of the state exercise power.

Critically, the approach of Southwark demonstrates that neoliberal precarisation is not inevitable, and that collective endeavours to ensure protection and safety have continued power, not simply as a last gasp tool to prevent insurrection, but as a central concern of governance. In this context, it is relevant that the immediate aftermath of the fire at Grenfell Tower has seen extensive public debate about the responsibility of the state to provide collective security. Such widespread discussion, taken together with the approach of Southwark to the Lakanal House fire, might suggest that, instead of a shift from liberal to neoliberal modes of governance, governmental approaches to the precariousness of shared life fluctuate, competing and co-existing. Additionally, and crucially, the emphasis on protection has not been exclusively framed by the protection of some and exclusion of others, as some of the policy announcements in relation to an amnesty for sub-letting[59] and on the immigration status of those involved have demonstrated.[60]

It is too early to analyse whether this reaction against deregulation and precarisation amounts to management of the potential for insurrection

[59] See Royal Borough of Kensington and Chelsea, 'Grenfell Tower: Amnesty from prosecution for illegal subletting' (*Royal Borough of Kensington and Chelsea*, 2017): www.rbkc.gov.uk/newsroom/all-council-statements/grenfell-tower-amnesty-prosecution-illegal-subletting.

[60] For example, see the announcement of a 12-month immigration amnesty for those involved. Alan Travis, 'Grenfell: 12-month immigration amnesty for survivors announced', *The Guardian* (London, 5 July 2017): https://www.theguardian.com/uk-news/2017/jul/05/grenfell-12-month-immigration-amnesty-for-survivors-announced.

arising out of the fire at Grenfell Tower, or is part of a more fundamental re-imagination of the relationship between collectively lived precarious lives and the care and protection of those lives. However, what the fire does highlight is the integral flaw of governance predicted on the isolation and precarisation of subjects; that it does not reflect the reality of lives lived in close proximity in a common space. Lorey's account of governmental precarisation—in which ever-lowering standards of safeguarding result from the state stepping back from intervention and protection/exclusion, instead accepting responsibility solely for managing and balancing disputes between competing claims—can only work if individuals do not see themselves as part of a collective. Lorey's endeavour to craft a response to governmental precarisation calls for an emphasis on common notions (drawn from Spinoza), 'formed by way of the affective connections of bodies, through what they have in common in their mutual affections.'[61] Once again, further work is needed to develop these themes in relation to the discussion above, but high rise living and responses to the deaths at both Lakanal House and Grenfell Tower highlight the existence of affective, emotionally founded connections built on home, family and immediate physical community. These fires, and the risk of such fires, make it all too clear that endeavours to isolate and compartmentalise people and space can never perfectly contain and manage lives lived collectively. They also demonstrate that accounts of precarious life have to engage with the role of space as both a potential disruptive element and also as part of the way in which precarity and precarisation is structured.

Lakanal House demonstrates both aspects. The fire both revealed the divisions built in law and space and showed the flaws in such efforts. However, the investigations, inquest and public response left law's role in compartmentation of life through tenure unchallenged, and the possibility of collective responses to the resulting vulnerability went unheard.

In this context the early signs of the approach of the state to the mass deaths in the fire at Grenfell Tower are not particularly encouraging. It appears that the work of making those who died count will fall to survivors, the bereaved and activists, to ensure that the engagement with the deaths at Grenfell goes beyond the technicalities and absence of a broader accountability which characterised the response to the Lakanal House fire. In addition, as I have sought to do in this chapter, critical scholarship must also play a small part, resisting endeavours to frame the deaths as tragic but inescapable, countering moves to de-contextualise and detach individual errors from underlying structures, and crucially, continually unpicking the technical to reveal the political.

[61] Lorey, *State of Insecurity* (n 1) 93.

Part IV

Global/Local Precariousness

10

The UK as a Precarious Home

RICHARD WARREN*

'I consider that the word "precarious" is an unsophisticated, unpretentious member of the English language. It denotes generally, something which is unstable, uncertain, fragile. It describes a state of affairs, condition or status which is bereft of guarantees and security. It is the antithesis of something which is stable, secure, certain. This is its ordinary and natural meaning'.

President of the Upper Tribunal (Immigration and Asylum Chamber)
—*Deelah* (section 117B—ambit) [2015][1]

'In some circumstances it may also be that even a person with indefinite leave to remain, or a person who has obtained citizenship, enjoys a status that is "precarious"...'

AM (s 117B) [2015][2]

I. INTRODUCTION

THE QUOTES ABOVE are taken from two recent cases considered by the Immigration and Appeals Chamber of the Upper Tribunal, in which senior immigration judges sought to define and apply the legal concept of 'precariousness' to non-nationals[3] who were seeking to remain in the UK on the basis of their family and private life. In these judgments the term 'precarious' is used as an unproblematic legal term, descriptive of a non-national resident's objective situation, rather than a term that conceals the power relationship between the state and a non-national resident. The judges consider that anyone with a time restriction on their leave to remain,

* Richard Warren, Caseworker and Assistant Lecturer, Kent Law Clinic, University of Kent, r.l.warren@kent.ac.uk.

[1] *Deelah and others* (section 117B—ambit) Mauritius [2015] UKUT 00515 (IAC).

[2] *AM* (s 117B) Malawi [2015] UKUT 0260 (IAC).

[3] The term non-national is used here to refer to a resident of the UK who has not acquired UK citizenship. This may include those born in the UK to non-citizen/non-settled parents as well as migrants to the UK with a variety of immigration statuses.

including those on a path to settlement can be described as having a precarious status. Furthermore in certain situations even those with indefinite leave or citizenship could be considered precarious. Under the Immigration Act 2014 the judges are mandated to give little weight to the private life of such a person when considering their claim to remain under Article 8 of the European Convention of Human Rights (ECHR).[4]

This chapter will consider how the UK itself may be conceived of as an increasingly precarious home. It will argue that it is now becoming more difficult for non-nationals to establish a secure right of residence even after many years living in the UK. Recent developments in UK immigration law, directed at strengthening border controls, can be seen as an attempt to reassure citizens that the UK is a secure home for them, at the expense of making it a precarious home for non-nationals. However, I will argue that creating a more precarious population of non-national residents does little to improve the security of citizens. In considering this I will draw on the work of Isabell Lorey and her discussion of how modern neoliberal governments 'govern through precarity'.[5]

This chapter is in three main parts. The first of these (section II) considers different approaches to the concept of home and the ideological role that the term plays in discussions surrounding immigration control. In recent years the UK Home Office has promoted an essentialist conception of 'home' as a fixed place of territorial residence to which an individual is bound by their nationality. The fact that a non-national resident is not 'at home' can rationalise conceiving of them as precarious, whilst masking the reality that their precarity is ultimately produced by the law. In contrast critical academic accounts have problematised home and instead developed a more nuanced account of home as a product of social activity.

Section III considers the recent history of UK immigration law. Whilst it may be argued that the status of non-nationals has theoretically always been precarious in law, in that the state retains the sovereign right to exclude any non-national, it is only comparatively recently that the monitoring of immigration status has entered almost all areas of civil society making it possible to subject resident non-nationals to the continual review of their status. At the same time deportation has gone from being a seldom used power to a 'normalized and standardized technique of state power'.[6] In recent years attempts to establish the right to a secure home have been pursued through the language of human rights, with individuals relying on a right to private life under Article 8 ECHR to prevent their removal. This has now been countered by the UK government which has formalised the category of the

[4] Nationality, Immigration and Asylum Act 2002 s 117B(5), inserted by s 19 Immigration Act 2014.

[5] I Lorey, *State of Insecurity: Government of the Precarious* (London, Verso Futures, 2015) 20.

[6] See N de Genova and N Peutz, *The deportation regime: sovereignty, space, and the freedom of movement* (Durham NC, Duke University Press, 2010).

'precarious migrant' into primary legislation. Today there is an increased conditionality attached to continued residence, where a failure to satisfy certain criteria may prevent settlement and lead to removal.

Section IV considers how the introduction of legislation which increases the legal precarity of non-national's residence is antagonistic to stated attempts to improve the integration of migrants into the UK.[7] Such an approach is contradictory and destabilising and does little to improve the security of citizens. It will be argued that the policies that drive this are themselves the result of fundamental contradictions in the UK's approach to immigration control.

II. 'TEXT "GO HOME" OR FACE ARREST'

Photograph © Rick Findler, www.rickfindler.photoshelter.com

In the Summer of 2013, the UK Home Office pioneered a new high-visibility marketing campaign targeted at migrants in the UK without legal status. Dubbed the 'Go Home vans', the giant roving billboards advised those in the UK unlawfully to text 'Go Home or Face Arrest—Text Home to 78070'. Widely criticised at the time by migrant welfare organisations and liberal commentators,[8] they have since become a symbol of the

[7] See Department for Communities and Local Government, *Creating the conditions for integration* (London, DCLG, 2012).

[8] A subsequent evaluation report found that only 11 individuals were persuaded to leave the UK. (See Home Office, *Operation Vaken Evaluation Report—October 2013* (London, Home Office, 2013).

The billboards were subsequently criticised by the Advertising Standards Agency for using misleading statistics. (See ASA Adjudication on Home Office (*Advertising Standards Agency*, 9 October 2013): www.asa.org.uk/rulings/home-office-a13-237331.html).

At the same time a campaign of sending text messages to those considered unlawfully resident asking them to send proof that they had bought a plane ticket 'home' was found to have wrongly included those with settled status and even British citizens. (See L Back and S Sinha, '"Go Home" texts expose anti-migrant British policy to the world', (*Shine A Light*, 26 October 2013): www.opendemocracy.net/shinealight/les-back-and-shamser-sinha/go-home-texts-expose-anti-migrant-british-policy-to-world).

'Hostile Environment' which it is now UK policy to create for unlawful migrants.[9] Yet for some of the intended audience—the unlawfully resident—this was a counter-intuitive message. 'Home' for them was not their country of nationality, but the UK—the country where they had spent the majority of their life and where their social networks and family live.

DW exemplifies this incoherence.[10] He arrived in the UK in 1966 as a four-year-old child. Having never returned to his country of origin, DW believed himself to be a British citizen. In 2009, faced with being asked to prove his immigration status, DW applied for a British passport and was surprised when he was told that he was not in fact a UK citizen though he was entitled to indefinite leave to remain in the UK and could confirm this by obtaining a stamp in a passport from his country of origin. DW duly applied for this stamp and after a lengthy delay in processing his application was even more surprised to receive in response a deportation order, effectively requiring him to 'Go Home' and prohibiting him from returning. The grounds for this were that over 13 years ago he had served a prison sentence for crimes which were now spent for other purposes. For DW, in his 50s with several British children, the UK was not considered to be his home.

Conceptually, home can be conceived of as operating on different scales. At the micro-level of the individual, a house or shelter associated with the self is called a home.[11] At the level of the state, the nation state where an individual is entitled to rights as a member is conceived of as the 'homeland'.[12]

The use of home in the 'Go Home' campaign is a clear example of a 'sedentarist' discourse in which the concept of home is essentialised and conceived of as an individual's intrinsic relationship to a fixed territory. In such a discourse, populations are conceived of as rooted and naturally belonging to a specific 'home' territory. The need for a fixed 'home' territory is viewed as being fundamental to an individual's secure identity and sense of belonging. Those who are unlawfully resident, even from birth or a young age, are considered to be indelibly marked with the nominal nationality of their birth, and therefore not really 'at home'. Within this model of rooted populations, movement across boundaries can be perceived as inherently violent and destabilising.[13] The deportation of a non-national,

[9] See David Bolt, Independent Chief Inspector of Borders and Immigration, *An inspection of the 'hostile environment' measures relating to driving licences and bank accounts, October 2016* (London, Borders and Immigration, 2016).

[10] Interview with experienced immigration law practitioner (Kent Law Clinic, 2 January 2017).

[11] P Tabor, 'Striking home' in J Hill (ed), *Occupying Architecture* (London, Routledge, 1998) 218, cited in D Morley, *Home Territories: Media, Mobility and Identity* (London, Routledge, 2000).

[12] ibid.

[13] S Jansen and S Löfving (eds), *Struggles for Home: Violence, Hope and the Movement of Peoples* (Oxford, Berghahn Books, 2009).

'out of place', back to their 'home' can be conceived of as restoring the natural order of things. It is evident therefore that home has an ideological aspect to it—it is associated with a sense of security, with stability and with being 'in place'. Walters[14] uses the term 'domopolitics' to describe the way in which states draw on a particular conception of the home to rationalise 'homeland security' measures. Home is associated with family, intimacy and safety in an uncertain and chaotic world and provides a ready metaphor for the nation.

Structural changes in the global economy, the dismantling of post-war welfare states and increasingly insecure working conditions have arguably led to a developing sense among some sections of the UK population that their home is no longer secure. In 2016 a YouGov poll reported that 37 per cent of the British public agreed with the statement that as a result of immigration, 'where they live doesn't feel like "home" anymore'.[15] In recent years appeals to 'secure the border' and 'take back control' have resonated with this demographic[16]—it is conceived that if immigration, a visible symptom of globalisation, can be curtailed, then perhaps the security of the national home can be restored.

Post-structuralist and anthropological critiques have problematised the concept of home.[17] Rather than focusing on the home as tied to a fixed space, home is conceived of as a product of social activity. Home can be conceived of as a matrix of social relations with wider symbolic and ideological meanings,[18] as a subjective sense of belonging or attachment to space or territory. To this end a number of scholars have explored the way in which migrants' subjective experiences of home develop in their country of residence.[19] By questioning the reification of home as a timeless fixed place of security, and migration as its antithesis, it can be recognised that for many, home-making is an ongoing process. Constructions of home are complex, sometimes contested and often negotiated against a background of legal and policy obstacles.

[14] W Walters, 'Secure borders, safe havens, domopolitics' (2004) 8 *Citizenship Studies* 237.

[15] YouGov, '37% of Britons say immigration has meant that where they live doesn't feel like home any more' (*YouGov*, 5 December 2016): yougov.co.uk/news/2016/12/05/many-europeans-say-immigration-has-meant-they-dont/.

[16] The phrase 'Securing the Border' now frequently appears in many UK Border Force publications. 'Take Back Control' was the official slogan of the successful VoteLeave campaign in the EU Referendum in 2016.

[17] Jansen and Löfving (n 13 above).

[18] A Blunt and R Dowling, *Home* (London, Routledge, 2006).

[19] See A Sirreyeh, *Inhabiting Borders: Routes Home: Youth, Gender, Asylum* (London, Routledge, 2013); N Rapport and A Dawson, *Migrants of Identity: Perceptions of Home in a World of Movement* (Oxford, Berg Publishers, 1998).

A. Establishing a Home in the UK

In the case of non-nationals residing in the UK the legal background against which attempts are made to construct a meaningful home, are the increasingly complex and regularly changing immigration rules. Academics have argued that far from simply enforcing the border, modern immigration controls—so called 'managed migration'—play a role in structuring and disciplining the workforce by facilitating the entry of 'precarious workers', who finding themselves in a situation of 'institutionalised uncertainty', are more easily exploited by employers.[20] Time-limited visas which may or may not lead to permission to settle, with limited access to state resources, can keep migrants living year by year with the knowledge that any home they make may necessarily be only a temporary one. Tying temporary workers to sponsors effectively creates a fixed-term contract, whose termination may lead to the removal of the worker, creating a greater power imbalance between the employee and employer. Workers find themselves dependent on the employer for continued lawful residence, and thus may find themselves in situations where there is no acceptable alternative than to continue working in an exploitative relationship. Workers with no legal status are highly vulnerable to exploitation, can be denied basic employment rights and have very limited means of challenging their treatment. Some have argued that the irregular migrant is the paradigmatic precarious worker, responding to the logic of neoliberal capitalism.[21] Yet as a result such workers may be seen as 'good employees' who are less likely to complain about conditions of service or agitate for improved employment rights.

Immigration controls may be deliberately designed to prevent settlement on the grounds that the migrant's labour is only wanted on a temporary basis—for example Germany's post-war *Gastarbeiter* programmes were designed on the basis that Germany was not a country of permanent immigration.[22] Alternatively, immigration routes may be designed to lead to settlement in theory (for example family reunion routes), but may nevertheless have a series of conditions that need to be met and a failure to meet them may result in delayed settlement or even removal. Even those non-nationals who secure settled status remain subject to the condition of good behaviour—they remain deportable should the state decide that they are no longer worthy of membership.

[20] B Anderson, 'British Jobs for British Workers? Understanding Demand for Migrant Labour in a Recession' (2010) 11 *The Whitehead Journal of Diplomacy and International Relations* 103.

[21] See discussion and criticism in HM Lewis, PJ Dwyer, S Hodkinson and L Waite, 'Hyper-precarious lives: Migrants, work and forced labour in the Global North' (2015) 39 *Progress in Human Geography* 580–600.

[22] See Y Algan, *Cultural Integration of Immigrants in Europe* (Oxford, Oxford University Press, 2012).

The next section will consider recent developments in the UK's immigration law and the effect they have had on enabling non-nationals to develop a secure sense of home.

III. THE UK AND PRECARIOUS MIGRANT STATUS

A. The Sovereign State and the Right to Remain

The principle that the sovereign state retains absolute power to admit or refuse foreign nationals at discretion was at one time unexceptional. In *Musgrove v Chun Teeong Toy* [1891] it was affirmed that there was no authority for the proposition that an alien[23] could establish a legal right to enter British territory.[24] The principle that the Crown as head of a sovereign state has the prerogative to exclude any alien was consolidated in domestic law.[25]

In the UK for many years it was very difficult for an alien to challenge an executive decision to deport them. The 1920 case of *Venicoff*,[26] concerned the deportation of a Russian who had been resident for over 30 years. The court held that there was no duty on the Secretary of State to hold an inquiry into an alien's deportation or provide an opportunity for them to be heard in order to rebut any allegations against them. Until rights of appeal were introduced in the 1969 Appeal Act, there was frequent criticism that the executive retained an arbitrary power to deport a non-national.[27]

In the case of *Schmidt* [1969],[28] which involved individuals who wished to extend their residence permits, it was stated that:

> when an alien approaching this country is refused leave to land, he has no right capable of being infringed in such a way as to enable him to come to this Court for the purpose of assistance ... In such a situation the alien's desire to land can be rejected for good reason or bad, for sensible reason or fanciful or for no reason at all.[29]

[23] The first modern immigration controls introduced with the 1905 Aliens Act applied to those defined as 'aliens'—ie, not British subjects. British subjects including those from the colonies and Commonwealth were not subject to deportation. Controls on the immigration of Commonwealth and colonial citizens began to be brought in during the 1960s with the Commonwealth Immigration Acts 1962 and 1968. The 1971 Immigration Act, which provides the modern framework of UK immigration law, finally consolidated the position of these citizens with that of aliens.

[24] Similar cases in the US further established this principle. See The 'Chinese Exclusion Cases' *Chae Chan Ping v United States* 130 US 581 (1889) and *Nishimura Ekiu v United States* 142 US 651 (1892).

[25] P Shah, *Refugees, Race and the Legal Concept of Asylum* (London, Cavendish Publishing, 2000) 28–29.

[26] *Venicoff v Leman Street Police Station Inspector* [1920] 3 KB 72.

[27] See Quintin Hogg MP, HC Deb 22 January 1969, vol 776 col 502.

[28] *Schmidt v Secretary of State for the Home Department* [1969] 1 WLR 338.

[29] ibid, Widgery LJ.

In giving the judgment, Widgery LJ drew on the analogy of a landlord who need not provide any explanation for refusing to extend a lease to a tenant. This posits the alien as a guest and the nation's immigration laws represent the exercise by the 'owners' of the national property of their collective right to use the property as they please.[30] A guest may be welcomed in, but he does not accrue tenancy rights.

As a result, it could be argued that the ability of a non-national to establish a home in the UK has always been precarious in that it is something that an individual can claim no right to do. Here it is illuminating to consider the etymology of the term precarious. The Latin word 'precarious' is derived from 'prex' meaning prayer. Precarious thus literally means 'obtained through prayer', though it became more generally used for something that was 'given as a favour', or 'depending on the favour of another person'; the earliest meaning of the English word precarious relates to the idea of being given something—the right to occupy land, or to hold a particular position—'at the pleasure of another person', who might simply choose to take it back at any time. Thus the favour given is not a permanent or inalienable right but is very much dependent on a relationship of power between the individual supplicant and their benefactor.

B. The Human Rights Counter-Narrative

The cases above illustrate the position prior to the Immigration Act 1971 which created the modern framework of UK immigration law. This established a system of published immigration rules which individuals must continue to qualify under if they are to be granted leave to remain. Those who are unable to meet the regularly changing immigration rules, those refused asylum, as well as settled residents convicted of criminal offences may find that even after a significant period of residence in the UK they become liable to removal. In recent years it has been argued that developing international human rights norms must place some limitation on the ability of governments to expel long-term residents who have made their homes in another state. In the UK over the past 15 years there has been an ongoing battle between the executive and the judiciary over where the limits to state action in immigration control should lie. Unlike other European states the UK is not a signatory to the EU Long-term Residence directive[31] which does provide some degree of legal protection to non-EU migrants who have resided legally in the host country for five years. Since the passing of the Human

[30] See SH Legomsky, *Immigration and the Judiciary* (Oxford, Oxford University Press, 1987) 316 for discussion of the 'guest theory' and to what extent it explains the UK courts traditional deference to the executive.

[31] Council Directive 2003/109/EC of 25 November 2003 concerning the status of third-country nationals who are long-term residents.

Rights Act 1998, claims to remain in the UK by those who are not able to meet the strict terms of the UK immigration rules have largely been articulated through the prism of Article 8 of the ECHR, which has developed as a legal counter-narrative, employed by those seeking to argue that with the passage of time, a migrant should be considered as acquiring the right to a secure home. This frames the argument in terms of an individual's right to private and family life, pitted against the wider public's right to control immigration or to deter and punish crime. But beneath the language of individual rights, what has always been at stake in these forums is whether the appellant has a claim to 'belong' in the UK—whether the UK should be recognised as their home.

It took some time for the European Court in Strasbourg to recognise the applicability of Article 8 in removal cases.[32] Even then the focus was primarily on family life, as opposed to private life. However, a growing number of cases have dealt with long-term resident migrants facing removal where arguments have been framed in terms of private life.[33] The concept of private life as developed by the jurisprudence of the courts has been held to encompass a wide range of factors such that it is not possible to attempt an exhaustive definition.[34] However, it certainly can include non-family relationships, extended family relationships, the ability to form such relationships in the future, work, voluntary activities, studies and community involvement.[35] Essentially it includes those aspects that constitute an individual's *home* in the wider sense. It can also cover an individual's physical and psychological integrity—'those features which are integral to a person's identity or ability to function socially as a person'.[36]

By the late 1990s optimistic authors were arguing that with the increased recognition of human rights norms we were entering an era of post-nationalism where increasingly rights are de-territorialised and attached to personhood rather than membership in a political community. As such, national citizenship had been superseded by new forms of local or regional belonging.[37]

[32] See M-B Dembour, *When Humans Become Migrants: Study of the European Court of Human Rights with an Inter-American Counterpoint* (Oxford, Oxford University Press, 2015).

[33] *Bensaid v United Kingdom* (2001) 33 EHRR 205; *Maslov v Austria*—Application no 1638/03 [2008] ECHR 546. Interestingly the concept of 'home' has not been considered in the context of removal cases.

[34] *Niemitz v Germany* (1992) 16 EHRR 97.

[35] 'It must be accepted that the totality of social ties between settled migrants and the community in which they are living constitute part of the concept of 'private life' within the meaning of Article 8'—*Uner v Netherlands* (Application no 46410/99) EHRR [59].

[36] *R (on the Application of Razgar) v Secretary of State for the Home Department* [2004] UKHL 27 [9].

[37] See R Hansen, 'The poverty of postnationalism: citizenship, immigration, and the new Europe' (2009) *Theor Soc* 38 for his critique of S Sassen, *Losing Control. Sovereignty in an Age of Globalisation* (Columbia, Columbia University Press, 1996); Y Soysal, *Limits of Citizenship. Migrants and Postnational Membership in Europe* (Chicago, University of Chicago Press, 1994).

In the UK there have been a number of progressive determinations by the House of Lords and subsequently the Supreme Court which strengthened the ability of non-nationals to rely on Article 8 to resist removal.[38] The critical question for any judge in deciding a case is whether the removal of the non-national is necessary in a democratic society and proportionate to the legitimate public aim sought. In situations where a settled migrant has committed a criminal offence there may be a greater public interest in removal, yet this must still be balanced against any well-established family and private life. Increasingly Article 8 has allowed migrants to challenge the assumption that they are eternal guests at the favour of the sovereign state and instead argue that their life in the UK should be protected from arbitrary interference.

In the case of *EB (Kosovo)*[39] the court addressed the issue of individuals without leave to remain who had nevertheless spent many years resident in the UK and developed relationships:

> An immigrant without leave to enter or remain is in a very precarious situation, liable to be removed at any time … A relationship so entered into may well be imbued with a sense of impermanence. But if months pass without a decision to remove being made, and months become years, and year succeeds year, it is to be expected that this sense of impermanence will fade and the expectation will grow that if the authorities had intended to remove the applicant they would have taken steps to do so. This result depends on no legal doctrine but on an understanding of how, in some cases, minds may work and it may affect the proportionality of removal.

Here we see the importance of temporality in the development of home. The passage of time is held to naturally diminish the precariousness of a migrant's residence. For a while it appeared that there was a growing recognition that migrants who had built a life for themselves in the UK over a long period of time were entitled to respect for the home they had established.[40]

However, other scholars have cast doubt on whether the discourse of human rights will ever be sufficient to protect those who make claims in states of which they are not members.[41] Arguably in the UK, the introduction

[38] *R (Razgar) v SSHD* [2004] UKHL 27; *Beoku-Betts* [2008] UKHL 3; *Huang* [2007] UKHL; *EB (Kosovo)* [2008] UKHL 4; *Chikwamba v SSHD* [2008] UKHL 40.

[39] *EB (Kosovo)* [2008] UKHL 41.

[40] See D Thym, 'Residence as De Facto Citizenship? Protection of Long-term Residence under Article 8 ECHR' in R Rubio-Marin (ed), *Human Rights and Immigration* (Oxford, Oxford University Press, 2014).

[41] See for example M-B Dembour, *When Humans Become Migrants: Study of the European Court of Human Rights with an Inter-American Counterpoint* (Oxford, Oxford University Press, 2015). Other scholars such as Dauvergne and Marsden have drawn on Arendt's argument that human rights discourse is a hollow promise for those who lack formal state membership and thus the 'right to have rights': 'The Ideology of Temporary Labour Migration in the Post-Global Era' (2014) 18 *Citizenship Studies* 224–42—http://commons.allard.ubc.ca/cgi/viewcontent.cgi?article=1087&context=fac_pubs.

of the Human Rights Act 1998 was not an abrogation of state sovereignty but merely a transfer of power from the executive to the judiciary, given that ultimately the enforcement of rights is left to individual states. Recent legislative developments mark an attempt by the executive to reclaim this power, and limit the efficacy of human rights based claims to remain.

In 2010 the Home Office under Theresa May, motivated by a manifesto pledge to reduce migration to the tens of thousands began a campaign against the successful use of Article 8 in immigration appeals. This included public warnings to the judges who 'misunderstood' how Article 8 should be applied, amendments to the Immigration Rules purporting to reflect how Article 8 'should' be applied,[42] and finally when these moves were less than successful, culminated in the 2014 Immigration Act which set out the government's vision of the 'public interest' for the purposes of Article 8. As a result the precariousness of the migrant's status is now formalised in law.

C. The Immigration Act 2014: Defining the Public Interest

The Immigration Act 2014 brought in significant changes to the rights of non-nationals to enter and remain in the UK. Most rights of appeal and grounds of appeal that had existed since the 1969 Appeals Act were swept away and replaced with a far more limited right to appeal based on having made an asylum or human rights based claim to remain.[43]

More significantly though is a part of the Act that seeks to define the public interest. Section 19 introduced a new Part 5A into the Nationality Immigration and Asylum Act 2002. Entitled 'ARTICLE 8 OF THE ECHR: PUBLIC INTEREST CONSIDERATIONS', it stipulates a number of considerations which all judges must have regard to when deciding human rights appeals. It seeks to guide the judiciary in how to conduct the proportionality assessment that is inherent in deciding whether an individual's claim under Article 8 should succeed. For example, the ability to speak English and to be financially independent so as not to be a 'burden on the taxpayer' are designated as being in the public interest. A distinction is made between family and private life, which are given separate consideration.

Of key importance is section 117B(5) which states: '(5) Little weight should be given to a private life established by a person at a time when the person's immigration status is *precarious*.' (emphasis added). This requires judges, when considering the proportionality of removal of a 'precarious migrant', to tilt the scales away from the migrant and towards the state. The Act itself does not address the definition of the term precarious, and indeed

[42] Statement of changes to the Immigration Rules: HC Deb 9 July 2012, vol 514.
[43] Section 15, Immigration Act 2014.

during the Parliamentary debates prior to the passing of the Act, the term was not discussed in debate. It was therefore left to the courts to define this term in law.

However, the Home Office was quick to issue guidance to its caseowners:

> For the purposes of this guidance, a person's immigration status is precarious if he is in the UK with limited leave to enter or remain but without settled or permanent status, or if he has leave obtained fraudulently, or if he has been notified that he is liable to deportation or administrative removal.[44]

This wide-ranging definition goes beyond that of temporary workers who are aware that their visas are strictly time-limited. It includes all those granted leave on an identifiable route to settlement such as spouses and skilled workers, who have every expectation that their leave will be extended if they continue to meet the relevant requirements. It would even include young children granted discretionary leave, where it has been decided that it is in their best interests to remain in the UK.[45]

It has been left to the courts to decide whether the Home Office's interpretation is appropriate. In the UK the Upper Tribunal (Immigration and Asylum Chamber) is the court of record that hears appeals from the First Tier Tribunal and produces guidance cases to be applied in future judgments. The court has now decided a number of cases in which the legal definition of 'precarious status' is defined.[46]

In *AM (s 117B)*[47] the first case to be decided, the Upper Tribunal accepted the Home Office position but went further still, considering even wider scenarios in which a person may be said to be precarious.

> A person's immigration status is 'precarious' if their continued presence in the UK will be dependent upon their obtaining a further grant of leave.
>
> In some circumstances it may also be that even a person with indefinite leave to remain, or a person who has obtained citizenship, enjoys a status that is 'precarious' either because that status is revocable by the Secretary of State as a result of their deception, or because of their criminal conduct. In such circumstances the

[44] Immigration directorate instructions. Chapter 13: criminality guidance in Article 8 ECHR cases. Version 5.0, 28 July 2014, 2.3.8.

[45] It is interesting to note that in the case of *Alladin v Secretary of State for the Home Department* [2013] EWHC 1406 (Admin), in which child claimants were arguing that it was in their interests to be granted immediate indefinite leave to remain rather than discretionary leave, government lawyers took the opposite position, arguing that in such cases the children's status could not be described as 'precarious'.

[46] *Deelah and others* (section 117B—ambit) [2015] UKUT 00515 (IAC) and *Forman* (ss 117A–C considerations) [2015] UKUT 00412 (IAC), which were presided over by the President of the Upper Tribunal, and *Terrelonge* (para 399(b)) [2015] UKUT 00653 (IAC). See also *BM and Others* (Returnees—criminal and non-criminal) Democratic Republic of Congo (Country Guidance) [2015] UKUT 00293 (IAC).

[47] *AM* (s 117B) Malawi [2015] UKUT 0260 (IAC).

> person will be well aware that he has imperilled his status and cannot viably claim thereafter that his status is other than precarious.[48]

Furthermore,

> Nor is there any merit in our judgement in the suggestion that the answer is to be found in an individual's subjective belief that they would in the future be able to extend the period of leave that had been granted to them. The test must be an objective one.[49]
>
> Indeed the ability of those who have not yet been granted indefinite leave to remain, to obtain a variation of their leave in the future, will probably always depend in part upon matters that are outside their control—whether that be the actions of others, or the future prosperity of themselves or others.[50]

A consequence of this is that even individuals on a route to settlement who can reasonably foresee that they will meet the requirements of the immigration rules are not entitled to any expectation that leave will be extended and are in fact defined as precarious. This state of existence will not naturally decrease with the passage of time, as was indicated in *EB (Kosovo)*, but will endure in some cases for a further 10 years, or longer until they are able to obtain indefinite leave to remain.[51] If the immigration rules change so as to make subsequent extensions of leave impossible, little weight should be given to their private life when considering the proportionality of their removal.

The issue has since been considered in a number of subsequent cases.[52] In a particularly compelling case involving an accepted child trafficking victim who faced returning to potential destitution in a country where he had no family after seven years' residence, the first-tier judge acknowledged that treating him as precarious 'would appear to contradict numerous policy statements made by the Secretary of State about the importance of stability, roots and relationships for such children'.[53] Yet this harsh impact was 'the unavoidable consequence of the legislative choice which Parliament has made'[54] and the appeal was dismissed.

The legal use of the term 'precarious' is derived from the case law of the ECtHR which has tended to apply it in cases involving the family life of

[48] ibid, headnotes (4) and (5).
[49] ibid para 25.
[50] ibid para 28.
[51] Some settlement routes now require a continuous period of 10 years lawful leave before settlement is possible. However, settlement application fees are now over £2000 per person and also require additional criteria to be met. If the fee cannot be paid a further extension of limited leave will be required, for which it is possible to apply for a fee waiver if destitute.
[52] n 46 above.
[53] *Miah* (section 117B NIAA 2002—children) [2016] UKUT 00131(IAC), para 20.
[54] ibid para 24.

migrants who either have no lawful status, who are on temporary admission pending a determination of an asylum claim, or who have already been notified of a decision to deport when they began their relationship. I have argued elsewhere[55] that it is questionable whether the term as defined by the Upper Tribunal is consistent with how the term has been applied by the ECtHR. As such, rather than clarifying how Article 8 should be interpreted, this interpretation of the term 'precarious' acts to significantly curtail the protection of Article 8.

The Court of Appeal has now given the concept some consideration. In the case of *Rhuppiah* [2016] it was accepted that a student on a time-limited visa may be classed as precarious but obiter remarks suggested that the court was not convinced by the Home Office's more expansive use of the concept of 'precariousness'.[56] The court also read down the requirement to give 'little weight' to private life in all cases where an individual's status was precarious, recognising that otherwise the provision could be incompatible with Article 8 in some circumstances. In *MS*[57] Justice Collins in the High Court went further and decided that an individual who was resident for over 20 years but still on limited leave should not be classed as 'precarious', though he was unable to offer any clear guidance as to the point at which precariousness ceased. It may be that the Supreme Court will resist the government's approach to Article 8, though one result of this may be to provide further ammunition to those in the government who seek to renounce the 1998 Human Rights Act and ECHR. However, the willingness by the tribunal to embrace such an expansive definition of the term is symptomatic of an underlying rationality that pervades considerations of the rights of non-nationals.

D. Constructing the Precarious Migrant

The Upper Tribunal judges adopt an 'unsophisticated, unpretentious' dictionary definition of the term 'precarious' equating it with 'unstable', 'fragile' or being 'bereft of guarantees and security'.[58] For them this describes the objective situation of a non-national granted temporary leave to remain. The notion that there is at the heart of the precariousness a power relationship has been lost; rather someone is precarious due to the uncertainties of an unforeseeable future—eg whether their relationship will endure, whether

[55] R Warren, 'Private Life in the Balance: Constructing the Precarious Migrant' (2016) 230 *Journal of Immigration, Asylum and Nationality Law* 124.

[56] See Sales LJ, para 44, *Rhupiah v Secretary of State for the Home Department* [2016] EWCA Civ 803.

[57] *MS v Secretary of State for the Home Department* [2016] EWHC 3162, paras 23–29.

[58] *Deelah and others* (section 117B—ambit) [2015] UKUT 00515 (IAC).

their earnings will continue at the same level, whether the economic situation will be such that they are still required by the state. The judges do not acknowledge the significant sociological literature that has developed concerning the concept of 'precariousness' as an academic term.[59]

Goldring and Landolt[60] have argued that the term 'precarious status' captures variable forms of irregular status and represents a better conceptual approach than adopting a binary categorisation of illegal/legal documented/undocumented, citizen/non-citizen as favoured by policy makers. They recognise that there are degrees between these two poles where individuals may still find themselves in a vulnerable position. For them precarious status is marked by absence of any of the following: 1) work authorisation, 2) right to remain permanently, 3) not having to depend on a third party for the right to remain, 4) social citizenship rights available to permanent residents (eg, public health, public education). They are concerned with how immigration law creates this condition, the purpose that this serves and the wider social consequences. It is regrettable that the UK government has effectively appropriated this concept, reified it in law and established a new binary distinction between precarious and settled migrants, as a means to devalue the rights of the former by limiting the weight to be attached to their private life.

Although migration may involve many uncertainties, it is by no means a natural consequence of the act of migrating that an individual becomes particularly precarious. Indeed, the 'homes' that migrants have left may themselves be sources of insecurity, and migration may provide the foundations to develop a more secure home through employment opportunities or reunion with family. After many years' residence (sometimes since birth) an individual may have developed a strong subjective sense of home and stability. States could operate on the basis that once accepted for admission as a worker or family member, a non-national is entitled to the same rights as UK citizens. The fact that some individuals are instead vulnerable to the loss of immigration status, social exclusion, incarceration and forcible removal is a consequence of the way in which the law operates to categorise them as precarious non-nationals.

Isabell Lorey (following Butler) draws a conceptual distinction between existential social precariousness and 'precarity' as a relationship of inequality. Because life is exposed to an existential vulnerability, the idea that one could be entirely legally protected is a fantasy.[61] However, what needs to

[59] See for example: G Standing, *The Precariat: The New Dangerous Class* (London, Bloomsbury Academic, 2011); P Bourdieu, 'La precaritie est aujourd'hui partout [Precariousness is everywhere nowadays]' in P Boudieu, *Contre-Feux (Acts of Resistance)* (Cambridge, Polity, 1998).

[60] L Goldring and P Landolt (eds), *Producing and Negotiating Non-Citizenship: Precarious Legal Status in Canada* (Toronto, University of Toronto Press 2013).

[61] Lorey (n 5 above) 20.

be understood is the way in which the law is applied to institute precarity for certain groups of people and the purpose that this serves. She argues that increasingly the state utilises precarity as an instrument of governing. Legitimising the protection of some requires increasing the precarity of those marked as 'other'.[62] As Butler argues, 'every political effort to manage populations involves a tactical distribution of precarity'.[63] It is therefore necessary to focus on the political decisions through which some lives are protected and others are not.[64] In the case of immigration controls, policies marketed to the citizen population as a means of increasing their security, increase the precarity of resident non-nationals. The final section will consider the wider social consequences of such an approach.

IV. PRECARITY VS INTEGRATION: THE UK'S CONTRADICTORY APPROACH

Whilst one might argue that restrictive immigration controls and strong rhetoric about border enforcement are an attempt to reassure certain sections of the UK population that as citizens they live within a secure home, it is my argument that the policies being pursued are contradictory and destabilising in their impact on citizens as well as non-nationals. Recent policies that are stated to address concerns over immigration levels have done little to reduce the overall number of migrants arriving,[65] but they have increased the precarity of those non-nationals already present.

A. Longer Routes to Settlement

Attempts by the UK government to undermine the protections of Article 8 have coincided with a more general move to conceive of immigration as a temporary and reversible phenomenon. In February 2012 it was announced that settlement would be restricted for skilled workers, with the immigration minister Damien Green stating: 'Settlement in the UK is a privilege. We are sweeping aside the idea that everyone who comes here to work can

[62] ibid 14.

[63] J Butler, 'Precarious Life, Vulnerability, and the Ethics of Cohabitation' (2012) 26 *Journal of Speculative Philosophy* 134, 148.

[64] I Lorey (n 5 above) 18.

[65] Despite the pledge to reduce net migration to the tens of thousands, net migration for the year ending June 2016 was 335,000. The figure has fluctuated between 200,000 and 300,000 for the past 10 years with the highest recorded figure in 2015. Office for National Statistics: *Migration Statistics Quarterly Report December 2016* (Office of National Statistics, 1 December 2016): www.ons.gov.uk/peoplepopulationandcommunity/populationandmigration/internationalmigration/bulletins/migrationstatisticsquarterlyreport/dec2016.

settle, and instead reserving this important right only for the brightest and best'.[66] It is now increasingly difficult for workers, spouses and others to gain settlement in the UK.

Until April 2006 many of those entering the UK as workers, had a viable route to settlement after four years. Students were able to extend their leave on post-study work visas and subsequently acquire settlement. Many of those routes to settlement have now been restricted, including for skilled workers who may be forced to leave the UK after a period of six years or more unless they are earning a salary of £35,000 or more. Those who entered the UK as spouses must now wait at least five years before applying for settlement.[67] A financial requirement, the highest in the Western world and an English language test must be met on entry and every 2½ years when an extension of leave is requested.[68] Should they fail to meet these new conditions, they may find themselves being removed from the UK. In March 2017 a new policy of actively reviewing refugee status after five years with a view to revoking it was introduced, increasing the insecurity of those already granted asylum who would normally have qualified for settlement.[69]

Those without leave, seeking to remain in the UK based on accumulated private life are now expected to have been resident more than 20 years, or half their life if under 25, or else show 'very significant obstacles' to their reintegration into their country of return, as well as meeting additional suitability requirements.[70] These are strict criteria to be met, and near misses will be refused. A successful application will lead to a further four periods of 2½ years' limited (ie precarious) leave before settlement can be considered. During this time an individual is now excluded from accessing public funds

[66] UKBA Press Release, 29 February 2012, 'Automatic settlement for unskilled workers to end'.

[67] Formerly those on spouse routes had a probationary period of 12 months (later increased to 2 years) prior to settlement, or in some cases could gain indefinite leave to remain (ILR) immediately if they had been living abroad with their spouse.

[68] The financial requirement, subject of litigation in the case of *MM and Others v Secretary of State for the Home Department* [2014] EWCA Civ 985 has been observed to be such that 45% of applicants would be unable to sponsor a foreign national spouse. Starting at £18,600, it increases to £22,400 with a child and a further £2400 for every additional non-British dependent child.

[69] Home Office, *Refugee Leave Version 4.0 March 2017* (London, Home Office, 2 March 2017).

[70] See Immigration Rules, para 276ADE on private life. It is worth noting that the test of 'very significant obstacles' is being interpreted as a very high threshold. Guidance issued to Home Office caseowners directs that not having lived in the country of return, having no friends, family or social network and not speaking the language would not necessarily constitute very significant obstacles. See Home Office, *Immigration Directorate Instruction Family Migration: Appendix FM Section 1.0b: Family Life (as a Partner or Parent) and Private Life: 10-Year Routes*, August 2015. In a recent unreported Upper Tribunal case it was held that very significant obstacles did not include an appellant's imminent death upon return due to a lack of vital healthcare (*Jallow v Secretary of State for the Home Department* (Gambia), Upper Tribunal (Immigration and Asylum Chamber) Appeal No: AA/05801/2014, 26 May 2015).

and must pay an additional surcharge to access the National Health Service. So even after succeeding with such a claim to remain, the leave granted does not provide a secure status such as to give the expectation of settlement.[71]

The insecurity is compounded in that those on lengthy routes to settlement are continually at risk of falling back into the status of the 'unlawful', due to the requirement to make repeated expensive applications.[72] Failure to apply in time, failure to pay the fee or a legal error in deciding the application will lead to the loss of leave to remain and the associated lack of rights—loss of right to work, right to rent, right to access healthcare or any state support, and requiring an applicant to start again on the 10-year route to settlement.[73] Under the Immigration Act 2016 any appeal against a refusal on human rights grounds may have to be exercised from outside the UK.[74]

B. The Hostile Environment

In October 2013 the Home Secretary announced her determination to create a 'really hostile environment' for those who are unlawfully resident which specifically sets out to exclude this category of residents from any participation in society.[75] This involves denying access to rented accommodation, health services, bank accounts and driving licences in an attempt to make it impossible to remain in the UK. At the same time most appeal rights were removed and so the consequence for a non-national who has their leave curtailed is to immediately find themselves in the hostile environment.

[71] Given the current commitment by the Government to repeal the Human Rights Act in favour of a British Bill of Rights, migrants who have succeeded in human rights based appeals and remain with a temporary legal status can have little confidence that their status is now secure.

[72] On a 10-year route an individual will need to make a further four in-time immigration applications, paying a fee and additional NHS surcharge. To obtain settlement a family of four at present rates would need to spend £33,076 on application fees. (See The Immigration and Nationality Fees Regulations 2017, SI 2017/515).

[73] Goldring and Landolt have described this, albeit in the context of Canada, as being akin to a game of 'chutes and ladders'. L Goldring and P Landolt, 'The Impact of Precarious Legal Status on Immigrants' Economic Outcomes' (IRPP Study, 2012): irpp.org/wp-content/uploads/assets/research/diversity-immigration-and-integration/the-impact-of-precarious-legal-status-on-immigrants-economic-outcomes/IRPP-Study-no35.pdf.

[74] At the time of writing the future of this policy of 'deport first—appeal later' had just been called into question by the Supreme Court. The case of *R (on the applications of Kiarie and Byndloss) v Secretary of State for the Home Department* [2017] UKSC 42 found that the deportation of long-term residents without a system in place to ensure that an appeal could be heard fairly breached Article 8 ECHR. It remains to be seen how the government will respond to this judgment.

[75] Alan Travis, 'Immigration bill: Theresa May defends plans to create "hostile environment"' (*The Guardian*, 20 October 2013): www.theguardian.com/politics/2013/oct/10/immigration-bill-theresa-may-hostile-environment.

For those long-term residents caught in its net, it involves an attempt to dismantle the social and physical infrastructure which they have come to regard as their home—a form of home *un*making.[76] Arriving at the same time as the 'Go Home' vans campaign, these policies can be seen as a crude attempt to demonstrate to voters that the government was 'taking control' of immigration.

The 2014 Immigration Act also introduced the concept of 'the right to rent'. However, this was not a benevolent attempt to increase access to affordable housing for UK residents. It was instead directed towards preventing those without lawful status from entering into a tenancy agreement. Under the Immigration Act 2016, landlords are to be directed to evict those who lose their leave to remain on the order of the Secretary of State and without the supervision of the courts,[77] and face criminal sanctions if they are found renting to those without lawful status.

The stated aim of these policies is to force unlawfully resident migrants to voluntarily depart, though NGOs are concerned that those in the most vulnerable positions, for whom leaving the UK is unthinkable, may be forced further into exploitative housing and employment situations. A 2009 study estimated that there are likely to be between 417,000 to 863,000 undocumented migrants in the UK.[78] It is believed 120,000 are under 18 years old, with 65,000 likely to have been born in the UK.[79] A number of those affected by the hostile environment are likely to have British partners, parents, children and other family members. Cumulatively these changes are likely to lead to more precarious classes of migrants; firstly unlawful migrants who are excluded from all aspects of society but the black market, and secondly a more precarious class of lawful migrants, temporarily resident or on various lengthy routes to settlement—lacking certainty over where their future ultimately lies.

C. Creating the Conditions for Integration: The UK's Contradictory Approach

In February 2012 the coalition government produced a paper entitled 'Creating the conditions for integration'[80] which professed commitment to

[76] See Introduction, section II, citing R Baxter and K Brickell, 'For Home *Un*making' (fn 14) this volume.

[77] Immigration Act 2016 s 40.

[78] LSE, *Economic impact on the London and UK economy of an earned regularisation of irregular migrants to the UK* (London, Greater London Authority, 2009).

[79] N Sigona and V Hughes, *NO WAY OUT, NO WAY IN Irregular migrant children and families in the UK* (Oxford, ESRC Centre on Migration, 2012).

[80] Department for Communities and Local Government, *Creating the conditions for integration* (London, DCLG, 2012).

creating an integrated society as being 'central to long term action to counter extremism'. However, the strategy paper had very little to say about steps to address the social exclusion of those long-term residents with a precarious immigration status. It specifically denies the role of law in promoting integration, stating that changes must come from society, rather than from the law.

Since this time there have been two further important reviews focusing on integration. The Casey review,[81] established to review integration and opportunity in isolated and deprived communities, made a number of recommendations including oaths of allegiance for public servants and a renewed focus on British values. The All Party Parliamentary Group on Social Integration,[82] reporting in the aftermath of the Brexit referendum, recommended improved local integration plans and integration for new immigrants to begin upon arrival in the UK. Yet neither of these reports engaged with the role of UK immigration controls in constraining or facilitating the development of a secure sense of home amongst non-nationals whose future in the UK remains uncertain.

The 2015 Migrant Integration Policy Index (MIPEX) measures policies to integrate migrants in all EU Member States as well as a number of other nations.[83] It notes how the UK has fallen significantly in the index of countries which promote integration and is now the hardest place in the developed world for separated families to reunite; with one of the most restrictive and expensive paths to settlement. The UK is now ranked 31 out of 38 developed countries in terms of the ability of migrants to gain permanent residence. They observe that integration has clearly fallen off the policy agenda.

A number of scholars have emphasised the importance of a secure status for facilitating integration and a sense of belonging,[84] and the difficulties that those with temporary status can face in accessing resources that will better enable them to participate in society. The Labour government in its 1998 White Paper 'Firmer, Faster, Fairer' had also recognised that: 'One measure of the integration of immigrants into British society is the ease with which they can acquire citizenship',[85] and recommended reducing routes to settlement which were considered to be 'unnecessary obstacles' to acquiring citizenship.[86] This would allow new arrivals to 'integrate more easily and

[81] L Casey, *The Casey Review: A review into opportunity and integration* (London, DCLG, 2016).

[82] A Kere and R Bell, *Interim Report into Integration of Migrants* (London, All Party Parliamentary Group on Social Integration 2017).

[83] *Migrant Integration Policy Index* (MIPEX): http://www.mipex.eu/.

[84] See S Da Lomba, 'Legal Status and Refugee Integration: a UK Perspective' (2010) 23 *Journal of Refugee Studies* 415; Sirreyeh (n 19 above).

[85] Home Office, *Firmer, Faster, Fairer—A Modern Approach to Immigration and Asylum* (Cm 4018, 1998) s 2.16.

[86] ibid s 10.1.

quickly into society, to the benefit of the whole community'.[87] Given repeatedly expressed concerns by politicians about the perceived lack of integration of migrants, the current approach of leaving migrants on precarious routes to settlement, denied equal entitlements and access to public funds, appears contrary to the stated goal of creating the conditions for integration. The potential dangers for community cohesion of a two-tier system of citizen owners and guest workers have long been recognised in academic literature.[88]

There are now a growing number of long-term residents trapped in a limbo of unlawful status, for whom there is no strategy to integrate but no realistic prospect that they will be imminently removed. This number includes those refused asylum but where removal is not possible.[89] It also includes those who have committed criminal offences but who have succeeded in human rights claims to remain. In such cases the approach is now one of toleration with a view to eventual removal rather than any attempt to encourage integration and rehabilitation.[90]

It is therefore necessary to question what has driven these seemingly contradictory policies.

D. The Future: 'Taking Back Control?'

In the aftermath of the 2008 financial crash, successive UK governments have remained committed to fundamentally neoliberal economic policies in

[87] ibid s 9.3. Following this White Paper, refugees were to be granted ILR immediately on arrival. It should be noted though that this policy was later withdrawn and refugees now need at least five years' residence. The current government has been consulting on increasing this period to 10 years. Labour subsequently legislated in 2009 for a far longer route to citizenship.

[88] See for example, M Walzer, *Spheres of Justice* (New York, Basic Books, 1983) 31–63.

[89] Gibney has termed this the 'deportation gap'—the difference between those liable for deportation and those who are actually removed. M Gibney, 'Asylum and the Expansion of Deportation in the United Kingdom' (2008) 43 *Government and Opposition* 146.

It has long been recognised that those refused leave to remain, particularly those coming from conflict zones, are often not removable due to practical or bureaucratic difficulties. Some individuals are de facto stateless, and whilst the UK does now have a procedure for recognising statelessness, reports show that many applicants are unable to satisfy the burden of proof to demonstrate their lack of nationality. See Asylum Aid Briefing, *The UK's Approach to Statelessness*, September 2016.

[90] UK law provides for the automatic deportation of foreign nationals who have been sentenced to more than 12 months in prison, regardless of their length of residence, unless the decision would breach the individual's rights under the ECHR, the Refugee Convention or EU law. In cases where removal is not possible, long resident individuals may find their indefinite leave to remain is revoked and they are instead granted a temporary (precarious) status, which requires regular expensive applications for renewal and denies them access to public funds. In the case of *Kardi v Secretary of State for the Home Department* [2014] EWCA Civ 934 it was reaffirmed that this policy is intended to 'plant road blocks' in the way of individuals, to emphasise their sense of impermanence and make it difficult for them to develop a private life, even in cases of long residence where removal is unlikely to occur and where they might ultimately be granted settled status in the future.

which business benefits from cheap, flexible labour, yet have found themselves confronted by a public concerned about the resulting dislocation to their communities. Such concerns are frequently translated into a hostility to migration as the most visible evidence of social change, amidst allegations that low-skilled migration undermines social cohesion and working conditions. This has been described as the 'neoliberal paradox',[91] with states embracing the logic of neoliberal free market economic policies whilst still attempting to maintain the boundaries and political closure of the nation state.

Across the West, anti-immigration parties such as the UK Independent Party (UKIP) have made significant gains and centre parties have competed with each other to demonstrate that they can 'control immigration'. This has led to policies that seek to further entrench a sharp distinction within the UK between the citizen and the outsider. However, the government's manifesto commitment to reduce absolute numbers of migrants to the tens of thousands has translated into policies that have failed to achieve this,[92] yet they have succeeded in increasing insecurity for lawful as well as unlawful non-national residents. This in turn leads to an even more precarious and exploitable migrant workforce, and as has been suggested, an insecure immigration status is a factor that inhibits integration. Thus concerns about a lack of integration and poor working conditions are likely to be exacerbated, feeding a self-reinforcing cycle that does little to make citizens feel more secure.

Whilst those with unlawful status have always been in a precarious position, this sense of uncertainty about the future is now being expanded to a growing number of legally resident non-nationals whose rights are being eroded and undermined. It is an example of what Lorey calls the 'normalisation of precarisation'. Precarity is no longer located at the margins but is spreading to areas of society that were formerly considered secure.[93]

The attempt by the Conservative Government to balance the demands of business for migrant labour with restrictionist anti-immigration rhetoric has now collapsed spectacularly in the UK, which is facing the consequences of the referendum on membership of the EU, a campaign that was dominated

[91] Varsanyi, 'Rescaling the "Alien", Rescaling Personhood: Neoliberalism, Immigration, and the State' (2008) 98 *Annals of the Association of American Geographers* 879. Varsanyi takes this idea from Hollifield, who talks of the 'liberal paradox'. JF Hollifield, 'Migration and international relations: the liberal paradox' in H Entzinger, M Martiniello and C Wihtolde Weden, *Migration between markets and states* (Burlington VT, Ashgate, 2004) 3.

[92] In the year ending December 2010 the annual net migration figure was 256,000. By the year ending December 2015 the figure was 332,000. Statistics taken from Office for National Statistics, *Provisional Long-Term International Migration (LTIM) estimates*. Available at: www.ons.gov.uk/peoplepopulationandcommunity/populationandmigration/internationalmigration/datasets/migrationstatisticsquarterlyreportprovisionallongterminternationalmigrationltimestimates.

[93] Lorey (n 5 above).

by calls to limit the free movement of EU citizens. Whilst this chapter has largely been concerned with the situation of non-EU migrants whose status is governed by UK immigration rules, at the time of writing, the future status of EU nationals is yet to be determined. At present they have strong rights of residence derived from EU law, but growing concern about their security of residence has led to increasing numbers of EU nationals applying for documentation confirming that they have acquired permanent residence.[94] Some have found that even after many years' residence in the UK they are unable to qualify as a result of the controversial way in which the UK interprets and applies the EU Citizens Directive through its own domestic regulations.[95] It has now been proposed by the UK government that all EU nationals will need to apply for a new status in UK law and so will effectively be in a similar position as other non-nationals.[96] Whilst it is difficult to speculate on the result of the present Brexit negotiations, it appears that another formerly secure group of residents may find that their home in the UK is no longer a right of EU citizenship, but a privilege—'given as a favour' and therefore precarious. It is highly questionable whether decreasing the security of approximately three million UK residents will provide any greater sense of security to UK citizens.

V. CONCLUSION

The institutionalisation of insecurity and an increased conditionality attached to the right to a secure home in the UK is a growing development in UK law. The recent attempt to formalise and define in law the category of the 'precarious migrant' can be seen as an attempt to immunise this logic from the challenge posed by an emergent human rights counter-narrative. By positing the lawful migrant as occupying a legally precarious existence, the social ties and connections that normally develop between an individual and a community in which they reside are devalued. The migrant can be

[94] Under EU law (Citizens Directive 2004/38), permanent residence is acquired automatically after 5 years' lawful residence. It is not necessary to apply for it, and until recently relatively few EU nationals have needed to do so.

[95] See J Shaw and N Miller, 'When Legal Worlds Collide: An Exploration of What Happens when EU Free Movement Law Meets UK Immigration Law' (2013) 38 *European Law Review* 137. Particular issues in recent years have been the UK's refusal to recognise access to the NHS as constituting comprehensive health insurance in order for students and the self sufficient to claim a right of residence, and attempts to make use of a minimum earnings threshold when calculating whether EU workers have been participating in 'genuine and effective work'. Since the UK does not in general remove EU nationals for lacking a formal right of residence under the Citizens Directive, the circumstances in which these issues emerge are when an EU national applies directly for permanent residence or makes an application for welfare benefits where they need to show 5 years' continuous lawful residence.

[96] The United Kingdom's Exit from the European Union: Safeguarding the Position of EU Citizens Living in the UK and UK Nationals Living in the EU (Cm 9464, 2017).

conceived of as an isolated unit of human capital—at once present in society for the purposes of labour but yet not permitted to develop meaningful social ties and a secure residence. Furthermore, an essentialised understanding of home as one's country of origin is utilised by the state to justify the removal of resident non-nationals, contradicting the lived experiences of those for whom home is an ongoing process.

I have argued that these developments are likely to be destabilising in the long term, since this agenda contradicts stated efforts to facilitate the integration of long-term residents. As the law is applied to disrupt and break the social ties between resident non-nationals and citizens, as these policies impact on the lives of the British partners, parents, children and other relatives of socially excluded migrants, it is possible they will have divisive consequences. Scholars have shown how the deportation of non-nationals, whilst seemingly aimed at defining the symbolic and normative boundaries of the national community can lead to increased contestation over who gets to define what it means to belong to a community.[97] This finds expression in a growing number of anti-deportation activist campaigns and on-line petitions seeking supra-legal means of challenging the state's refusal to recognise individual's claims of belonging.[98] As the UK becomes an increasingly precarious home for non-national residents, it will be increasingly necessary to study and understand the wider social impact.

[97] M Gibney, B Anderson and E Paoletti (eds), 'Boundaries of Belonging: Deportation and the Constitution and Contestation of Citizenship' (2011) 15 *Citizenship Studies* 547.

[98] See for example C Patler and R Gonzales, 'Framing Citizenship: Media Coverage of Anti-deportation Cases Led by Undocumented Immigrant Youth Organisations' (2015) 41 *Journal of Ethnic and Migration Studies* 1453.

11

Precarious Home and Institutional Ambiguity in China's Urbanisation

TING XU* AND WEI GONG**

I. INTRODUCTION

URBAN LAND IN China, one of the most important state-owned assets, became leasable in the late 1980s via the establishment of the land use rights ('LURs') system, which has separated ownership and use rights pertaining to urban land.[1] The transfer of LURs has given rise to the emergence of an urban property market. In parallel with changes to the urban land system, the urban housing sector has undergone fundamental transformations: In the 1980s there was massive construction of public housing and the dominant form was public rental.[2] The housing was built on land owned by the state, and work units[3] or urban Real Estate Administration Bureaus represented the de facto 'public owners'.[4] In the late 1980s, however, based on the LURs system, urban households in China were given the opportunity to purchase their flats or houses for the first time. In March 1998, Premier Zhu Rongji introduced a package of reforms that included the abolition of housing provision and allocation by work units.[5]

* School of Law, University of Sheffield, ting.xu@sheffield.ac.uk.
** School of Law, University of Sheffield, w.gong@sheffield.ac.uk.

1 The duration of LURs varies from 40 to 70 years, depending on the types of land use.

2 Youquin Huang, 'The Road to Homeownership: A Longitudinal Analysis of Tenure Transition in Urban China (1949–1994)' (2004) 28 *International Journal of Urban and Regional Research* 774, 778.

3 Work units (*danwei*) are a special form of social organisation, which play an important role in urban governance in China. See eg, Xiaobo Lü and Elizabeth J Perry (eds), *Danwei: The Changing Chinese Workplace in Historical and Comparative Perspective* (Armonk NY, ME Shape, 1997); Lu Feng, 'The Work Unit: A Unique Form of Social Organization' in Michael Dutton (ed), *Streetlife China* (Cambridge, Cambridge University Press, 1998) 53–58; Andrew G Walder, *Communist Neo-Traditionalism: Work and Authority in China Industry* (Berkeley CA, University of California Press, 1986).

4 Tim Murphy and Ting Xu, 'Home Ownership and its Consequences: Some China-UK Comparisons' (2013) 7 *Journal of Comparative Law* 194, 198.

5 David Zweig, 'China's Stalled "Fifth Wave": Zhu Rongji's Reform Package of 1998–2000' (2001) 41 *Asian Survey* 231.

The subsequent direction of the housing reform has been to let the individual household purchase the houses, and the private housing market has since been flourishing. In 2000, housing began to be commodified in China.[6] As Huang Youqin points out, a class of homeowners began to emerge.[7] The formation of the urban property market has transcended many entrenched boundaries in China's governance system such as public vs. private. However, due largely to the formation of a dual-track land use rights allocation system and the complexity embedded in the governance structure, some of the old boundaries such as rural vs. urban have been strengthened, and new boundaries such as property owners vs. non-property owners have been generated. Many people simply cannot afford properties because of the increasing housing prices.

In contrast to the development of the formal property market, in many areas a de facto property market is emerging that consists of affordable properties called 'minor rights properties', which does not constitute a formal legal concept. These sorts of properties are built by farmers on collectively-owned land that is reserved for agricultural purposes or farmers' residential use according to the classification of land use control,[8] and which cannot be commodified in the sense of being transferred on the formal property market according to relevant provisions of the Land Administration Law (2004) and the Property Law (2007).[9] Buyers (most are rural migrants) of such properties can obtain an ownership certificate issued by the township government. However, the 'legality' of such ownership certificates is highly contested, as according to the law, only governments at the county level or above have the authority to issue the ownership certificates and register

[6] For housing commodification see eg, Min Zhou and John R Logan, 'Market Transition and the Commodification of Housing in Urban China' in John R Logan (ed), *The New Chinese City: Globalization and Market Reform* (Oxford, Blackwell Publishers, 2002) 137–52.

[7] Huang, 'The Road to Homeownership' (n 2 above) 774.

[8] According to Article 4 of the Land Administration Law (2004), the state controls the purposes of the use of land. The state formulates overall plans for land utilisation, and classifies the purposes of land use into agriculture, construction use and unused. Article 4(1) of Land Administration Law provides: '"Land for agricultural use" refers to land directly used for agricultural production, including cultivated land, woodland, grassland, land for farmland water conservancy and water surfaces for breeding; "land for construction use" refers to land on which buildings and structures are put up, including land for urban and rural housing and public facilities, land for industrial and mining use, land for building communications and water conservancy facilities, land for tourism and land for building military installations'.

[9] According to the Land Administration Law (1986, revised 1998, 2004), only farmers can build houses on the collectively-owned land, whereas people with urban *hukou* (urban household registration) including property developers are not allowed to do so. Article 43 of the Land Administration Law stipulates that any work unit (*danwei*) or individual who needs land for construction purposes should apply to the government for the use of the land owned by the state. Article 63 of the Land Administration Law stipulates that no right to the use of the land owned by 'rural collectives' may be assigned, transferred or leased for non-agricultural construction.

these properties.[10] When purchasing these properties, rural migrants cannot use mortgages or apply for bank loans to support their purchase.

Despite the hurdles that the potential purchasers of minor rights properties may face, the minor rights property market is flourishing, due in large part, it seems, to the fact that prices are low and more affordable compared to those available on the formal urban property market. There were already 6 billion m^2 of minor rights properties nationwide by June of 2010.[11] In Shenzhen, for example, approximately 50 per cent of properties have minor property rights.[12] Buyers of minor rights properties are attracted to their relatively low price, which only constitutes approximately ⅓ of that of commercial housing.[13]

This chapter examines the emergence of precarious home ownership in China's rapid urbanisation and its relationship with institutional ambiguity. It focuses on a seemingly self-contradictory governance strategy; that is, the state has created numerous boundaries such as the rural–urban divide for controlling its population; and in the meantime, the state also accommodates, or even encourages the existence of a significant degree of 'ambiguity' in its governance structure, which in effect transcends some of the old boundaries but generates new ones. This governance strategy has given rise to the increasing extent of 'precarity', ie a condition of vulnerability relative to contingency and the inability to predict,[14] in home ownership in China. Considering the position in China underlines Ettlinger's point that precarity is not limited to post-welfare states, notably in Europe and the United States.[15]

Although some of the purchasers of minor rights properties are investors who want to buy these properties for rental purposes, they are not the super-rich, in the sense that they could not afford to invest in the formal property market. Most purchasers are pensioners, young professionals who have just started their careers, and rural migrants in the city who cannot afford the

[10] Article 10 of the Property Law (2007), promulgated by the National People's Congress; Article 4 of the Methods of Housing Registration (2008), issued by the Ministry of Construction on 22 January 2008.

[11] 'There are 6 billion m^2 Minor Rights Properties in China' ['zhongguo xiao chanquanfang huo da 60 yi pingfang mi']: house.ifeng.com/special/xiaochanquanfang/focus/detail_2010_06/03/1580970_0.shtml.

[12] Juan Zhang, 'The Dilemma of the Property Market in Shenzhen: Should We Buy Minor Rights Properties?' ['Shenzhen loushi de ganga: xiaochan quan fang daodi gai bu gai mai'?], (24 August 2012): toutiao.szhome.com/detail/97930.html.

[13] See 'What is Minor Rights Property?' ['shenme shi xiao chanquan fang?'], Renminwang Theory Channel (Renmin wang), (22 February 2012): theory.people.com.cn/GB/49154/49155/17190374.html.

[14] Nancy Ettlinger, 'Precacity Unbound' (2007) 32 *Alternatives: Global, Local, Political* 319, 320.

[15] Ibid.

high price of commercial housing, and in the meantime want to own their houses.[16] As a result, purchasing minor rights properties has been a reasonable and legitimate choice. According to a survey conducted by Jin Zhifeng and others in Nanjing, 98 per cent of households who have bought minor rights properties simply want an adequate standard of housing for living.[17] Moreover, the source of their funds comes from savings, and they are therefore able to avoid the risk of being too reliant on bank loans, or of being in debt to loan sharks. In some ways, accordingly, they are less precarious that other home owners.

However, our argument is that the context of institutional ambiguity—from the central and local governments, the law-makers, the courts—emerging in the governance of this rapid social change illustrates a form of 'governmental precarization'.[18] In particular there is a choice similar to that taken by property guardians[19] where legal certainty is sacrificed for a lower cost. The chapter has four further sections. Section II looks at the formation of the rural-urban divide in governing China's population and its links with the dual track LURs allocation system. Section III examines institutional ambiguity manifest in the complex central–local relationship. Section IV probes the nature of precarious home ownership via a case study of minor rights properties in China. Section V engages with key cases concerning disputes over minor rights properties, using data only recently made publicly accessible.

For cases concerning disputes over minor rights properties, we have chosen to focus on those cases occurred in Henan province, where preserving arable land while providing land for constructing houses for its increasing population has become a real tension.[20] We have explored the database 'China Judgments Online' launched by the Supreme Court in 2013.[21] Searching cases using the keywords 'minor rights property', 'civil cases', 'disputes occurring in Henan province' and 'cases heard at the local court/at the first instance',[22] we have gathered 369 results with 93 cases concerning

[16] Qiren R Zhou, 'Minor Property Rights, Big Opportunities' ['xiao chanquan, da jihui'], *The Economic Observer ['jingji guancha bao']* (27 August 2007).

[17] ZF Jin et al, 'Research on the Activities of Minor Rights Properties' Buyers: A Survey Based on Nanjing' ['Xiao chanquan fang yezhu goufang xingwei yanjiu: jiyu Nanjingshi de wenjuan diaocha'] (2015) 36 *Shanghai Land & Resources [Shanghai guotu ziyuan]* 40.

[18] Isabell Lorey, *State of Insecurity: Government of the Precarious* (Verso, 2015) 13.

[19] See Hunter and Meers, Chapter four this volume and Mara Ferreri, Gloria Dawson and Alexander Vasudevan, 'Living precariously: property guardianship and the flexible city' (2016) 42 *Transactions of the Institute of British Geographers* 246.

[20] Henan has the largest population in China. It is located in the central part of China, as the hub of transportation in China. It is regarded as the breadbasket of China and one of the most important producers and processors of food products in China. Henan Statistics Bureau, 'Introduction to Henan Province' (Henan Statistics Bureau): www.henan.gov.cn/hngk/system/2006/09/19/010008384.shtml.

[21] China Judgements Online, 'Homepage' (n.d): wenshu.court.gov.cn/.

[22] According to Chapter Three of the 2004 Constitution, the structure of governance in China consists of five tiers: the central government, provinces, cities, counties and townships.

property transactions. In our analysis of these cases, 34 cases are identified by the court as cases concerning disputes over the transaction of minor rights properties. The discrepancies in the perceptions of the 'legality' of the transfer of minor rights properties between the parties and the courts indicate the difficulties in determining the nature of minor rights property.

II. THE RURAL–URBAN DIVIDE AND THE DUAL-TRACK LURs ALLOCATION SYSTEM

The rural–urban divide has become entrenched in the Chinese governance system in the post-1949 era. The Maoist regime, although it claimed to be pro-village and anti-city, 'was fundamentally urban after all'.[23] Industrialisation was the priority in the making of the modern state, and the transfer of rural resources to subsidise the industrial sector enlarged the gap between the rural and urban areas. The mobility of rural people to cities was controlled by the state through the household registration system (*huji zhidu*), whereby people registered as rural households were treated as 'second-class citizens' in terms of their entitlements to social security, education and health care provision. As a result, the Maoist regime became deeply alienated from the countryside.[24] Further, the rural–urban divide has been closely linked to two different land systems—the rural land system and the urban land system. In the post-Mao era, and especially in the post-Deng period (1992–), large-scale rural–urban migration and rapid urban expansion have led to the relaxation of legal and administrative distinctions between urban and rural. For example, 17 provinces, autonomous regions and municipalities have abolished the category of rural household (*nongye hukou*).[25] Yet the land system still remains as an obstacle to bridging the gap between the rural and urban areas.[26]

In correspondence with the first four tiers, the court system in China is divided into four levels: the Supreme Court, the court at the high level, the court at the intermediate level, and the court at the local level. Some courts at the local level have established detached tribunals in townships with large populations. The tribunals function as the constituent of the court at the local level and their judgments constitute the body of judgments of the court at the local level. See Articles 2, 17, 19, 22 and 25 of the Organic Law of the People's Courts (1980, amended 1983, 1986, and 2006).

[23] David Strand, 'New Chinese Cities' in Joseph W Esherick (ed), *Remaking the Chinese City: Modernity and National Identity, 1900–1950* (Honolulu, University of Hawaii Press, 2000) 211, 223.

[24] See Kate X Zhou, *How the Farmers Changed China: Power of the People* (Boulder CO, Westview Press, 1996) 243–44.

[25] '17 Provinces, Autonomous Regions and Municipalities Have Published Local Plans to Reform the Household Registration System' ['17 shengfen chutai difang ban hugai fangan'], (Xinhua.com, 9 June 2015): news.xinhuanet.com/finance/2015-06/09/c_127893419.htm.

[26] For more discussion, see Ting Xu, 'The End of the Urban-Rural Divide? Emerging Quasi Commons in Rural China' (2010) 96 *Archiv für Rechts und Sozialphilosophie [Archives for Philosophy of Law and Social Philosophy]* 557.

Before 1978, urban land was not a commodity, and was allocated by administrative methods. The state granted LURs to its agencies, for example, governments, state-owned enterprises (SOEs), hospitals, and universities.[27] These state agencies were not just land users, but also held management rights and functioned as the de facto owners.[28] One important means of administrative allocation of urban land was through public-sector employers, that is, work units.[29] Until 1999, most of China's urban residents lived in state-owned housing, built and distributed by work units.

Urbanisation has speeded up since the late 1980s, leading to the dramatic increase in the commercial value of urban land in the 1990s. This change called for a new mechanism to improve the market efficiency of the urban land system while maintaining the doctrine of state land-ownership. It was in response of this challenge that the LURs system emerged. The establishment of the LURs system also served as an engine to boost economic growth.[30] For example, urban land was leased to foreign investors so that they could access and use the land for a certain period of time.[31] The LURs system attracted foreign direct investment (FDI), which contributed to the construction of Special Economic Zones (SEZs) such as Shenzhen. The LURs system, along with the change in housing provision, has led to the formation of the urban property market in China.

The lease of state-owned lands has been legalised via the promulgation of the Land Administration Law (1986). In April 1988 the Constitution was also amended to provide that 'the right of land use can be transferred in accordance with the law' (Clause 4 of Article 10). However, rather than establishing a LURs system based on market principles, a 'dual-track' LURs allocation system was introduced to assign LURs in urban areas. A dual-track allocation system means that LURs are assigned in two ways: allocation (*huabo*) and assignment (*churang*). Allocation is the transfer of LURs to state-owned users without either time-limits or land leasing fees; assignment is the transfer of LURs to non-state users for a fixed period (40 years for commercial purposes, 50 years for industrial purposes and 70 years for residential purposes) and for payment of land leasing fees.[32]

[27] See eg, You-tien Hsing, 'Land and Territorial Politics in Urban China' (2006) 187 *The China Quarterly* 575, 579.

[28] ibid, 580.

[29] Public-sector employers included government agencies, service units (for example, educational and cultural institutions), large state-owned enterprises, and other social organisations affiliated with the government.

[30] Fulong Wu and Laurence JC Ma, 'The Chinese City in Transition: Towards Theorizing China's Urban Restructuring' in Laurence JC Ma and Fulong Wu (eds), *Restructuring the Chinese City: Changing Society, Economy and Space* (New York, Routledge, 2005) 260, 267.

[31] Chengri Ding, 'Land Policy in China: Assessment and Prospects' (2003) 20 *Land Use Policy* 109, 112.

[32] Article 12 of the Interim Regulations Concerning the Assignment and Transfer of the Right to the Use of the State-owned Land in the Urban Areas (1990). See also Samuel PS Ho

Together allocations and assignments of LURs constitute the primary property market. The transfer of LURs via sale has, in effect, created a secondary property market.

The Urban Real Estate Administration Law of the People's Republic of China (PRC) was promulgated in 1994 (amended in 2007), for the purpose of administering urban land and real estate in China. It confirms the functioning of the dual-track LURs allocation system and the existence of the dual property market. Article 3 of the Real Estate Administration Law stipulates that the state shall adopt a paid transfer of LURs system for the use of state-owned land for a limited period, except in instances where LURs are obtained through the state land allocation system in accordance with this Law. Article 12 provides that the assignment of LURs could adopt tender, auction, and negotiation. Under the dual allocation system, the property market is largely controlled by administrative power.

Chapter 13 of the Property Law (2007) deals with LURs to rural residential plots, but fails to clarify the issue of the transfer and sale of these use rights (in instances where the plot has not been reclaimed by the state first). As a result, many informal norms concerning the transfer and sale of LURs have emerged at the grassroots level.

When the central government suppresses the development of minor rights properties, it fails to distinguish two categories of minor rights properties—those built on rural land where construction has been authorised by the state, and those built on agricultural land. According to the state control of land use, the state restricts conversion of land for agriculture purposes to land used for construction, in order to keep the total area of the land for construction under control and to provide special protection for agricultural land. For example, Article 63 of the Land Administration Law (2004) stipulates that no right to the use of land owned by rural collectives may be assigned, transferred or leased for non-agricultural construction. This is in line with China's land policy and the pressing need to feed 1.3 billion people.[33] Building minor rights properties on agricultural land changes the use of the land and is against the law.[34]

Due largely to the existence of the rural–urban divide and the dual-track LURs allocation system, land acquisition by the state has become the only

and George CS Lin, 'Emerging Land Markets in Rural and Urban China: Policies and Practices' (2003) 175 *The China Quarterly* 681, 687.

[33] Preserving 1.8 billion *mu* (1 hectare = 15 *mu*) of arable land in order to ensure the country's food supply is a national policy, but arable land only constituted 12.7% of the total land in 1996, and this figure had decreased to 11.3% (around 1.6 billion *mu*) in 2013. The World Bank, 'Arable Land (% of land area)': data.worldbank.org/indicator/AG.LND.ARBL.ZS/countries.

[34] Xiaojun W Chen, 'Minor Rights Properties Are Illegal and Cannot be Transferred' ['Xiao chanquan fang bu hefa bu neng jiaoyi'], *Economic Information Daily [Jingji cankao bao]*, (31 October 2014).

way through which farmers' land use rights can enter into the market.[35] The Land Administration Law (2004) states that compensation shall be given in accordance with the original use of the acquired land,[36] and the compensation is dispensed through a package that includes compensation for the land, resettlement subsidies and compensation for fixtures to, and young or green crops on, the acquired land. Article 42 of the Property Law (2007) expands the scope of compensation to 'the premiums for social security of the farmers' in order to guarantee their normal lives and safeguard their lawful rights and interests. However, and in spite of this, it is not specified that the compensation is to be paid at full market prices, and nor is it mentioned that the value added to the land via development is to be recognised.[37]

III. CENTRAL–LOCAL RELATIONSHIPS AND INSTITUTIONAL AMBIGUITY

Since the market reform that commenced in 1978, the power to control and mobilise resources that was once held by the central government has been gradually decentralised and shifted to local governments. The central–local divided is manifest in the *tiao-kuai* system. This system consists of the vertical administrative line (*tiao*) of government bureaus or ministries and the horizontal line (*kuai*) of local governments.[38] State agencies are often subject to dual supervision of both the *tiao* and the *kuai*, which means that a state agency may be controlled by both a higher-level agency and a local government at the same administrative level.[39] The extent to which a state agency is subject to the control of either the *tiao* or the *kuai* depends on the source of its funding and the power of appointing 'the chairman in command' in that state agency—whether it is vested in the *tiao* or the *kuai*. For instance, a taxation bureau is in effect subordinate to their vertical higher levels, which have the authority to allocate funding to taxation bureaus at lower levels and to control their personnel appointments. Another important example is that although the revised Land Administration Law

[35] Both Article 10(3) of the Constitution 2004 and Article 2(4) of the Land Administration Law (2004) specify that the state, in the public interest, may lawfully acquire land owned by collectives. This establishes the mechanism for compulsory land acquisition.

[36] The Land Administration Law (2004), Article 47.

[37] For land development rights in China, see Ting Xu and Wei Gong, 'Taking as Giving, Appropriation as Access: Transfers of Land Development Rights and China's Recent Experiments' (2013) 64 *Northern Ireland Legal Quarterly* 411.

[38] Carolyn Cartier, 'Scale Relations and China's Spatial Administrative Hierarchy' in Lawrence JC Ma and Fulong Wu (eds), *Restructuring the Chinese City: Changing Society, Economy and Space* (New York, Routledge, 2005) 21–38, 26.

[39] ibid.

(1998) was designed to centralise power held by the State Council to enable better management of land, power is dispersed between different levels of government.[40] For example, at the national level, the Ministry of Construction and the Ministry of Land and Resources, under the State Council, may coordinate with each other in regulating the property market. However, real estate and land management departments at the provincial and local levels are directly responsible to provincial or local governments.[41] The Ministries at the central level do not have direct control over these local departments, other than providing working guidance. There are often conflicts between the central and the local, as well as between *zhengfu* (local governments) and *bumen* (departments or ministries).[42]

Competition for financial resources constitutes one of the most important reasons for the increasing tensions between the central and local governments. There are many sources of revenue that can be extracted from land; for example, tax. A tax sharing system was adopted in 1994 in attempts to enhance the revenue of the centre and to increase the transparency of tax revenues. However, local governments are reluctant to share land revenue such as value-added tax with the central government.[43] Moreover, in order to collect more tax revenue, local officials have a range of tools in the name of accelerating the pace of urbanisation, for example, seizure of farmland and extension of infrastructure in urban expansion, which may contribute to the property market boom but harm farmers' rights and interests. Land has become an important source of local government revenue and the main vehicle for them to compete and bargain with the central government in the fiscal and administrative decentralisation.[44]

As the property market develops, more important sources of revenue have been generated that could be extracted from land, which, under the current system, local governments do not have to share with the central government, for example, local taxes and land use rights transfer fees.[45]

[40] For example, Article 6 of the Real Estate Law defines the functions and powers of government departments at various levels. See Ling Li, *Urban Land Reform in China* (London, Macmillan, 1999) 32.

[41] Li, *Urban Land Reform in China* (n 40 above) 32.

[42] For the *tiao-kuai* system and the disputes between the central and the local, see eg, Jonathan Unger, 'The Struggle to Dictate China's Administration: The Conflicts of Branches vs. Areas vs. Reform' (1987) 18 *Australian Journal of Chinese Affairs* 15; Richard Baum and Alexi Shevchenko, 'The "State of the State"' in Merle Goldman and Roderick MacFaquhar (eds), *The Paradox of China's Post-Mao Reforms* (Cambridge MA, Harvard University Press, 1999) 333–62, 340–42.

[43] Qingshu Xie, AR Ghanbari Parsa and Barry Redding, 'The Emergence of the Urban Land Market in China: Evolution, Structure, Constraints and Perspectives' (2002) 39 *Urban Studies* 1392.

[44] Hsing, 'Land and Territorial Politics in Urban China' (n 27 above) 576.

[45] See eg, Samuel Ho and George Lin, 'Emerging Land Markets in Rural and Urban China' (2003) 175 *The China Quarterly* 681; You-tien Hsing, 'Brokering Power and Property in China's Townships' (2006) 19 *The Pacific Review* 103, 108.

Further, the income from selling LURs has become the major source of off-budgetary or self-raised revenue (*zichou zijin*) for local governments.

The price of commercial housing is high, and this is in part due to the fact that when using state-owned urban land to construct housing, property developers need to pay land leasing fees to the government;[46] and it is further due to the fact that commercial housing developers also want to make high profits. The fees and profits all increase the price of 'legal' urban housing. The development of minor rights properties has a huge impact on the profits accrued by the property developers on the commercial property market, and it also indirectly affects the government's income drawn from land leasing. As a result, the central government leaned toward the curtailment of minor rights properties.

The emergence of competing and even conflicting rules in dealing with property issues has increased the degree of precarity in home ownership. For the minor rights holder their lack of certainty compounds the precariousness of their situation.[47] Further, the complexity embedded in the governance system has generated institutional ambiguity in the process of economic reform, which the central government has to tolerate. The state has even deliberately introduced a significant degree of ambiguity in the process of law-making as a governance strategy: national law only provides general principles and needs to be complemented by various kinds of regulations made by a complex hierarchy of legislative organs for implementation (see Figure 1 below).[48] Specifically according to the Legislation Law of the PRC (2000), the National People's Congress and Standing Committee exercise state legislative power (Article 7); only national laws may be enacted in respect of matters relating to 'acquisition of non-state assets' (Article 8(6)). The State Council enacts administrative regulations in accordance with the Constitution and national law in order to implement the law (Article 56). Various ministries and commissions under the State Council also exercise regulatory power and make administrative rules in accordance with national law, administrative regulations, and decisions and orders of the State Council in order to implement administrative regulations (Article 71).

[46] See Article 8 of the Interim Regulations Concerning the Assignment and Transfer of the Right to the Use of the State-Owned Land in the Urban Areas (1990) and Article 8 of the Urban Real Estate Administration Law (1994, revised 2007).

[47] Laurie Berg, *Migrant Rights at Work: Law's Precariousness at the Intersection of Immigration and Labour* (London, Routledge, 2015) 44.

[48] Ting Xu and Wei Gong, 'The Legitimacy of Extralegal Property: Global Perspectives and China's Experience' (2016) 67 *Northern Ireland Legal Quarterly* 189, 205. According to the Chinese Legislation Law (2000), the State Council can make regulations. Article 56 of the Chinese Legislation Law reads: 'The State Council enacts administrative regulations in accordance with the Constitution and national law.' Administrative regulations may provide for the following: '(i) matters for which enactment of administrative regulations is required in order to implement a national law; (ii) matters subject to the administrative regulation of the State Council under Article 89 of the Constitution.'

The Local People's Congress and Standing Committee make local decrees, and local governments make local rules within their authorities (Articles 68 and 71). In theory, the Constitution has the highest authority, followed by national laws and administrative regulations, which have higher authority than local decrees and administrative or local rules (Article 79). Local authorities tend to make law that suits local interests but not the national interest. Moreover, both the central government and local authorities tend to issue policies rather than laws and regulations in order to deal with matters flexibly. Such flexibility allows for local experiments and initiatives, but it may also be utilised to supress those experiments if they contravene vested political and economic interests.

Figure 1: The hierarchy of law-making in China

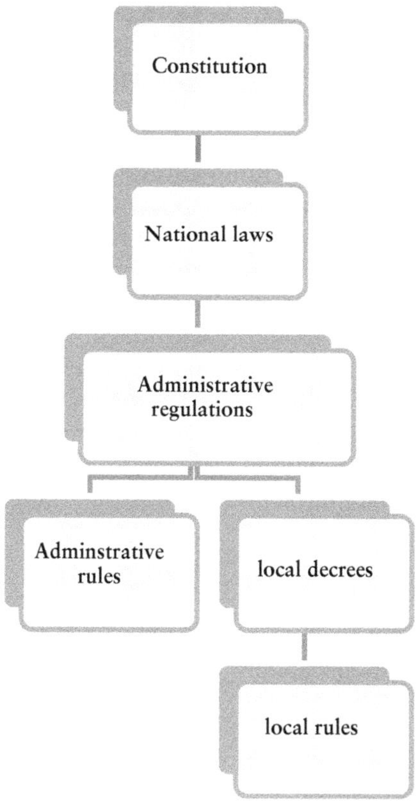

IV. MINOR RIGHTS PROPERTY AND PRECARIOUS HOME OWNERSHIP

As discussed in the Introduction and Section II, minor property rights are essentially property claims that are not recognised by the law.

In terms of minor rights properties built on rural land for construction purposes, there are also two kinds of properties. One is built by the village committees on village communal land; the other is built by farmers on their residential plots.[49] The former are mostly for commercial purposes rather than for farmers' residential use, and contravene the law of land use control. In the 34 cases on disputes over minor rights properties we have analysed, only one case (2.94 per cent) concerns minor rights properties that are built on village communal land.[50] However, if we look at those minor rights properties built by farmers on their residential plots—their purpose is not for large-scale commercial sale; there are no issues with any violation against the control of the use of the rural land. 15 cases (44.12 per cent) out of the 34 cases concern this type of minor rights property.[51]

Potential purchasers of minor rights properties face many hurdles, due largely to the central government's critical scrutiny: these properties cannot be registered, and buyers cannot use mortgages or bank loans to support their purchase.[52] By contrast, township governments clearly acquiesced in the development of these properties, a fact which not only reflects an increasingly complex relationship between central and local government, but also indicates a significant degree of ambiguity embedded in the development of the land system. Township governments do not have the authority to grant LURs, and therefore they cannot profit from collecting the land leasing fees. As a result, township governments have managed to find an alternative source of income by encouraging the development of the minor rights properties, thereby competing for income from land with the superior levels of government.[53]

There are actually no laws prohibiting farmers from selling these properties. Article 62 of the Land Administration Law (2004) merely stipulates that one rural household can only have one residential plot; if they have sold or leased their houses their application for other residential plots should not be approved. Further, farmers' selling of their houses is not against the

[49] SJ Huang, 'Minor Rights Properties: Reasons and Solutions' ['Xiao chanquan fang: Chengyin yu chulu'] in JH Pan et al (eds), *A Report on the Development of Chinese Cities, No. 4 [Zhongguo chengshi fazhan baogao, No.4]* (Beijing, Shehui kexue wenxian chubanshe, 2011) 273–96.

[50] *Ding Ping v. Ding Zhanhua*, People's Court at Yuanhui District, Luohe City, Henan Province, 26 June 2014.

[51] Other 18 cases do not specifically address the purpose of land use; they just give the information that the disputed minor rights properties are built on collectively-owned rural land.

[52] The Ministry of Land and Natural Resources, 'New Policies on Residential Plots: It is Impossible to Legalise Minor Rights Property' ['Zhaiji di xin zhengce: Xiao chanquan fang zhuanzheng wuwang'], *Beijing Youth Daily [Beijing Qingnian bao]*, (Beijing, 12 December 2013).

[53] For the role of township governments in relation to property rights, see eg, You-tien Hsing, 'Broking Power and Property in China's Townships' (2006) 19 *The Pacific Review* 103.

Property Law (2007).[54] The subsequent ban on farmers' selling of their own residential properties was issued in the form of a series of policy documents formulated by the central government.[55] The fact that the central government has issued various policies concerning how best to deal with minor rights properties, indicates the ambiguous attitude of the higher-level authorities toward the status of minor rights properties.

Turning to the issue of whether urban residents, including rural migrants, can buy minor rights properties, no laws prohibit them from doing so. Before 1998, it was legal for urban residents to build houses on the collectively-owned rural land as long as they obtained approval from the county government and fulfilled several requirements (Article 41 of the Land Administration Law (1986)).[56] However, when the Land Administration Law was revised in 1998, this article was deleted, and the city residents' right to build houses in rural areas was thus abolished. That said, the law does not explicitly forbid urban residents from buying properties located in the rural area. Again, prohibition was issued via the publication of a series of policy documents.[57] From the above analysis, we can see that only documents issued by the State Council prohibit the transfer of the minor rights properties, but these policy documents do not constitute administrative regulations.

[54] For example, Article 39 of the Property Law (2007) provides that owners of immovables or movables shall be entitled to possess, use, benefit from and dispose of the immovables or movables according to law. Article 153 of the Property Law also stipulates that laws such as the Land Administration Law and the relevant state regulations shall be applicable to the obtaining, exercising and transferring of the right to the use of the residential plots.

[55] For example, Article 2 of the Circular on 'Strengthening the Administration of the Transfer of Land Use Rights and Prohibiting Speculative Land Dealings', issued by the General Office of the State Council in May 1999, provides that: farmers cannot sell their houses to urban residents, and applications from urban residents to use farmers' collectively-owned land to build houses shall not be approved. Similar prohibitions issued by the General Office of the State Council include the following: Article 2 of the Circular on 'the Stringent Implementation of the Laws and Policies Concerning the Use of Rural Collective Construction Land' (No. 71, 2007) and Article 3(6) of the Circular on 'the Active and Steady Promotion of the Reform of the Household Administration System' (No. 9, 2011). The same ban can also be found in Article 13 of the Opinions on 'Enforcing the Management of Rural Residential Plots' (No. 234) issued by the Ministry of Land and Resources on 2 November 2004.

[56] Those requirements include that the area to be used shall not exceed the standards set out by the provinces, autonomous regions, and municipalities; that users should pay compensation and resettlement fees just like those provided for farmers when their land is acquired by the state for the purpose of national construction.

[57] The State Council issued 'the Decision on Deepening the Reform and Strengthening the Management of Land' (No. 28) on 21 October 2004. Article 10 of this Decision prohibits urban residents from buying residential plots in rural areas. The Ministry of Land and Resources Management also issued many rules banning the issuing of ownership certificates to the owners of minor rights properties, including the Circular on 'Strengthening the Management of Construction Land' issued on 11 August 2009.

V. DISPUTES OVER PRECARIOUS HOME OWNERSHIP

In China, when a property is transferred, the purchaser's ownership of the property depends on a valid contract and registration of ownership. Because minor rights properties cannot be registered, of the 34 cases on disputes over minor rights properties we have examined, most disputes surround the validity of contracts. Among the 15 cases concerning minor rights properties built on the residential plots, only three cases concern requesting the court to confirm ownership of minor rights properties.

In *Nan Xiaohua and Nan Xiaowu v Nan Xiaoming*, the plaintiffs and the defendant are brothers; all claim ownership of a minor rights property.[58] The defendant built a house on the residential plot to which all brothers have use rights, and the plaintiffs contributed to the fund that was used to build the house. However, when the construction work was completed, the defendant refused to share the property with his two brothers, who then brought the suit to the court. The case was dismissed on the basis that building a minor rights property was illegal; the defendant was required to return the money that the plaintiffs had contributed to building the house.

In *Li Chao v Chen Hua, Lin Zubing, and Wang Xinchao* (as the third party), Li Chao bought a minor rights property from Wang Xinchao, who then had a dispute over the property with Chen Hua and Liu Zubing, and the property subsequently became subject to enforcement action.[59] Li Chao then filed a lawsuit and required confirmation of his ownership of the property. The court rejected his claim on the basis that use rights to the residential plot can only be enjoyed by members of the collective economic organisation; Li Chao, as an outsider of that collective economic organisation, could not obtain use rights to the residential plot and claim ownership of a property built on the plot.[60] Therefore the contract between him and Wang Xinchao concerning the transfer of the minor right property was void.

[58] People's court at Neixiang County, Nanyang City, Henan Province, 17 June 2015.

[59] People's court at Wuzhi County, Jiaozuo City, Henan Province, 9 June 2015.

[60] Article 60 of Property Law (2007) provides: 'with respect to the land, forests, mountains, grasslands, wasteland, tidal flats, etc. owned by the collective, the right of their ownership shall be exercised in accordance with the following provisions:

(1) For those owned by the collective of farmers of a village, the collective economic organization of the village or the villagers' committee shall exercise the right of ownership on behalf of the collective;
(2) For those respectively owned by two or more collectives of farmers within a village, the collective economic organizations or villagers' groups concerned within the village shall exercise the right of ownership on behalf of the collectives; and
(3) For those owned by the collective of farmers of a town or township, the collective economic organization of the town or township shall exercise the right of ownership on behalf of the collective.'

The case of *Li Xiaohong v Li Yumei and Sun Xiaojin* concerns another dispute over ownership of minor rights properties.[61] Li Xiaohong paid Li Yumei to buy a property that was reserved for Li Yumei's resettlement in his village. Li Xiaohong chose to purchase the property in this way, because as an outsider of the village, she was not entitled to purchase such kind of property. The two parties signed a contract that confirmed this arrangement. However, due to the increase in property prices, Li Yumei refused to transfer the property to Li Xiaohong. Li Xiaohong filed a lawsuit. Compared with the two other cases discussed above, the court reasoned differently in reaching its decision: the contract was valid, but the issue was with the ownership of the property. As the property was only for the villagers' resettlement, an outsider who had purchased the property only obtained use right to property. This was the only instance where the court did not rule against the validity of the contract, and in effect acquiesced in the transfer of minor rights properties.

A careful reading of Chinese law gives another explanation of the validity of this sort of contract that is different from the majority opinion of the court, which adheres to policy documents issued by the central government. The validity of a contract is determined by ascertaining whether certain necessary elements have been met. We are looking at situations where the transaction completes and the purchaser occupies the property in most cases; consequently, we are concerned with contracts that meet requirements such as the validity of execution and performance, etc.[62] We now focus on some other elements, which include the following: firstly, the parties should have legal and mental capacity;[63] secondly, the vendor should be the owner of the subject-matter for sale or have the right of disposal;[64] thirdly, the subject-matter should be lawful;[65] and fourthly, it must not be included in any of the circumstances stipulated by Article 52 of the Chinese Contract Law (1999).[66]

61 People's court at Wuzhi County, Jiaozuo City, Henan Province, 12 June 2015.

62 This sort of contract usually meets the requirement of formalities.

63 Article 9 of Chinese Contract Law (1999) reads: 'The parties shall, when making a contract, have corresponding capacity for civil rights and civil conduct'.

64 Article 132 of the Chinese Contract Law (1999) reads: 'The seller shall own the subject matter for sale or have the right of disposal. For a subject matter the transfer of which is forbidden or restricted by laws or administrative regulations, the provisions therein shall govern'.

65 ibid.

66 Article 52 of the Chinese Contract Law (1999) reads:

'A contract is invalid under any of the following circumstances:

(1) either party enters into the contract by means of fraud or coercion and impairs the State's interests;
(2) there is malicious conspiracy causing damage to the interests of the State, of the collective or of a third party;
(3) there is an attempt to conceal illegal goals under the disguise of legitimate forms;

In our consideration of the contract concerning the transfer of the minor rights property, we can set aside the question of whether the parties have legal and mental capacity. And from the above analysis, we reach the conclusion that farmers have the right to sell these properties and these properties are lawful. Clearly, a contract concerning the transfer of minor rights properties does not fall into the first four circumstances specified in Article 52 of the Contract Law. In terms of the fifth circumstance in that Article, as discussed above, the current laws do not prohibit farmers from disposing of their use rights to their residential plots and selling properties built on these plots. The fact that minor rights properties cannot be registered[67] does not affect the validity of the contract.[68] Further, although the transfer of properties needs to be based on a valid contract and registration, the prohibition of registering minor rights properties does not deny the 'lawfulness' of these properties. It is more appropriate to characterise minor rights properties as 'extra-legal' property, ie, not *against* the law, but not recognised by the law.[69]

VI. CONCLUSION

With the introduction of the LURs system and the emergence of the urban property market, some of the entrenched boundaries in China's governance system have begun to disappear or fade. However, LURs are still allocated administratively to both primary and secondary property markets. Whilst state agencies get LURs free or at low prices and without time-limits, 'new economic players' now bid or negotiate for urban LURs for a fixed period,[70] and they have to cultivate a good relationship with local governments in order to secure sufficient LURs for development projects.

The state has managed to get rid of the burden of providing public housing in the process of the development of the private housing market, but the

(4) harm is done to social and public interests; or
(5) mandatory provisions of laws and administrative regulations are violated.'

[67] Article 9 of the Property Law (2007) reads: 'the creation, alteration, transfer or extinction of the property right shall become valid upon registration according to law; otherwise it shall not become valid, unless otherwise provided for by law'. Article 14: 'Where the creation, alteration, transfer and extinction of the property right of the immovables are required to be registered according to the provisions of law, they shall become valid as of the time when they are entered in the register of the immovables'.

[68] Article 15 of the Property Law (2007) reads: 'The contract made between the parties concerned on the creation, alteration, transfer or extinction of the property right of the immovables shall become valid as of the time when the contract is concluded, unless otherwise provided for by law or agreed upon in the contract; and where the property right is not registered, it shall not affect the validity of the contract'.

[69] Xu and Gong, 'The Legitimacy of Extralegal Property: Global Perspectives and China's Experience' (n 48 above).

[70] Ho and Lin (n 45 above) 705.

empty space it has left behind has not been filled in properly. Due to the lack of a well-functioning social welfare system, ordinary people spend most of their savings on the expenses of education, housing and medical care; the rural and urban poor seldom receive sufficient support from the government for affordable housing. The development of the urban property market has stalled between the plan and the market, and it has also given rise to new distinctions such as property owners vs. non-property owners.

Highly motivated by the desire to benefit from the development of the property market, farmers are keen to build housing independently for the purposes of sale and gaining more income; rural migrants are also keen to buy the minor rights properties for affordable housing, since they cannot afford the high price of commercial housing. Neither the vendor nor the buyer should be treated as 'invaders' under the formal legal system. In many cases these 'property outsiders' are forced to become 'extra-legal' as a result of being excluded by the formal legal system. The purchaser has the right to buy and the vendor has the right to dispose of his or her property, but they have no recourse to the formal legal system to enforce their rights. In this way they are in a similar position to migrant workers in the West who find themselves unable to control their lives.[71]

The emergence of minor rights property has challenged the status quo of the land system, and has begun to transcend the entrenched boundaries in Chinese property law. Beneath the existence of minor rights property lies the complex governance structure and ambiguous governance strategy. As one of the grassroots initiatives, minor rights property may propel the reform of the current land system. However, minor rights property is still regarded by the central government as 'insecure' tenure and in many cases bitterly suppressed by the central government. As the process of economic reform struggles to strike a balance between party policy and law as well as between central and local law-making, it remains unclear whether the legitimacy of minor rights property will be recognised by the central government. The status of precarious home ownership therefore depends largely on how to govern institutional ambiguity in the rapid socio-economic transformation in China.

[71] Mimi Zou, 'Hyper-Dependence and Hyper-Precarity in Migrant Work Relations' in Tindara Addabbo and others (eds), *Labour And Social Rights. An Evolving Scenario (Proceedings of the Twelfth International Conference in Commemoration of Marco Biagi)* (Turin, Giappichelli Editore, 2015).

12

On Shaky Ground: Homes as Socio-Legal Spaces in a Post-Earthquake Environment

ANN DUPUIS,* SUZANNE VALLANCE** AND DAVID THORNS***

I. INTRODUCTION

NEW ZEALAND, SOMETIMES referred to as the Shaky Isles, is no stranger to earthquakes. Recognising this, the New Zealand government established the Earthquake and War Damage Commission in 1945 as a way of ensuring earthquake insurance for all property insured against fire loss. Now called The Earthquake Commission (EQC), this government-owned Crown entity provides privately insured residential property owners, primary natural disaster insurance of up to NZ$100,000 (+GST)[1] for each dwelling, with any further amount above that to be paid by the policyholder's insurance company. However, it was not until the severity of the Canterbury earthquakes of 2010–2011 that massive problems with this unique, compulsory, government indemnified insurance scheme, became apparent.

On 4 September 2010, the Canterbury region of New Zealand was rocked by a magnitude 7.1 earthquake. Since then the area has experienced many thousands of aftershocks, including the magnitude 6.3 earthquake of 22 February 2011 which caused major destruction, killing 185 people, injuring several thousand more, damaging more than 100,000 homes (or approximately half the housing stock of greater Christchurch, New Zealand's second largest city) and damaging the inner city to the extent that more than 1,200 buildings in the Central Business District required demolition.

* Honorary Research Fellow, School of People, Environment and Planning, College of Humanities and Social Sciences, Massey University, New Zealand.

** Lecturer in Urban Studies, Faculty of Environment, Society and Design, Department of Environmental Management, Lincoln University, New Zealand.

*** Emeritus Professor of Sociology, University of Canterbury, New Zealand.

[1] Goods and Services Tax.

Immense infrastructural damage also occurred to schools, hospitals and rest homes, road networks, water mains and sewer pipes.[2] In the weeks immediately after the February earthquake, approximately 70,000 people left Christchurch, as basic services were disrupted or they were deeply traumatised by the effects on employment, schools, family and community life, and sleep patterns.

The structural damage to homes and the problems and issues in dealing with EQC and private insurance companies had a profound impact on the way many Cantabrians came to understand the meaning of home. Living in an environment of extreme uncertainty, and faced with the threat of more quakes and aftershocks, their sense of ontological security, long associated with the home, was shattered. Similarly, their faith in the future viability of their homes as material structures and as part of a wider neighbourhood was also challenged as, in their attempts to repair their homes, they had to deal with an array of unfamiliar insurance, geo-technical, legal and regulatory issues.

It is within the context of this natural disaster that we explore the notion of home, not as a haven or respite from external threats as so frequently depicted, but as a socio-legal space in which the consequences of external threats in the form of a natural disaster are debated, disputed and laid bare. This exploration centres on the issues of insurance in a post-earthquake context, and discusses the complex and often contradictory interests of the state, private companies and individuals in this situation. This chapter argues that conceptualising homes as socio-legal spaces, the Canterbury earthquakes have exposed new vulnerabilities for home owners and tenants, thus adding to the literature on the precariousness of home. As a consequence, the notion of the home takes on new meanings. This view has implications for the way the home is secured and serviced and raises major questions of where responsibility lies in these processes.

II. THE THEORETICAL BACKDROP

The theoretical backdrop to the current chapter draws on two sources. The first is Mallett's excellent literature review on 'understanding home', which examines dominant and recurring themes about home, one of which is 'home as haven'.[3] Mallett notes that home as haven is based on a number of related ideas including: the distinction between the public and the private, with home representing a safe and secure private space; home as the place

[2] Canterbury Earthquake Recovery Authority (CERA), 'Briefing for the Incoming Minister' (CERA. 2011): www.eqc.govt.nz/sites/public_files/min-briefing-11.pdf.

[3] Shelley Mallett, 'Understanding Home: A Critical Review of the Literature' (2004) 52 *The Sociological Review* 62, 70.

associated with family, differentiated from public space as being associated with paid work and political activity; and home as an intimate space where close, caring relationships are developed. She also outlines the challenges to home as haven that abound in the literature, all of which 'reject the idealized view of home perpetuated' by such binary oppositions as inside/outside, work/home, public/private, and safe/unsafe.

The second source drawn on is the authors' previous work, together and with others, on the meanings of home, home ownership and ontological security.[4] In our 1998 paper we extended existing work in the broad area of the meanings of home and made the argument that 'home ownership offers individuals a means through which they can attain a sense of "ontological security" in their everyday lives'.[5] In our attempt to operationalise the proposition we argued that ontological security can be maintained when the following four conditions are met:

(1) home as the site of constancy in the social and material environment;
(2) home as a spatial context in which the day-to-day routines of human existence are performed;
(3) home as a site where people feel most in control of their lives because they feel free from the surveillance that is part of the contemporary world;
(4) home as a secure base around which identities are constructed.

Included within the discussion of these four conditions were issues to do with house and home, family, the economic and psychological security associated with home ownership, family rituals and gatherings and seasonal routines like gardening, privacy, and identity, especially gendered identities and the home. The notion of home as a refuge and a haven can be seen as embedded in each of these conditions.

In our 1996 paper we made the point that meanings of home are context-specific and open to change, and emphasised that 'experiences of home ownership that give rise to certain widely held meanings of home are facilitated by specific political and legal frameworks and shaped by specific sets of historical experiences'.[6] In a subsequent article[7] we analysed the leaky

[4] Ann Dupuis, 'Ontological Security' in Susan Smith and others (eds), *The International Encyclopedia of Housing and Home* (Elsevier 2012); Ann Dupuis and David Thorns, 'The Meanings of Home (1996) 3 *Housing Studies* 485; Ann Dupuis and David Thorns, 'Home, Home Ownership and the Search for Ontological Security' (1998) 46 *The Sociological Review* 24; Harvey Perkins and Davis Thorns, *Place, Identity and Everyday Life in a Globalizing World* (Palgrave Macmillan, 2012).

[5] Dupuis and Thorns (n 4 above) 25.

[6] Dupuis and Thorns (n 4 above) 486.

[7] Ann Dupuis and David Thorns, 'Living in Risk, Living with Risk: A Sociological Perspective on New Zealand's Leaky Building Syndrome' in Steve Alexander et al, *The Leaky Building Crisis: Understanding the Issues* (Thomson Reuters, 2011).

building crisis in terms of managing risk in an environment where the trust in experts has been challenged by system failures, contradictory advice, and the failure of the institutional protections that were once provided by local authorities, legislation and inspectorial practices. In this work we posed the question of how can trust and certainty in social institutions be rebuilt after such a disaster in order that people can recreate and maintain their sense of ontological security? Using this framing, the current chapter raises further challenges to the notion of ontological security in circumstances of a 'natural', rather than a 'human-made' disaster.

III. THE SHAKY ISLES: EARTHQUAKES IN NEW ZEALAND

New Zealand lies directly on the circle of activity around the Pacific Ocean known as the Ring of Fire, where most of the world's earthquake energy is released. Part of the boundaries of the two huge tectonic plates, the Pacific and Indo-Australian Plates, run the length of New Zealand and slide under and past each other. As a consequence, there are major fault lines running the length of New Zealand ensuring the country is extremely earthquake prone.[8]

Historically, earthquakes were recognised in Māori tradition through stories of Rūaumoko, the god of earthquakes, instigating subterranean rumblings and shaking as he walked about under the earth's surface. Some earthquakes were also said to be the work of *taniwha*, or supernatural creatures, taking a lizard-like form. Early European visitors and settlers soon became aware of New Zealand's propensity for earthquakes.[9] From the nineteenth century on, a number of major earthquakes were recorded as having caused injury and death and damage to towns, cities and land forms. As shown in Figure 1 these include:

— a magnitude 8.2 earthquake that occurred in 1855 in the Wairarapa, an area east of Wellington. This was the most powerful earthquake ever recorded in New Zealand and resulted in between five and nine deaths.

— a magnitude 7.8 earthquake in 1929 in Murchison, a small town north west of Christchurch. It was felt throughout the country and caused damage in Nelson, Westport and Greymouth. The small town of Murchison itself was severely damaged by landslides, which killed an estimated 17 people.

[8] Bulletin of the New Zealand National Society for Earthquake Engineering (NSEE), 'Changes to Disaster Insurance in New Zealand' vol 26 (1993) 437.

[9] Eileen McSaveney, 'Historic Earthquakes', *Te Ara: The Encyclopedia of New Zealand* (2014): www.TeAra.govt.nz/en/historic-earthquakes.

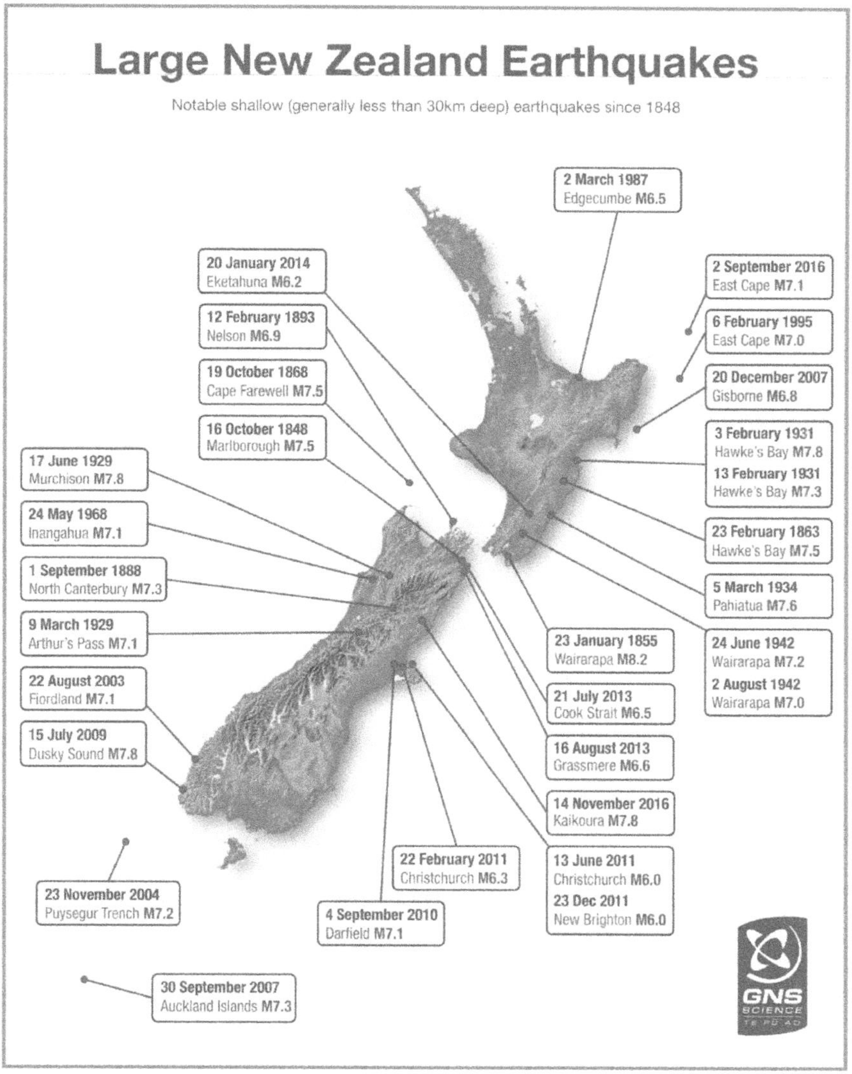

Figure 1: Large New Zealand earthquakes since 1848
Source: GNS Science, 'Large New Zealand Earthquakes' (November 2016).

— New Zealand's worst earthquake in terms of fatalities was in Hawke's Bay in 1931. A magnitude 7.8 quake, it claimed 258 lives and dramatically altered the landscape of the city of Napier. The aftershocks continued for months. One outcome of this, however, was that it led to a greater understanding of the hazards of living in a geological danger zone. It also led to a huge improvement in design and within two years the city was rebuilt in the styles of the 1930s and is now known as the 'art deco capital of the world'.

— two in the Wairarapa in 1942, 7.2 and 6.8 in magnitude, which caused damage in Masterton, Wellington, and other population centres.
— a 7.1 magnitude earthquake in 1968 in Inangahua, a small South Island West Coast town, which caused considerable damage to roads and bridges.
— a 6.3 magnitude earthquake in 1989 in Edgecombe in the Bay of Plenty. Although smaller, this quake caused major industrial damage. Dozens were injured and a huge crack appeared in the Rangitāiki Plains.

While this brief list indicates New Zealand's vulnerability to major earthquakes, there are also huge numbers of smaller tremors. For example, each year there are over 15,000 earthquakes, of which only about 100 to 150 are significant enough to be felt, with the others being recorded by seismographs. Historic trends and records dating from the 1840s show that, on average, New Zealand can expect several magnitude 6 earthquakes every year, one magnitude 7 quake every 10 years, and a magnitude 8 every century.[10] This vulnerability to large earthquakes led to the state implementing the earthquake insurance scheme, features of which are discussed in the following section.

IV. NEW ZEALAND'S EARTHQUAKE INSURANCE SCHEME

In most aspects of our lives, most of the time, we tend to do the right thing and in New Zealand it is recognised that insuring one's home is the right and necessary thing to do. It could be said that it is taken-for-granted in New Zealand where approximately 90 per cent of private homes are insured, a very high rate by world standards. This observation was borne out in the Canterbury earthquakes where some 97 per cent of homes were insured.

The New Zealand government has similarly done the right thing. In 1945, it established the Earthquake and War Damage Commission under the Earthquake and War Damage Act of 1944. This Act came into law not long after the 1942 Wairarapa earthquakes, responding to the concern that many of the uninsured and damaged homes and buildings had not been cleared away in the subsequent two years, let alone rebuilt. Before 1945, earthquake insurance was voluntary and few people took it out. However, the government of the time deemed a compulsory national disaster scheme was necessary, to ensure all owners were equally protected and that all

[10] 'Earthquakes' (GNS Science): www.gns.cri.nz/Home/Our-Science/Natural-Hazards/Earthquakes.

owners contributed. Under the Act, coverage was mandatory for all property insured against loss from fire, and all contributors paid the same amount, regardless of their individual risk.[11] In 1993 the Earthquake and War Damage Act was replaced by the Earthquake Commission Act, and the Earthquake and War Damage Fund with the Natural Disaster Fund. The original system was changed for a number of reasons. In its original form, the government was legally obliged to pick up any costs that the EQC fund could not cover. The potential liability costs were therefore very large and successive governments have attempted to reduce this. By 1993, political attitudes too had changed, with a much stronger market focus and a more limited government role in the economy. Moreover, the homeowner insurance industry had changed in its approach.

Under the 1993 Act the EQC was established as a Crown entity to provide insured residential property owners with 'primary natural disaster insurance' of up to a cap of NZ$100,000 (+GST) for each dwelling. Any further amount above that is paid by the policyholder's insurance company, when homeowners (or businesses) take out fire insurance with an insurance company. EQCover (previously disaster insurance cover) also applies to contents, if a current private insurance policy for contents includes fire insurance. Apart from earthquake insurance, EQCover insures against loss or damage from: a natural landslip, a volcanic eruption, hydrothermal activity, and a tsunami. It insures residential land (within limits) against storm and flood damage and also insures for fire resulting from any of these natural disasters. EQCover costs 15 cents (+ GST) for every NZ$100 of home or contents fire insurance that owners pay to a private insurance company, which then passes it on to EQC. At the time of the earthquakes, the maximum amount of earthquake levy per year a policyholder paid for one home and its contents was $180 (+ GST).[12] This provided the maximum cover of $100,000 (+ GST) for a home, $20,000 (+ GST) for contents, and cover for insured residential land. EQCover is government guaranteed, providing assurance to consumers that if EQC has a very large number of claims, and cannot cover its obligations from the Natural Disaster Fund and its reinsurance, then the New Zealand Government will pay the shortfall.

New Zealand's EQC is unique. No other private or government earthquake insurance scheme offers such extensive coverage at such an affordable price. However, since 1993, as New Zealand's private insurance industry has become increasingly competitive, there has been a considerable gap between the premiums received by these companies and the coverage offered. In the post-earthquake environment, this situation was exemplified

[11] NSEE (n 8 above).

[12] In the May, 2017 budget, the New Zealand government announced an increase in the levy from 15 cents to 20 cents for every NZ$100 of cover.

by AMI Insurance, the company which had covered a high percentage of dwellings and contents insurance in Canterbury. With the large number of earthquake claims and reinsurance requirements, the company became insolvent. However, to ensure the interests of all AMI policyholders were protected and all claims would continue to be met under the terms of their policies, the insurance company was bailed out by the New Zealand Government. AMI thus separated into two companies. Southern Response became government owned and AMI was taken over by IAG.[13]

V. PREPAREDNESS PRE-SEPTEMBER 2010

Despite extensive knowledge of New Zealand's vulnerability to earthquakes, despite knowledge that the possibility of a major earthquake hitting Christchurch was relatively high, despite knowledge of the propensity for widespread liquefaction[14] in the area, and despite having set up the Natural Disaster Fund, EQC was spectacularly unprepared for the severity of the September 2010 disaster and what was to follow. Up to that time the planning for dealing with earthquake damage was based on probability models. For example, in 1999, EQC identified that its greatest earthquake risks were in the Wellington region and in Christchurch. It was estimated that over the next 50 years there was a 20–25 percent probability of a large earthquake occurring in the Wellington region and a 50–75 percent probability of the same intensity of earthquake occurring in Christchurch. Popular wisdom however, suggested that were there to be a 'big one' it would be in Wellington, New Zealand's capital city which is built directly on a known major fault line. It appeared that EQC concurred and in its planning anticipated that a large-scale Wellington quake could result in about 150,000 claims and claims settlements of at least $6.8 billion. In retrospect, we now know the claims for the September 2010 earthquake alone were comparable to the largest event EQC had planned for—a large Wellington earthquake.[15]

Pre-2010, EQC's planned response to a large-scale natural disaster was termed the Catastrophe Response Programme, the objective of which was 'to achieve a successful response to a major natural disaster'. Indicators of successful responses were that: all claimants were able to lodge claims with EQC within the statutory 30-day period; claims were to be settled within an

[13] IAG refers to the insurance company, Insurance Group of Australia Limited. Southern Response, 'Background': southernresponse.co.nz/here-for-you/about-us/background.

[14] Liquefaction refers to the process which often occurs in an earthquake whereby water-saturated sediment temporarily loses strength and acts as a fluid. By undermining the foundations and base courses (the layer of material directly under the surface layer) of infrastructure, liquefaction can cause serious damage. See US Geological Survey, 'Earthquake Glossary' (USGS): earthquake.usgs.gov/learn/glossary/?term=liquefaction.

[15] CERA (n 2 above).

acceptable time frame and to standards of individual and overall fairness; essential office services were to be efficient; and the health and welfare of staff should be maintained to avoid stress.[16] It is patently clear from official documents that the programme planners did not envisage the extent of the catastrophe that was to occur.

Part of the catastrophe planning comprised measures for settling housing claims. Potentially, settlements can be accomplished in a number of ways: by cash settlement; through replacement of a house; through reinstatement of a house or repairs to return a house to its state before the natural disaster; or by relocating and then reinstating a house. Pre-2010, EQC's plan was to outsource the services it would require to settle cash claims and to this effect, had a service-level agreement set in place with an Australian-based claims administration company, which covered the provision of claims administration, including back-office support, to approve and settle claims. The outsourcing agreement assumed the capability for handling 60,000 claims for each year, operating in normal business hours, and using the provider's own staff. Additional staff and extended working hours would be used to handle a claims load exceeding 60,000 for each year.[17] As the aftermath of the earthquakes showed, this planning too was woefully inadequate.

The Catastrophe Response Programme was reviewed in 2009. One significant recommendation from the review was 'the need to have extraordinary measures planned for the largest natural disasters EQC could face'. In June 2010, according to the then Chief Executive of the EQC (who was appointed in February 2010), as a result of the review, EQC's Claims Team was looking for ways to increase their capacity to process claims should there be a significant event,[18] appearing to also assume that EQC would need to respond to a single event.

In sum, as of 4 September 2010, the EQC was in a state of almost complete unpreparedness. As noted, their first settlement option was cash for payments, on the grounds that it would be the option of administrative simplicity and have the potential for minimising EQC's costs and liability. Yet the EQC itself had not been provided with either specific legislative or Ministerial expectations about the scale of event they were to be prepared for and had been given no indication from government which of the range of possible responses available under the Act, was preferred.

[16] Office of the Auditor General, 'Earthquake Commission: Managing the Canterbury Home Repair Programme' (Office of the Auditor General, 2013): www.oag.govt.nz/2013/eqc/appendix2.htm.

[17] DA Middleton, 'EQC's use of computer modelling in a catastrophe response' (NSEE, 2002): www.nzsee.org.nz/db/2002/Paper31.PDF.

[18] Office of the Auditor General (n 16 above).

VI. POST-SEPTEMBER 2010: AN IMMEDIATE RESPONSE

Referring to the September 2010 earthquake, one newspaper headline of 2011 claimed, 'Extent of disaster never imagined'.[19] It was clear that despite the scientific and technical knowledge and the relatively sophisticated modelling EQC had to draw on, the sheer scale of the September earthquake and the on-going damage caused by the huge number of subsequent quakes and aftershocks was overwhelming. A disaster of this kind was beyond the imagination of the EQC professionals involved and certainly beyond the imagination of almost everyone who has any Christchurch or New Zealand connections.

Possibly because the Canterbury earthquakes were unimaginable, EQC had extremely limited capacity to handle a major disaster. On 1 September 2010, three days before the first major earthquake, it employed only 22 core staff members and 27 assessors in reserve. By way of comparison, by 2013 it had more than 1,800 staff, although numbers had reduced to 1161 by June 2014.[20] Following the September earthquake there were estimated to be 50,000 houses with damage in the range of NZ$10,000 to $100,000, the EQC cap. With the agreement of Ministers, the EQC Board decided that a Project Management Office (PMO) should be set up to manage these residential repairs, a decision made on the grounds that settling most claims in cash, as had been the pre-September 2010 plan, was simply unfeasible. EQC itself did not have the capacity to manage housing remediation and a PMO deemed the best way to ensure quality, mitigate inflation and facilitate equitable access to qualified labour. EQC identified 15 possible organisations that did have the skills and capacity for the task and issued a Request for Proposal to these organisations. It was expected that the PMO would: act as a primary contractor; source, subcontract and manage the necessary skilled contractors; ensure a single point of contact for stakeholders, including homeowners; develop an approved pricing mechanism; report to EQC; and manage the repairs for all EQC residential claims. In October 2010, Fletcher Construction, New Zealand's largest construction company with a long history in construction project management, won the tender to manage the repair process (as 'Fletcher EQR') on behalf of EQC. Although this system was set in place clients could opt out of it if they so wished. EQC would ensure their costs were reasonable by benchmarking them to Fletcher EQR costs. Organising consents and ensuring quality of repair then became their individual responsibility (Office of the Auditor General, 2013).[21]

[19] Ben Heather 'Extent of Disaster Never Imagined', *The Press* (Christchurch, 4 September 2011).

[20] EQC, 'EQC staff numbers and rates' (EQC, 2011): www.eqc.govt.nz/news/staff-numbers-rates.

[21] Office of the Auditor General (n 16 above).

In theory establishing Fletcher EQR as the PMO seemed like a very sensible start to addressing the consequences of the September earthquake.

As time went on, however, and the spate of aftershocks and earthquake events continued, a range of unanticipated residential insurance situations arose—each of which required resolution. To add further context, it should be noted that after September 2010, many people had lost homes or had homes badly damaged, or were living in terrible circumstances, with no proper washing, toilet or laundry facilities. Some homes had been awash with liquefaction which had to be cleaned up. And the relentless onslaught of aftershocks led to widespread symptoms of post-traumatic stress disorder. However, the full realisation of the extent of the disaster and its implications came only after the February 2011 earthquake, and subsequent series of quakes and tremors.

In scale, and in monetary terms, the costs have been eye watering. For example, in 2011 the New Zealand Treasury estimated the total cost of the earthquakes at around NZ$30 billion, approximately 15 per cent of New Zealand's GDP.[22] To put this estimate in context, the March 2011 earthquake off the north-east coast of Japan, although larger in physical terms, is estimated to have caused damage equivalent to around three to five per cent of Japan's GDP. Since 2011, the estimation of costs has risen to well in excess of NZ$40 billion, equivalent to 20 per cent of current GDP.[23] The earthquakes rank as one of the most costly natural disasters for insurers worldwide, and the fifth biggest insurance event in the world since 1953[24] and has been described by Munro as the 'largest claims management and settlement exercise in the world undertaken by a single insurer'.[25] It is against this backdrop of tragedy that we explore some complicated earthquake insurance issues.

VII. POST-DISASTER INSURANCE ISSUES

In this section four insurance-related issues are discussed. The first, apportionment, deals with the problem of decision making over responsibility of payment for repairs. Related to apportionment is the issue of assessment of damage. Third, is an examination of the tricky issue of multi-unit titles,

[22] EQC 'Earthquake Commission Briefing to the Incoming Minister' (EQC, 2011): www.eqc.govt.nz/sites/public_files/min-briefing-11.pdf.

[23] Deloitte Access Economics, 'Four Years on: Insurance and the Canterbury Earthquakes' (Vero Insurance, 2015).

[24] New Zealand Parliament, *Economic Effects of the Canterbury Earthquakes* (Parliamentary Support, Research Papers, New Zealand Parliament 2011).

[25] Jamie Munro, 'The Year in Review: General Insurance Industry Overview 2013' (KPMG, 2013), p 2: img.scoop.co.nz/media/pdfs/1311/NZ_Insurance_Update_2013_V10.pdf.

specifically cross leases and unit- or strata titles. Fourth, is the length of time it took for remediation decisions to be made and the accompanying tensions and stress for Canterbury residents.

A. Apportionment

For our purposes, apportionment can be defined as the process by which EQC determined who was liable to pay claims under the Earthquake Commission Act. The issue of apportionment arose as a consequence of having multiple earthquakes in the same area, the uncertainty of the extent of damage that could be attributed to each event, and the uncertainty as to EQC's responsibility versus the responsibility of a private insurer. After the deadly February 2011 earthquake, EQC acknowledged publicly that they were unsure whether their insurance cover was limited to one NZ$100,000 cap in any 12-month period, or whether their cover was automatically reinstated after each separate 'event'. The issue is summed up as one of either continuing cover or immediate reinstatement of cover. This mattered, as depending on the resolution of this issue, either EQC or private insurers were liable for larger losses. It also mattered to both EQC and private insurance company reinsurers who had significant interests in the outcome. And it mattered to home owners, as without a resolution they were prevented from moving forward in the recovery process.

To seek resolution the EQC and the Insurance Council took the issue to the High Court. In September 2011, the Court judged that EQC were liable for multiple capped claims in any one 12-month period.[26] Once this issue was clarified an associated issue arose. What methodology could be developed that could apportion the percentage of damage done between each of the events. Initially, a working group was established to develop an apportionment model. However, they were unable to come to agreement. The issue was summed up by one insurance manager as 'unique in the world … where you have a first loss non-proportional co-insurance position with billions of dollars at stake and you are trying to agree on a simplistic model to help make claim settlements more efficient'.[27] As a consequence of this decision the EQC were liable for multiple capped claims in any one 12-month policy period. Pertaining to this ruling four earthquake events

[26] *Earthquake Commission v The Insurance Council of New Zealand Inc, Vero Insurance New Zealand Ltd, IAG New Zealand Ltd* (CIV-2011-485-1137); *Tower Insurance Ltd v Earthquake Commission* (CIV-2011-485-1116).

[27] John Lucas, *Removing the Roadblocks to Claims Success* (AICLA/ANZIIF Claims Convention, 1 August 2013, Insurance Council of New Zealand): www.icnz.org.nz/removing-the-roadblocks-to-claims-success.

were recognised: those of 4 September 2010, 22 February 2011, 13 June 2011, and 23 December 2011.

Even with this decision the issue arose of how to assess the extent of damage that was caused by each individual earthquake event. Had a claim been made and a home assessed after each event it might have been straightforward. In reality, what frequently occurred was that there was no time to collect information about the damage done by one earthquake event before the next major earthquake event occurred. As a way of addressing this issue EQC used a variety of methods to establish how damage should be apportioned including: comparing the damage done to a particular property with the damage done to other properties in the area where damage had been assessed; and information provided by the home owner in terms of photographs or verbal description.

For many thousands of Christchurch homeowners there was a difference of opinion between ECQ and private insurers as to the real cost of repair. In these circumstances a complex process, Joint Review, was followed. This usually entailed each side hiring a range of professionals such as assessors, surveyors, contractors and even lawyers to determine the outcome. Given the complexity of the situation and the number of professionals involved, this process often took a long period of time. In the meantime, the householders involved, owners or renters, were left to face often very challenging circumstances.

B. Assessors and Estimators

The task of establishing the extent and timing of damage was accomplished by two categories of people: estimators and assessors. Estimators were trade qualified builders whose task was to identify and provide a preliminary view and costing of the damage and the possible repair strategies. The role of assessors was to arrange meetings, ensure all relevant parties attended, complete the necessary paperwork and liaise with customers. In theory, these roles seem rational and logical. However, in practice any number of problems quickly became obvious.

In order to respond to the massive number of claims EQC had to find and train people with the expertise to do these tasks. It was reported that builders were brought out of retirement to act as assessors and retired policemen, who were supposedly good at observation, listening and taking notes, were hired as estimators. The thousands upon thousands of stories reported regarding the incompetence of these people, and the inconsistency of outcome their work produced, led to them frequently coming under scrutiny, and broader questions being raised about the robustness of the process employed. The case study included later in this chapter (section VIII) highlights the kinds of problems that could occur in this area.

C. Strata Titles and Cross Leases

By 2013 a special Multi-Unit Building Team was operating at EQC to address the very complex situations of dwellings that form part of a multi-unit; defined as two or more homes that share at least one common element, such as a wall, garage, roof or foundation. Like the leaky building syndrome referred to earlier, the repair of damage to one unit will almost invariably impact on the neighbouring unit(s). Earthquake damage can affect neighbouring units differently, with one unit perhaps manifesting only cosmetic damage, while the adjacent unit can have significant structural damage. In 2013, EQC noted that many multi-unit homes were on earthquake-compromised land and often housed the elderly or vulnerable population groups.[28]

Examples of multi-unit buildings include: units on cross-lease titles, such as flats attached by a party wall, terraced housing, townhouses and apartments;[29] and unit-title (or strata title) developments, which can take the same form of accommodation as cross-lease titles, but are owned and managed in accordance with the Unit Titles Act 2010. Insurance issues pertaining to cross-lease properties are especially problematic, as owners of adjoining units could all be insured with different private insurance companies—or even uninsured. For cross-leased properties, if earthquake damage exceeded the cap then owners could not only be insured by different insurance companies, but they could also hold different types of policies—some indemnity policies and some replacement policies. Because of their complexity, cross-lease claims figured significantly in the number of claims still not settled in 2016.

Insurance issues related to unit-title properties are potentially less difficult to address than those related to cross leases. In practice however, as we have seen in the leaky building disaster, complex insurance difficulties have arisen. Under section 135(1) of the 2010 Unit Titles Act, bodies corporate, the legal entities comprising the owners of all units, are responsible for the maintenance of common property. Bodies corporate are a form of management structure designed to ensure decisions affecting the shared aspects of developments can be made jointly by the owners. As part of their function bodies corporate are required to insure all buildings and other improvements to their full insurable value. In some cases, this might mean indemnity value, but in most cases it is full replacement value. Section 136(4) of the Act also stipulates that insurance pay-outs must be used for reinstatement of

[28] Sumner Community, '10 May 2013 Update', *Sumner Community* (Christchurch, 10 May 2013).

[29] A cross lease is where a number of people own an undivided share in a piece of land and the homes that they build on the land are leased from the other land-owners (normally for a term of 999 years). The houses are usually flats or townhouses.

the units, unless the body corporate decides otherwise by special resolution at a general meeting, ie 75 per cent of the eligible voters who vote on the resolution. Insurance issues have also been particularly complicated relating to rest homes and retirement villages, given the specificities of the right to occupy title that many retirement village occupants hold.

D. Delays in Decision Making

The impact on homeowners of the delays in responses and decision making of both EQC and private insurance companies has been regularly documented and, in the earlier years, documented daily in the local Christchurch newspaper. In addition, countless thousands of blog and Facebook entries have been posted, letters, books and articles written, meetings held, television programmes made and so on, that have all described the impacts on local people. For example, one woman whose home was uninhabitable for nearly four years following the September 2010 earthquake reported in her blog site that she had received over 31 separate visits to her property, involving more than 70 people, all from her private insurers. In addition, she was denied requests to her insurer to record meetings she had with company personnel.[30]

After the earthquakes, much seismological research was undertaken and previously unknown faults, like the Greendale Fault, were very quickly better understood, as was the interrelatedness of the faults. In the areas of Christchurch where land was most susceptible to liquefaction, long delays were experienced while geotechnical assessors evaluated options for land remediation. These ranged from remediating individual lots to large-scale solutions. There was also much work to be done establishing how building, and in particular foundation repairs, should be undertaken. In preparation for both land remediation and foundation/house repairs soil tests had to be done. As the capacity for such testing was limited, long waits for responses were common.

Given the on-going nature of the quakes and aftershocks, insurers certainly did not rush into repairs when they were faced with the experience of multiple claims resulting from the various events and the possibility of already completed repairs having to be re-repaired. In contrast to the 'official' response that rested on the uniqueness and complexity of the situation, many Cantabrians came to believe that the tardiness of response was deliberate on the part of insurers. A widely accepted view was that people were effectively ground down by the process, leading them to accept lower

[30] Sarah Miles, *The Insurance Aftershock: The Christchurch Fiasco Post-Earthquake 2010–2016* (2nd edn, Labyrinth Publishing, 2016).

than expected payments so they did not have to go through the trauma of protracted court cases and so they could get on with their lives, even if for some this meant more or less starting again.

VIII. ONE COUPLE'S EXPERIENCES

The purpose of this section is to move from a more abstract discussion to illustrate the experiences of one Christchurch couple.[31] Don and Grace (pseudonyms), a couple in their sixties were overseas when the September 2010 earthquake struck. On their return, they submitted a minor damage claim to EQC and their private insurer, AMI. Between September and February AMI informed Don and Grance that they, not the insurers would be responsible for the remediation of damage outside their home, such as damage to fences, paths, terraces and garden structures.

The February earthquake, centred in the eastern part of Christchurch, where Don and Grace lived, caused extensive damage through flooding and liquefaction. A huge sinkhole, so large a car was stuck in it, opened in their street. Like so many other houses in their area, Don and Grace's house was also hit badly. The terracotta tile floors in the entrance, kitchen and other service areas were cracked. The contents of their fridge and pantry were strewn all over the kitchen floor by the severity of the earthquake, with the floor awash from the mess of broken glass and the contents of jars and bottles. Other breakages included the computer monitor. A further claim was made to EQC and AMI for both house and contents.

Prior to the major earthquake of 13 June, Don and Grace had an EQC inspection, followed by a one-page handwritten report describing mostly minor damage to the floor tiles and some cracks above windows and indicating that the cost of repairs would be below the NZ$100,000 cap and therefore EQC's responsibility. After the 13 June quake, there was further damage to the floors of their house. Another inspection ensued which was much more thorough and the subsequent report recommended a rebuild on the basis of concerns over the extent of the floor cracks visible in the expansive tiled areas, and evidence that showed that floor levels at one end of the house had sunk.

On receipt of the report Don and Grace contacted EQC who, in September, revisited them and did another scope of works. On this occasion, they raised the amount of the value of repairs, but still maintained it was under the $100,000 cap. However, despite Don and Grace's concern over the possible damage to their concrete foundations, still no one looked under

[31] Interview conducted by the first author.

the carpets to investigate the extent of cracking that had occurred to the house's foundations.

In the interim Don had been in hospital with a serious health condition. Soon after his release the 23 December 2011 earthquake occurred and more damage resulted. Pictures fell off the walls, the bookcase in their study collapsed and their piano danced across the floor and punched a hole in the wall. New claims were therefore made to both EQC and Southern Response, who had taken over from AMI.

In June 2012, a full year and nine months after the September 2010 earthquake, Don and Grace received a joint inspection with one representative from EQC and one from Arrow.[32] They spent about an hour inspecting the house. Still deeply troubled by the obvious cracks in their floors, and worried that the house's concrete foundation would be similarly damaged, Don and Grace were appalled when an assessor poked a nail in the lounge carpet, commenting he 'could not feel any cracks'. The outcome of the inspection was again unsatisfactory as no agreement could be reached. The Arrow assessor confirmed a rebuild but the EQC assessor still insisted that the value of repairs would come in under the cap.

In September 2012 Don and Grace received a call from Fletcher EQR to arrange a time to come and do a scope of works with the builder to finalise repairs. This necessitated the couple contacting both Southern Response and EQC to point out they were still in dispute. Two further inspections took place over the next few months. Prior to the final resolution there was a requirement to have a geotechnical assessment of the ground around the house. The report that followed was almost incomprehensible.

Finally, in June 2013, Southern Response initiated a final inspection by Arrow which confirmed a repair could be done under the cap. At the time of the last independent inspection organised by EQC the carpets were finally lifted and checked, as were the floor levels, and it was decided the differences in levels were within an acceptable range and the floor cracks could be repaired with epoxy resin.

Repairs were finally undertaken in September and October 2013. Southern Response covered the cost of temporary accommodation for six weeks while the couple were out of the house, as well as the costs of the removal and storage of their household contents. The final out-of-scope work, ie non EQC repairs, on their driveway and patios was done in March and April of 2014. At that time Don and Grace took a financial settlement from Southern Response and organised their own contractor. As they live down a right of way, they had to negotiate with their two sets of neighbours, who both had different insurers, but had received cash settlements and contributed their third of the cost.

[32] The company that project-managed Southern Response's building remediation.

This exhausting experience was drawn out over three and a half years. For long periods of time, periods when the world around them was shaking, they were by and large ignored, left uncertain about the nature of the damage to their house or the possible road to recovery. Despite their best efforts, their communication with their insurers was minimal. In the meantime, with Don's health deteriorating, they were living in a house that they had carefully planned and built for their retirement, but that was repeatedly being shaken by thousands of aftershocks and that could possibly have been so damaged that it had to be rebuilt.

IX. CONCLUSION

This chapter has canvassed the proposition that in the circumstances of a natural disaster home can be understood as a socio-legal space, a view very different from home as a haven, and one that directly addresses the book's theme of the precariousness of home. Early in the chapter the basic tenets of home as a haven were set out: the distinctions between the public and the private, with home representing a safe and secure private space, differentiated from the outside world, often represented as a set of binary opposites like inside/outside, work/home, public/private, and safe/unsafe. It was also argued that the psycho-socio concept of ontological security was of value in understanding the meanings of home as an entity of our own creation. Through habits, practices, routines and relationships we create and maintain a sense of ontological security within the home. This concept also links the affective dimensions of home with the material dimensions. We work to protect the material aspect of home in any number of ways—regular upkeep, gardening, maintenance and home improvement. But perhaps the most fundamental means through which the home is protected is through insuring it against damage from human or natural causes. The knowledge that homes are adequately insured strengthens our sense of ontological security.

The natural disaster of the Canterbury earthquakes severely disrupted most Cantabrians' sense of ontological security. As the world repeatedly and violently shook around them their homes were damaged. For some the damage was irreparable, and for some the damage to the land on which their homes were built was such that the government deemed it unfit for building on. This chapter discussed issues of whose responsibility it was to assess the extent and nature of the earthquake damage to homes; whose responsibility it was to oversee and pay for repairs; the length of time taken to settle claims; and the particular difficulties in settling claims where the property in question was located in a multi-unit development.

Like other New Zealanders, Cantabrians before the earthquake felt secure in the knowledge that their homes were insured against such disasters as fires and earthquakes. In the aftermath of the earthquakes, it soon became evident that the measures the state had set in place to protect them were incapable of doing so. The constant tales of insurance companies, and others, delaying, prevaricating or attempting to shift responsibility to others, laid bare the extent to which insurance activities (whatever their slick, accompanying rhetoric) are underpinned, not by an ethos of protection, but by the commercial imperative of profit. The insurance scheme in its 2010 form was incapable of dealing with the extreme trauma of the earthquakes. A crucial point identified in the chapter was the break-down in trust people felt for the institutions that had previously believed would protect them. Moreover, the government's actions in classifying Christchurch and its environs into coloured areas had a similar effect. Almost all owners of more than 7,000 residences in the residential red zone, where rebuilding was not permitted, took up the government's offer to purchase their properties. The few who were uninsured have not fared well. A small number chose to remain or hold out for a better offer from the government. Furthermore, those housed on land zoned as TC3—a technical category describing land which, if there were to be another large earthquake, may suffer moderate to significant damage from liquefaction)—have been impacted in that the value of their land has fallen, rather than risen as in the TC1 zone (where land is categorised as unlikely to incur future damage from liquefaction) and the TC2 zone (where standard foundations for concrete slabs and timber floors are acceptable, although in some cases, some minor additional foundation works may be required such as providing more reinforcement).[33] Questions arise therefore, of the implications for civil society when there is a break down in trust and when the state intrudes in ways that further disturb people's sense of ontological security.

> A TC1, TC2, or TC3 land zoning means that the land is zoned green, however, the technical category describes how the land is likely to move and react if there was another large earthquake. TC3 land may suffer moderate to significant land damage from liquefaction. But the real relevance of the TC3 zoning is the standard required to repair damage to foundations or building foundations for new buildings.
>
> So what does it really mean for you? Should you purchase a house in TC3? What impact will it have on you going forward? What will your bank say? What will your insurance company say?

And what of the future? The frequency and intensity of the aftershocks have settled. Most severely damaged buildings in the city's Central Business District, and elsewhere, have been taken down, the rubble cleared and new

[33] Building Performance, 'Getting to Grips with the Canterbury Residential Guidance' (Ministry of Business, Innovation & Employment): apps.building.govt.nz/canterbury-guide/m10/index.html.

buildings are being erected. There is an official, if controversial, plan for the rebuild of the central city which is slowly being set in place. There is hope that over the next decades the city of Christchurch will emerge in a new guise.

Although most homes have now been repaired a number of insurance issues are still evident. Nearly 3,000 'over-cap' residential claims are still to be settled. Because of the complexity of some cases delays were inevitable, particularly those pertaining to multi-unit dwellings, where homeowners shared land ownership and had different insurance companies. A proportion of cases have turned litigious. There have also been class actions where insurance companies have been taken to court. The 7.8 earthquake that struck in November 2016 in Kaikoura, a small town some 180 kilometres north of Christchurch, was of such magnitude that it was felt strongly by Christchurch residents and tsunami warnings were set in place for the eastern coast of the South Island. As Christchurch had begun to settle back down to some normality, the Kaikoura earthquake further demonstrated that stability is still not something Christchurch residents can be assured of.

Unresolved housing issues will likely reappear in the future. First, there is the issue of non-repair. Some owners have found the whole ordeal of the earthquakes too difficult to deal with. Others have been paid out insurance settlements but have used their insurance money for other purposes, and homes are being sold privately on an 'as-is-where-is' (caveat emptor) basis. Initially these tended to be cheaper homes, possibly bought with an eye to financial gain from the rapidly burgeoning rental property market, aimed at the large numbers of especially foreign workers attracted to Christchurch as part of the rebuild. But as this market diminishes, what will become of these properties? Questions have also been raised pertaining to the poor quality of workmanship of some repairs. It has been suggested that in the future a situation as disastrous as the leaky building syndrome could occur and, in a similar fashion, there will be no one to take responsibility as the repair companies will have been wound up or dissolved and the small contractors who have done the shoddy work will have long gone from Christchurch.

The case study of the Canterbury earthquakes of 2010–12 has illustrated a number of ways in which the concepts of home as haven and ontological security have been profoundly shaken. The impact of this series of natural disasters has shown just how permeable the home can be. As a material structure, homes were cracked, damaged and open to the elements, which seeped and intruded into the interiors. The chapter has also highlighted another form of invasion; the invasion by representatives of the institutions set up ostensibly to protect home owners. Hence, the chapter's descriptions of insurance company representatives, assessors, estimators and the like, as they visited, and often intruded into people's homes and lives. The lack of clarity and disagreements among these various interested parties around apportionment and assessment frequently left home owners confused, exasperated, angry and exhausted. Worse, for some, it was as if their very homes had turned against them or become the battle-ground over which the fight for constancy, routine, control and identity was being fought. In addressing the book's theme of the precariousness of home, we have focused on the home as a vulnerable socio-legal space. Consequently, those with a concern for home as haven and ontological security may do well to attend to these vulnerabilities, as could those with more practical socio-legal responsibilities.

Part V

Resistance and Strategies

13

Precarity and Defiance in Temporary Accommodation: The King Hill Hostel Campaign, 1965–66

LAURA BINGER*

I. INTRODUCTION

ON 26 MAY 1965, Joan and Stan Daniels and their four children became homeless when the landlord of their private rented home told them to leave so that he could move into the property. Kent County Council (KCC) provided Joan and her children with temporary accommodation for a maximum of three months at King Hill Hostel (KHH), but KCC policies prohibited men from living at the hostel, so Stan was not accommodated with them. When the time limit of three months for the family's stay came to an end, 43 families were staying at the hostel, which had room for 71. Regardless, officials from KCC, aware that Joan had no other place to live, arrived at KHH prepared to evict Joan and take the children into care. Joan refused to leave and Stan had moved into the hostel with her. As officials attempted to persuade her to obey, residents gathered in the corridors to support her. When the KCC officials left, they found that their car tyres had been slashed. Residents took down the rules posted at the hostel, made a barricade of dustbins, and invited a reporter to cover events. Two weeks later officials from KCC wrote that 'staff were no longer in effective charge of the hostel'.[1] Over the coming year, many other residents would join Joan and Stan in defying the rules of the hostel and demanding changes in what became known as the King Hill Hostel Campaign (the Campaign).

* Kent Law School, University of Kent. Email: l.m.binger@kent.ac.uk. The author is grateful for the comments of Prof Helen Carr, Prof Sarah Blandy, Prof Caroline Hunter, Dr Ed Kirton-Darling, Nick Piska and Richard Warren.

[1] Kent History and Library Centre: CC/C-A/11/1/86, 15 September 1965.

KCC had a duty to provide temporary accommodation for homeless families under the National Assistance Act 1948 (NAA 1948). The provisions of the NAA 1948 that dealt with family homelessness were vague and gave wide discretion to the counties tasked with implementing them. Family homelessness fell within the purview of the Ministry of Health at the level of central government and the Ministry had issued circulars and had used some of its financial powers to pressurise local authorities, including KCC, into making specific changes in how they provided temporary housing, but these steps were frequently ineffective. The NAA 1948 also delegated additional powers to the Ministry of Health to implement its provisions, but it had traditionally not used those powers. Hilary Rose wrote that during the Campaign the Minister of Health held the view 'on somewhat conservative legal advice ... that he was unable to use the powers in this situation'.[2]

The Campaign was complex and dynamic, using a wide array of tactics over the year it was active. A Residents' Committee represented the families living at the hostel and worked alongside a group of supporters from outside the hostel called the Friends of King Hill. KHH had been the subject of public criticism before, but this was the first time that residents had organised to voice criticism and make demands on KCC. Residents' demands differed in important ways from those of many non-residents who were not connected to the Campaign, although many of their concerns overlapped.

This chapter proceeds in two parts. First (in section II) it describes life at KHH using the framework of precarity and drawing on sources that include traces of residents' critiques of life and governance at KHH. During the Campaign, residents described and critiqued life at KHH and publicly made demands for changes in communications with KCC and the Ministry of Health, in leaflets published by the Campaign, and in interviews with the press. The Campaign therefore provides a glimpse into how homelessness was experienced by families in Kent in the 1960s that would not otherwise be available. The residents' Charter to Make King Hill Hostel Fit for Human Habitation (the Charter) listed a number of their concerns and demands and is central to the analysis in this section. The concerns and demands were particular to the experience of living at KHH and were addressed directly to KCC rather than central government. Some, like those that discuss the splitting up of families, would certainly have resonated with homeless families living in many other English counties at the time and would continue to have public attention brought to them after the Campaign. Others, like the demand for a bus stop, were more specific to this hostel. By concentrating

[2] Hilary Rose, *Rights, Participation and Conflict* (London, Child Poverty Action Group, 1971).

on this campaign I can analyse locally specific dimensions of precariousness that would be difficult to see if the focus were wider.

Isabell Lorey's work on precarity plays a central role in this analysis, as the chapter attempts to describe not only the specific ways that life was precarious at the hostel but also the relationships within which this precariousness existed. Precariousness is created, sustained, and changed within relationships, and this chapter argues that describing these relationships is important not only to understanding the experiences of precarious life at KHH that residents brought attention to, but also to understanding how precariousness was resisted and recreated at the hostel. The focus here, as the focus was in the Campaign, is on the relationship between KCC and KHH residents, but I am attentive to how this relationship was complex and shifting and existed in the context of a complex web of other relationships.

The second part of the chapter (in section III) contrasts Lorey's descriptions of precarity with historical narratives of housing in Britain that assume the benefits of the ossification and solidity of the welfare state. The 'wobbly pillar' metaphor especially, with its vivid invocation of precarious imagery to describe and critique housing within the welfare state, portrays precariousness as destructive and dangerous, in contrast to Lorey's argument that precariousness is not necessarily positive or negative. This chapter argues that this difference in part stems from the wobbly pillar narrative's spotlight on central government policy changes and obscuring of the role of local-level policies, changes, and struggles. It is hard to see how the wobbly pillar metaphor would have space to recognise the KHH Campaign. For those interested in describing the efforts people make to resist, remake, and manage precariousness in their everyday lives by struggling for changes in the buildings, housing estates, and localities where they live, this is problematic.

II. PRECARIOUS, PRECARITY, AND PRECARISATION AT KING HILL HOSTEL

The framework for thinking about precariousness that Isabell Lorey sets forth in her book *State of Insecurity* guides this analysis of the King Hill Hostel Campaign in raising questions about the conditions of life at KHH and the relationships in which that precariousness existed. Lorey adopts specific vocabulary, distinguishing between precariousness, precarity, and governmental precarisation, and this chapter follows her use of these terms in its analysis of residents' descriptions of life at KHH, beginning with a discussion of precariousness at KHH before moving on to discuss precarity and governmental precarisation.

A. Precariousness of Life at KHH

Lorey defines precariousness as 'the term for a socio-ontological dimension of lives and bodies' that 'can be described in the broadest sense as insecurity and vulnerability, destabilization and endangerment'.[3] At KHH, people experienced precariousness in multiple, intertwined, and particular ways. Unlike some recent social movements, residents did not specifically invoke or highlight the word 'precarious' in their struggle, but themes of instability, vulnerability, destabilisation, and endangerment run throughout their descriptions of life at KHH. These themes are apparent in the Charter to Make King Hill Hostel Fit for Human Habitation.[4] In the early days of the Campaign, residents organised themselves into a Residents' Committee that presented KCC with its demands in the form of the Charter, which was signed by almost all residents living at the hostel at the time. The Charter critiqued policies and rules, governance structures, and material conditions at the hostel. The Charter was not necessarily a comprehensive or objective list of all of the ways precariousness existed at KHH, but it does reveal something about residents' own priorities and critiques.

The Charter began by demanding the '[i]mmediate removal of the threat of eviction and of the 3 month limitation of stay rule'.[5] KCC maintained that residents had licences to live at the hostel during these three months, which they believed enabled them to make residents leave at short notice with little process. The policy to limit stays had been in place since 1952 and had been strictly enforced until the start of the Campaign, yet prior to Joan's refusal to obey officials' demand that she leave at the end of this time limit, there are no references in the KCC archives to residents refusing to comply with these demands. This was because of KCC's power over the families. Frequently, residents were unable to find alternative accommodation before the time limit expired, and when this happened they were pressurised into agreeing that KCC take their children into care. Parents were told that if they did not agree to leave KHH and voluntarily place their children into care, their children would be taken into care involuntarily. This was a very real risk faced by many families; in 1965, 245 children from Kent were taken into care due to homelessness.[6] This interweaving of instability of housing with threats to family relationships was emphasised by residents.

[3] Isabell Lorey, *State of Insecurity: Government of the Precarious* (Aileen Derieg (trans), London, Verso 2015) 10–11, citing Judith Butler, *Frames of War: When is Life Grievable?* (London, Verso, 2004).

[4] Kent History and Library Centre: CC/C-A/11/1/86, 'A charter to make King Hill Hostel fit for human habitation'.

[5] ibid.

[6] Colin McGlashan, 'Battle of King Hill Nears Its Crisis Point', *The Observer* (London, 8 May 1966).

In the Charter, they followed their demand for removal of the time limit with demands for '[a]n acknowledgment of the fact that the constant threat of being parted from their children is making mothers sick with worry, and an assurance that no family will be broken up while accommodation is available at King Hill'.

The intertwining of housing precariousness with precariousness of family relationships was also clear in relation to KCC's ban on men living at the KHH. This was the second KCC policy that residents took up in the Charter, and it was the issue at KHH that received the most press attention during the year-long campaign.[7] In the Charter, residents referred to the rule as 'the inhuman separation of husbands and wives' and emphasised that it 'deprives children of their fathers and leads to the breaking up of families'.[8] Residents were concerned about potential long-term break-ups of their families, but also with the ways that even temporary separation strained life at KHH. Direct action and protests by the residents and their descriptions of the rule's impact on their lives add depth to their concerns. During one action that garnered attention in the national press, a group of men, who were already the subject of injunctions, held a 'sleep-in' at the hostel. One news story began by describing how '[t]wo lonely husbands cooked breakfast for their wives and children yesterday after defying a "love curfew" imposed on them by a judge'.[9] A press release connected to the sleep-in signed by 11 men whose families lived at the hostel, explained that '"[w]e have discussed the situation and we are agreed that it is our primary duty as husbands and as men, to be with our wives and families during this period of great strain and humiliation"'.[10] Here, the emphasis is on how the rule prohibiting men from living at the hostel compounded an already precarious situation. One man in a statement prepared to be read in court emphasised his wife's resolve that he should live with his family and described the impact his absence had on his children, saying, 'Two of my children fret for me so much that they become ill.'[11] Residents also criticised the rule for endangering women and children. For example, a newspaper quoted one father expressing his desire to protect his family, who he said had been 'scared out of their wits by prowlers at night'.[12]

[7] The prominence of this issue comes out in the reference to KHH simply as the '"no husbands" hostel' in one article covering the Campaign. 'Dingley Dell Families March on Minister', *Daily Mirror* (London, 6 December 1965) 7.

[8] Above n 4.

[9] 'Lonely Men Defy "Love Curfew"', *Daily Express* (London, 15 November 1965) 6.

[10] Andy Anderson and Jim Radford (eds), *KCC versus the Homeless* (London, Radical Press 1966) 39.

[11] ibid.

[12] '14 Husbands in "War Council" on Order to Quit', *Daily Mirror* (London, 5 October 1965) 4.

Men's voices dominated much of the media coverage surrounding this issue, which frequently reported developments in the courts relating to injunctions, but women also criticised the ban. At times, women spoke with reporters about the rule banning men from the hostel, sharing their support for their husbands' actions. In one story a mother living at the hostel explained, 'The judge wanted my husband to apologise to the county council for continuing to stay at the hostel. He refused and I am behind him all the way'.[13] Her husband was sent to Brixton Prison for defying the injunctions against him, and eight months after her initial comments, the *Daily Express* reported that she and her children had given her husband a note saying, 'We love you. Please stick it out'.[14]

Because there was only one hostel in Kent, many families had to relocate a long distance from where they had lived before. KHH was a little over one mile from the centre of West Malling, a village six miles north-west of Maidstone. This meant that a family from Thanet, for example, would have moved over 50 miles to live in KHH. As a result, many residents were separated from the support of friends and relatives that they had previously relied on; some would have been forced to give up paid work at now distant jobs; many children stopped attending school during their stays; and some families lost their places on waiting lists for council housing due to harsh 'local connection' policies put in place by urban and rural districts who were responsible for council housing allocation. In these ways and others, precariousness at KHH involved simultaneous destabilisations in residents' lives caused by the relocation to the edges of West Malling. In the context of referring to 'the isolated nature' of KHH, the Charter demanded the installation of a phone kiosk and provision of a school bus.[15] Although there was a phone at KHH, its use was controlled by staff.[16] The demand in the Charter for collaboration between KCC and local authorities to rehouse people also sought to address the problem that residents could lose their places on waiting lists for council housing.

Not even KCC officials disputed that conditions at KHH were poor, though perhaps at times they disputed the severity of the problem. The wooden 'hutments' that housed KHH residents sat on the grounds of a derelict former workhouse. The oldest of the hutments were built after the workhouse building was damaged by bombing during the Second World

[13] ibid.

[14] '"Stick to It" Plea for Jailed Father', *Daily Express* (London, 13 June 1966) 5.

[15] Above n 4.

[16] Phone access remained an issue throughout the Campaign. In April 1966, residents complained that hostel staff had denied a woman access to the phone when she was having a miscarriage, telling her she had to wait until the morning for medical attention. She miscarried that evening hours before a doctor arrived. Kent History and Library Centre: CC/C-A/11/1/88, 26 April 1966.

War and were intended to be used only temporarily. Over the years, KCC built additional wooden hutments on the site, and had no plans to replace the temporary structures with more permanent structures.

These poor conditions were part of what made life at KHH precarious. Sickness had been common at KHH, a problem that KCC officials had noted even before the start of the Campaign.[17] In their Charter, residents demanded that KCC provide a 'trained nurse' and a 'hostel sick bay with full facilities for preventive medical attention for over 100 children'.[18] Residents also requested 'separate washing and toilet facilities for each family' and hot water in the evening, noting that up to 19 people at KHH had to share one bath and two basins.[19] When the Campaign began, electricity meters in different units were running at different rates, some of which exceeded the maximum amount allowed, and residents demanded their removal.[20] They also demanded '[v]entilated storage cupboards for food' and '[t]he repair of leaking roofs and walls' and of windows which could not be opened. Demonstrating their general frustration with conditions at the hostel in December 1965, the Campaign posted Christmas cards featuring a 'particularly squalid' photo of the hostel to local and national politicians, officials, and even the Queen with the words 'We hope that you and your family are enjoying the festive season … We are not at King Hill'.[21]

Lorey emphasises that precariousness is *socio*-ontological; it is 'always relational and shared *with* other precarious lives' (emphasis added).[22] How was precariousness at KHH relational? There could be many ways of answering this question: the precariousness residents faced could be located in relation to local government, individual people who worked at KCC, elected officials, the Ministry of Health, Parliament, or more broadly 'the state'. Here, perhaps it is important to take seriously that residents addressed their demands for change directly to KCC. This shows that they viewed their precariousness to be relational to the county. Residents did address their concerns to other institutions and people including the Minister of Health, MPs, and district councillors, but these demands were made in order to increase pressure on KCC. For example, the Campaign maintained its focus on KCC even in demonstrations in front of the house of the Minister of Health. A sign at one of those demonstrations asked 'Will the Labour government save us from the Kent County Council?' and another read 'Rachman is not dead. He is on the Kent County Council'.[23]

[17] Kent History and Library Centre: CC/C-A/11/1/89, Response to Press Coverage.
[18] Above n 4.
[19] ibid.
[20] Kent History and Library Centre: CC/C-A/11/1/97, 14 January 1966.
[21] 'Unseasonable Greetings for Hostel', *The Guardian* (London, 24 December 1965).
[22] Lorey (n 4 above) 12.
[23] Anderson and Radford (n 11 above) 25.

Residents' decision to address their demands to KCC is important and distinguishes their approach from many other campaigns around homelessness, particularly those that focused on legislative change (eg that undertaken by the Joint Charities Group in the 1970s).[24] Yet, it is also clear that residents' actions show that they were aware that their relationship with KCC did not exist in a vacuum, but instead existed in a context of other complicated relationships.

B. Precarity and Life at KHH

While precariousness is necessarily a part of life, it manifests itself in different ways and is distributed in unequal and hierarchised striations. 'Precarity' is the term Lorey uses to refer to this ordering—'the hierarchized difference in insecurity'.[25] This ordering of striations of precariousness is accompanied by processes of 'othering'.[26] Lorey argues that logics of securitisation are employed to react to the vulnerabilities of others, and that the effects of securitisation create these striations. She writes that '[i]n a historically different way the precarious thus represent both the cause and effect of domination and security'.[27]

A move to KHH for residents was a move between these striations of precariousness rather than a move from the secure to the precarious. Residents entered the hostel after other housing arrangements failed, and because KCC allowed residents to stay at the hostel once per year, some had lived there before. KCC kept records with summaries of residents' previous living arrangements, and some residents spoke about their housing history publicly during the campaign. These sources show that residents' housing arrangements were strikingly varied and how they were eventually unsustainable.[28] Families came to King Hill Hostel from private rented accommodation, council housing, caravans, stays with friends or relatives, accommodation tied to a job, and in one case from living in an old van. Some residents had moved around quite a bit before entering the hostel as successive arrangements collapsed, sometimes very quickly. Other residents had lived for significant amounts of time at one place prior to their move to the hostel. At times KCC officials portrayed residents' house histories in a negative light, highlighting families that had been evicted for rent arrears. These portrayals were repeated in court decisions and press coverage, but

[24] Lorraine Thompson, *An Act of Compromise: An Appraisal of the Effects of the Housing (Homeless Persons) Act 1977—Ten Years on* (London, SHAC and Shelter, 1988).

[25] Lorey (n 3 above) 21.

[26] ibid 12.

[27] ibid 11.

[28] Kent History and Library Centre: CC/C-A/11/1/97.

the records KCC itself kept of residents' housing histories contradict these accounts. KCC's own data on the residents for the year of 1964 showed that only six per cent of families who stayed at KHH had been evicted for rent arrears and in these cases, the reasons that families had accumulated rent arrears varied.[29] Whether residents had been evicted from private rented or council housing, or after losing a job that came with accommodation, or had lost accommodation upon breakdown of a relationship, fleeing abuse, or after being told to leave by friends or relatives, their earlier arrangements had been precarious, as was demonstrated by their eventual need to move to KHH.

It is not possible here to thoroughly identify and discuss the various striations of the precarious home that were present during the 1960s in Britain, but it is still possible to understand something about how precariousness at KHH was distinguished from precariousness in these other housing arrangements. The rules that governed everyday life at the hostel were generally unlike those that governed life outside. A sign at a protest outside a KCC official's home brought attention to this disparity: 'While Dr. Elliott sleeps with his wife, the homeless are jailed for sleeping with theirs'.[30] Regardless of where residents had lived before they entered the hostel, at least where they had been living they had a last resort still available in KHH. But once in KHH, residents were in that place of last resort with nowhere else to fall back on with no sure other option to be housed if forced to leave. One man was quoted in the *Daily Mirror* after a judge granted an injunction against him explaining the predicament he was in: 'I've been at the hostel four months. I'd like to stay, but it looks as though anyone disobeying the judge's order would go to prison. Nobody would stay at the hostel through choice. But we've got nowhere to go'.[31]

This sense among residents of being at a place of last resort was accompanied by the sense that they were at the bottom of the social hierarchy. A letter to the Minister of Health from the Residents' Committee stated, '[u]ntil we became homeless we did not know that this would automatically make us second class citizens'.[32] One resident's comments to a reporter for *The Guardian* expressed this feeling in a slightly different way:

> 'I have just left the Navy after 12 years' service. I came out because we wanted some normal home life for the children, but this is what we've got. We knew things might be hard, but in a few weeks of looking for a home we've sunk right to the bottom of the barrel'.[33]

[29] Kent History and Library Centre: CC/C-A/11/1/95, 13 May 1966.
[30] Anderson and Radford (n 10 above) 26. See text to fns 39–42 below.
[31] '14 Husbands in "War Council" on Order to Quit' (n 12).
[32] Anderson and Radford (n 10 above) 43.
[33] '14 Husbands in "War Council" on Order to Quit' (n 12).

Lorey writes that

> [w]ithin the framework of its welfare-state paradigm of protection, liberal governmentality was based on multiple forms of precarity as inequality through *othering*: on the one hand, on the unpaid labour of women in the reproduction area of the private sphere; on the other hand, on the precarity of all those excluded from the nation-state compromise between capital and labour—whether as abnormal, foreign or poor.[34]

For example, home ownership had remained out of reach for the many residents who were single mothers, affordable private rented accommodation had been impossible to find, and these residents were also 'likely to be denied access to local authority waiting lists'.[35]

The conditions of precariousness at KHH were connected with particular ways of othering homeless families, and precariousness and these forms of othering justified and reinforced each other. In her brief article providing background to the Campaign, Audrey Harvey wrote that homeless families at the time were treated as 'the lowest of the low', and she attributed this to welfare authorities who 'had always looked on their proper business as that of caring for old, blind and disabled people.'[36] In this context, she described homeless families as 'unwelcome cuckoos in the welfare nest'.[37] These process of *othering* were apparent in KCC officials' frequent use of the 'problem family' frame to describe KHH residents. Examples of how this happened appeared in memoranda and letters saved in the archive of KCC, in comments that officials made to the press, and in court judgments. Though officials typically couched their language so as to leave the possibility that not all residents were problem families, they had next to nothing to say about those who were not and much to say about those who were. In one document from 1961, KCC's County Welfare Officer defended the three-month time limit by stating that 80 per cent of those affected by the rule were from the 'problem family category'.[38]

When the Chief Welfare Officer, Aldred Elliott, discussed the men staying at the hostel in one report, he suggested that some were 'the most undesirable characters'.[39] In the same report, he wrote that

> there are some groups of people, ranging from train robbers to some parents of homeless families, who show no desire to conform to acceptable standards of life and who pursue anti-social attitudes in defiance of society so long as they can.[40]

[34] Lorey (n 3 above) 36.

[35] Patricia Kennett, 'Women, Housing, and Citizenship in Great Britain', *Women and Housing: An International Analysis* (London, Routledge, 2011) 371.

[36] Audrey Harvey, 'Background to Homelessness', *KCC versus the homeless* (London, Radical Press, 1966) 5.

[37] ibid.

[38] Kent Library and History Centre: CC/C-A/11/1/84, 1 November 1961.

[39] Anderson and Radford (n 10 above).

[40] ibid.

During the early months of the Campaign he produced a report that offered the following reason for the rule: 'some of the persons using the Hostel have standards of behaviour, particularly in relation to sexual matters, that are difficult to describe or comprehend'.[41] KCC officials' emphasis on the sexual behaviour of residents at KHH was present also in comments that one official made to a reporter months before the Campaign started. The newspaper reported that large families were not offered additional rooms despite there being vacant rooms 'because of sex problems caused by teenaged boys living at the hostel'.[42] On the same day, a KCC official told a reporter from another paper that 'some of the "husbands" are not husbands at all'.[43]

KCC officials blamed 'problem families', rather than shortages of housing, for homelessness and even the poor conditions at the hostel were attributed the families that resided there. If conditions at the hostel were better than those outside, if men were allowed to stay with their families, or if stays were not temporally limited, 'problem families' would be attracted to KHH and never leave. This was an argument that Lord Denning endorsed in his judgment upholding the injunctions KCC had sought against men staying at the hostel. According to Lord Denning,

> The council's experience was that when a family was homeless the best way to deal with it was to put the wives and children in this hostel, but not the men, because the men could get accommodation for themselves much more easily; but if the men and the whole family once got in, goodness knew when they could be induced to leave.[44]

This provided one example of how the 'problem family' frame justified harsh policies that intensified precariousness at KHH.

Just as residents exposed, critiqued, and struggled against precariousness at KHH, they also struggled against the othering processes that accompanied precariousness. The preamble of the Charter included the phrase, 'recognizing our status as human beings'.[45] Hilary Rose quoted a resident at KHH describing how her participation in the Campaign challenged how she felt about where she stood in the social hierarchy. The resident said that participants in the Friends of King Hill organisation were 'of a higher level of society than we are, but they treated us like human beings. It makes me feel we are not at rock bottom. People outside have called us dirt'.[46]

Lorey also emphasises the role that securitisation plays in the process of stratifying precariousness, and the desire for security at times was used both

[41] ibid.
[42] '"Belsen" Hostel Puts Ban on Love', *Daily Mirror* (London, 3 February 1965) 5.
[43] 'Few Comforts in Home for Homeless', *The Times* (London, 3 February 1965) 7.
[44] 'Husbands Must Leave Hostel', *The Times* (London, 9 October 1965) 14.
[45] Anderson and Radford (n 11 above) 35.
[46] Rose (n 2 above) 10.

to justify and respond to precariousness at KHH. The state's commitment to provide housing for children through the Children Act 1948 provided security for the children, but KCC's threat to take children into care became a threat to parents as they approached the end of their stays. Logics of security were used to justify rules that banned 'dangerous' men from staying at the hostel. KCC also portrayed its role as one of providing security to people outside the hostel from the problem families who it framed as responsible for family homelessness. To this end it claimed that it needed to closely govern the lives of people living at the hostel in order to rehabilitate them. Precariousness in KHH residents' lives then was variously 'both the cause and effect of domination and security'.[47]

KCC's temporary accommodation policies sent other messages to people not living at the hostel. KHH can be read as an example of what Angela Mitropoulos describes as 'both [the] persistent threat and circumstance' of poverty.[48] The threat of life at KHH was felt by renters and even homeowners. In this sense, it could be traced back to the Poor Laws and the workhouse, the spectres of which haunted residents of the hostel in 1965 as it had in a different way the population more generally before the National Assistance Act 1948.

Lorey is concerned that social-security logics have the potential to trap social movements as people resist precariousness.[49] Many of the demands made by the Campaign can be read as attempts by residents to gain security at KHH. Yet some of these demands were qualified and others do not easily fit within securitising logics. An example of the former can be found in the Charter's demand for a removal of the time limits on stays. The demand ends with a qualifier that families should not be broken up 'while accommodation is available at King Hill'.[50] This showed residents' unwillingness to gain their own security if it were to come at the expense of others' precariousness.

Residents made other demands that cannot be interpreted as straightforward attempts to lessen precariousness at KHH. These demands at times differed significantly from the changes proposed by non-residents who shared many of their criticisms of KCC policies. This comes out, for example, in the visions that residents had for addressing KHH's isolated location and poor conditions. As discussed earlier, residents who were unhappy with conditions at the hostel demanded a variety of amenities that would allow them to live at the isolated site more easily, including the provision of a phone kiosk and school bus. A few politicians, some of whom had visited

[47] Lorey (n 3 above) 11.
[48] Angela Mitropoulos, 'Precari-Us?' (*transversal: 'Precariat'*, March 2005) www.transversal.at.
[49] ibid 7.
[50] Anderson and Radford (n 5 above) 35.

and spoken up about KHH before the campaign began, clearly shared many of the residents' concerns. The Liberal MP from Orpington, Eric Lubbock, triggered a spate of press coverage prior to the Campaign when he compared KHH to a concentration camp. He explained,

> The phrase was not mine. It was used in a letter sent to me by one of the residents. But I wholeheartedly endorse it. I have seen Belsen and I have seen the hostel. And from their appearance it would be difficult to distinguish between them.[51]

Upon visiting KHH, Anne Kerr, a Labour MP from Rochester and Chatham, told *The Times*, 'This place should be razed to the ground'.[52] She was not alone in pushing for KCC to stop using the hostel. The Ministry of Health's opposition to KCC's sole use of KHH to provide temporary accommodation to homeless families had preceded the onset of the Campaign. For this reason, it had refused to assist KCC in obtaining loans to fund the expansion of KHH in 1963.[53] Throughout the Campaign the Minister of Housing maintained a consistent focus on pressuring the county to wind down KHH and replace it with smaller hostels sprinkled around the county.[54] These demands are important, because they had some influence on KCC. In January 1966 KCC was still pursuing men for violating injunctions and women for staying past the time limits, but KCC had already indicated that it hoped to provide two additional hostels in Kent.[55]

The Campaign, in contrast, opposed winding down KHH. The Friends of King Hill, who worked closely with the Residents' Committee throughout the Campaign, were at last offered a chance to meet with KCC officials in the autumn of 1966, and the minutes of that meeting portray deep concern over this issue.[56] The Friends did not trust KCC, and shared their fears that it would use the change as an opportunity to cut back on the total amount of accommodation available for homeless families in Kent.

III. GOVERNMENTAL PRECARISATION

Lorey explains that governmental precarisation refers to bio-political modes of governing that destabilise 'the conduct of life and thus of bodies and modes of subjectivication' in an 'ambivalence between subjugation and self-empowerment.'[57] Here she draws heavily on Foucault's work on

[51] 'Unjustified Slur on Hostel', *The Times* (London, 31 December 1964) 8.
[52] 'MP Protests over Hostel Conditions', *The Times* (London, 14 December 1965) 6.
[53] Kent History and Library Centre: CC/C-A/11/1/84, 2 July 1963.
[54] 'Kent Plan to Help Homeless', *The Times* (London, 26 January 1966) 7.
[55] ibid.
[56] Kent Library and History Centre: CC/C-A/11/1/88, 15 September 1966, Meeting Minutes.
[57] Lorey (n 3 above) 13.

governmentality and bio-politics, which she connects specifically to precariousness and precarity. Lorey emphasises the importance of speaking not only about subjugation, but also about self-empowerment in governing, because 'self-government can always enable immanent struggles over the manner of leadership'.[58] While precariousness and precarity offer no necessary space for resistance on their own, this mode of governing does. '[P]recarized deviance' contradicts liberal governmentality and has 'repeatedly distorted and disturbed the stabilization dynamics between freedom and security and has frequently triggered collective counter-behaviour and struggle'.[59] Lorey argues that precarisation in the present day is characterised by its move from precarisation of deviant 'others' to normalising precarisation.[60]

Self-governance certainly played an important role at KHH. Before moving into the hostel, residents had to sign agreements with KCC. The agreements for residents were all the same, used the word 'licence' and included promises to follow the rules of the hostel. When KCC went to the courts to force Joan Daniels to leave KHH, they argued that she had agreed to obey the rules of the hostel, including the three-month time limit on her stay by signing the agreement. Joan Daniels' lawyer argued that she had signed the agreement under duress, but this did not persuade the judge who decided on her case.[61] Instead, the court interpreted Joan's agreement to abide by the rules as a free decision. When residents reached their time limits, KCC's strategy, as discussed earlier in this chapter, was to pressurise residents into voluntarily placing their children into care and to persuade women to leave. So long as residents continued to sign and abide by the agreements KCC confronted them with on arriving at KHH and to voluntarily put their children into care at the end of their stays, KCC was able to see its policies implemented. So long as KCC was holding onto a frame that blamed problem families rather than a housing problem for family homelessness, it was able to justify laying responsibility on the shoulders of residents for accommodating themselves when their three-month time limits came to an end. But when Joan Daniels had to leave when asked, KHH residents' critiques of and refusal to cooperate with this self-governance structure left KCC in a situation they had not faced in the past and for which they had no plans. The failure of this self-governance structure revealed purposes for KCC's rules and policies that they had not articulated in the past. KCC officials and others were no longer only concerned with the rules accomplishing their ostensible goals (eg rehabilitation), but were increasingly concerned with restoring order, and KCC's control over residents and the hostel itself. Lord

[58] ibid 35, citations omitted.
[59] ibid 38.
[60] ibid 39.
[61] *Kent County Council v Daniels* (1966) 198 *Estates Gazette* 787 (Queen's Bench Division).

Denning noted that the rules preventing men from living at KHH had a role to play in protecting KCC's ability to govern the hostel. According to him, '[o]ne could well see that once rules of this kind were broken, there could be a good deal of disorder'.[62]

A. Precarisation, the King Hill Hostel Campaign and Historical Narratives of Housing

How might the struggle over precarity at KHH fit into or challenge historical narratives of housing and the welfare state? To answer this question, this part of the chapter discusses Lorey's framework of precarisation and then moves to the 'wobbly pillar' metaphor, which has attracted considerable discussion amongst housing scholars in the UK. The chapter argues that though much of the work on precarity has focused on precarity in the context of neo-liberalism, this does not mean precarity did not exist prior to this. The KHH Campaign provides an example of the limits of periodisations of security and precarity in the welfare state. The chapter argues that the wobbly pillar metaphor obscures the role of the KHH Campaign and other local-level actions. In other words the Campaign shows the limits of the metaphor's explanatory power.

B. KHH and Periodisations of Precarity

The choice to focus on events that took place in the mid-1960s when discussing the precarious home resists framing precarity as a condition peculiar to neo-liberal times. The previous section, after all, described precarisation at KHH during the Campaign which took place from 1965 until 1966. Lorey states that '[t]he normality of the minimum developing in the neoliberal paradigm stands in a continuous line of precarious working and living conditions in place since the formation of capitalism'.[63] She does, however, allow room for retaining portrayals of the 'golden age' of the welfare state by leaving open the possibility that the Fordist welfare state could be considered 'as a historical exception against the background of' 'the becoming-normal of precarization'.[64] To be clear, Lorey recognises that any exception was limited in its scope. 'The exceptional safeguarding through the welfare state guaranteed livelihoods and social advancement for many in different ways, reproducing and manifesting at the same time classifications and

[62] 'Husbands Must Leave Hostel' (n 44 above).
[63] Lorey (n 3 above) 68.
[64] ibid.

subdivisions of labour according to naturalized gender attributes and characteristics of origin'.[65] Yet periodisations of the welfare state that highlight or assume transformations from security to precarity are so common that this deserves further discussion.

Some have argued against exceptionalising the post-war welfare state. Daniel Wincott, for example, writes against how a 'general historiography has come to be dominated by the idea of a (Golden) Age of the welfare state' as post-war 'commentators and analysts imagined Britain as the original, exemplary, and pre-eminent welfare state, which was leading the world towards the New Jerusalem'.[66] While more accepting of the possibility that such an exception may have existed to a certain extent in France, Piketty in his analysis of wealth and income inequality, sees differences in Britain and the United States, in relation to which he says 'neither the economic liberalization that began around 1980 nor the state interventionism that began in 1945 deserves such praise or blame … The most one can say is that state intervention did not harm'.[67] Aside from these critiques of this periodisation, the welfare state is coherent neither in how it developed nor in how it functioned in different spheres (eg health, housing, education) or within those spheres (eg by providing poor relief or social security).[68] It is also internally complex, dynamic, and even contradictory, existing on multiple scales and with shifting departmental jurisdictions. This one micro-level history cannot bear the weight of arguing against any exceptionalising of the post-war years, but it may provide a helpfully critical perspective on the tendency to emphasise the exceptionalism of the post-war years.

Another limit to golden age conceptions of the welfare state has been communicated through images of precariousness and articulated in the work of housing researchers, many of whom have long argued that housing has been an exception within the welfare state in that it provided something less than other spheres of the welfare state in the way of security or de-commodification. The Campaign, however, challenges the ways that this exception has been portrayed. In the frequently cited 'wobbly pillar' metaphor, housing is described as one of multiple foundations of the British welfare state, but one which is more precarious (wobbly) than the others.[69]

[65] ibid.

[66] Daniel Wincott, 'Images of Welfare in Law and Society: The British Welfare State in Comparative Perspective' (2011) 38 *Journal of Law and Society* 343–75, 344.

[67] Thomas Piketty, *Capital in the Twenty-First Century* (Cambridge MA, Harvard University Press, 2013) 98.

[68] For further discussion of the lack of coherence in the welfare state, see Peter Malpass, 'The Wobbly Pillar? Housing and the British Postwar Welfare State' (2003) 32 *Journal of Social Policy* 589, 591–93.

[69] Metaphors that evoke a precarious welfare state extend beyond the realm of academic scholars. For an analysis of institutional representations of the 'welfare state' in cartoons with images of crumbling stone and sinking ships, see Wincott (n 66 above).

Torgerson and Malpass each invoked this image to specifically refer to housing being 'the least de-commodified and most market determined of the welfare state services.'[70] The metaphor was originally used to explain how change happens in welfare state housing policy. Using the wobbly pillar metaphor, the lack of de-commodification of housing provision in the welfare state becomes the root of wobbles that make this pillar of the welfare state especially vulnerable to erosion. Malpass writes that in the UK 'the lack of housing rights, the retention of user charges and the persistence of a predominant market sector all contributed to the distinctive position of housing in relation to the welfare state and subsequently made the public sector vulnerable to attack from governments less committed to public provision.[71] Malpass argues that the wobbles did not first appear at the start of neo-liberalism, but were built into the pillar from its start. The wobbly pillar metaphor has been invoked by other housing researchers and far as I am aware, always in the same negative light, although not necessarily clearly tied to the specific arguments about housing policy that Torgerson and Malpass developed. Perhaps one could argue that the continued need for KHH and the attention the Campaign brought to its problems exposed the wobbles in the housing pillar of the welfare state. However taking the metaphor further, for example, using it in a discussion of the relationships of power between residents and KCC, stretches it beyond its intended use because the notion of the wobbly pillar has been used primarily to describe housing policy in the context of *central* government.

Up until now I have primarily discussed precariousness as a condition of life of the residents at KHH, but it is not only humans that are precarious, institutions are also precarious. This chapter has already discussed how precariousness at KHH was relational, but the Campaign's ability to disrupt and even change governance of the hostel highlights the simultaneous precariousness of KCC itself. Lorey's theory of precarisation pushes us to pay attention to this. In doing so, it may provide open up different perspectives on the wobbly pillar metaphor. To begin with, precarity requires a shift of focus—onto how peoples' lives (or in this case homes) are made precarious (or wobbly) by the socio-political. In the case of KHH this includes, but is not limited to, the laws, policies, and practices of a complex, multi-level, peopled and horizontally- as well as vertically-networked welfare state. The traditional wobbly pillar metaphor is concerned with housing provision by the welfare state, but assumes that the strength and security (ie reduced precariousness) of the housing arm of the welfare state means housing is

[70] Ulf Torgersen, 'Housing: The Wobbly Pillar under the Welfare State' (1987) 4 *Scandinavian Housing and Planning Research* 116; Malpass (n 68 above).

[71] Peter Malpass, 'Housing and the New Welfare State: Wobbly Pillar or Cornerstone?' (2008) 23 *Housing Studies* 604.

less commodified.[72] Successful attacks on the housing pillar of the welfare state expose it as a precarious institution in the metaphor, but Lorey's theorisation does not assume that the extent to which it is precarious would necessarily correspond directly with how it securitises or precarises, commodifies or de-commodifies homes. While this conceptualisation of a precarious welfare state may capture something about the welfare state's vulnerability to 'Thatcherite zealotry and Blairite modernisation',[73] it also shifts emphasis away from the relationship between the welfare state and the people it precarises/securitises, occluding agency of the latter, and subsequently only portraying precariousness in the welfare state as negative. The occlusion of agency of those who rely on the welfare state for their housing means that events like the Campaign, particularly those that primarily encounter the welfare state at the local level, have no way of changing housing policy.

IV. CONCLUSION

Lorey argues against exclusively negative approaches to precarity. For her '[t]he question is … where, within these governing mechanisms, cracks and potentials for resistance are to be found'.[74] In her framework, there may be potential in the cracks, wobbles, and precariousness of the welfare state, even if the same cracks Malpass identified are not those that have opened up spaces for resistance from below. A wobbly pillar with cracks allowing resistance by those in subordinate relationships to it may allow for productive, rather than destructive processes. Conversely, perhaps even if the cracks that Malpass noted were filled, the welfare state would remain precarious. The precarious cannot be eradicated, because, after all, the welfare state continues to operate in social relationships.

The shift away from assuming that a precarious welfare state only leads to its erosion allows for an analysis of the power relationship between the institutions of the welfare state and the people who encounter it in their everyday lives, and that shift is important to understanding struggles like the Campaign and more generally to allowing us to see agency of the residents of KHH. So long as KHH was hidden from public view, so long as its residents remained individualised and obedient, so long as homelessness remained conceptualised as a problem of the 'other' and so long as residents did not make demands envisioning an alternative, the pillar's wobbles may have been hard to see. But that changed when Joan Daniels refused to leave

[72] In another variation, this is treated differently. The cornerstone sees housing (especially the expanded home ownership sector) as a cornerstone for a transforming welfare state. Peter Malpass (n 72 above).

[73] Malpass (n 68 above).

[74] Lorey (n 3 above) 2.

the hostel. In this narrative of potential for change in the welfare state, the wobbliness of the pillar could lead to an unknown future. It is not only Thatcher and Blair that wobbled the pillar or participated in its remaking, and it is no longer clear whether that future will be one with better or worse distributions of precarity.

A further problem with retaining the wobbly 'pillar' metaphor remains. A pillar conveys a sense of a unitary, static, coherent, and solitary state institution, which might not pose problems to some analyses of top-down change, but obscures precarisation and its resistance at King Hill Hostel. Images of state institutions as unitary and coherent only capture their precariousness on one scale, and assume a coherent intra-institution structure that misses out on the possibility of complex power relations, contestation, and contradiction. These images also hide the spaces where people directly encounter a decentralised state in their everyday lives, where they find 'cracks' from which to resist, and where they do indeed resist.

14

Responding to the Precarisation of Housing: A Case Study of PAH Barcelona

GABRIELE D'ADDA,* LUCIA DELGADO** AND EDUARD SALA***

I. INTRODUCTION

'PRECARISATION' IS ONE of the characteristic features of the contemporary world and neoliberal governance. As Lorey explains, precarisation is no longer an exception but has come to be considered the rule. It exposes people to contingency and insecurity, not just in the field of work, but also in areas that were previously considered secure, at least for the majority of people in Western Europe.[1] Ferreri, Dawson and Vasudevan, in their analysis of the connection between labour precarity and the increasingly precarious access to housing, speak about precarisation as a spatial process that generates and sustains a varied geography of insecurity, flexibility and temporariness, at once intensifying and normalising precarity.[2]

As Marcuse and Madden say:

> Housing is under attack today. It is caught within a number of social conflicts. Most immediately there is a conflict between housing as lived, social space and housing as an instrument for profit making—a conflict between housing as home and as real estate.[3]

* PhD student at Kent Law School, University of Kent: g.d'adda@kent.ac.uk.

** Independent researcher, a founder member of PAH – *Plataforma Afectados por la Hipoteca*: luciad02@gmail.com.

*** PhD student, Universitat Autònoma de Barcelona: edusala123@hotmail.com.

[1] Isabell Lorey, *State of Insecurity: Government of the Precarious* (London, Verso, 2015).

[2] Mara Ferreri, Gloria Dawson and Alexander Vasudevan, 'Living precariously: property guardianship and the flexible city' (2016) 42 *Transactions of the Institute of British Geographers* 153.

[3] David Madden and Peter Marcuse, *In Defense of Housing: The Politics of Crisis* (London, Verso, 2016).

Real estate attacks housing through a process of commodification that means a subordination of the social use of housing in favour of its economic value. Referring to the contemporary situation, Marcuse and Madden talk about 'the age of hyper commodification' and they identify three main factors that contributed to this evolution:

1. Deregulation—understood as the removal of restrictions on real estate as a commodity.
2. Financialisation—which implies the increasing role in the housing sector of actors and firms that engage in profit accumulation through the servicing and exchanging of money and financial instruments.
3. Globalisation—which causes the residential real estate to be increasingly dominated by economic networks that operate on a global scale.[4]

II. PRECARIOUS HOUSING—THE SPANISH CONTEXT

Using this theoretical framework to analyse the housing sector in Spain, we see that in the context of hyper commodification, the right to housing has become increasingly more precarious as a result of combination of concrete factors such as the increasing of prices both to rent and buy property, the almost non-existence of social housing, and the huge number of repossessions caused by the mortgage crisis. This process is neither new nor recent in Spain, but the global economic crisis and its consequences caused an impressive acceleration.

In the 1950s the housing market in Spain was roughly equally divided between rental and ownership, with rental units being slightly ahead at 51 per cent of total housing stock. The increasing tendency toward homeownership can be explained as having resulted from public housing policies. Changes in housing laws in this direction can be traced to the early democratic period (post-1975). From 1978, Spanish legislation favoured ownership over renting by creating different sets of tax advantages for buyers, while, simultaneously, insecurity in renting laws jeopardised the rental market.[5] Subsequently the political system continued to promote tax advantages for buyers along with the emergence of new family models, the arrival of migrants linked with an increased availability of jobs in the sector of construction, and the purchase of housing by foreign retirees.

[4] Ibid.

[5] Antònia Casellas and Eduard Sala, 'Home eviction, grassroots and citizen empowerment in Spain' in K Brickell, F Arrigoita, M Vasudevan (eds), *Geographies of forced eviction: dispossession, violence, insecurity* (Basingstoke, Palgrave Macmillan, 2017).

As Naredo explains, housing and construction policies in Spain have been characterised by the objective of encouraging the development of the financial market and real estate. For this reason, it has promoted a housing model which focuses primarily on private property through tax breaks for buying and general and extremely easy access to credit. The result of this strategy is that currently 83 per cent of homes are owned homes and only 17 per cent are for rent.[6] Furthermore, public housing has always been marginal and nowadays is clearly below the European average, at one per cent.[7]

At the same time, during recent years rents have grown significantly, producing what has been described as a rent bubble.[8] This has been linked, in cases like Barcelona, to gentrification processes with the massive arrival of tourists, reaching historic heights in 2016.[9]

At the international level a speculative global market with the securitisation of mortgages was created during the 1980s[10] as a result of the financialisation of housing. In Spain there were a number of policies designed to promote owner-occupation, such as tax advantages for buyers.[11] Urbanisation became a tool for speculative economic growth during a period in which successive administrations established insufficient regulations to integrate urban development.[12] By 2007, 87 per cent of families were owner-occupiers, when the European average was 60 per cent.[13]

During this 'golden age' of easy access to credit, not only the banks and financial companies, but also the political system in general, saw mortgages as the best way to extend the right to housing. Buying a house in a period of economic growth, even with a long mortgage term, looked like a safe

[6] JM Naredo, 'El modelo inmobiliario español y sus consecuencias' in Mireia Belil, Jordi Borja and Marcelo Corti (eds), *Ciudades una ecuación impossible* (Barcelona, Icaria, 2012).

[7] Elena Herrera, 'infoLibre' (23/06/2015): www.infolibre.es/noticias/politica/2015/06/24/amnistia_denuncia_que_espana_cuenta_con_solo_de_vivienda_social_34431_1012.html.

[8] Miguel Ángel Maestro, 'El Periódico' (18/11/2016): www.elperiodico.com/es/noticias/entre-todos/burbuja-esta-aqui-maestro-articulo-5635616; Max Jiménez, 'El Periódico' (13/11/2016): www.elperiodico.com/es/noticias/economia/burbuja-precios-alquiler-llega-grandes-ciudades-5621351.

[9] 'La Vanguardia' (12/01/2017): www.lavanguardia.com/economia/20170112/413295264824/espana-turistas -extranjeros-record-2016.html.

[10] Saskia Sassen, *Expulsiones. Brutalidad y complejidaden la economía global* (Buenos Aires, Katz Editores, 2015).

[11] Ada Colau and Adrià Alemany, *¡Sí se puede!* (Barcelona, Destino, 2013).

[12] José Taboada, 'La explosión de la burbuja inmobiliaria en España', *TYS Magazine*, 15/01/2014.

[13] Dan Andrews, Aida Caldera Sánchez and Asa Johansson, *Housing markets and structural policies in OECD countries: OECD Economics Department Working Papers, No. 836* (Paris, OECD Publishing, 2011).

investment for the future. These factors facilitated the over-indebtedness of the middle class. The average debt to buy a home increased, during the period 1997–2007, from 55 per cent to 130 per cent of the family's disposable income. The average loan also increased during the same period to €149,007 from €50,786 and the average term of repayment for the loan passed from 19 to 28 years.[14]

The official statistics produced by the Spanish INE (National Institute of Statistics)[15] provides further details of the trend. In 1997, 479,237 mortgages for home purchase were recorded; by 2004 the figures exceeded one million for the first time, and reached a maximum in 2006 with 1,342,171 new mortgages recorded. Since then there has been a decline, slow at first, then accelerating as the crisis worsened. By 2009 the number of mortgages (650,889) had halved, and the decrease continued until it reached a minimum in 2013 with 199,703 mortgages recorded. From 2000 to 2007 a total of 7,854,562 mortgages have been recorded, while in the following period (2008–15), when the consequences of crisis became more evident every day, the total was 3,427,949. Taking into account the period 2003–07 that represented the culmination of this phenomenon, we have an average of 1,187,115 per year and a total of 5,935,777 mortgages granted.

The steady growth in the unemployment rate from eight per cent in 2007 to almost 27 per cent in 2013[16] and the specificities of Spanish legislation on mortgages, led to a huge number of mortgage repossessions. Details of repossessions are provided by the data of the *Consejo General del Poder Judicial*.[17] The report published on 20 June 2016 covers the years from 2007 until 2015. It is clear that from 2007 the number of repossessions has increased quickly. Since 2007 in Spain 672,624 repossession proceedings have been started.[18] According to the data produced by *Consejo General del Poder Judicial*, from 2008 to 2016, the completed repossessions numbered 327,228.[19]

With the bursting of the credit bubble in the United States in 2008, connected with subprime mortgages, the financial crisis quickly spread worldwide. In Europe it had its greatest effects in the peripheral countries that had

[14] Ada Colau y Adrià Alemany, *Vidas hipotecadas. De la burbuja inmobiliaria al derecho a la vivienda* (Barcelona, Angle Editorial, 2012).

[15] 'Instituto Nacional de Estadística': www.ine.es.

[16] 'Instituto Nacional de Estadística': www.ine.es/en/prensa/epa_tabla_en.htm.

[17] 'Poder Judicial España': www.poderjudicial.es/cgpj/es/Poder_Judicial.

[18] The data available regarding the period before 2007 shows that between 2001 and 2006 the number of repossession proceedings started was 88,414.

[19] 'Poder Judicial España': www.poderjudicial.es/cgpj/es/Temas/Estadistica-Judicial/Estudios-e-Informes/Efecto-de-la-Crisis-en-los-organos-judiciales/.

the most real estate speculative activity: Portugal, Ireland, Italy, Greece and Spain.[20] One of the most important consequences of the 2008 financial crisis in Spain was a mortgage crisis linked to subprime mortgages that involved hundreds of thousands of families who found themselves, overnight, facing a real risk of losing their home.

If we look beyond the data we can begin to understand how the right to housing that should be granted by the international,[21] European,[22] and Spanish[23] legal framework, in Spain, was put into question for hundreds of thousands of people affected by the mortgage crisis and at risk of losing their homes. The instinctive and spontaneous reaction of people affected by the mortgage crisis was a mixture of despair, helplessness, shame, and guilt that often resulted in depression, family crises and, in the most dramatic cases, even suicide. This can lead to what Madden and Marcuse call, 'residential alienation' a source of fear, stress, anxiety, and disempowerment for many affected people.[24]

III. THE PAH (*PLATAFORMA AFECTADOS POR LA HIPOTECA*)

In the autumn of 2006 in Madrid, following a massive spontaneous street-sitting protest, many groups against the precarious housing condition joined Barcelona's 'V de Vivienda'[25] movement. The 'V de Vivienda' organisers employed sophisticated social media networks and campaign strategies. The movement remained active until the crisis transformed their claims from access to affordable housing to defence of mortgage victims. Members of 'V de Vivienda' became directly involved in the creation of the PAH on the 22 February 2009.[26]

[20] Vicenç Navarro, 'Ataque a la democràcia y al bienestar' (Barcelona, Anagrama, 2015).

[21] Article 25 of United Nations Universal Declaration of Human Rights (1948) states that: 'Everyone has the right to a standard of living adequate for the health and well-being of himself and of his family, including food, clothing, housing and medical care and necessary social services, and the right to security in the event of unemployment, sickness, disability, widowhood, old age or other lack of livelihood in circumstances beyond his control.'

[22] Article 34 of Charter of Fundamental Rights of the European Union (2000) affirms that: 'In order to combat social exclusion and poverty, the Union recognises and respects the right to social and housing assistance so as to ensure a decent existence for all those who lack sufficient resources, in accordance with the rules laid down by Community law and national laws and practices.'

[23] Article 47 of Spanish Constitution declares that: 'All Spaniards are entitled to enjoy decent and adequate housing. The public authorities shall promote the necessary conditions and shall establish appropriate standards in order to make this right effective, regulating land use in accordance with the general interest in order to prevent speculation. The community shall participate in the benefits accruing from the urban policies of the public bodies'.

[24] David Madden and Peter Marcuse (n 3 above).

[25] 'Vivienda' translates to 'House'.

[26] Casellas and Sala (n 5 above)

The platform defines itself as a citizen movement, independent from political parties and structured through assemblies. People directly affected by the mortgage crisis and people who wanted to express solidarity with those people organised themselves in order to denounce and change this situation. Since its creation, up until 2017, 230 branches have been created throughout Spain and thousands of evictions have been blocked. According to Spain's mortgage laws, when a bank repossesses a property, the outstanding debt is not automatically discharged. Therefore, many families who lose their homes remain tied to a huge debt, and thus face social exclusion. To respond to this situation PAH helped people to avoid evictions and to negotiate directly with banks to obtain a resolution of their cases through different strategies. The objective of these negotiations is often a 'dación en pago'; that is, the cancellation of the debt by handing back the property of the mortgaged house to the bank. If the bank has already repossessed the mortgaged house through an auction, then the main objective is the 'condonación de la deuda', which is the cancellation of the remaining debt. These objectives are often accompanied by the request for 'Alquiler social'; that is, a rent contract that permits the affected person to stay in the mortgaged house, on an affordable rent base, after the bank have repossessed the house.

Over the years, PAH developed several strategies to secure a law with three main demands: 1) to stop evictions, 2) grant the 'dación en pago', and 3) grant 'Alquiler social'. To these requests two more were subsequently added: 4) guaranteed basic supplies such as gas, electricity and water, and 5) increase the public housing stock; all together forming the so-called '5 of PAH'.

PAH works actively through actions, assemblies and collective advice, in order to empower people affected by the mortgage crisis, becoming one of the reference points in the urban resistance to evictions in Spain.[27] It has become an important social movement that has demonstrated that, through a combination of a process of collective awareness and individual empowerment, it is possible to successfully conclude negotiations with banks and find a solution for thousands of people who, because of the mortgage crisis, risked losing their homes. It has generated strong interest from both local and international media.[28] There have also been academic

[27] Jordi Mir-Garcia et al, 'Fundamentos de la Plataforma de Afectadospor la Hipoteca: activismo, asesoramiento colectivo y desobediencia civil no violenta' (2013) *Educación Social: Revista de Intervención Socioeducativa* 55.

[28] Julie de Weerdt and Marisol García, 'Housing Crisis: The Platform of Mortgage Victims (PAH) Movement in Barcelona and Innovations in Governance' (2015) 31 *Journal of Housing and the Built Environment* 471.

investigations which have analysed some aspects of the 'empowerment process',[29] mobilisation,[30] and the relation between PAH and the institutional actors.[31]

In our analysis of PAH we focus on four main questions:

1. Who has come to PAH over the years?
2. Why at some point did these people stop paying their mortgages?
3. What are the main causes of this phenomenon?
4. What are the objectives of the negotiations? And what are their results?

IV. METHODOLOGY

In answering these questions, we use a mixed methodology. First, we use the notes that we took during our ethnographic work based on an observant participation process during attendance at the weekly 'welcome assemblies'. Furthermore, we participated in several action and mobilisation campaigns. This field-work gave us the opportunity of being involved in a great number of assemblies and actions and helps us explain how awareness and empowerment are promoted. We use the notes that we took in our diaries, therefore the quotes are not verbatim.

There is a 'welcome commission' in PAH Barcelona, which handles the welcome assembly every week. A group of people are in charge of the different parts of this presentation and the roles can change every week. For simplicity, we will use as an example an explanation led by a fictitious activist called 'Paula' to summarise PAH's activities in general and how the three phases of a negotiation are presented in the welcome assembly every Monday. We chose a feminine name because women play a central role in the welcome commission such as in all PAH activities.

Secondly, we will analyse a database summarised in the report: '*Exclusión Residencial en el mundo local: Informe de la crisis hipotecariaen Barcelona*

[29] See Julie Lawton 'Preserving Homeownership Through the Power of the Collective: Lessons for Barcelona' (2015) 297 *Revista de Derecho Urbanístico y Medio Ambiente* 31 and Lluís Mangot, 'La Plataforma de Afectadospor la Hipoteca. De la Crisis a la Estafa. Del Prozac al Empoderamiento' (2013) 2 *Clivatge* 56.

[30] Cristina Flesher Fominaya, 'Redefining the Crisis/Redefining Democracy: Mobilising for the Right to Housing in Spain's PAH Movement' (2015) 20 *South European Society and Politics* 465–85.

[31] Eduardo Romanos, 'Evictions, Petitions and *Escraches*: Contentious Housing in Austerity Spain' (2014) 13 *Social Movement Studies* 296–302.

(2013–2016)' produced by Observatory DESC and PAH Barcelona.[32] We collaborated in the production of this report over the last two years. The goal of this report is to analyse the consequence of the mortgage crisis in Spain from another perspective—namely, that of the families and the people affected. To do this, the report analyses the data on negotiation of 957 cases of people who have turned to PAH Barcelona between 2013–16. From the methodological point of view, we used different tools, in different periods, to monitor the personal situations and the negotiation process followed by those people. In a first phase, we focused on the very first time they arrived at the PAH's Welcome Assembly, which takes place every Monday; on this first occasion, the affected people filled out a questionnaire on their situation (sociological profile, characteristics of mortgage contract, stage of negotiation, objectives, etc). This data was then saved in a database that was regularly updated during the process of negotiation between affected people and banks.

Finally, every affected person was contacted by phone between January and March 2016 to make a final update of their database file. After this, the cases considered for the data analysis were 957 in number. Those cases don't represent just 957 people who have turned to the PAH however; if we consider also the families of those people, this study analyses the consequences of the mortgage crisis for 3206 people, of whom 745 are minors.

Thus, to analyse the awareness and empowerment process developed by PAH, in this chapter we merge an ethnographical reconstruction of the weekly 'welcome assembly' of PAH Barcelona with the results of the database analysis.

V. FROM 'AFFECTED TO ACTIVIST': THE AWARENESS AND EMPOWERMENT PROCESS PROMOTED BY PAH

In this section, we describe the welcome assemblies of PAH that take place every Monday at the movement headquarters. The assembly is a central space in which people that have problems related to the right to housing have their first contact with PAH. Furthermore, the welcome assembly is a key moment for the development of the awareness and empowerment process that helps the affected people arriving for the first time at PAH in their negotiation. The welcome assembly has gradually evolved over the last few years, and there are more and more people coming to PAH for the first time with problems that are not strictly related to mortgages.

[32] Observatori DESC and PAH (2016), *Exclusión Residencial en el mundo local: Informe de la crisis hipotecaria en Barcelona (2013–2016)*: http://observatoridesc.org/es/nuevo-informe-exclusion-residencial-mundo-local-crisis-hipotecaria-barcelona-2013-2016.

Nevertheless, we will focus our analysis solely on those people affected by the mortgage crisis and on the negotiation process promoted by PAH.

Although PAH currently has more than 200 branches throughout Spain, we focus on the Barcelona PAH. It is really important to point out that the assemblies, commissions and actions that are described in this chapter, are part of the organisational structure of this local PAH. Although the basic structures of all PAH are similar, their functioning and organisation may vary depending on the number of people involved.

The PAH of Barcelona is a space for meeting, seeking mutual help and action, that is organised in different groups, commissions and assemblies. There are always two weekly assemblies that form the organisational structure of the PAH of Barcelona: the welcome assembly and the coordination assembly.

Every Monday at 6.00 pm the local PAH of Barcelona welcomes about 80–90 people. For many of them this is their first contact with the PAH. This open assembly takes place in a space where chairs are placed in a circle, whenever possible, so that people can look at each other and feel included in the group. The business of the meeting is structured in three parts:

First, a welcome and contextualisation part, where the nature of PAH is explained, along with its demands, its campaigns and the different commissions and groups in existence. The timetable of future events is detailed and some 'veteran' activists explain how to take part, and also give information on the situation of the right to housing, using news and topics. People who are responsible for providing such information use inclusive language, for example by using 'nosotras' ('the feminine form of 'us'), that is a way of visualising the patriarchal social problem. The objective is to create a sense of community and family, open to dialogue and which encourages people to participate and to speak. Furthermore, this helps break the feeling of loneliness and shame that accompanies people arriving at PAH for the first time. Also, personal examples are used, highlighting phrases and keywords such as:

> 'PAH is free',
>
> 'si se puede' ('yes, it is possible' which is the main slogan of PAH),
>
> 'actively listen, normally the other's problem will be similar to yours',
>
> 'PAH doesn't provide individual advice',
>
> 'you have not done anything wrong; you are not a criminal',
>
> 'do not despair, it's a long process but you are not alone.'

A second part of the meeting explains the stages of the mortgage enforcement procedure and eviction process and what can be done during each of the different phases. These pieces of information are also on the posters displayed on the PAH headquarters' walls and summarised in the

PAH Green Book.[33] This handbook briefly summarises what PAH is and how it works, and gives some suggestions on how to manage the negotiation process at every different stage. At the end of the assembly there are copies available to all those who want one. The usefulness of this 'guide' is twofold. On the one hand, it is a tool intended for people who come to PAH for the first time who can use it to understand what strategies can be put in place at different stages of the negotiation with the banks. On the other hand, it is also a valuable tool for 'veteran' activists who use it as a basis for the presentation of PAH as well as to explain the three stages of negotiation during the welcome meeting.

The people in charge of explaining each phase do so in colloquial language, using their personal experiences and encouraging the 'veterans' to explain their cases and how they solved them. They use key phrases such as:

> 'within PAH none will be left homeless',
>
> 'the best lawyer for you is you',
>
> 'you are the best person to defend yourself',
>
> 'you will never be alone',
>
> 'listen and ask',
>
> 'Concluding a negotiation in a positive way is not an easy goal',
>
> 'You have to fight for it and it's important to be aware of this',
>
> 'Before you get a positive answer you will have many negatives',

etc.

The final part of the meeting involves collective advice. During this part of the welcome assembly, people affected explain their case and express their concerns. This phase is crucial for them as they feel that their individual problems are really tackled in a collective way. They lose their fear and shame; they acquire the knowledge and tools needed to fight for their case in order to get a satisfactory solution to their problem. The fact of sharing their case, talking about it and possibly addressing worries, for the majority of people, is therapeutic and it is part of a process of liberation from the feelings of guilt and personal failure that for many people represents a necessary first step to be able to face the difficult situation they are in.

In this last phase of the welcome assembly, every Monday, expressions such as:

> 'together, yes we can',
>
> 'first of all you have to feed your children',

[33] The PAH green book is available on the PAH website 'Afectados por la Hipoteca': www.afectadosporlahipoteca.com/wp-content/uploads/2014/01/LibroVerde-PAH-32.pdf.

'you are not alone',

'you have to lose the fear',

'You have to insist, insist, insist',

'do not despair',

'with the PAH you can find a solution'

are used.

There is no one person in charge, the role is performed in rotation by activists who generally are, or have been, directly involved in a negotiation process with a bank. These people know exactly what problems and feelings those who are coming to PAH for the first time are experiencing. This means they give a number of concrete examples with reference to themselves or other activists, who may be called upon to explain certain points, talking about their own cases. PAH supports and collaborates with people in their negotiations with the banking entities, but it is absolutely necessary that the person affected undertakes first-hand the process of negotiation with the bank. This key point is repeated several times during the welcome assembly.

VI. THE FIRST PHASE OF THE NEGOTIATION PROCESS

This begins when people realise that they can no longer pay the instalments of their mortgage, and therefore decide to stop paying. This decision is hard because many people feel guilty about the difficulties they face and they often try everything to avoid taking this decision. Many families try to reduce other expenses, some ask relatives to help, others ask the bank for a new loan, but sooner or later the majority of people stop paying.

The first phase ends when the affected person receives the documentation that officially launches repossession proceedings. When activists illustrate this phase, they also explain the objectives the affected person can pursue and what actions can be taken to reach them.

Paula (our fictitious activist) makes clear that the first phase is the one in which the bank is more willing to negotiate. However, to begin a negotiation it is necessary to have already stopped paying the mortgage repayments.[34] If a person continues paying, the bank will not take an attempt to negotiate seriously. Paula explains that it is fundamental to stop paying immediately when you realise that you can no longer bear the weight of the payments. Do not procrastinate because each quota that is not paid at 100 per cent is treated like an unpaid quota.

[34] ie the monthly repayment sum.

She adds that it is also necessary to move all money in current accounts or savings to other banks to prevent it from being blocked by the bank with which you are negotiating. Generally, in this first phase the main objective is the 'dación en pago' which is the cancellation of the debt relating to a mortgage in exchange for the return of the mortgaged house to the bank: 'To request a "dación en pago" you have to present to your bank a document that can be downloaded from the PAH website.'[35]

Paula then quickly lists a series of practical tips to negotiate more effectively and to reassure the affected people:

> You have to remember that no one goes to jail or can be deported for stopping their mortgage payments. It is not a crime, you have done nothing wrong, and you are not a criminal. Repossession is a long procedure, eviction does not occur immediately. It's a long process, so don't despair. You have the time to negotiate with your bank and to try to find a solution, but you must have clear in mind the goal you want to achieve when you start a negotiation, and pursue it with patience and perseverance without being discouraged by the difficulties.

These simple concepts are repeated several times during the assembly to reassure newcomers and make them understand that the process of negotiating with banks is long and complicated. The importance of the fact that each proposal of the bank must be submitted in writing at least 72 hours in advance of the deadline for signature is also repeated many times.

Paula concludes the presentation of the first phase of negotiations, giving some advice that can be useful for every affected person:

> During a negotiation you can use some tricks to put some pressure on the bank. The first-one it is to openly declare to the bank with whom you are negotiating that you are a member of the Plataforma Afectados por la Hipoteca. By doing so, the counterparty is aware that they are not negotiating with a single person or family, isolated and often frightened. On the contrary, there is a specific organisation which has dealt with this issue for years, concluding hundreds of fruitful negotiations and using a range of pressure tactics to get banks to negotiate and achieve agreement. Another useful strategy is to go to your bank wearing the PAH green shirt, a true symbol of the organisation, to put pressure on them.

VII. THE SECOND PHASE OF THE NEGOTIATION PROCESS

The second phase begins when the documents commencing the repossession procedure arrive. This means that the mortgaged house will be auctioned

[35] 'Afectados por la Hipoteca': www.afectadosporlahipoteca.com/documentos-utiles/#dacion-en-pago.

so that the bank can recover all or part of the remaining debt. According to Spanish mortgage law the debt is not completely extinguished when the bank repossesses the mortgaged house or property. For example, if the bank recovers only part of its credit (which also includes interests and legal fees) after a devaluation of the mortgaged house and its auction, the remaining part of the debt remains with the person who signed the mortgage contract and on their guarantors.

The documents which begin the procedure indicate the date of the auction. This must be notified at least 20 days beforehand to all the signatories and the guarantors of the mortgage. Paula explains that the first thing to do is to ask for free legal representation:

> It is really important to ask for a public defender. First, to avoid paying the legal costs of the procedure, which can be very high, and secondly to gain a little time, since while the application for it is under consideration, the repossession is suspended. If the public defender is not granted following the first request, you have to insist because it is possible to file an appeal, and you can find the necessary documents on the PAH website.[36]

Even at this stage, at least up to when the house is auctioned, the priority objective of the negotiation is the 'dación en pago'. When describing these steps, there is a strong emphasis on the need to remain calm, even when the mortgage execution procedure begins, because it does not mean an imminent expulsion. The length of the proceedings may vary from several months to several years. Paula and other activists who speak about this point insist that even after the house has been auctioned, it should not be abandoned.

> You have to remain in the house. It is essential because otherwise you and your family have to find a different solution. At the same time staying in the house gives you greater bargaining power with the bank. You have to leave the house only when the police come to evict you by force.

When a house is auctioned the bank can keep 70 per cent of the 'valor de efectos de tasación de subasta' a value that is stated in the mortgage contract. It is therefore important to check this value. If it covers all the remaining debt then the bank can recover the house for 60 per cent of this value.[37] Paula adds ironically:

> What is sure is that the bank, once they recover money from the mortgaged house, will not give you any of it back, ever! You have to know that at the beginning of

[36] 'Afectados por la Hipoteca': www.afectadosporlahipoteca.com/documentos-utiles/#denegacion-justicia-gratuita.

[37] 'Boletin Official del Estado' (08/01/2000): www.boe.es/buscar/act.php?id=BOE-A-2000-323.

> the mortgage crisis banks could recover houses at auction for 50 per cent of their value. The fact that later it was increased to 70 per cent is the result of struggles and mobilisations of the PAH.

If you don't get a 'dación en pago' through negotiation process, the second phase ends with the auction of the mortgaged house. Paula insists a lot on the fact that during the negotiation phase the affected person is the first person that has to get engaged in the negotiation.

> During the negotiation process, it is a priority to put an increasing pressure on the banks. At first, you start by bringing them the documents to ask for the 'dación en pago', then you should go as often as possible to your bank wearing the green t-shirt of PAH. For example, some affected people used to stand in front of their bank every day with a poster with the photo of their family with the sentence: 'This bank wants to evict my family'. Actions like these can be very effective because banks generally don't want bad publicity. If the negotiation is blocked, there are several tools that you can use. For example, you can try to speak with your bank manager, accompanied by other activists of PAH that have more experience in negotiation. If a situation is complicated we can also decide to organise a specific action to try to unblock it. You have to remember that you are not alone in this fight. But the first thing that you have to do is come here every Monday to listen to the experience that other activists share, and start using the things that you learn here in your own negotiation.

Another important aspect of all the stages of the negotiation that is often taken up by the various interventions is the need to turn to social services and public administration to obtain all documents that can demonstrate to the bank the economic difficulties people are going through.

Before illustrating the third phase, Paula repeats again that, if the negotiation with the bank succeeds in one of the previous stages and one obtains the 'dación en pago', there will not be a third phase. Another important strategy is to always link the demand for 'dación en pago' with a demand for an 'alquiler social'. This means undertaking to pay a rental fee to the bank in order to stay for a specified time in the mortgaged home, even after the bank has completely recovered title to the property. The duration of 'alquiler social' and its amount varies from one case to another depending on the socio-economic situation of the affected family. If a family doesn't get a 'alquiler social' they have to leave the mortgaged house.

VIII. THE THIRD PHASE OF THE NEGOTIATION PROCESS

The third phase begins when the house has been auctioned and, in most cases, becomes the property of the bank. The objective of the negotiations becomes the 'condonación de la deuda'. However, the most urgent issue related to this third phase is possible eviction from the house, now owned by the bank. Paula said that auctioning the house does not automatically mean eviction from it, which can only occur after several months.

Once the eviction notice has been issued, there is a whole series of tools to suspend the eviction. These tools are explained step by step in the PAH Green Paper, and are summarised every week by Paula:

> You must not despair. Stay in the house, even after the auction, and continue to negotiate and put pressure on the bank. Remember that the eviction is not automatic and that there are some different tools that you can use to avoid or postpone it: ask for a public defender; appeal to the court to stop the eviction; apply to the court for the cancellation of the debt; go to social services and request a temporary suspension of the eviction.

Once the illustration of the three phases has been completed, the assembly is interrupted for 10 minutes during which those who wish to present their cases tell it to a person responsible for preparing a list of cases to be dealt with. Each case is the subject of a collective consultation process where PAH 'veteran' activists answer technical questions and give advice on how to resolve the different issues. In this process, people who participate in the meeting and listen to the presentation of the different cases and the solutions proposed, gradually acquire skills, thus relating to the experience of others who have had the same problems and difficulties.

People who have already confronted and resolved a complicated part of a negotiation are more than willing to share the strategies they adopted and the solutions achieved. This collective consultation process is essential for people who are getting involved with PAH for the first time in order to understand a little better how to behave in relation to their own case, also on the basis of the testimonials of other affected people. For this reason, there is often an emphasis on the need to participate as much as possible in welcoming meetings every Monday. Even if the welcome meeting mainly involves people who are having their first contact with PAH or who have recently started to follow its activities, there will always be about 15–20 PAH 'veteran' activists who explain the objectives of PAH, how it is organised and how it works. The approach is therefore rather didactic and there is a clear separation, also visible in the occupation of space, between the two categories of 'expert' and 'newcomer' activists.

The other central moment of PAH activities is the Coordination assembly that takes place every Tuesday at 6.00pm. In this assembly between 40 and 60 people meet at PAH Barcelona to discuss issues related to the overall strategy of the Platform, its organisation, campaign monitoring and to hear reports on current issues. These assemblies, which are facilitated by a couple of people, usually the same each week, are structured in three blocks. The first block consists of welcome and distribution of roles of the assembly (eg person who takes minutes, person who takes notes on the board) and weekly rotating tasks (for example, the cleaning of the headquarters). A second block comprises agenda items, where each person or commission can propose a point to discuss in the assembly previously prepared and communicated to the person facilitating the meeting.

The third part of the meeting is dedicated to actions, accompaniments and evictions. Here is when people affected are directly involved: people are asked to help stop an imminent eviction; to accompany the person concerned to negotiate with the bank or the administration; or to organise and participate in a protest at a bank's offices in case the negotiations are stalled.

As explained earlier, during the PAH assemblies people are advised that the best and most effective strategy in a negotiation with a bank is to put progressively increasing pressure on the banks through different actions. There is a pattern that is always repeated:

— The affected person has to have the main goal of the negotiation (such as 'dación en pago', condonacion, a renegotiation of the mortgage contract, etc) clear in their mind.
— People should bear in mind that they have to be informed, listen and know their own case the best they can, carefully reading the different documents and asking questions in the welcome assembly. Information is the best weapon.
— Firstly, go alone to the bank to request the solution chosen, with the corresponding document that can be found on the website of the platform.
— Insist, insist, insist, and follow the indications of the Green Book. Participate in the activities promoted by the PAH.
— If the bank does not respond positively, organise an action to publicise your situation, for example distributing leaflets in front of the bank.
— If the bank gives a response but it is not the one that the affected person wants, they should request someone to go with them for support in a coordination meeting.
— If the bank still does not give the desired solution, organise more forceful actions (occupy the bank indefinitely until a solution is found, communicate to the media about the personal case …).

These actions can either be individual, for a single case, or collective, to unravel different cases of the same financial entity. The goal is to put pressure on the bank to enhance the negotiation. It has been found that 'small victories', as they call the resolution of cases, are obtained by exerting pressure on the street and practising civil disobedience, since the current laws in Spain do not oblige administrations and banks to grant the right to housing.

IX. WHO ARE THE AFFECTED PEOPLE THAT CAME TO PAH OVER THE YEARS?

It is possible to try to answer to this question by using the data collected in the report *Exclusión Residencialen el mundo local: Informe de la crisis hipotecariaen Barcelona (2013–2016)*[38] to structure a profile of the people that take part in the welcome assembly.

Of the 957 people who answered to the questionnaire, 52.1 per cent are women and 47.9 per cent are men. More than 68 per cent of affected people are between 35 and 55 years old, eight per cent are under 36 years of age, and 17 per cent are over 56 years.

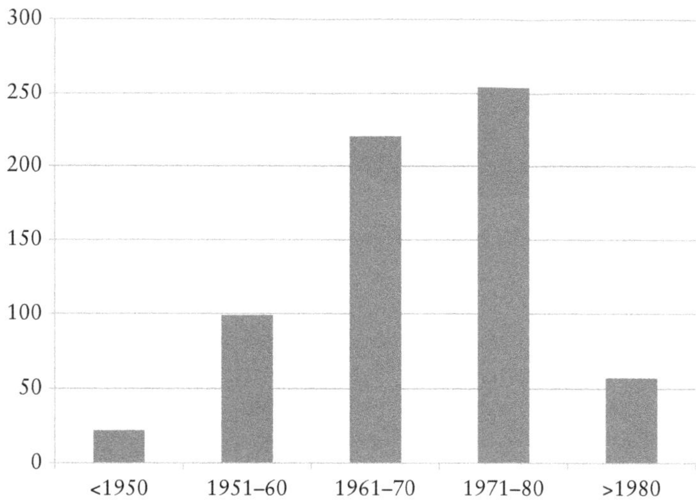

Figure 1: Year of birth of the people affected
Data taken from the Report.

About half of the people affected are Spanish (52 per cent). Among those who are migrants, there is an important presence of people from Latin America, with 23 per cent of Ecuadorian origin, three per cent of Colombian and seven per cent Peruvian. Finally, 14 per cent of people have a different nationality (figure 2). 24.5 per cent of respondents have a second nationality, and in 95 per cent of these cases the second nationality is Spanish. Thus, by considering this data, the percentage of people with Spanish nationality raises to almost 76 per cent of the people interviewed.

[38] Observatori DESC (n 32 above) ('the Report').

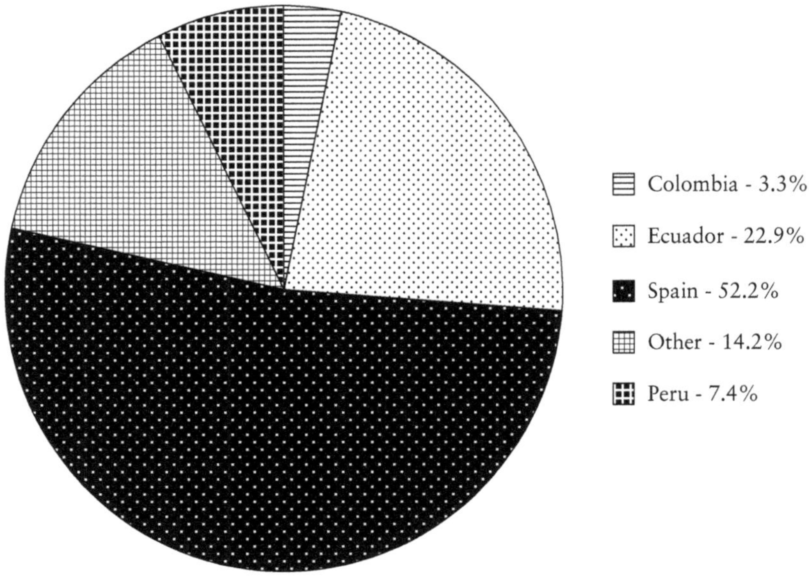

Figure 2: Nationality of the people affected
Data taken from the Report.

Mortgage problems do not only directly affect the people who signed the mortgage contract, 'los titulares'[39] but also the people who guaranteed them, 'los avaladores'[40] who are co-responsible.

In most of the cases analysed (57 per cent) two people are joint holders of the mortgage. In 23 per cent there is just one holder, and in the remaining 20 per cent there are more than two. In total, the number of shareholders affected in the cases of this report is 1,623. That is that 98 per cent of people who filled out the questionnaire were mortgage holders, and only two per cent were guarantors. Nevertheless, often, the guarantors participate in the PAH assemblies to know more about the procedure and to try to understand how to resolve the case in which they are involved.

39.7 per cent of mortgages do not have guarantors, 53.4 per cent have at least one and 6.9 per cent have more than two. 15.2 per cent of guarantors are friends, 9.9 per cent are parents, 19.2 per cent other relatives and 9.9 per cent unknown (when there are unknown guarantors usually in the mortgage contract there is a cross-guarantee clause). In total, the guarantors involved in the cases totalled 606.

Problems with mortgages also affect families indirectly. So, it is interesting to analyse the characteristics of the families of the people who turned to PAH Barcelona to solve their problems with mortgages. Most family units

[39] 'los titulares' can be translated as 'the mortgagors'.
[40] 'los avalistas' can be translated as 'the guarantors of the debt'.

are formed of two (24.9 per cent) or three people (24.6 per cent). 14.2 per cent of those affected live alone, while 21.9 per cent are families of four people and the rest, 14.4 per cent, are families of five or more people. In total, the number of family members affected in this analysis is 2,600. In 61.6 per cent of the families there are minors. Of these, 29.5 per cent there is one minor in the family, in 26.1 per cent of the cases, two and in 7.1 per cent, three or more. So, the total number of minors affected considered in this report, is 745. Furthermore, in 10.1 per cent of the families, there is a person over 65 years old and in 2.6 per cent, there are two. In 12.2 per cent of the families there are also people with some form of dependency.

The concept of residential alienation proposed by Madden and Marcuse[41] perfectly fits with the data with regard to the way in which mortgage problems had a negative impact on the health of people: 17.8 per cent of those interviewed claimed that they suffer from insomnia, 49.5 per cent from anxiety, 33 per cent from depression and 11 per cent told how these difficulties caused family tension.

X. WHY DID THESE PEOPLE STOP PAYING THEIR MORTGAGE AT SOME POINT? AND WHAT ARE THE CHARACTERISTICS OF THESE CONTRACTS?

50 per cent of the mortgages analysed in the study were signed in 2005 (26 per cent) and in 2006 (27 per cent), in the middle of the real estate bubble. If we consider the period 2004–07 covered by this data 84 per cent of mortgages signed in Barcelona were considered in our sample. After the outbreak, the figure dropped to seven per cent (figure 3).

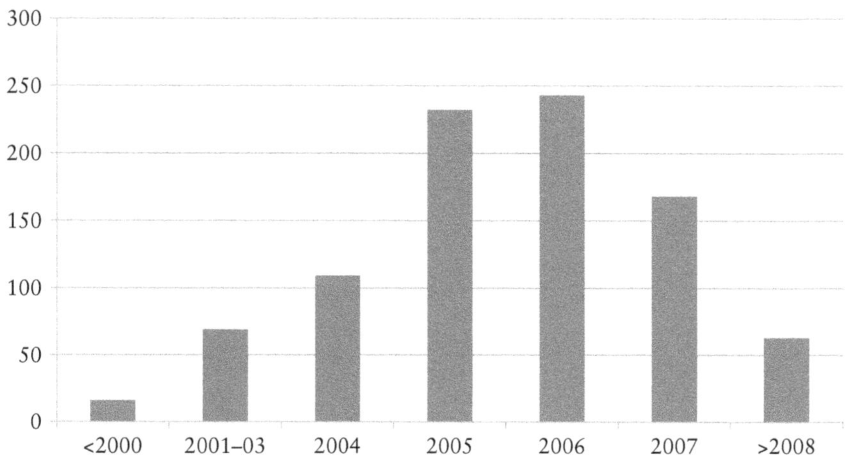

Figure 3: Year of signature of mortgage contract
Data sourced from the Report.

[41] David Madden and Peter Marcuse (n 3 above).

The median contracted loan amounted to €200,000–250,000 (figure 4) and there were payment terms of 26 to 30 years in more than half of the mortgages contracted (51 per cent), 39.2 per cent being over 30 years (figure 5).

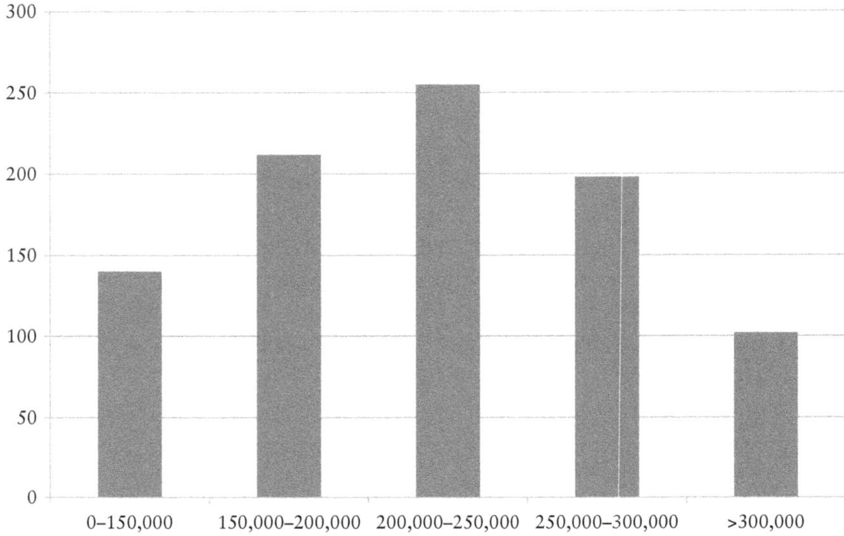

Figure 4: Original amount of the mortgage loan expressed in euro
Data sourced from the Report.

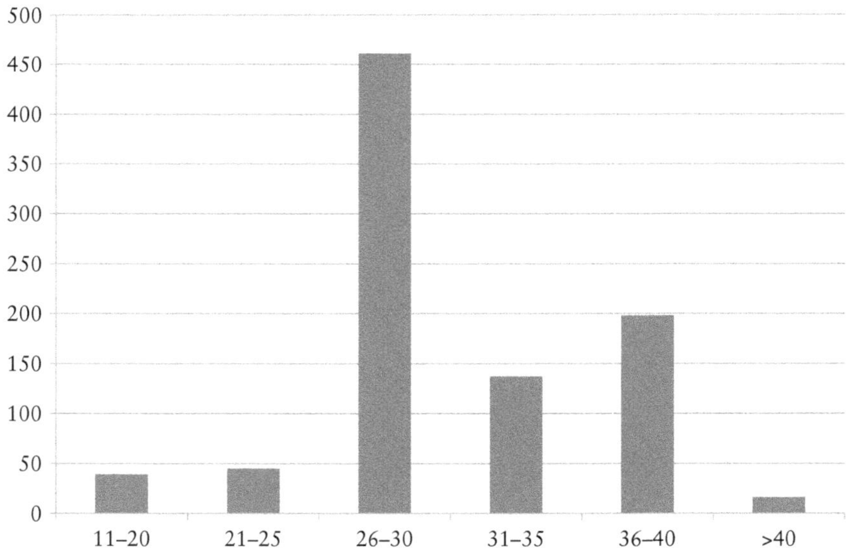

Figure 5: Duration of the mortgage loan, expressed in years
Data sourced from the Report.

With regard to the analysis of the reasons that have led mortgage holders to default on repayment it is important to highlight the following situations:[42]

— 68.1 per cent of the cases were caused by loss of work or unemployment situation.
— 22.3 per cent of the cases were caused by divorce and/or separation. Of these, 64 per cent are women and 36 per cent men.
— 3.4 per cent were due to illness.
— 43.1 per cent were as a result of the increase in Mortgage repayment.
— 32.1 per cent caused by many accumulated debts (in addition to the mortgage).

To understand why people are not able to continue to pay their mortgage it is also important to focus on the economic situation of the families affected. The net income of families in this study is on average, €939 per month. In 70 per cent of cases the net family income is less than €1,200. 10 per cent of households surveyed have no income as a consequence of unemployment, while the seven per cent of households are entering between €400 and €800 per month. Of these, a quarter gain only €426 from family support for unemployment. In 11 per cent of cases, income monthly is over €1,600.

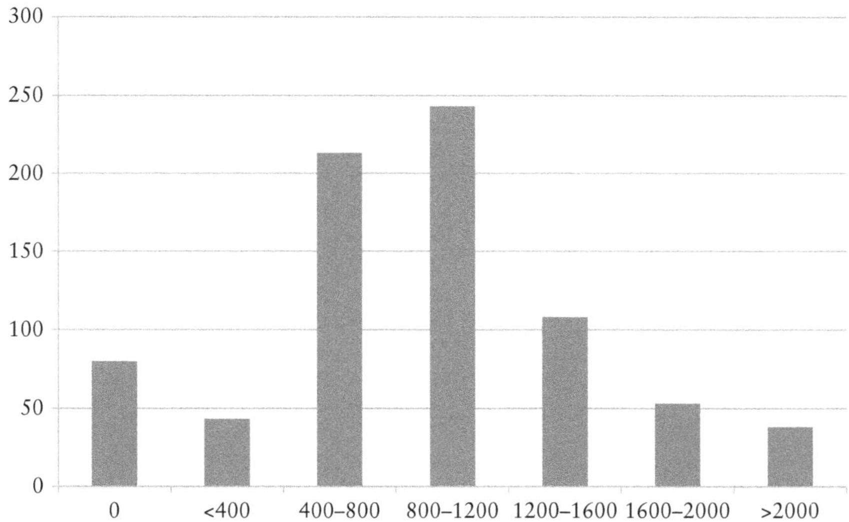

Figure 6: Total monthly income of the families, expressed in euro
Data sourced from the Report.

[42] Methodological note: This question was of a multi-causal type; therefore multiple responses were possible.

Cross referencing the income data with the data regarding the characteristics of the families, the result is that 55.4 per cent of families with three or more members have no income. 58.8 per cent of families living on between €400 and 800 per month are made up of three or more members, the same as the 61.3 per cent of the families living with revenues between €800 and 1,200. And the families with income over €1,600 correspond to 71 per cent of families with three or more people.

At the same time, the average monthly payment to be paid is €1,065, being in 60 per cent of cases a monthly fee between €800 and 1,600. Cross referencing household income with mortgage rates, it is understood that 53.9 per cent of the households would have than to meet a repayment higher than the monthly income total of the family. This means that even by using all their monthly income, more than half of the families are not able to cover the monthly mortgage payment, and they run out of finance to cover the rest of their basic needs. On the other hand, 2.4 per cent earn the same amount as the repayment that they have to make and another 22.4 per cent paying the monthly repayment would have less than €400 remaining. Only 8.6 per cent of families after having made the repayment have more than €800 left, and 12.9 per cent would be left with a sum between €400 and 800 per month to cover all their basic needs (figure 7).

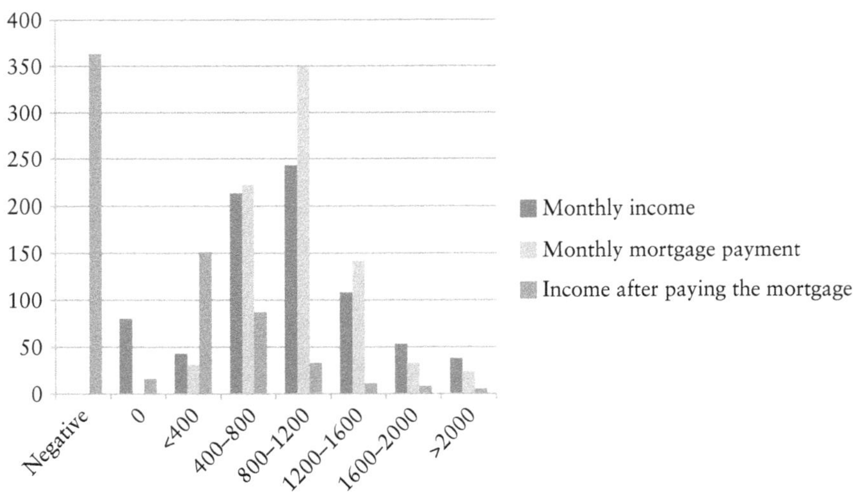

Figure 7: Total monthly income of the family, monthly payment for the mortgage, and income available after the payment

Data sourced from the Report.

The most important consideration that emerges from this comparison is that more than half of the families (54 per cent) do not have sufficient income to pay the monthly mortgage. In 24.8 per cent of the cases, by paying the monthly mortgage payment, the family would retain less than €400, which is obviously not enough to meet the basic needs of an entire family. Another confirmation in this sense is that seven per cent of the people affected receive aid to feed their family from the Food Bank or from their parents, or from Caritas.[43] This data suggests why 88 per cent of respondents, sooner or later, have stopped paying the mortgage. Furthermore 93 per cent of respondents confirm having difficulty meeting basic needs such as food, clothing and supplies.

XI. WHAT IS THE SITUATION OF THE AFFECTED PEOPLE WHEN THEY ARRIVE FOR THE FIRST TIME AT PAH, AND WHAT ARE THEIR OBJECTIVES?

People affected by inability to meet mortgage payments approached PAH at different stages of the repossession process. By the time they first arrive at PAH, 53 per cent of the families had already stopped paying the mortgage, 23 per cent had received court papers, while 13 per cent continued to pay their mortgage instalments, seven per cent had had their house already auctioned and four per cent had already received the eviction order (figure 8).

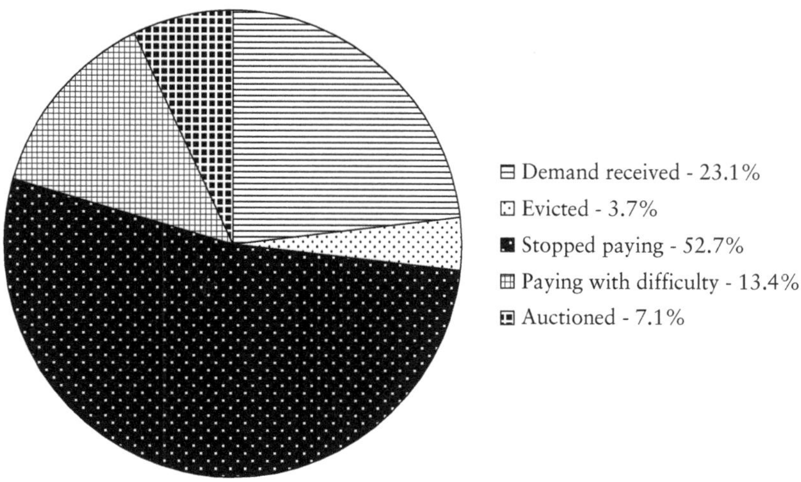

Figure 8: Situation of people when they arrived at PAH
Data sourced from the Report.

[43] Caritas is a charity organisation of the catholic church: www.caritasbcn.org/es/.

People affected by the mortgage crisis who approach PAH have different objectives[44] related to their negotiations with banks: 80 per cent want a 'dación en pago', 53 per cent want a social rent in the same mortgaged house, 14 per cent want the erasure of the debt remaining after the auction and just seven per cent want a renegotiation of the mortgage contract.

XII. WHAT ARE THE RESULTS OF NEGOTIATIONS BETWEEN AFFECTED PEOPLE AND BANKS?

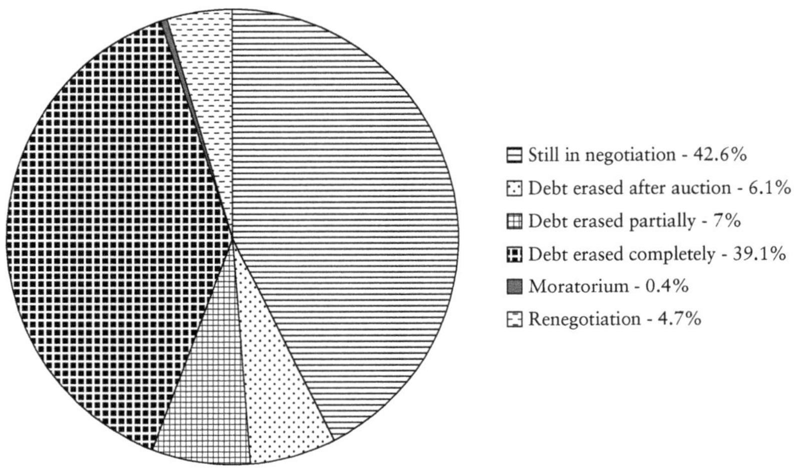

Figure 9: Negotiation results regarding debt
Data sourced from the Report.

According to the data, 57 per cent of the people affected who took part in this study have already resolved their mortgage problem in some way, while 43 per cent are still involved in the negotiation process. Of the cases solved, 68 per cent (39 per cent of the total) have obtained a full 'dación en pago', 11 per cent (6.1 per cent of the total) a 'condonación de la deuda' and 12 per cent (seven per cent of the total) have received a partial 'dación en pago', eight per cent (4.7 per cent of the total) obtained a renegotiation of their contract. Furthermore, 27 per cent of the cases have also obtained a social rent with the bank and live in the same mortgaged dwelling.

[44] Methodological note: This question was of a multi-causal type; therefore multiple-responses were possible.

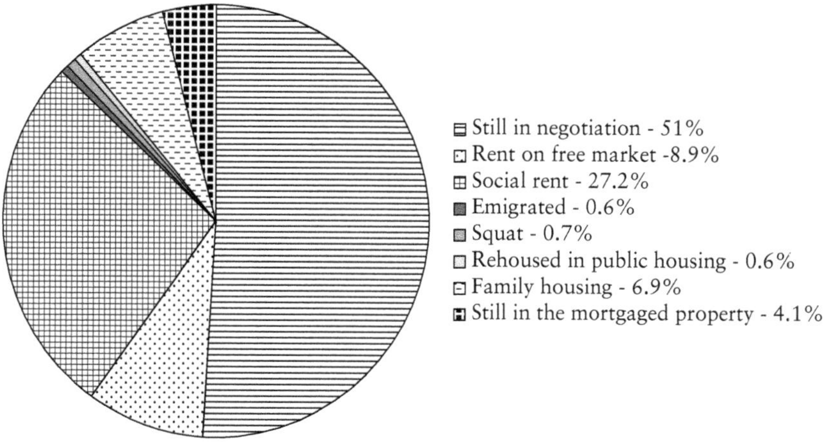

Figure 10: Negotiation results regarding housing
Data sourced from the Report.

Finally, it is also interesting to consider the data on auction and evictions executed. There was a procedure of auction in 11.1 per cent of the cases treated in this section of the study: 61.8 per cent were executed but in the other cases the auction was suspended. During the negotiation process there was an eviction procedure in 4.3 per cent of the cases: 56.6 per cent of these evictions were executed and 43.3 per cent suspended. This data shows that in the majority of the cases, during the negotiation process between affected people and banks there was no auction or eviction procedure and even when the procedure was begun, in more or less 40 per cent of the cases they were suspended thanks to the pressure exerted by PAH.

XIII. CONCLUSIONS

We have shown how in Spain, in a context of hyper commodification of housing, the mortgage crisis affected hundreds of thousands of people, questioning and making their right to housing increasingly precarious. Entire families, often with children, faced the real risk of losing their home and—in the worst cases—they were evicted. In this situation, PAH has often represented the only form of help and support for these people.

Madden and Marcuse affirm that the claim of the right to housing has to be radical, a transformative demand, and they state that: 'an actual right to housing necessarily implies fundamental challenge to the existing system.'[45]

[45] David Madden and Peter Marcuse (n 3 above).

PAH challenged the system refusing the public blame of people affected and involving them in a process of awareness and empowerment that is at the core of the PAH political action in defence of the right to housing. Refusing the idea that people were guilty because they tried to live beyond their possibilities and underlining the responsibilities of the financial and political system, PAH succeeds in building an effective counter-narrative on the mortgage crisis.

PAH challenged the rules. Bypassing Spanish mortgage law, which overprotects the creditors, which in the majority of cases are banks, PAH has successfully promoted thousands of individual and direct negotiations between affected people and banks.[46] These negotiations are preceded and accompanied by a collective awareness and empowerment process developed through the weekly welcome assembly but also during the actions, the interventions to block evictions and the mobilisations promoted by PAH. The affected people gradually lose their sense of guilt and the fear of losing their home that often accompanies them when they first arrive at PAH. At the same time, they realise that they are not alone and, listening to other people's situations, they learn strategies that they can use in their own negotiations. Furthermore, by taking part in actions and mobilisation, affected people feel a sense of community and they become aware that, being part of the PAH, they can count on other people and on the forces of the movement.

In this way, the strategy employed by PAH effectively counteracts both the effects of 'residential alienation' described by Madden and Marcuse[47] and the 'individualisation' and 'isolation' of the affected people described by Lorey as one of the characteristics of the contemporary process of precarisation.[48]

This 'transformation' from affected to activist is fundamental for the negotiation process and explains why in many cases, even after the resolution of their own case, these people continue to participate in meetings and actions of PAH.[49]

By using the data summarised in the report *Exclusión Residencial en el mundo local: Informe de la crisis hipotecaria en Barcelona (2013–2016)*,[50] we focused on the profile of the affected people that came to PAH, on the reasons that forced them to stop paying their mortgage, on the objectives of their negotiation with banks and on the results of these negotiations. The data concerning the reasons behind the choice to stop the mortgage

[46] Jordi Mir-Garcia et al (n 27 above).
[47] David Madden and Peter Marcuse (n 3 above).
[48] Isabell Lorey, *State of Insecurity: Government of the Precarious* (n 1 above).
[49] Lluís Mangot (n 29 above).
[50] Observatori DESC (n 32 above).

payment and the relationship between incomes of families and their mortgage repayment (figure 7) on one hand confirm that the majority of families were affected by unemployment (68.1 per cent of families), and on the other explain that to stop paying the mortgage was not a choice. Finally, data concerning the results of direct negotiations (figures 9 and 10) show that the strategy of PAH is effective and has produced positive results in most cases.

Since 2009, PAH and the people affected from the mortgage crisis have challenged the law, blocking evictions, occupying banks and organising civil disobedience action to 'win' thousands of individual negotiations with banks.

Nevertheless, the mortgage crisis is only one aspect of the 'housing crisis'. PAH also decided to challenge the political system through several proposals to change the law, both at national and regional level, to grant everyone the right to housing. These proposals, until now, have always been blocked by the Popular Party, but in April 2017 PAH has put to all the parties represented in the Spanish Parliament a new proposal for a law based on the '5 of PAH'.[51] This proposal will be supported by a mobilisation campaign to put pressure on the different parties in order to get it approved. Whether or not this is successful, the struggle of PAH to block evictions, win negotiations, change the law and grant the right to housing to everyone continues every day.

[51] See above, section III.

15

Returning Home?

DANIE BRAND*

I. INTRODUCTION

IN SOUTH AFRICA the concept of home and in particular the precariousness of home has over the last several years featured prominently in legal scholarship and judicial work where one would expect it to: in the context of evictions law. Here South African courts have for example had to grapple with questions such as: when occupation of land constitutes a home, so that it attracts the protection of constitutionally mandated evictions legislation;[1] whether restoration of the physical structure of a house after an eviction is overturned on appeal is sufficient to remedy the loss of home occasioned by the original eviction;[2] and whether temporary emergency accommodation provided to evictees after an eviction by the state to ameliorate the immediate effects of an eviction must show the basic characteristics of a home rather than only be physical shelter.[3]

However, home and precarious home, although not explicitly so, has also featured strongly in the operation of law in another area: the process of restitution of land rights that were discriminatorily dispossessed during Apartheid. Although the word 'home' appears neither in the constitutional provisions founding the restitution process[4] nor in its enacting legislation;[5] and although the scope of that process—intended as it is to enable restitution of any 'rights in land' dispossessed under Apartheid[6]—stretches wider than simply the home, because the destruction and dispossession precisely

* Professor Danie Brand, University of Pretoria, danie.brand@up.ac.za.

[1] See eg *Zulu and Others v Ethekwini Municipality and Others* 2014 (4) SA 590 (CC); and *Fischer and Another v Persons whose identities are to the applicants unknown and who have attempted or are threatening to unlawfully occupy Erf 150 (Remaining extent) Philippi In re: Ramahlele and Others v Fisher and Another* 2014 (3) SA 291 (WCC).

[2] *Mathale v Linda and Another* 2016 (2) SA 461 (CC).

[3] *City of Johannesburg v Dladla and Others* 2016 (6) 377 (SCA).

[4] Section 25(7) of the Constitution of the Republic of South Africa, 1996 ('the Constitution').

[5] The Restitution of Land Rights Act 22 of 1994 ('the Restitution Act').

[6] Section 2 of the Restitution Act enables the restitution of 'rights in land' and 'rights in land' is defined broadly to include 'any right in land, whether registered or unregistered'.

of homes was so characteristic of spatial apartheid, many restitution claims in terms of the process are intended in the first place at retrieving some conception of a home lost under Apartheid or at least to redress the injustice specifically of the loss of a home.

In this chapter I look at one such claim—that of the Baphiring Community for the restoration of their erstwhile home, the farm 'Old Mabaalstad' in the North West Province of South Africa, that gave rise to a decision of the Supreme Court of Appeal in *Baphiring Community and Others v Tshwaranani Projects CC and Others.*[7] Against the background of readings of the claim and the case as indicating the taking over of restitution jurisprudence by an instrumentalist, developmental 'good governance' ethic,[8] I propose that it simply illustrates in the context of restitution the radical precariousness of home. It shows that home is radically precarious in the sense that once it is destroyed, it is practically impossible to restore a home. It also shows (and here I draw on Andre van der Walt,[9] Cherryl Walker[10] and Karin van Marle)[11] that home is radically precarious in the more uncomfortable sense that it may simply be inappropriate to restore a home once it is destroyed.

II. BACKGROUND[12]

In the late 1800s, a community of people affiliated to the larger Baphiring tribe[13] (the Baphiring Community) bought approximately 7,700 hectares of farming land in the North West Province near the rural town of Koster, which they named Mabaalstad. Unusually for the time, when it was becoming more difficult for black South Africans to own land in their own name, the majority of the different portions of the farm were registered in title to the Baphiring tribe, rather than, as was the practice, the land being

[7] *Baphiring Community and Others v Tshwaranani Projects CC and Others* 2014 (1) SA 331 (SCA) ('the *Baphiring* case').

[8] J Pienaar, 'Restitutionary Road: Reflecting on Good Governance and the Role of the Land Claims Court' (2011) 14 *Potchefstroom Electronic Law Journal* 30; J van Wyk, '"Feasibility of restoration" as a factor in land restitution claims' (2010) 25 *Southern African Public Law* 590.

[9] AJ van der Walt, *Property and Constitution* (Pretoria University Press, 2012).

[10] C Walker, *Landmarked: Land Claims and Land Restitution in South Africa* (Johannesburg, Jacana Media, 2008).

[11] K van Marle, 'Counter-archive as staging dissensus' in S Motha and H van Rijswijk (eds), *Law, Memory, Violence: Uncovering the Counter-Archive* (Routledge, 2016) 116.

[12] My description of the claim, its background and its resolution is drawn from the different decisions of the Land Claims Court and the Supreme Court of Appeal and from the record of the case that served before the Supreme Court of Appeal, which was kindly made available to me by Louise du Plessis of Lawyers for Human Rights, the instructing attorney in the case.

[13] I use the term 'tribe', with all of its problematic connotations only because of the absence of a more suitable word.

registered in title to the state or another private nominee, which held it in trust for tribes or communities.[14]

Here they settled, with each family allocated a plot on which to build a home and to farm. Houses were built with bricks baked from the clay found on the farm, with roofs made of thatch also cut on the farm. Families engaged primarily in crop farming, producing among other things maize, sorghum, beans, sugar beans, potatoes, spinach and water melons. Water was plentiful and the soil fertile, so that families were easily able to produce enough food for their own needs, often with a surplus that could be sold commercially. Families also kept small numbers of cattle—primarily for ploughing—and some also sheep and goats. The community cooperated with each other in farming: families that did not have enough cattle for ploughing shared cattle with other families (a custom known as '*letsema*'). Crops were also shared, so that the community as a whole was self-sufficient. Smaller children attended a primary school on the farm, while older children travelled to Koster township to attend high school. In the 1960s a slate mine was established on the farm at which a number of community members found employment.

In short, as they had intended to do, the Baphiring Community had, in the inhospitable centre of rural white South Africa and during the height of the establishment of statutory spatial Apartheid managed to create for themselves a home: homes for the families making up their community, but also a home for the community as such.

This home they managed to maintain in the face of Apartheid for a little over 70 years. In 1971 Mabaalstad was identified by the Apartheid government as a so-called 'black spot'. In October of 1971 the entire community, then numbering some 450 households, was forcibly removed to land about 80 kilometres away, which they called 'New Mabaalstad' to distinguish it from their erstwhile home, now 'Old Mabaalstad'. Their houses and other improvements on the land were destroyed; Old Mabaalstad was newly subdivided and sold off to white commercial farmers. In 1972 Old Mabaalstad was formally expropriated, with the Baphiring Community receiving the land at New Mabaalstad (now, however, registered in title to the state, which held it in trust for the Baphiring tribe) and a further approximately R170,000 in cash as compensation, in addition to R10,670 for the loss of

[14] I have been unable to determine why the Baphiring were in this position. Certainly at the time the norm was that communities of black South Africans who wanted to acquire land would buy the land through a nominee, who held title on their behalf; or title would be registered in the state, that would hold the land in trust for the broader tribe of which the community was part. For a discussion of this practice see S Mnwana and G Capps, '*No Chief Ever Bought a Piece of Land' Struggles over property, community and mining in the Bakgatla-ba-Kgafela Traditional Authority Area, North West Province Society*, Work and Development Institute Working Paper 3 (March 2015).

the mineral rights to Old Mabaalstad. The combination of the market value of New Mabaalstad and the cash compensation surpassed the market value at the time of Old Mabaalstad in purely monetary terms. However, the Baphiring Community received no compensation for the trauma of the loss of their home, nor anywhere near adequate support for their resettlement.

Whatever its market value, New Mabaalstad was also a poor substitute for their erstwhile home. With difficult access to water, poor soil and smaller plots per family, farming, compared to the extent that it was possible on Old Mabaalstad, became impossible and the community lost its economic independence. There was no material from which to build brick houses as was the case at Old Mabaalstad, so that families now lived instead in corrugated iron shacks, vulnerable to heat and cold. With their self-sufficiency destroyed, the community soon started to disperse. Some people found work on neighbouring white farms and moved there. Others moved to the city in search of a livelihood. In short, in very little time, the community and its home and the homes of its members were destroyed.[15]

After the nominal fall of Apartheid in 1990, in August 1993 a group of about 360 erstwhile residents of Old Mabaalstad and descendants of the original community took steps to claim back their home. They instituted a land claim, first with the Advisory Commission on Land Allocation, established in terms of the Abolition of Racially Based Land Measures Act,[16] but which was later converted into a claim in terms of the Restitution Act.

Their claim faced a number of initial hurdles. First, the competency of the claimant group to claim the land on behalf of the broader Baphiring Community was disputed by the current owners of Old Mabaalstad. Given that the claimant community was a small fraction of the larger Baphiring tribe, the objection was that they could not claim back rights that were initially lost by the tribe as a whole, nor were they properly authorised to act on behalf of the broader Baphiring tribe. The Land Claims Court held that they were competent to do so as a discrete part of the broader tribe, on the understanding that, although they were not acting on behalf of the tribe, any benefit that might accrue from the claim would be accessible to the entire Baphiring tribe and New Mabaalstad—from which the entire Baphiring tribe had benefitted—would not have to be relinguished should their claim for Old Mabaalstad be successful.[17] Although at this stage the claim was openly supported by the formal traditional leadership

[15] See the brief discussion below of the decision in *Baphiring Community v Uys and Others* (Unreported) case number LCC 64/98 [2003] ZALCC 27 (5 December 2003), where it was held that, despite receiving fair market value, the Baphiring were not justly and equitably compensated for their loss.

[16] Abolition of Racially Based Land Measures Act 108 of 1991.

[17] *Baphiring Community v Uys and Others* (Unreported) case number LCC 64/98 [2002] ZALCC 4 (22 January 2002).

of the Baphiring tribe, in the person of Chief Lucas Manyane Mabelane, the challenge to the capacity of the claimant community to bring the claim does echo a long-standing dispute between that part of the Baphiring who called Old Mabaalstad their home and regarded it as their property, and the traditional leadership structures of the tribe. About this, more below.[18]

After the issue of capacity had been dealt with, a further objection was raised that the Baphiring had at the time of their dispossession been adequately compensated, so that they were precluded from claiming any further restoration or compensation now.[19] The Land Claims Court again held in their favour, determining that, although the market value of New Mabaalstad, with the monetary compensation they received in addition at the time of expropriation, exceeded the market value of Old Mabaalstad at the time of its loss, the lack of financial or other support for their relocation and viable resettlement on New Mabaalstad meant that the compensation received at the time was nevertheless not 'just and equitable' as the Restitution Act requires.

With these two obstacles out of the way, their claim had been recognised. However, a final hurdle remained. The Restitution Act determines that a successful land claimant can receive one of two forms of relief: the default option is always restoration of the actual land lost; but in the alternative, if, for example a claimant does not want the land back, or restoration of that land is physically impossible, the relief may take the form of 'equitable redress', including but not limited to a grant of alternative land, or monetary compensation.

The Baphiring Community's intention was always to achieve restoration of Old Mabaalstad itself, so that they could return to and re-establish their home there, rather than to receive alternative land, monetary compensation or any other form of 'equitable redress'. For this reason, the 'right in land' that they claimed was ownership of Old Mabaalstad, which would vest in a communal property association created for that purpose.

In their claim for restoration of Old Mabaalstad the Baphiring Community were opposed by the new occupiers and owners of the land: white commercial farmers who had acquired the land at various stages after the dispossession in 1971 and had established commercial crop and stock farms and who would have to be expropriated should the land be restored.

Here the Land Claims Court held against the Baphiring, concluding that the restoration of the land was not 'feasible' as required by the Restitution Act. Whereas previously the Court's approach in determining the feasibility of restoration had been to take into account only the extent to which

[18] See Section II, text accompanying n 25 below.

[19] *Baphiring Community v Uys and Others* (Unreported) case number LCC 64/98 [2003] ZALCC 27 (5 December 2003).

the claimants' intended use of the land was compatible with how the land and surrounding area had been developed since dispossession, it cast its net much wider in *Baphiring*, taking into account also: the high cost of acquiring the land and successfully resettling the Baphiring on Old Mabaalstad; the track record of the relevant state department in achieving successful resettlements on claimed land; the likely lack of proper financial support from the state for the resettlement; the impact that restoration and resettlement would have on the current owners and the communities of farm workers currently living on the land; the likely overcompensation that would result if restoration were to occur without the Baphiring relinquishing New Mabaalstad; and even the impact that restoration and resettlement would have on food production on the farm and national food security.[20]

On appeal to the Supreme Court of Appeal, this decision was overturned. Although the Supreme Court of Appeal confirmed the Land Claims Court's new, more wide-ranging approach to determining the feasibility of restoration, it held that the Land Claims Court did not have sufficient information before it at the time of its judgment to determine the feasibility of restoration in terms of this broader approach. It referred the case back to the Land Claims Court for reconsideration and ordered the state to furnish the Land Claims Court with a comprehensive report on a number of specified questions, including the cost of resettlement and the impact of restoration to inform its decision.

Back before the Land Claims Court the case stalled. The state proved unable to make the wide-ranging and detailed factual determinations required of it in terms of the order of the Supreme Court of Appeal. After a number of appearances before the Land Claims Court the parties settled. The state agreed to buy the farms comprising Old Mabaalstad from their current owners and to transfer them in ownership to the Baphiring Community's communal property association. At the time of writing negotiations within the Baphiring Community over the manner in which the land will be used, and between the Community and the state about resettlement assistance were ongoing and no actual resettlement had as yet taken place.

III. ANALYSIS

The *Baphiring* decisions of the Supreme Court of Appeal and Land Claims Court raise a number of important technical legal questions about the purpose of the land claims process and the manner in which just and equitable relief may be determined for successful land claimants. In this respect, most

[20] *Baphiring Community v Uys and Others* (Unreported) case number 64/98 [2010] ZACC 9 (29 April 2010).

scholarly engagements with the two judgments have focused on the extent to which they signal a move from a primary theme of redressing past injustice to a more instrumental and perhaps pragmatic 'good governance' theme in judicial work in the restitution arena—a move, that is, from 'redress and restitution' to 'economic development and sustainability' as animating themes. Juanita Pienaar has, for example, described the decision of the Land Claims Court as indicative of the appropriate approach for the court to take in achieving a balance between 'the conflicting discourses of redress/restitution on the on hand and economic development/sustainability on the other'.[21] In a similar vein, Jeannie van Wyk has detailed the shift from earlier cases such as *In re Kranspoort Community*,[22] where compatibility of use was still the overriding consideration, to broader developmental and sustainability issues such as cost and economic impact brought about by the Land Claims Court decision in *Baphiring*.[23] Whether or not *Baphiring* indeed signals this shift and if so, whether or not that is appropriate are no doubt important questions—but they do not detain me in this chapter. I am more interested in what the case, and more broadly the Baphiring Community's claim, says about the concept of home in the context of past dispossessions of home and claims for return specifically to home.

Because this is what the Baphiring's claim amounted to. Their claim was not in the first place economically motivated—although for some of the claimants return to the land could provide a way out of continuing poverty, many had by the time the claim was brought already re-establish economic independence elsewhere. It was also not, in the first place, intended to acquire a physical space within which to live as a community. By the time the claim was instituted most of the claimants had managed to settle successfully at New Mabaalstad, or had moved elsewhere and established homes there and only some of the claimants intended actually to return to Old Mabaalstad.

Instead their claim was primarily motivated by a spiritual bond to Old Mabaalstad as opposed to any other place *as their home* (the home of their individual families; of their community as a whole; and of their ancestors)—by the need to address the injustice of the loss of that home and by the dream of returning to that home. This purely spiritual or, as it has been called 'nostalgic' aspect of their claim appears poignantly from the following excerpt from the testimony of a member of the claimant group, Mr Ferdinand Mabelane in the case before the Land Claims Court. Mr Mabelane grew up in his grandparents' home on Old Mabaalstad and was present during the forced removal in 1971, at which time he was

[21] Pienaar (n 8 above) 43.
[22] *In re Kranspoort Community* 2000 (2) SA 124 (LCC).
[23] Van Wyk (n 8 above).

10 years old. Asked to explain how the loss of Old Mabaalstad had affected him (how it had changed his thinking), he answers:

> The forced removal was the highlight of emotions—I remember I visited my grandmother and how angry I got for how they treated her ...
>
> The idea to return is something that has its origins recently ... I always had the dream. When I use[d] to work in Mafikeng [a nearby town], I would travel back and stop my car to look at the farm. I continued to do it for a long period of time.

As Karin van Marle has pointed out, the claim for restoration of Old Mabaalstad in this light had both a political, more public-minded or 'reflective nostalgic' aspect and an intimate, more privatist, 'restorative nostalgic' aspect to it.[24] In addition to the yearning for a personal return to a family home lost, to an idyllic childhood, as reflected in the quote above, Old Mabaalstad was also a powerful symbol of the Baphiring's political identity and of their resistance to Apartheid governance. The claim is clearly motivated by a strong desire to correct an historical, intergenerational injustice not only at the personal level. In addition, the claim can be seen as the continuance of the Baphiring's century-old political struggle against Apartheid indirect rule through the traditional governance structures of the paramount tribe, the Bafokeng. Although Old Mabaalstad was bought in 1872 by the actual community of people who ended up living on it, the broader tribe in 1906 asserted ownership over it through the person of the then Chief, August Mokgatlhe. In collusion with the colonial government of the time, that regarded him as sufficiently pliable to ensure effective government control over his subjects, Mokgatlhe obtained a court order in 1908 recognising title of the tribe over Old Mabaalstad, against the protestations of the buyer community. Since its institution, the land claim to Old Mabaalstad was explicitly asserted as a continuance of this struggle against control from traditional governance quarters.[25] At its heart therefore, it was not a claim for actual compensation or housing or economically productive land. It was a claim for return to home in both an individual and a communal, identity-based, political sense.

What to say of the claim so described?

Despite, or perhaps precisely because of its clarity and forcefulness in this respect, this aspect of the Baphiring Community's claim illustrates for me the precariousness of home in this context—the context of forced dispossession of homes in the past and a process of restoration of, or return to, home now.

It does so firstly and perhaps obviously in practical terms. Quite simply, the Baphiring's claim as a claim for a return to and re-establishment of their

[24] Van Marle (n 11 above).
[25] ibid 131–32.

erstwhile home is probably impossible, but at best very difficult to realise. Expert testimony before the Land Claims Court showed that the resettlement of the Baphiring Community as an economically viable community would be a major undertaking, both in terms of the amount of money required and the necessary 'post-settlement' support. It was shown that not one such community post-restitution resettlement in the North West Province, where Old Mabaalstad is situated, has as yet been successful. These resettlement plans and estimates, furthermore, all focused on the re-establishment of an economically viable community, without taking account at all of the social aspects of recreating a home in the spiritual sense.

In addition, it is clear from the testimony of members of the claimant group before the Land Claims Court that a major element of the drive to return home is a drive to re-establish or to salvage the community of Old Mabaalstad—the close-knit collective that had lived and worked together around a shared ethic, with a shared purpose and around a shared set of rules and practices—that had in fact formed the core of the home that was lost. All indications are that this community is irrevocably lost. The competence of the claimant group (all original inhabitants of Old Mabaalstad or their direct descendants) to bring the claim was initially, as set out above, challenged. Although the Land Claims Court in this respect held in favour of the claimant group, the claimants had to make significant concessions as to who would benefit from the claim should it be successful, essentially placing themselves in the position of claimants on behalf of, and so for the benefit of, the entire broader tribe. This resurrects the century-old conflict about 'real ownership' of Old Mabaalstad that had reached its zenith shortly after the turn of the previous century, referred to above.

From very early on it was also clear that not even all the members of the claimant group would in fact return to Old Mabaalstad should it be restored to them, with some electing to remain in the new homes they had established for themselves and others saying that they would only retire at Old Mabaalstad. Once the land had indeed been bought and restored to the Baphiring, it soon became clear that different factions within the claimant group had different ideas about what to do with Old Mabaalstad, with some favouring economic use only and others indicating that they in fact wished to return. In short, the community that was the core of Old Mabaalstad as a collective home, seems no longer to exist. The conclusion is one of the radical practical precariousness of home in this context: once a home has been broken and a certain amount of time has passed, although it is possible at great expense and effort perhaps to recreate the physical characteristics of that home again, precisely the spiritual and social, collaborative aspects of that home, which are what the Baphiring Community seek to have restored, cannot be restored.

More importantly, perhaps, the idea or concept itself of return to home, claimed by the Baphiring Community, is precarious.

In his 2012 book, *Property and Constitution*, Andre van der Walt describes his vision of a new, transformed property system for South Africa. His point of departure is that 'property should be approached from the systemic rather than the individual perspective'.[26] He envisages 'a property system that is characterised by an equitable balance between the property interests of the individual property holder and the social or public interest.'[27] Rather than that property law should be about the identification of discrete individual rights to things such as land and the allocation of legal remedies to vindicate those rights, the property law *system*'s aim should be to regulate overlapping interests and rights to land and in particular the relationship between individual rights and the public interest. Land reform legislation, sourced in the Constitution, provides for him an example of this kind of regulative system of property in operation. Focusing on the Restitution Act and its source, section 25(7) of the Constitution, Van der Walt points out the difference between private law restitution remedies such as the *rei vindicatio* or spoliation and constitutionally mandated restitution—the purpose of the former being to vindicate private rights, with the latter intended to correct a 'public wrong'—to address the effects of Apartheid dispossessions.[28] Consequently, he continues, in the constitutional restitution process

> the important thing is not just restitution of what was lost (which would be the focus of a private law remedy) but also the larger process of legal and social restoration (which might well extend beyond narrow restitution of what was lost). Since the intended restitution process is about wider notions of justice than is the case with private law restitution remedies, and because it includes a symbolic element of restorative justice, the constitutional provision in section 25(7) restricts neither the objects of the dispossession nor the objects of restitution, to land or to particular property or rights. In contrast with private law remedies, the restitution process in terms of section 25(7) does not follow the logic of restoring a particular object to the person who had lost a particular right in it; its logic is purposive, determined by the transformative objectives of the Constitution; and contextual, determined by the historical context of apartheid dispossessions and by the personal circumstances of those affected by the original injustice, rather than just by their or anybody else's legally vested rights.[29]

In a similar vein, Cherryl Walker has criticised what she describes as the 'master narrative of loss and restoration' that underpins the constitutional restitution process in South Africa: the basic intuition that the process is aimed at specific people who lost land in the past due to government conduct and is intended to '[get] the land back to th[ose] people'.[30]

[26] Van der Walt (n 9 above) 131.
[27] ibid 129.
[28] Van der Walt (n 9 above) 134.
[29] ibid 135–36.
[30] Walker (n 10 above) 11.

To Walker this master narrative in its basic elements rings true, but she cautions that as a guideline for the resolution of historical land injustice in South Africa, it is too simple. It is too simple first, because it focuses exclusively on the story of forced removals under Apartheid. That is, it includes only those people who had rights to land to lose and lost them due to discriminatory state action within a set period, offering them the remedy of full restoration, but excludes those who lost rights to private action (farmer evictions) and all those who had no rights to lose in the first place, who might qualify for much more tenuous redistribution or tenure reform assistance. As such 'it isolates the history of forced removals under apartheid … as a story on its own, instead of an important chapter in a much larger and more complex history not only of dispossession but also of social change.'[31] It is too simple secondly, because it focuses on the moment of dispossession itself, disregarding developments that occurred in the intervening time between dispossession and the time in the early 1990s when restoration became possible. In this intervening time the circumstances of specific dispossessed people, of dispossessed communities and of the land that was taken from them changed considerably. The master narrative 'fails to deal with [these] specificities'.[32] It is too simple finally, because it makes no links between the restitution process and other social development programmes such as housing, social assistance or environmental conservation and does not relate itself to 'other constitutional commitments to justice, socio-economic development and equality', or to economic development in its relationship with social redress.[33]

Thus, Walker concludes

> as a guide to practical action … the master narrative could be dangerous. The simple story of forced removals, leads to a narrative of restitution that is constructed around the equally ingenuous idea of reversal. The task becomes simply to turn those elements of dispossession in the past around—to … restore those who were uprooted to the land from which they were torn, and reconcile those who lost with those who gained. Underpinning this is the naïve hope that through this act of reversal our society will indeed reach its promised land and thereby overcome the entrenched poverty, suffering, alienation, ignorance and conflict we see all around us.[34]

Finally, Karin van Marle considers whether the Baphiring Community's claim for a return to home—by its nature nostalgic in the sense that it reflects 'a community's longing to return to the land from which they were evicted under apartheid law'[35]—can be described as reflexively nostalgic or

[31] ibid 16.
[32] Walker (n 10 above) 16–17.
[33] ibid 17.
[34] ibid 17.
[35] Van Marle (n 11 above) 129.

restoratively nostalgic. If reflexively nostalgic, the claim would be motivated by an ironic remembrance of the past home, and the longing for a return to home would be seen in the current context, in a way that does not stand in the way of broader social transformation. If restoratively nostalgic, the claim would instead simply be for a return of that which was lost, remembered uncritically; in a sense, a turning back of time to what was before.[36]

Van Marle sees hints of reflexive nostalgia in the Community's ostensible continuance of a century-old struggle to obtain title for themselves to Old Mabaalstad, counter to the claim of the leadership of the Bafokeng tribe, which was upheld by the courts in 1906. However, she detects at the same time a restorative nostalgia, reflecting 'a longing for home, belonging and a rediscovery of identity'.[37]

Common to Van der Walt, Walker and Van Marle's accounts of the restitution process is a concern that the process should not be seen in a one-dimensional, privatist sense, as intended only to right specific wrongs done to specific people or groups in the past, but instead as a process bound up with and embedded in a broader history of injustice and more general current programme or drive for transformation and the creation of a new, post-Apartheid society.

Seen in this light, the Baphiring's claim for a return to home is not only precarious in a sense of practical feasibility as related above, but seems also to be a precarious idea, in the sense that it is, in the current context, inappropriately individualistic and one-dimensional.

This is so in a number of different, but related ways.

First, and most obviously, restoration of Old Mabaalstad to the Baphiring Community will of necessity lead to a new dispossession and dislocation: not only of the new, relatively well-off white farmer-owners of the land, but also of a quite large number of poor black farm workers who have over the last 40 years settled there and made lives for themselves. To be sure, some of these farm workers are members of the claimant community and will benefit from the claim, but the position of the majority of them was sufficiently unclear that the Supreme Court of Appeal made a determination of their status and of the impact that restoration would have on them one of the requirements of its order and referral of the matter back to the Land Claims Court. In addition, probably the majority of this group are excluded from the claimant group and won't benefit from the restoration, precisely because they have been in this precarious position all along—that is, they are some of those referred to by Walker, who lost nothing specific under Apartheid, because they had no rights to lose.

Secondly, it remains unclear who is included and who excluded from the claimant community which would benefit from restoration. Despite a

[36] ibid 116.
[37] Van Marle (n 11 above) 132.

significant number of people who were actual inhabitants of Old Mabaalstad at the time of dispossession remaining, and it being possible to draw clear lines of descendance to identify other members of the broader community (as required by the Restitution Act), the fact is that the community that existed at dispossession no longer exists, and the community that has developed around the claim is fractured and disputed, as shown by tensions that have surfaced after restoration was agreed. In addition, the century-old dispute between the core Old Mabaalstad community and the broader Baphiring tribe around title to Old Mabaalstad seems to persist. It remains unclear how the restoration that has now been engineered extra-curially, to use Walker's terms, takes account of these specificities.

Thirdly, although the peculiarities of the restitution process in some ways mandate this (what are restored are the rights that were lost—so if title was lost under Apartheid, title is restored), it seems incongruous that the Baphiring Community's claim for restoration of their ancestral home should be asserted in the form of a claim for vindication of ownership in the absolutist privatist sense.

This concern, which might seem motivated by a need for ideological neatness, is placed in relief if one takes account of the fact that, in terms of private law logic, the Baphiring Community was near to fully compensated for the expropriation of Old Mabaalstad at the time of dispossession. Restoration of Old Mabaalstad without the Community relinquishing at least part of New Mabaalstad (and this has never been on the cards) will in purely monetary terms result in significant over-compensation. If one further takes account of the tremendous additional cost that viable resettlement would entail for the state, Walker's concern over the concentration of public resources on people who are only able to claim restoration because they had something tangible to lose under Apartheid (stated bluntly, the Baphiring Community owned land under Apartheid and is only for that reason able to claim it back today), to the exclusion of all those who, although also suffering under the injustice of Apartheid, at the time had nothing, clearly rears its head.

Fourthly, and finally, one must take account of the undoubted impact that restoration will have on economic development as a prerequisite for broad social redress and viable transformation. Although it is unclear what impact restoration will eventually have on the economically productive capacity of Old Mabaalstad as commercial agricultural land, it is clear that there will be a significant impact. Old Mabaalstad in its current incarnation is farmed successfully on a significant commercial scale. It is unclear what exactly the plans are for the Baphiring Community with the land, but it is clear that there is no consensus and no plans to continue with such large-scale commercial farming. The track record of restoration programmes where they have occurred—even in those cases where the plans were to continue economically productive activity on restored land—is also dismal. Here one is not so much, or at least not in the first place, concerned with the impact on agricultural productivity and food production at national level as with the role that the current agricultural business on Old Mabaalstad plays in the local economy, creating jobs and feeding into and from broader local economic networks.

IV. CONCLUSION

In the end then this is what the Baphiring community's claim illustrates for me: if a restitution claim in the context of historical unjust dispossession is aimed at restoring or recreating a community's home specifically—the sense of belonging, of identity and of community that their initial link to the land embodied—then it is impossible. Home in this context is radically precarious. Even were a community to have their physical home restored to them, as was eventually the case with the Baphiring, it is precisely the intangible aspects of home that the community is concerned with that are practically impossible to recreate. What is more, the claim for this kind of restoration of those aspects of home sits uncomfortably with the broader demands of social transformation facing a society such as South Africa that is in the process of dealing with past injustice and its legacies. In short, this kind of claim, given the context, simply seems inappropriate.

This is in no way to blame the Baphiring Community or to deny the 'justness' of their claim. In concert with Walker I am convinced that the 'constituent elements' of this narrative of dispossession and restoration are true. Instead, it is to emphasise and place in stark relief the tragedy that the loss of home that South Africa's forced removals caused for so many.

Index

www.ingramcontent.com/pod-product-compliance
Ingram Content Group UK Ltd.
Pitfield, Milton Keynes, MK11 3LW, UK
UKHW020236290926
15470UKWH00002B/573